Integrating Regions

Integrating Regions

ASIA IN COMPARATIVE CONTEXT

Edited by Miles Kahler and Andrew MacIntyre

Stanford University Press • Stanford, California

Stanford University Press
Stanford, California

Printed on acid-free, archival-quality paper

Library of Congress Cataloging-in-Publication Data

Integrating regions : Asia in comparative context / edited by Miles Kahler and Andrew MacIntyre.
    pages cm
  Includes bibliographical references and index.
  ISBN 978-0-8047-8364-4 (cloth : alk. paper)
    1. Regionalism—Asia. 2. Asia—Economic integration. 3. Regionalism (International organization) 4. International economic integration. I. Kahler, Miles, 1949– editor of compilation. II. MacIntyre, Andrew J., 1960– editor of compilation.
  JZ5333.I57 2013
    337.1'5—dc23   2013013480

    ISBN 978-0-8047-8930-1 (electronic)

Typeset by Classic Typography in 10.5/13.5 Bembo MT Pro

Contents

Contributors

Amitav Acharya holds the UNESCO Chair in Transnational Challenges and Governance and Chair of the ASEAN Studies Center in the School of International Service at American University.

Jorge I. Domínguez is the Antonio Madero Professor for the Study of Mexico at Harvard University and a past president of the Latin American Studies Association. He is co-editor (with R. Fernández de Castro) of *Contemporary U.S.-Latin American Relations* (Routledge, 2010) and co-editor (with C. Lawson) of *Mexico's Pivotal Democratic Election: Candidates, Voters, and the Presidential Campaign of 2000* (Stanford University Press, 2004).

Stephan Haggard is the Krause Distinguished Professor at the Graduate School of International Relations and Pacific Studies at the University of California, San Diego. In addition to work on regionalism in East Asia and Latin America, he is the author of *Pathways from the Periphery: The Politics of Growth in the Newly Industrializing Countries* (1990) and, with Robert Kaufman, *The Political Economy of Democratic Transitions* (1995) and *Development, Democracy and Welfare States: Latin America, East Asia and Eastern Europe* (2008).

C. Randall Henning is Professor in the School of International Service, American University and a Visiting Fellow at the Peterson Institute for International Economics.

Simon Hix is Professor of European and Comparative Politics in the Department of Government at the London School of Economics and Political Science. His main research interest is the design of democratic political institutions, in the European Union as well as elsewhere in the world. He has written eight books, including "What's Wrong with the EU and How to Fix It" (Polity, 2008), more than 40 articles in peer-reviewed journals in political science, and numerous reports for public and private organizations.

Miles Kahler is Rohr Professor of Pacific International Relations and Distinguished Professor of Political Science in the School of International Relations and Pacific Studies (IR/PS) and the Department of Political Science, University of California, San Diego (UCSD). He was Founding Director of the Institute for International, Comparative, and Area Studies at UCSD. Recent publications include "Asia and the Reform of Global Governance" (*Asian Economic Policy Review*, December 2010) and *Networked Politics* (editor).

Judith G. Kelley is Associate Professor of Public Policy and Political Science at the Duke Sanford School of Public Policy. She is the author of *Ethnic Politics in Europe: The Power of Norms and Incentives* (Princeton, 2004) and *Monitoring Democracy: When International Election Monitoring Works and Why It Often Fails* (Princeton, 2012).

Andrew MacIntyre is Professor of Political Science and serves as College Dean and Director of the Research School of Asia & the Pacific at the Australian National University.

John Ravenhill is Head of the School of Politics and International Relations, Research School of Social Sciences, Australian National University.

Erik Voeten is the Peter F. Krogh Associate Professor of Geopolitics and Justice in World Affairs at the School of Foreign Service and the Department of Government. Voeten's research on the United Nations, the European Union, the European Court of Human Rights, and broader issues of international law and cooperation has been published in journals such as the *American Political Science Review*, the *American Journal of Political Science*, *International Organization*, *International Studies Quarterly*, the *Journal of Politics,* and the *Journal of Conflict Resolution*.

Acknowledgments

Asia has had a longstanding reputation as a region averse to formal institutions; an inventory of significant regionwide institutions made fifteen years ago would have been relatively short. Since the Asian financial crisis, however, institutional development has accelerated. As part of its larger investigation of the progress of Asian economic integration and the region's institutions, the Asian Development Bank (ADB) sponsored a trilogy of studies; the last of these, *Institutions for Regional Integration*, was published in 2010.

This volume grows out of that wider ADB project on the future of Asian regional institutions. We are grateful to the ADB for its institutional and financial support of the background papers and report on which this volume is based. In particular, we wish to acknowledge the support of ADB President Haruhiko Kuroda, who initiated and encouraged the project. Jong-Wha Lee, Chief Economist, ADB Economics and Research Department, and Srinivasa Madhur, Senior Director and Officer-in-Charge, Office of Regional Economic Integration (OREI), provided essential leadership for the project. Special thanks are due to Giovanni Capannelli, OREI Principal Economist, for his tireless support and management of the project from beginning to end, and to Sabyasachi Mitra, OREI Senior Economist, for his valuable advice.

Outside the ADB, our greatest debt is to our colleague and collaborator, Barry Eichengreen, who served as the lead consultant for the ADB project and provided essential intellectual leadership. The late Hadi Soesastro and Tan See Seng were the other principal consultants and key collaborators. We deeply regret that Hadi was unable to see this product of our collaboration. Although many members of our respective ADB teams are represented in this volume, we wish to thank the other members of our teams who contributed their expertise to the working papers and to workshop discussions that improved early drafts of the papers: Richard Baldwin, Helen Nesadurai, Jon Pevehouse, Etel Solingen, and Yong Wang.

Finally, we wish to recognize Stacy Wagner, Acquisitions Editor, Geoffrey Burn, Executive Editor, and Jessica Walsh, Editorial Assistant, at Stanford University Press, whose oversight and support were essential in bringing this volume to life. We are pleased to acknowledge the contributions of the Press's anonymous referees; their comments have strengthened the volume. Thanks are also due to Paula Percival at the Australian National University, for her invaluable assistance in preparing the final manuscript.

MK

AM

Integrating Regions

ONE

INTRODUCTION

1

Regional Institutions in an Era of Globalization and Crisis

MILES KAHLER

During three decades of globalization, regional integration and institutions have flourished.[1] In the 1990s, Europe embarked on the Economic and Monetary Union, the United States and its neighbors ratified the North American Free Trade Agreement (NAFTA), and the largest economies of South America founded the Common Market of the South (MERCOSUR). Asia seemed to stand apart, producing a trio of regional institutions that were far more modest in scope than their counterparts elsewhere—Asia-Pacific Economic Cooperation (APEC), the Free Trade Area (AFTA) of the Association of Southeast Asian Nations (ASEAN), and the ASEAN Regional Forum (ARF). The Asian financial crisis at the end of the 1990s appeared to mark a turning point, however, exposing the region's vulnerabilities and the ineffectiveness of its institutions. The first decade of the new century produced three new institutional developments: region-wide economic arrangements, such as ASEAN Plus Three (APT), which were limited to Asian members; innovation in monetary and financial collaboration (APT's Chiang Mai Initiative and Asian Bond Market Initiative—ABMI), and a proliferation of bilateral and plurilateral preferential trade agreements (PTAs).[2]

Despite this apparent catching-up in Asian institution building, many saw a mismatch between high levels of regional economic interdependence and formal region-wide institutions that continued to lag other regions. An organization gap persisted in Northeast Asia, where multilateral security structures were absent and three of Asia's largest economies have failed to complete a free trade agreement that would deepen their existing economic links (Calder and Ye 2010). The wider gap between interdependence and institutions in Asia has "stubbornly refused to close, despite the recent proliferation of bilateral and minilateral PTAs and security dialogues" (Aggarwal and Koo 2008, 286, 288). The new Asian regionalism now confronts the aftershocks of the Great Recession of 2008–2009, a global economic crisis that hardly brushed the largest emerging economies in Asia and failed to set back the economic progress of the region. The crisis could increase incentives for defensive institution-building to safeguard against future shocks from the global economy; deeper regional economic integration may also provide the best prospects for high economic growth, as Asia's export markets in North America and Europe enter a period of sluggish growth.

This volume explains and evaluates the new Asian regionalism and its institutions in the context of other regions and their institutional architecture.[3] It is an opportune moment for such a reassessment, as the highly elaborated European regional model faces a sovereign debt crisis, and Asian economies seek more secure sources of growth among their immediate neighbors. The three sections of the volume investigate variation in regional institutions, comparing Asia to Europe, the Americas, and other regions. The first section outlines the key dimensions of institutional design and their implications for the performance of regional institutions, in Asia and elsewhere. A rigorous comparison is impossible without agreement on precisely defined features of the institutions that are to be compared. In the second section, the regional trajectories of Europe and the Americas are compared to Asia in an effort to explain their respective constellations of regional institutions. In light of these comparisons, in the third section and conclusion, Asia's regional institutions are evaluated: have they contributed to regional integration and cooperative outcomes? Will the region sustain a different model of institutionalization, convergent on the rest of the world, given changes in the regional and global environments?

The Design of Regional Institutions

Three key dimensions of institutional design vary across regional institutions: decision rules; commitment devices, such as legalization and enfranchisement; and membership rules. These design features reflect regional characteristics, the dynamics of regional economic integration, and the interests of cooperating governments. They also influence the effectiveness of these institutions in forging and implementing cooperative bargains to promote regional economic integration.

Depending on the elements of their design, institutions can contribute to at least three ends related to economic integration: *consolidating* existing liberalization gains, undertaken unilaterally or multilaterally; *deepening* integration, by expanding the scope of regional agreement, and particularly including the removal of barriers to exchange behind national borders; and *widening* economic integration, through the development of infrastructure or the incorporation of new members in existing or new regional regimes. Institutions with different decision rules, commitment devices, and membership rules will be more or less effective in the promotion of these ends.

Decision Rules: Winning Consent to Cooperative Agreements

Although the international legal regime posits the sovereign equality of states, any regional or global institution must contend with disparities in underlying bargaining power among its members. Decision rules reflect those disparities. A one country, one vote system, based on majoritarian decision rules, is unlikely to satisfy more powerful member states with significant outside options. One solution awards more powerful members greater influence over outcomes of particular interest to them through informal rules (Stone 2011). Another relies on consensus decision-making, which permits opposition from any member to defeat proposed actions or commitments.[4] Even institutions that adopt formal majoritarian or qualified majoritarian decision rules are likely to introduce other mechanisms to produce de facto consensual outcomes. Among regional groupings, the European Union (EU) has ventured further than any other in adopting decision-making by qualified majority. As Hix (chapter 2) points out, however, national governments in Europe have carefully hedged those outcomes by requiring a unanimity rule for delegation of additional authority to European institutions, by insuring equal representation on the EU's executive body, and by instituting checks and balances and high thresholds for decision.

Consensus decision rules guard against defection—from the organization or from its decision—on the part of discontented minorities. They also discourage backsliding, since cooperative commitments can only be modified through the same procedures. Consensus imposes a steep tradeoff between commitment and decisiveness, however. The prospect of an agreement that is difficult to change or one that will be effectively enforced may produce protracted bargaining and frequent failures of collective action (Fearon 1998). In the face of a crisis or a rapidly changing environment, institutions that strain for consensus may fail to produce timely changes of course. The disappointing record of Asian regional institutions during the Asian financial crisis has been attributed in part to the region's attachment to consensus decision-making.

Commitment Devices: Political Engagement, Legalization, and Enfranchisement

The history of regional agreements is littered with ambitious commitments that are not implemented. Particularly when new commitments deepen economic integration, extending regional collaboration into domains of domestic sensitivity that arouse political opposition, current or future governments may renege on those agreements or slight their implementation. To counter such temptations, regional institutions often contain embedded commitment mechanisms and instruments for monitoring and enforcement.

The mobilization of high-level *political commitment*, particularly at the launch of new institutions and new national undertakings, is one such device. Involvement of top political leaders signals possible costs to those within the government who fail to implement the new agreement and engages the reputation of leaders in the success of the regional enterprise. Regional commitments are also reinforced if national political institutions, such as legislatures and bureaucracies, are part of the process of ratification and implementation, rendering regional institutions truly intergovernmental rather than "inter-executive" (Dominguez, chapter 5; Martin 2000). Successful regional institutions that affect significant national policy domains are seldom purely technocratic; visible domestic political commitments are required to sustain them.

Legalization is another institutional instrument for bolstering commitment. Legalization is measured on three dimensions: precision of international commitments; obligation or the degree to which those commitments are legally binding; and delegation of authority to third parties, such as global or regional institutions, to interpret, monitor, and enforce those commitments (Goldstein, Kahler, Keohane, and Slaughter 2001). Delegated authority is often interpreted as a marker of whether regional institutions are strong or weak. The other dimensions of legalization can substitute for delegation, however. Precise and binding commitments, such as those in NAFTA, may produce high levels of compliance without substantial delegation of authority to regional institutions. Delegation risks the creation of institutional agents who will pursue their own interests rather than those of the contracting governments. Member states of the EU, for example, have designed additional institutions and rules to hedge against such drift away from their preferences (Hix, chapter 2). Elaborate institutions do not always signify substantial delegation. Despite a proliferation of regional courts, Erik Voeten (chapter 3) confirms that they are rarely used to resolve interstate disputes. In Latin America, delegation to supranational regional institutions has been most helpful in specialized domains; ambitious region-wide institutions have often failed to exercise the powers awarded them on paper (Domínguez, chapter 5).

Enfranchisement of non-governmental actors, such as corporations or citizens, also serves as a commitment mechanism in regional governance. Compliance constituencies, mobilizing outside the self-protective cartel of national governments, use courts and other dispute settlement mechanisms to reactivate the integration process, to interpret agreements, and to prevent backsliding by governments. As Voeten (chapter 3) describes, rules for enfranchisement in regional courts contribute directly to their effectiveness. Commitments by governments are rendered more credible by the ability of non-state actors to participate in enforcement.

Membership Rules and the Widening of Regional Institutions

Judith Kelley (chapter 4) describes two membership models that dominate the universe of regional institutions. The club model imposes strict admission criteria based on prior policy change and thereby awards leverage to existing members over the candidate member's policies. The convoy model is more permissive, basing membership on geographical proximity (ASEAN) or on ad hoc and flexible rules (APEC). Policy change is rarely required in advance of institutional membership. As regional institutions contemplate admission of new members, both models may have strengths. Convoy membership organizations rely on socialization to shape the behavior of members after they are admitted; Acharya (chapter 9) argues that socialization has succeeded in key Asian cases. The effectiveness of convoy membership rules appears to be greatest in the domain of security, where inclusiveness often has positive effects. The EU is a notable example of the club model of membership, in which a wider array of tools can be deployed before membership to change the policies of a national candidate (Kelley 2004 and chapter 4).

Manipulation of membership rules is an important means of introducing flexibility into regional institutions when some members wish to pursue new and more ambitious cooperative bargains (Kelley, chapter 4). New institutions may be spun off by the "cooperators," or the existing organization may adopt different categories of membership. If members agree on integration goals but disagree on timing, multi-speed integration will allow transitional periods for new members. If disagreement over the aims of integration is more profound, variable geometry or à la carte regionalism may be introduced. Under those membership rules, a single institution recognizes different "integration spaces." For example, some members of the EU have opted out of monetary union indefinitely (variable geometry); new members must fulfill policy requirements before adopting the Euro (multi-speed membership). A risk of fragmentation lies in such flexibility, undermining institutional goals of policy harmonization and economic integration.

Widening, which may produce a larger membership with more heterogeneous preferences, might also appear to undermine future deepening of regional cooperative bargains. That tradeoff is dependent on membership rules, however: regional organizations with club membership rules can wield those rules to exclude members who have not signaled their cooperative intent and harmonized their policy preferences with those of incumbent members. Institutional devices, such as the introduction of new decision rules, may also offset some of the effects of widening. In Europe, an extension of qualified majority voting served to enhance decision-making efficiency as membership grew. Finally, new members may be the most enthusiastic cooperators in certain policy domains. The EU's newest members in central and east Europe were eager to join its monetary union, despite demanding entry conditions. In Asia, India has backed regional agreements that liberalize trade in services and establish rules governing foreign direct investment, two areas of deeper integration that existing Asian trade agreements have often excluded (Debroy 2009).

The Distinctive Design of Asia Regional Institutions

Although Asian regional institutions have increased in number during the latest wave of regional institution building, they have remained, in the eyes of observers outside the region, "shallow" or "thin" (Haggard, chapter 8). The preceding review of the dimensions that define such institutions permits a more precise description of their common institutional design.

Although Asia's regional institutions are hardly uniform, certain characteristics define an "Asian way" of institution building. Decision rules emphasize building consensus, a process that emphasizes persuasion and deliberation rather than decisiveness. Regional arrangements are rarely legalized through precise and binding obligations, and governments are reluctant to delegate substantial authority to regional institutions. As a result, the monitoring and enforcement powers of most regional institutions are limited. The Asian Development Bank (ADB) is a rare regional example of consequential delegation to an Asian institution. ASEAN has a small secretariat whose operational autonomy has been carefully circumscribed by member governments. The leadership of APEC's secretariat, which is even smaller than ASEAN's, is seconded from member governments. Despite its economic importance, Asia has no regional courts (Voeten, chapter 3). Asian regional institutions are also exclusively intergovernmental: non-state actors, whether individuals, corporations, or non-governmental organizations (NGOs) are not formally enfranchised in regional institutions. Finally, Asian regional organizations have adopted a model of membership that produces heterogeneous convoys rather than homogeneous clubs. In all of these characteristics, Asian regional institutions emphasize preservation rather than pooling of sovereignty; regional institutions avoid intrusions into domestic politics and policy.[5]

Regional Comparisons: Europe, Latin America, and Asia

Whether this institutional syndrome is a complex that is distinctively Asia requires careful cross-regional comparison. Certainly, each of the enumerated features of Asian institutions can be found in other regions. Contemporary Europe has too often served as the benchmark for Asian institutions. As Kevin O'Rourke (chapter 6) describes, however, Europe of the 1950s and 1960s provides a more satisfactory benchmark for comparison. It was in those decades that Europe took the key decisions that directed its future away from free trade agreements—the most common regional economic arrangement in Asia and elsewhere—and toward the more elaborate institutions of today's EU. Jorge Domínguez (chapter 5) provides an equally illuminating comparison, juxtaposing Asia and the Americas. Like Asia, the Americas combine a major industrialized economy with middle-income developing countries. The Americas, however, have both a longer post-colonial history than Asia and a record of more institutional experiments. Three clusters of variables provide candidate explanations for contrasting institutional design in these three regions: structural characteristics of regional economies and their politics; regional dynamics that reinforce or undermine institution building over time; and contingencies, such as economic crises, that have inflected institutional development. Explanations for institutional variation provide a starting point for predictions of future regional trajectories, in particular whether the Asian way of institutional development will persist.

Regional Structure and the Pattern of Institutional Development

Three structural characteristics shape the configuration of regional institutions: determinants of convergence or divergence in national preferences; distribution of economic and military power; and relative openness of a region to the influence of extra-regional powers.

Heterogeneous Asia and Preferences for Regional Economic Cooperation

Although increasing economic integration in Asia points to growing national demand for cooperative regional arrangements, two other features of Asian politics—disparities in national income levels and heterogeneity of political regimes—serve as structural constraints on regional institution building. Functional, demand-driven models of institutional development would predict a higher level of institutionalization than currently exists in Asia. The level of economic integration in the region remains subject to dispute, depending on the measure employed (MacIntyre and Ravenhill, chapter 10). On several measures of regional economic integration, however, Asia approaches Europe and the Americas (ADB 2008, 40–43). Economic integration in this case, however, has not produced an interest-driven process of institutional creation. A top-down process of building regional institutions, directed by governments, has been offered passive support at best by domestic political and economic coalitions that support linkage to the international economy (MacIntyre and Ravenhill, chapter 10; Solingen 2009).

Other comparative indices of national preferences suggest greater heterogeneity in Asia. Asia displays a wider divide between its richest and poorest members than the Americas or Europe (ADB 2009, 30). Overall, Asia is less homogeneous in its domestic political institutions than other regions, which have been predominantly democratic (Europe and the Americas) or authoritarian (the Middle East and North Africa). More direct measures of preference convergence produce a mixed comparative assessment. Individual citizen's values (as measured in survey data) display variance that is roughly similar to that in the 27 members of the European Union, particularly attitudes toward protection of the environment and wealth accumulation (Hix, chapter 2). Surprisingly, identification with the region is also at similar levels in the two regions. Despite this evidence of popular preferences, "overall, the level of political, economic and ideological convergence is lower in East Asia than in Europe" (Hix, chapter 2).

Distribution of Economic and Military Power

In contrast to Europe and the Americas, Asia is home to a handful of countries that have much larger populations and economies than other countries in the region, a reasonable proxy for a multipolar regional distribution of power. The effects of power distribution on the design of regional institutions are contested, however.[6] On the one hand, great powers may provide supply-side benefits that promote cooperation: regional public goods and a focal point for coordination of national policies. After the Asian financial crisis, for example, Japan provided financial leadership in Asia through the New Miyazawa Initiative. In Europe, the German deutschmark served as the coordination anchor for the European Monetary System before the creation of a common European currency. On the other hand, larger countries have been less willing to delegate authority to regional institutions, and great power leadership that is perceived as overbearing may produce a backlash against the aspiring leader and its policies.[7]

A simple measure of power distribution may be less important for the configuration of regional institutions than the dynamic of power relations (the rapidity of shifts in economic and military power) and rivalries among the dominant regional powers. Regional cooperation in Asia may be disadvantaged by both the rapid readjustment of economic hierarchies over time (China's overtaking of Japan) and longstanding national rivalries. The former adds uncertainty to regional security relations and a bias toward free-riding by emerging powers in regional economic cooperation. The latter may produce liberalization through competition in the creation of exclusive bilateral and sub-regional arrangements. At the same time, rivalry among the most powerful states undermines efforts to construct more inclusive regional arrangements, since deeper economic integration may require sturdier institutions with greater delegated authority, based on consensus among the major economies. MacIntyre and Ravenhill (chapter 10) trace the recent surge in Asian preferential trading arrangements to political rivalry between China and Japan for regional leadership; United States backing of the Trans-Pacific Partnership adds another element to regional competition.[8]

Open Regionalism and the Influence of Outside Actors

Peter Katzenstein (2005) has described contemporary regionalism as "porous": infiltrated by the forces of globalization and the pervasive influence of the United States. Intervention by outside actors has had positive and negative effects on regional collaboration and institutionalization. During the Cold War, for example, the United States lent critical support to the building of European institutions and made clear to its close allies, such as Britain, that participation in the European project was favored. (O'Rourke, chapter 6) In Asia, on the other hand, the United States favored bilateral security and economic relations with its principal allies and trading partners; it offered weak support for regional multilateralism.

Although regions are no longer as permeable as they were during the Cold War, they vary in their vulnerability to the strategies of extra-regional powers.

In the Americas, for example, the United States has played an erratic and occasionally influential role in democracy promotion over time; it has had relatively little influence on regional economic institutions, apart from NAFTA.
The production networks of Factory Asia, on the other hand, remain dependent on American and European export markets, although that dependence
may decline over time.[9] Four Asian states also have military alliances with the
United States; several others have informal, trans-Pacific defense relationships.
Given the growing economic weight of the region, outside powers will be interested in Asia's institutional choices; they may also have the means to influence those choices.

Dynamic Processes and Institution Building Across Regions

Although structural variables have constrained regional collaboration and
its institutional manifestations, regional institutions develop from dynamic
processes that are (path) dependent on divergent historical starting points.
Institutional trajectories over times are marked by political and economic
feedback effects, distinctive links between security and economic integration, and differing weights assigned to global, regional, and sub-regional institutions. Contingencies—exogenous shocks from economic crises and the
emergence of regional political entrepreneurs—have also had demonstrable if
unpredictable effects on the building of regional institutions.

Historical Context and the Origins of Regional Institutions

Regional institutional design has been marked by global and domestic politics at the time of their foundation. Europe faced unfavorable initial conditions after World War II: high levels of insecurity after catastrophic interstate
war and the emergence of Soviet power in central Europe coupled with a
relatively closed international economy. Regionalism seemed to provide an
essential response: liberalization of trade and investment through global negotiations would be slow; most of the initial work of lowering barriers to cross-
border exchange had to occur at the regional level, reinforced by nascent
European institutions (O'Rourke, chapter 6). Western Europe's status as the
first industrial region also shaped institutional design. A spare free trade agreement could not accommodate the interventionist demands of agriculture and
other national sectors; the linked bargains required at the foundation of European institutions pointed toward supranational institutions with substantial
authority. For regional institutions founded in the Americas and Asia during
the 1990s and 2000s, a different logic applied: the end of the Cold War and

an open global economy offered many more options to political elites who embarked on programs of liberalization.

Feedback Effects and the Demand for Regional Institutions

Prescriptions for the sequencing of regional economic arrangements and institutions often resemble crude diagrams of the ascent of man: an inevitable and formulaic progression from free trade agreement to customs union to common market and common currency. The theoretical and empirical basis for these predictions is suspect. More compelling is a positive analysis of the regional spillovers and feedback loops produced by economic integration and its accompanying institutions, processes that may or may not reinforce both institution building and broaden the scope of cooperative bargains.

Based on the experience of Europe and other regions, Richard Baldwin has identified several feedback mechanisms of varying strength; their sequencing may produce more or less institutionalization in the course of expanding trade and investment (Baldwin 1993, 2011). These interest-based models assume that initial decisions for trade liberalization increase the political weight of export interests within national political economies and produce demands for more liberalization. Trade-dependent economic interests may also create a domino effect on applications for membership in an expanding Free Trade Association (FTA) or customs union because of the threat of trade discrimination. Another feedback mechanism links trade and exchange rate cooperation. Via the policy trilemma, national governments (and trade-dependent economic interests) become more attracted to stable exchange rates as economies become more open to international trade and capital controls are removed (Frieden 1991; Eichengreen 1996; Baldwin 2011). Institutional feedback, the ability of regional institutions to amplify and channel demands for integration into further institutional elaboration, is subject to more demanding conditions: regional institutions must possess both a mandate from national governments to further economic integration and delegated authority to carry out that mandate. Even without an explicit mandate, institutions may serve to create or dampen demands for further institutional development by their effectiveness or shortcomings.

These feedback effects, based on demands from export interests and strategies of regional institutions, had a powerful influence on the trajectory of regional institutions in Europe. Economic and institutional feedback effects created political support for widening the agenda of liberalization within the European Economic Community (EEC). A domino effect tipped governments against the European Free Trade Association (EFTA), as the larger and more dynamic EEC exerted its attraction on trading interests outside the Community (O'Rourke, Chapter 6). Similar effects also operated outside Europe. Latin American regional institutions were often born after an initial, unilateral round of liberalization by national governments. In certain cases, such as the Central America Free Trade Agreement (CAFTA) or MERCOSUR, liberalization then spurred regional cooperation by providing a costly signal of intent for trading partners as well as reflecting the growing political power of exporters. As Dominguez (chapter 5) points out, however, feedback effects in Latin America did not extend beyond trade liberalization to agreements for deeper economic integration or monetary union.

In Asia, the feedback link between trade expansion and regional institution building was even more tenuous. No regional core with a comprehensive and discriminatory trade arrangement emerged as equivalent to the EEC, serving to attract prospective members. A strong substitution effect undermined the link to regional institutions, since demands for further liberalization by exporters could be satisfied in global trade negotiations rather than regional FTAs. In any case, regional institution building in Asia seldom resulted from strong political pressure from organized business or other non-governmental actors (MacIntyre and Ravenhill, chapter 10; Nesadurai 2010).

In the domain of regional monetary and financial cooperation, the European model of demand-driven exchange rate cooperation, intensified by the removal of capital controls, applies only weakly, if at all, to other regions. Despite a decline in intra-MERCOSUR trade following the Brazilian and Argentine exchange rate crises (1999–2002), no progress was made toward regional economic policy coordination or exchange rate collaboration. As they had in trade governance, Asian governments once again chose a substitute for regional monetary cooperation: pegging to the dollar or to a basket of currencies. Recent regional financial cooperation in Asia has followed a path even more distant from predictions of a trade-based feedback dynamic. The shock of the Asian financial crisis and discontent with the response by global institutions produced the regional Chiang Mai Initiative (CMI), an instrument for offering financial support to members of ASEAN Plus Three (APT) during financial crises. Recent multilateralization of the CMI suggests that monetary and financial cooperation may produce spillovers to other areas of regional economic cooperation rather than the reverse, a pattern found in other monetary unions in the developing world.

At key moments, European economic integration was promoted by institutional feedback—actions taken by European institutions to promote economic integration (Baldwin 2011). Europe's initial conditions, which awarded it a panoply of influential regional institutions, also gave those institutions unique possibilities for deepening economic integration. That driver of regional institution-building was largely absent in other regions. Neither Asian nor Latin American regional institutions have possessed the delegated authority of the European Court of Justice or the European Commission, authority that allowed those institutions to strengthen regional economic cooperation. Despite MERCOSUR's relatively elaborate institutions, trade expansion produced little pressure to increase the scope of the customs union by including such areas as trade in services, competition policy, or coordination of social policy (Domínguez, chapter 5). The North American Free Trade Agreement (NAFTA) did not develop a more elaborate institutional architecture as regional trade expanded. Modest innovations, such as multilateralization of swap lines among the United States, Canada, and Mexico, were driven by concern over Mexican financial crises, not by NAFTA institutions.

The dynamics of regional integration and institutional development varied across regions. Europe's progression from trade liberalization and a common market to financial liberalization and monetary union may not be the only path to further institutional development; feedback mechanisms that have driven regional integration in Europe may not operate to the same effect elsewhere.[10] Two features of Latin America and Asia have distinguished their regional dynamics from those of Europe. Trade-dependent constituencies were less influential politically, particularly in Asia: this necessary correlate of trade expansion was weak or absent. The relative weakness of political demands may have resulted from reliance on potent substitutes for strengthened regional institutions. For example, unilateral liberalization, participation in global trade rounds, and bilateral exchange rate pegs offered functional substitutes in Asia for Europe's regional institutions. A central unanswered question is whether the Asian dynamic of institution building—including its reliance on such substitutes—will provide more substantial regional governance if a new agenda of deeper economic integration targets a wider array of sensitive domestic policies.

Economics and Security: Integration, Reinforcement, Separation

No region has directly managed core economic and security issues in a single regional institution. Nevertheless, the interrelated dynamics of economic integration and security provision have influenced the creation and strengthening of regional institutions. Conflict has affected economic exchange: negative effects of unresolved territorial disputes on levels of trade, for example, have been documented in Latin America (Simmons 2006). In other circumstances, careful linkage of peace building—the gradual winding down of regional rivalries—and economic integration has reinforced both economic and security dynamics in a cooperative direction. Regional institutions have built on an association between economic opening and a reduction of military tensions, reinforcing that linkage through the risk of economic loss if political or military conflict disrupts regional collaboration.

Although Europe does not have a single, multipurpose pan-regional organization, the region nevertheless *integrates* security and economic issues. As described earlier, initial security conditions in Europe favored regional institutions with substantial delegated authority. Even so, an early institutional effort to integrate defense policies and national militaries, the European Defense Community, failed. The region's key security provider became the North Atlantic Treaty Organization (NATO), a highly institutionalized alliance dominated by an extra-regional power; the alliance's membership overlapped substantially with membership in the European Economic Community. The EU has played a major indirect role in reinforcing regional security through its expansion into Eastern Europe. Regional security is also sustained by a network of regional institutions, such as the Council of Europe and Organization for Security and Cooperation in Europe (OSCE), that complement and coordinate with the EU (Kelley, chapter 4). Recent institutional changes in the EU, such as the appointment of a High Representative of the Union for Foreign Affairs and Security Policy and a planned European External Action Service, aim to give additional weight to the EU's Common Foreign and Security Policy.

The Americas display a second pattern of economic and security linkage, in which peace building and economic integration have *paralleled* one another in a mutually reinforcing relationship. The most successful regional economic institutions, particularly MERCOSUR and NAFTA, were preceded by resolution of longstanding security and political conflicts among their members (Domínguez, chapter 5). At the same time, regional institutions divided clearly between rules and forums governing intra- and interstate conflict and those dealing with regional economic integration. The Organization of American States (OAS) has had a longstanding role in dispute mediation and settlement. More recently, it became the principal institutional guarantor of democratic constitutionalism, authorizing regional intervention in the domestic affairs of its members. The OAS played no role, however, in regional or subregional agreements to liberalize trade and investment. On the other hand, until MERCOSUR limited membership to democracies through a treaty amendment in 1997, economic integration treaties had not included clauses that constrained the domestic political ordering or foreign policy behavior of their members (Domínguez 2007). Regional institutions dealt with both security and economic issues, but a clear division of labor existed.

Those regions and sub-regions without robust mechanisms for conflict prevention and resolution often found that insecurity created negative spillovers for economic integration, a third pattern of linkage between economics and security. In certain sub-regions of Latin America, such as Central America, as well as the Middle East, South Asia, and Africa, conflict *undermined or slowed* regional institution building and integration. In the Central American Common Market (CACM), regional insecurity and conflict were coupled with declining intraregional trade in the 1980s. Persistent militarized disputes hindered further development of existing regional institutions. Sustained peace was not required, however, to produce trade liberalization and expansion in this and other cases, such as the Andean Group (Dominguez, chapter 5).

For East and Southeast Asia, links between economics and security display a fourth pattern. Relations in these two domains run on *distinct tracks*, neither interfering with nor reinforcing one another. On the one hand, political conflict and militarized disputes are seldom allowed to inhibit mutual economic interests in expanding trade and investment. The most striking example of this agreed divorce between deep political conflict and rapidly growing interdependence is the relationship between China and Taiwan. In the rest of Northeast Asia, this separation has permitted the growth of trade, investment, and economic cooperation in the face of persistent territorial and political disputes. Regional governments avoid economic sanctions or economic statecraft aimed at changing the policies of a target state. ASEAN's unwillingness to endorse U.S. and EU sanctions against Myanmar is only one example of this preference for separating economic exchange from political relations. Regional economic institutions also reflect this separation, with few connections between institutions that deal with economic issues and those, like the ASEAN Regional Forum (ARF), that address security concerns.

Despite the economic benefits of a two-track approach to economics and security, Asian avoidance of linkage has not promoted political reconciliation or military confidence building of the kind that has either preceded or accompanied regional initiatives in Europe and Latin America. ASEAN may have created positive economic spillovers through creation of a code of state conduct (ASEAN's Treaty of Amity and Cooperation or TAC) and bolstering norms of cooperative behavior. Those economic benefits were unintentional, however, not the product of a regional or national strategy that linked security and economic cooperation.

Competition and Complementarity Among
Institutions: Global, Regional, Sub-regional

The emergence of protectionist trade blocs in the 1930s produced a long-standing suspicion of regional trade arrangements among proponents of globe trade liberalization. Renewed interest in regional economic arrangements in the 1990s heightened concerns that global institutions might be undermined.[11] In certain issue-areas, such as trade, there are explicit rules governing competition between global regimes and regional institutions (General Agreement on Tariffs and Trade [GATT] Article XXIV in trade, for example); such rules are absent in the sphere of monetary and financial cooperation.

The competition offered by robust global institutions to the development of regional governance has received less attention. Substitution effects, described earlier, may weaken the demand for regional institutions. A preference for global rules is particularly apparent in Asia, where economies have been uniquely successful in connecting to international markets and global production networks. With few exceptions, Asian governments have sought membership in key global institutions, and they have made use of their dispute settlement mechanisms. Europe and the United States had turned toward regional economic alternatives decades before the major Asian economies—Japan, South Korea, and China—embarked on regional trade initiatives. Other regions are more reliant on regional institutions (Europe); more wary of global institutions (Latin America's unhappy history with the International Monetary Fund [IMF]); or remain suspicious of membership in any regional or global institutions with substantial authority (the Middle East's reluctance to embrace either the World Trade Organization [WTO] or effective regional institutions).

Asia's embrace of global institutions has fluctuated over time. Disenchantment with global financial institutions during the Asian financial crisis spurred negotiations for the CMI and other regional financial initiatives. The Great Recession did not produce either a new push to complete the Doha Round, a breakdown in global trade rules, or a rush toward new, defensive regional trade initiatives. The financial crisis of 2007–2009 and the subsequent threat to the Eurozone elevated the role of the IMF in financial crisis management and demonstrated that regional institutions could not provide insulation from financial globalization. Given the openness of the Asian regional economy, global institutions will remain attractive forums for negotiation and cooperation, particularly for the largest economies in the region.

Sub-regional organizations are also potential competitors with region-wide institutions, in Asia and elsewhere. Institutional competition is most damaging to regional integration when sub-regional organizations have over-lapping memberships and similar mandates or when their memberships and mandates closely resemble those of regional institutions. Where a clear division of labor exists among sub-regional institutions or between those institutions and region-wide organizations, institutional relationships are more likely to be complementary than competitive. In Europe, the European Community's greater economic weight produced a domino effect created by trade discrimination against non-members, ultimately attracting most members of the EFTA to membership. EFTA was reduced to four small economies, confirming the EEC/EU model for regional integration (O'Rourke, chapter 6; Baldwin 2011). The EU became a region-wide institution with both a political role, in advancing democracy and enhancing security, and a dominant economic role in European integration.

Region-wide institutions elsewhere are primarily political; sub-regional organizations have taken the lead in the integration of regional economies. The OAS, for example, has mediated disputes among its Latin American members and promoted democracy, but it has not played a significant role in economic liberalization. Because of this implicit division of labor between sub-regional economic institutions and region-wide political and security organizations, little overt friction has resulted in the Americas between peak regional organizations and those promoting regional economic integration. When broader regional economic initiatives, such as the Free Trade Agreement of the Americas (FTAA) were proposed, sub-regional competition was not an important obstacle to their successful negotiation and implementation.

Unlike most other regions, Asia does not support a region-wide, political institution or institutions in addition to a population of sub-regional economic institutions. The recently inaugurated East Asia Summit may eventually become a central region-wide political organization, but it lacks institutional permanence, and its membership remains in flux. The Asian sub-regional institutional landscape is also unusual. Northeast Asia, its most important economic sub-region, lacks any significant institutions; ASEAN, representing a smaller sub-regional economy, has played a leading role in designing region-wide initiatives (APT, ART). In addition, Asia has proliferated bilateral and plurilateral trade agreements over the past decade, unconstrained by region-wide agreement on their contents. This pattern of sharp variation in sub-regional institutional strength and relative weakness in region-wide institutionalization creates the possibility of future competition between sub-regional group and future region-wide institutionalization.

Contingency: Political Entrepreneurs and Economic Crisis

Two contingencies may accelerate or arrest the dynamics of regional integration and institution building. Political entrepreneurs seek to exchange public policy initiatives for electoral support and public recognition. They may promote regional initiatives, calculating domestic political benefits in excess of any regional public good that might be provided.[12] Wedded to robust European institutions, Christian Democratic leaders in Europe played a central role in European integration during the crucial decade of the 1950s (O'Rourke, chapter 6). In Asia, Prime Minister Mohammed Mahathir of Malaysia argued for an East Asian Economic Group in the early 1990s, an idea that was realized in the creation of ASEAN+3 later in the decade. More recently, two former Prime Ministers, Yukio Hatoyama of Japan and Kevin Rudd of Australia, backed visions for, respectively, an East Asian Community and an Asia Pacific Community. Their lack of success demonstrated that political entrepreneurs are highly dependent on the regional and global environment, particularly the attitude of the major powers.

Economic crisis often creates a dramatic shift in the regional environment that provides openings for such entrepreneurs. Henning (chapter 7) finds that, under certain conditions, economic and financial crises promote regional institution building. Crises that originate within the region and attract extra-regional support for regional governments are unlikely to promote regional collaboration. On the other hand, several regional characteristics are likely to contribute to post-crisis institutional development: a substantial secretariat tasked to promote regional integration, significant market integration, functional spillovers across issue-areas, and disenchantment with global institutions.

Explaining Regional Institutions: Asia, Europe, and the Americas

Comparison with Europe and the Americas underlines the distinctiveness of Asian regional institutions. The same comparison also indicates that Asian regionalism shares several characteristics with other developing regions in which intraregional trade and investment have grown rapidly during the past two decades. Asia seems even less of an outlier if African and Middle Eastern regional institutions are added to the comparison set.[13]

As outlined by O'Rourke, the backers of the EEC benefited from both structural and contingent historical circumstances in the crucial decades of the 1950s and 1960s. Europe's grim history of insecurity, its status as the first industrialized region, and a world economy that remained relatively closed for two decades after 1945—all pointed to regional demand for more robust institutions to promote economic integration. As its economies liberalized, the Asian regional economy confronted a very different starting point, one in which the end of the Cold War, minimal welfare states, and a relatively open global economy, sustained by a strengthened global trade regime, reduced the incentives for more elaborate regional institutions.

Apart from growing regional economic integration, structural variables have had a negative or neutral effect on Asian integration: heterogeneous preferences based on political and economic disparities; leading powers that view each other as rivals; and a region open to influence by outside powers that provide its with market access and security guarantees. Europe, and later the Americas, founded regional integration advances on political reconciliation and a reduction in intra-regional military threats. Although ASEAN has pursued a similar path toward regional institution-building, negotiating a Treaty of Amity and Cooperation and extending its reach, political and military rivalries still beset Northeast and South Asia. For foreign policy reasons, the United States, the outside actor with the most leverage over Europe, consistently supported regional initiatives that might have placed its economic interests at risk. In Asia, the United States constructed a bilateral alliance system and often viewed regional initiatives as threats to that security architecture. None of these structural features of the Asian region are an absolute barrier to a different model of regional institutions, but they may set limits to institutional change in the near term.

Following the creation of the European Economic Community and its institutions by the Treaty of Rome, both economic and institutional feedback effects reinforced future institutional development. A ratchet effect consolidated economic liberalization and hindered backsliding, even in the face of such powerful skeptics as Charles de Gaulle and Margaret Thatcher. Pro-liberalization interests, such as export-oriented business, found multiple points of entry to European regional institutions. As described by Hix (chapter 2), the Single European Act (1986) was a critical juncture, in which institutional innovations were introduced to manage deeper economic integration. On each of the institutional dimensions described earlier—decision rules, legalization, and membership—European institutions moved further away from the minimalist FTA model than any other region.

Although regional institutions in the Americas diverge less from their Asian counterparts, their trajectory differs in three key respects. First, regional economic institutions incorporate more commitment mechanisms. Unilateral liberalization was important in both Asia and the Americas. In Latin America, however, national decisions to reduce trade barriers were often followed by regional agreements that confirmed those commitments. Legalized agreements—precise, binding, with clear timetables—reinforced liberalization commitments in NAFTA and other free trade agreements (Domínguez, chapter 5). In MERCOSUR and other cases, high-level political commitment (or intervention) served as commitment devices. Latin America's historical policy volatility—swings in national policy between populism and closure on the one hand and free-market openness on the other—may explain its greater demand for regional commitment mechanisms. A second difference between the two regions lay in the pursuit of peace building in the Americas, a dampening of historical rivalries that preceded or accompanied regional economic collaboration. In North America, peace building among Canada, the United States, and Mexico began in the nineteenth century; in Latin America, rapprochement between Argentina and Brazil was a key departure of the 1980s. That decade also produced a third development that set regional institutions in the Americas apart from those in Asia: nearly universal democratization. Political opening across Latin America contributed to preference convergence in favor of liberalization and empowered pro-liberalization interests and their demands for regional commitments that would reinforce the new policy orientation.

In light of these regional comparisons, another explanation for the Asian way of regional institution building can confidently be set aside: greater sovereignty costs. As Hix (chapter 2) demonstrates, even among the post-modern states of Europe, governments carefully construct checks and balances to insure that their preferences guide European institutions. In other regions, postcolonial sensitivities regarding sovereignty have marked regional institutions from their inception. In Latin America, the founding principles of the OAS included the protection of national sovereignty and maintenance of existing borders (Domínguez 2007, 90–93). Generalizations regarding Asian governments, sovereignty, and international institutions are also refuted by Asia's record of participation in global institutions: Japan's support for a strengthened dispute settlement mechanism at the WTO; China's negotiation of a WTO protocol of accession that imposed stringent requirements of change in domestic regulations and laws; willingness of ASEAN member states to turn to the International Court of Justice for the resolution of territorial disputes (while ignoring ASEAN's own dispute settlement mechanism).

A final explanation for the distinctiveness of Asian institutions is more difficult to dismiss: the Asian institutional model may simply be more effective than many Western critics allow. Determining the influence of regional institutions on national policies, the most convincing measure of their effectiveness, requires grappling with a daunting counterfactual: what would national policies have been in the absence of regional institutions? Both Kelley (chapter 4) and Haggard (chapter 8) provide a skeptical overview of arguments that convoy membership rules and soft law, of the kind promoted by Asian institutions, may be as effective in certain contexts as binding membership requirements and hard law. Jon Pevehouse (2009) has estimated the effects of regional institutions, operating through several avenues of influence, on national policies. In the domain of anti-corruption policies, his findings support those of Kelley (chapter 4): club membership rules and pre-accession conditionality—the European model—appear to be more effective. He also confirms the conclusions of Domínguez (chapter 5) on Latin American regional agreements: a willing national "consumer" of policy change reinforces institutional influence.

Amitav Acharya (chapter 9), on the other hand, argues forcefully that the design features of Asian regional institutions—convoy membership, multi-issue agendas, consensus decision-making and deliberation—are more conducive to socialization of members than more formal and legalized structures. Based on outcomes for three large Asian countries—Vietnam, China, and India—in three different issue-areas, Acharya finds progressive adoption of community rules and norms over time. The effects of socialization on national behavior in such institutions as ASEAN and the ASEAN Regional Forum (ARF) are central to the positive case for Asian institutional design.[14]

Asian Institutions: Deeper Economic Integration and the Prospects for Change

Recent changes in key Asian regional institutions suggest that their distinctive features are not fixed. ASEAN, the institutional model for many institutions in the region, has adopted a charter that self-consciously models itself on the vocabulary and template of the European Union and formally empowers its secretariat to monitor compliance by member countries. The CMI has been transformed during the global financial crisis into the CMIM. Its new multilateral design is marked by the first move toward majoritarian decision rules in an Asian regional institution. Adoption of its new voting formula may permit more decisive action in a future financial crisis and at the same time protect the interests of its largest members. These modest changes hardly suggest a revolution in Asian regional institutions, but they confirm that regional governments continue to question the performance of existing organizations and aim at improving their effectiveness.

Which of the variables that produced Asia's particular brand of regional institutions could change and, in changing, accelerate institutional development in the region? Structural variables by definition change slowly, but the Great Recession of 2008–2009 may encourage Asian governments to depend less on extra-regional export markets for their politically essential high rates of growth. Over time, growth strategies based on domestic demand could make regional markets more attractive and access to those markets a higher priority. Extra-regional influence over future institutional development would also decline. Democratization would empower non-state actors and spur interest in deeper integration, but political change in the region's authoritarian states is likely to be incremental and geographically limited. MacIntyre and Ravenhill (chapter 10) emphasize the larger political and strategic fissures in the region as a barrier to sturdier regional institutions. Linking economic and security issues, the recently expanded East Asia Summit may provide the necessary forum for dampening and resolving intra-regional rivalries over time. The evolution of its spare institutional framework to become the "foundational security and political institution for Asia," as described by former Secretary of State Hillary Clinton, is only likely in the long run.

For the authors in this volume, radical change in Asian regional institutions is unlikely, and none recommend ambitious blueprints that are designed to fail. For contemporary Asia, the likeliest route to change in its regional economic institutions will be elite-based and demand-driven: a calculation that the agenda of deeper integration—dealing with barriers to exchange that lie behind national borders and are often deeply embedded in domestic politics and policy—is necessary for buoyant economic growth and political survival. Regional institutional change would follow from a second estimate: deeper economic integration requires a different model for regional governance. In regions outside Europe, either unilateral national decisions to reduce trade barriers or commitments undertaken at the GATT/WTO have typically been more important than regional institutions in the expansion of regional trade and investment. A key question for Asia is whether its model of regional economic integration, based largely on unilateralism and WTO commitments, has been exhausted, pointing to a need for new regional initiatives and institutions.

Developing regions have seldom moved beyond free trade agreements to negotiate an agenda of deeper economic integration. As Domínguez points out, Latin American regional groupings have not achieved common markets that create more integrated economic spaces, despite their successful implementation of free trade agreements. Industrialized countries have been the principal advocates for more ambitious regional economic agendas. Most recently, the United States has advanced the Trans-Pacific Partnership as a model agreement of this kind.

From the very limited array of regional institutions that have pursued an effective deeper integration agenda, several paths to institutional effectiveness are apparent. European analysts agree that deeper integration—the creation of a true common market—required greater delegation to supranational institutions, even though the particular institutional model of the European Union may not be optimal for other regions.[15] Without the institutions of the EEC, Europe might well have remained a large and successful free trade area. In the case of NAFTA, a more extensive agenda of economic integration did include some delegation to third-party adjudicators, but its alternative to supranationalism on the European model was reliance on the precise and binding character of the NAFTA agreement. Finally, Australia and New Zealand have pursued an ambitious agenda of deeper economic integration since 1983 through their agreements on Closer Economic Relations.[16] The two economic partners have not built substantial bilateral institutions to govern their deepening interdependence, however. Exceptional circumstances appear to explain the absence of institutionalization in this case: similar political institutions, national preferences that clearly converged to favor liberalization, and limited mutual economic vulnerability.[17] For Asia, a region absent those characteristics, an institution-free move toward deeper integration is unlikely.

The authors in this volume propose several incremental steps that would build institutions for a future of deeper economic integration in Asia. First, as a large and heterogeneous region, Asia is not likely to proceed toward more intensive cooperation under the umbrella of a single organization. Haggard (chapter 8) suggests that adjustment of memberships may be more important to future collaboration than adjustment of rules, permitting smaller groups of cooperating governments to develop more ambitious economic agendas. Kelley (chapter 4) outlines the ways in such groups of cooperators could deploy membership rules flexibly to promote their new agenda, by creating tiered memberships, changing membership requirements, and creating multiple institutions.

Voeten (chapter 3) proposes initial steps to introduce useful judicial institutions to a region without such institutions, allowing courts to offer advisory opinions on the interpretation of existing rules and standards. Should the region or some part of it embark on a deeper integration agenda, regional rules would probably create rights and obligations for private parties, as they have elsewhere, and regional courts could undertake the interpretation of new treaty obligations. Haggard (chapter 8) emphasizes a different and equally modest set of institutional innovations, centered on delegation. Paralleling Voeten's recommendations, some involve the introduction of non-state actors into regional governance. Compliance boards that include non-governmental representatives could serve to illuminate failures to implement negotiated agreements. Their work could be complemented by independent assessment and evaluation on the effectiveness of regional institutions. Private parties could be granted standing in dispute settlement mechanisms, even in the absence of full-blown regional courts. Just as changes in membership rules could amplify the influence of those in favor of more ambitious cooperative bargains, such innovations in delegation would open regional political dynamics to private parties who have incentives to promote compliance with negotiated agreements.

Incremental steps to change existing institutions have already confirmed that Asia is willing to consider changes in its institutional models to accommodate new economic circumstances. ASEAN's plans for an ASEAN Economic Community by 2015 will be an important first test of the link between deeper economic integration and institutional change; progress of the Trans-Pacific Strategic Economic Partnership (TPP) will be another. If Asia—or, more likely, some group of Asian governments—successfully undertakes the challenge of deeper economic integration with its political risks and concomitant institutional demands, the choice will have profound economic and strategic consequences for the region. Depending on their design, regional economic institutions can promote peace as well as economic integration (Kahler 2012). Asia's choices in regional governance will not only shape its own prospects, they will also affect, for better or worse, a system of global economic governance that has long sustained Asian economic development and its growing contribution to international prosperity.

Notes

1. The regional institutions of principal interest in this volume are economic institutions, although cross-regional variation in the linkage between economics and security is examined.

2. By January 2010, the number of preferential trade agreements with at least one Asia-Pacific member was 112; an additional 60 were under negotiation (ADB 2010, 61, Table 2.13).

3. The remainder of this chapter is based in part on the author's contribution to ADB 2010, especially chapters 3 and 5.

4. Consensus rules can be distinguished from unanimity rules, which require active support from all members.

5. The "Asian Way" closely resembles the ASEAN institutional model described in Khong and Nesadurai 2007, 36, 41–42; Johnston 2008, 161–163.

6. Compare Mattli 1999: 56; Acharya and Johnston 2007a, 258–259; and Dominguez 2007, 123.

7. Smith (2000) documents the influence of more powerful state on the design of dispute settlement mechanisms. Khadiagala (2009) points to the resentment of Nigerian leadership within the Economic Community of West African States (ECOWAS). Similar resistance to regional leadership has periodically confronted India in South Asia and the United States in the Americas.

8. See also Solís, Stallings, and Katada (2009).

9. These economic relationships are documented in Asian Development Bank (2008).

10. See, for example, Wyplosz 2006: 274, for a dissent from the necessity of trade integration rather than monetary cooperation as a prerequisite for deeper economic integration.

11. For contrasting views, see Barton, Goldstein, Josling, and Steinberg 2006, 54–55; Bhagwati 2008; Lawrence 1996.

12. On the role of the political entrepreneur in the creation of international institutions, Keohane 2001.

13. On Africa, Khadiagala 2009; on the Middle East, Solingen 2009. These regions do not display the same level of regional economic integration as the Americas or Asia.

14. On socialization in international institutions, see Checkel 2005 and Johnston 2008.

15. Hix, chapter 2; Baldwin 2009; Wyplosz 2006.

16. Closer Economic Relations (CER) replaced an existing Free Trade Agreement between Australia and New Zealand. In its first phase, CER aimed at achieving free trade in goods and services. After a 1988 review, when that agenda was substantially complete, the two partners embarked on the deeper integration agenda, which included harmonization of business law and regulatory practices, customs procedures, government purchasing, and technical barriers to trade.

17. Kahler 1995, 109–111.

TWO

THE DESIGN OF REGIONAL INSTITUTIONS

Institutional Design of Regional Integration
Balancing Delegation and Representation

SIMON HIX

Introduction

Regional economic integration is both a deregulatory project, involving the removal of barriers to the movement of goods and services, as well as a re-regulatory project, involving the adoption of new common standards. The removal of trade barriers may be achieved by bilateral or multilateral agreements, as the network of trade agreements in East Asia demonstrates. However, the adoption of common rules—such as competition rules, minimum product standards, and environmental rules—requires the delegation of agenda-setting and enforcement to independent bodies. Put another way, regional integration is unlikely to progress from free trade to a genuine single market without a certain degree of delegation.

Such delegation has thus far been resisted by governments in East Asia. There are many reasons why sovereign states in the region have resisted this step. One reason is the fear that delegation to a "supranational body," like the European Union (EU) Commission, would lead to policy outputs beyond the intentions of the governments. Such a step would compromise the national sovereignty of these states. East Asia is simply different from Europe, where citizens and state officials share a post-national conception of sovereignty.

I challenge this reasoning. In both regions governments primarily seek to protect their national interests. Moreover, delegation to an independent body, if designed carefully, can promote the collective interests of the states rather than undermine national sovereignty. Specifically, "policy drift" by an independent executive beyond the intentions of the governments can be limited by careful institutional design of delegation and representation.

To make the case that regional economic integration in East Asia could be promoted by institutional design, this chapter is organised as follows. Section 2 explains how regional economic integration is primarily an exercise in market regulation, and how delegating agenda-setting and enforcement is critical for the promotion of market integration. Section 3 then explains how institutional mechanisms can be designed to limit "policy drift." Section 4 discusses whether state preferences are sufficiently convergent in East Asia for such delegation to take place, and section 5 turns to the design of representation in a potential East Asian Economic Union. Finally, section 6 looks at the current institutional arrangements in East Asia, and particularly the Chiang Mai Initiative Multilateralization.

Regional Economic Integration as a Regulatory Project

A free trade area involves the removal of barriers to trade in a particular set of goods or services, via the reduction or abolition of import tariffs and quotas. All free trade agreements exclude particular sectors of the economy. In contrast, genuine regional economic integration, for example, in the European "single market," involves the removal of all barriers to the free circulation of goods, services, capital, and labour as well as the implementation of a set of common regulations to enable a market to function efficiently and effectively (European Commission 1985).

Setting up a single market beyond the nation-state consequently involves both deregulation and re-regulation (Dehousse 1992; Majone 1996). On the deregulatory side, legal obligations as set out in a free trade agreement commit governments to abolish tariff barriers and "behind-the-border" (non-tariff) barriers on the free movement of goods, services, and capital, such as capital controls, import quotas, and customs duties. In addition, "mutual recognition"—the principle that if a good or service can be sold in one state it can be sold in all other states—puts indirect pressure on governments to remove non-tariff barriers.

On the re-regulatory side, to enable goods and services to circulate, certain product and process standards need to be adopted, to correct potential market failures and a potential regulatory "race to the bottom," as states compete to cut the costs for their own industries or to attract foreign direct investment. Product regulations include things like product safety standards, labelling rules, and packaging and waste disposal standards, while process regulations include rules on health and safety at work, environmental pollution, labour market rules, and gender equality and other non-discrimination rules. There is little empirical evidence of a regulatory race-to-the-bottom, but these effects are difficult to identify and the political perceptions of such a race are potent (esp. Baldwin 2009).

How should these common rules be adopted? According to the normative theory of regulation, the aim of market regulation should be to promote the public interest (e.g., Mitnick 1980; Sunstein 1990). In classical economic theory, free markets are naturally pareto-efficient. In the real world there are, of course, market failures, and regulation can be used to correct these failures. For example, technical standards enable consumers to gain information about the quality of products, environmental standards reduce negative externalities, and competition policies prevent monopolistic markets and anti-competitive practices. If these policies are made through representative institutions—such as a council of states deciding by majority rule—they are likely to promote private interests rather than the public interest.

Applying this logic to regional economic integration, most scholars advocate the delegation of agenda-setting and enforcement to independent bodies (e.g., Moravcsik 1998, 1999; Pollack 1997, 2003; Mattli 1999). First, delegating agenda-setting facilitates the resolution of a coordination dilemma. Each state has an interest in having its domestic standards established for the market as a whole. This can lead to conflict if states' domestic standards are considerably different. However, all states benefit from an agreement on a common set of standards rather than no agreement, as any common standard would enable a single market to function in a particular sector whereas no agreement would mean that trade could not take place. In this situation, an independent agenda-setter helps resolve the conflict, by working out which set of regulations are best to correct potential market failures, and then proposing these rules as the harmonized standard. In building the European single market, despite differing national regulatory standards, the European Commission was able to secure common rules that were above the average level in Europe.

Second, delegating enforcement to an independent body resolves another type of collective action problem (a prisoner's dilemma). Even if the benefits for a state of the other states opening their markets are greater than the costs of opening up its own market, there is a collective action problem because the best response of each state is not to apply the rules, in the expectation that the other states would do the same. The likely outcome is that all states fail to implement the common agreement. However, delegating enforcement to an independent actor changes these cost-benefit calculations, as each state is then aware that they could be punished for failing to apply the rules. For example, in the EU context, the Treaty of Rome delegated to the European Commission responsibility for monitoring the enforcement of the collective rules, and referring any state which breached the rules to the European Court of Justice. A similar logic applies in the operation of the Dispute Settlement panels of the World Trade Organization. In this way, delegating enforcement is a "commitment device" as each state is then aware that once an agreement has been reached on a new set of common regulations, there is a high likelihood that all states will have to apply these rules.

Institutional Mechanisms to Limit Policy Drift by a Supranational Executive

Once powers have been delegated to independent institutions, however, these institutions are likely to have their own institutional interests and policy preferences, which might not be identical to the preferences of their principals (cf. Stigler 1971). For example, agencies can try to increase their influence in the policy process, their budgets, or their independence from political control. Delegating agenda-setting and enforcement might consequently lead to "policy drift."

Nevertheless, institutions can be designed to limit the potential of policy drift (cf. McCubbins and Schwartz 1984). In the EU context, for example, the institutions have been carefully designed to limit the possibility that the Commission will act as a "runaway bureaucracy" (esp. Moravcsik 1998). More precisely, three institutional mechanisms limit the policy independence of the EU Commission. First, *the initial decision to delegate is taken by a unanimous intergovernmental decision.* Amendment of the EU treaty is required to either add a new policy competence to the EU or to change decision-making in a policy area from unanimity amongst the governments to qualified-majority voting (QMV)—which would give genuine independent agenda-setting power to the Commission. And, reform of the treaty requires unanimity amongst the governments as well as national ratification, either by a parliamentary vote or by a national referendum, or both. This is a very high threshold.

This threshold means that there is already a high level of consensus amongst the EU governments in all the policy areas where the Commission has been given agenda-setting power (e.g., Franchino 2007). It also means that any potential losers from delegation have been able to demand "side-payments." These side-payments to purchase unanimous support for a market integration project can be in the form of "hard cash," from those states who expect to gain most from market integration (the net exporters) to those states who expect to gain least (the net importers). For example, when the single market programme was agreed, the periphery states (Italy, Spain, Ireland, Portugal, and Greece) demanded a doubling of regional aid via the EU budget as a price for signing up to market integration. Moreover, side-payments can also be policy "trades" in the original intergovernmental package deal. This trade involves those states who expect to gain most from market integration, allowing other states to add issues to the agenda which they feel promote their interests at the expense of the net exporting states. For example, the agreement to create a single market also contained a trade between a centre-right free market agenda for Europe and a social democratic policy of promoting a "Social Europe" (such as workers' rights).

And, the high thresholds for delegation mean that highly sensitive issues remain largely intergovernmental in the EU, as there is insufficient consensus to enable agenda-setting to be delegated on these issues. The EU heads of state and government, who meet in the European Council four times a year, set the medium- and long-term policy agenda of the EU and play an essential role in resolving disputes. Intergovernmental bargaining also dominates negotiations over the EU's multi-annual budget. Furthermore, supranational delegation and decision-making only operate on a limited set of issues which relate to the creation and regulation of Europe's continental-scale market. And, even within this set of policy issues, heads of state and government are involved on every highly salient issue, which they resolve through classic intergovernmental consensus-building and horse-trading.

Second, the rules governing the election of, and representation in, the supranational executive ensure that the preferences of the executive are close to those of the governments. Under the Rome Treaty design, the President of the Commission—the most powerful post in the EU—was chosen by unanimous agreement amongst the heads of state and government of the EU states. Since 1994, the nominee of the governments must also receive the backing of a majority in the European Parliament. And, since 2004, the governments can nominate a Commission President by QMV, although in practice they try to reach a consensus. These rules ensure that the governments are likely to choose a Commission President who they can work closely with and who shares their vision for the EU. In this respect, Jacques Delors was the exception rather than the rule, in that all Commission Presidents before and since Delors have been far more consensual and less ambitious. The three

Commission Presidents since Delors—Santer, Prodi, and Barroso—have been less willing to confront the big member states in major constitutional, policy, or budgetary battles.

Regarding the other members of the Commission, there has always been at least one Commissioner per EU member state—hence replicating the preferences of the governments inside the EU executive. Under the Rome Treaty design, the large states (Germany, France, Italy, and the UK) had two Commissioners each and the other states had one each. With the prospect of enlargement of the EU to 27 states, there was pressure to reduce the number of Commissioners. It was first agreed that there would be only one Commissioner per member state, which was implemented in the Barroso Commission in 2005. Then, in the failed Constitution for Europe it was proposed that the number of Commissioners would be less than the number of EU states. However, this became a salient issue in the rejection of the Lisbon Treaty in a referendum in Ireland, where Irish voters were concerned inter alia that they would lose a Commissioner. One result of the No vote in Ireland is a new protocol between the governments which ensures that every member state will retain a Commissioner.

Third, *high decision-making thresholds and multiple checks-and-balances for the adoption of legislative proposals of the executive ensure that policy outcomes are highly consensual.* At the same time as delegating new agenda-setting powers to the EU Commission and extending the use of majority voting in the EU Council, the EU governments reformed the treaty to increase the checks-and-balances in the legislative process, to ensure that no policy could be adopted without broad national and political support. In the main legislative procedure of the EU—known as the "ordinary legislative procedure"—legislative proposals of the Commission must pass a simple majority in the Commission, an oversized-majority in the Council, and a simple majority in the European Parliament. Furthermore, because governments are represented in the EU Council while parties are represented in the European Parliament, the EU legislative system guarantees that policies cannot be adopted without the support of a broad coalition of both governments and political parties.

In the Council, for example, where the EU governments are represented, the QMV rules ensure that an oversized-majority is required for policies to be adopted. And, even when QMV is used, the EU governments prefer to agree by consensus, as they know that they will be responsible for implementing policies once they have been passed, and that implementation will be more difficult if they have been outvoted in the Council (Mattila and Lane 2001; Hayes-Renshaw and Wallace 2006). This does not mean that EU governments "give in" to a majority of other states, but does suggest that every government has an incentive to compromise to achieve a broad consensus.

In the European Parliament, meanwhile, coalitions are formed along transnational party lines rather than national lines. The Members of the European Parliament (MEP) sit as transnational "political groups" rather than as national delegations. Moreover, as the powers of the European Parliament have increased, the political groups have become more powerful as the incentives to organise and mobilise to shape EU policies have increased. As a result, voting in the European Parliament is primarily along transnational political lines rather than along national lines (Hix et al. 2007, 2009).

In sum, economic integration beyond the nation-state is primarily an exercise in market regulation. The main policy aim of such regulation should be to create a level playing field for economic competition and to correct potential market failures. These goals are best secured through a particular institutional design. First, agenda-setting and enforcement should be delegated to an independent supranational executive (like the EU Commission). Second, the potential independent action of this body should be restricted via a particular institutional design, where (1) unanimous intergovernmental agreement is needed before any powers are delegated (and intergovernmental deals at the highest political level are used to resolve disputes even after delegation has taken place); (2) the procedure for appointing the head of the executive and the structure of representation in the body ensure a close match between the preferences of the executive together with the government principals; and (3) high decision-making thresholds for the adoption of policy proposals from the body ensure highly consensual outcomes.

What is remarkable in the European context is that the EU has been able to progress so far with such a high level of national and political consensus. This is partly a result of a convergence of preferences between the governments and the main political parties in Europe, relative to the status quo of no regional economic integration. However, it is also a result of the careful design of representation in the EU institutions to facilitate consensus. These two aspects—preferences and institutions—are hence the focus of the next two sections.

Convergent Preferences in Europe and Asia

The main reason why the states of Western Europe unanimously agreed in the mid 1980s to create a single market, and to delegate significant powers to the EU Commission to achieve this goal, was that there was a dramatic convergence of preferences at that time (esp. Moravcsik 1998). By the mid 1980s there was a consensus in favour of a single market which included every major political party and political leader. On the right, the British conservative government of Margaret Thatcher realised that the impact of British privatisation and deregulation would be much greater if these policies could be spread to the Continent. On the left, following the failure of radical socialist economic policies in the early 1980s, the French socialist government of François Mitterrand turned in the mid 1980s to the creation of a European-wide market as a way of promoting the rationalization of European industry and the emergence of European industrial champions.

This political consensus was also supported by a broad consensus amongst economists. By the mid 1980s most economists agreed that national Keynesian policies had failed, as these policies had not helped Europe recover from the recessions of the 1970s and early 1980s as quickly as the United States and Japan had. The solution, most felt, was the creation of a European-wide market that would force national governments to liberalize their economies and lead to enormous economies of scale. For example, a group of economists produced a famous report on *The Cost of Non-Europe*, which claimed that a single market would add 4.5 percent to the gross domestic product (GDP) of the EU member states, reduce prices by 6 percent, and create 1.8 billion new jobs (Cecchini et al. 1988).

Multinational corporations across Europe mobilized to lobby their governments to support this agenda (e.g., Sandholtz and Zysman 1989; Middlemas 1995). And, after the so-called "Eurosclerosis" years of the 1970s, there was widespread public enthusiasm in most countries for a renewed effort to integrate Europe. This was partly driven by optimistic expectations about the positive economic benefits of European integration. But, the new ideological commitment to European integration was also driven in the mid 1980s by growing antipathy in many countries to the Reagan administration in Washington.

In other words, a particular and potentially unique set of factors came together in the mid 1980s in Western Europe to create the environment for political leaders to embark on an ambitious programme of regional economic integration. Could something similar happen in East Asia? Tables 2.1 and 2.2 present data on socio-economic and political characteristics of states in Europe and Asia and citizens' preferences in the two regions. The most obvious inference from these data is that the level of heterogeneity in the size of states and economies is much smaller in the EU than in East Asia (e.g., Kahler 2009). By global standards the EU has 6 medium-sized states of more or less equal size (Germany, France, United Kingdom, Italy, Spain, and Poland) and 21 small or very small states. In contrast, if one takes the 16 states in the East Asian Summit, there is enormous diversity between the 2 most populous countries on the planet (China and India), 1 state with a huge economy but a medium-sized population (Japan), 6 states with either medium-sized economies or medium-sized populations (South Korea, Indonesia, Philippines, Thailand, Vietnam, and Myanmar), 2 relatively small-population states with medium-sized economies (Australia and Malaysia), and the remaining 5 states with either small economies or small populations, or both (Singapore, Cambodia, Laos, Brunei, New Zealand).

However, these size imbalances may present more of a problem for the design of representative institutions—which is the subject of the next section—than whether there can be a convergence of basic economic, social, or political preferences in a region. On these issues, the data in Tables 2.1 and 2.2 present mixed evidence. Measured in terms of standard deviations from the inter-state means, there is not much difference in the level of heterogeneity in the EU and East Asia. However, the difference between the highest and lowest values is larger in Asia than in the EU for almost all measures. For example, the gap in GDP per capita (in terms of purchasing power parity) between the richest three and the poorest three states in the EU27 is $39,000, whereas the same gap in East Asia is $44,000. Also, whereas no EU state has a GDP per capita less than $10,000, 11 states in the East Asian Summit are poorer than this level. Also, the level of income inequality within states is much higher in East Asia than in Europe. As a result, regional economic integration in East Asia must address issues relating to the alleviation of poverty and basic economic development, whereas these are secondary issues in the EU.

The heterogeneity in terms of the political characteristics of states is also smaller in Europe than in East Asia. The average level of public spending in the EU27 is 43.6 percent of GDP, with only a 6.6 percent standard deviation and a gap of only 20 percent between the average of the three highest public spenders (Sweden, France, and Hungary) and the three lowest (Romania, Estonia, and Lithuania). In East Asia, the average level of public spending is 23.2 percent of GDP, with 9.4 standard deviation and a gap of 26.5 percent between the average of the three highest spenders (New Zealand, Japan, and Australia) and the three lowest (Myanmar, Cambodia, and Singapore).

Moreover, the differences in public spending in the EU are mainly related to economic development, with poorer states spending less than richer states, rather than ideological policy choices. In East Asia, in contrast, the difference in public spending between Japan, Australia, New Zealand, and India, on the

TABLE 2.1.

Preference heterogeneity in the European Union

Country	Socio-Economic Characteristics					Political Indicators				Citizens' Values		
	Pop'n (mil.)	GDP, ppp (US$m)	GDP/cap. ppp (US$)	Income inequality (GINI)	Public spending as % GDP	Economic freedom	Level of democracy	Rule of law	Citizen of EU	Religion is important	Environmental protection rather than growth	Wealth accumulation is okay
Germany	82.2	2,910,490	35,407	28.3	45.4	70.5	10.0	1.8	51.4	28.2	45.4	48.0
France	62.3	2,130,383	34,196	32.7	53.4	63.3	9.0	1.3	57.9	36.4		
United Kingdom	61.6	2,230,549	36,210	36.0	44.6	79.0	10.0	1.8	25.8	36.7		56.3
Italy	59.9	1,814,557	30,293	36.0	50.1	61.4	10.0	0.4	60.1	72.1		28.3
Spain	44.9	1,396,881	31,111	34.7	38.6	70.1	10.0	1.1	54.3	50.1	57.5	28.3
Poland	38.1	666,052	17,482	34.5	43.9	60.3	9.6	0.9	66.2	83.9	50.6	48.6
Romania	21.3	270,330	12,692	31.0	31.6	63.2	8.4	-0.2	62.6	79.1	57.1	54.8
Netherlands	16.6	675,375	40,685	30.9	46.1	77.0	10.0	1.8	33.2	37.8		
Greece	11.2	341,127	30,458	34.3	42.3	60.8	10.0	0.7	36.4	68.3		
Portugal	10.7	235,904	22,047	38.5	46.4	64.9	10.0	1.0	51.3	76.1		
Belgium	10.6	389,518	36,747	33.0	48.9	72.1	9.8	1.5	65.8	47.6		
Czech Republic	10.4	262,169	25,209	25.4	43.6	69.4	9.6	0.8	41.0	21.4	59.3	33.0
Hungary	10.0	196,074	19,607	26.9	51.9	66.8	10.0	0.7	50.5	41.5	34.9	44.1
Sweden	9.2	341,869	37,160	25.0	55.6	70.4	10.0	1.9	43.6	35.0	78.2	56.1
Austria	8.4	28,571	39,116	29.1	49.3	71.2	10.0	1.9	42.0	54.9		
Bulgaria	7.5	93,569	12,476	29.2	37.1	64.6	8.7	-0.1	42.8	47.7	46.6	34.7
Denmark	5.5	204,060	37,102	24.7	51.5	79.6	10.0	2.0	43.8	27.0		
Slovakia	5.4	119,268	22,087	25.8	37.7	69.4	9.2	0.4	42.0	57.4	52.1	30.0
Finland	5.3	190,862	36,012	26.9	48.8	74.5	10.0	1.9	25.2	41.9	46.1	48.5
Ireland	4.5	188,112	41,803	34.3	34.2	82.2	10.0	1.8	49.9	76.2		

	Pop'n	GDP	GDP/cap	Income inequality (GINI)	Public spending as % GDP	Economic freedom	Level of democracy	Rule of law	Citizen of EU/Asia	Religion is important	Environmental protection rather than growth	Wealth accumulation is okay
Lithuania	3.3	63,625	19,280	36.0	34.0	70.0	10.0	0.5	35.5	56.8	36.4	48.7
Latvia	2.2	38,764	17,620	37.7	37.2	66.6	8.0	0.6	45.3	34.3	52.8	71.6
Slovenia	2.0	59,316	29,658	28.4	45.3	62.9	10.0	0.8	49.9	36.5	49.8	41.4
Estonia	1.3	27,207	20,928	35.8	33.0	76.4	7.0	1.0	32.4	21.6	48.7	69.8
Cyprus	0.9	22,703	25,226	29.0	43.9	70.8	10.0	1.0	25.8	77.6		47.0
Luxembourg	0.5	40,025	80,050	26.0	39.0	75.2		1.9	62.0	43.8		
Malta	0.4	9,806	24,515	28.0	44.1	66.1		1.6	50.9	91.2		
Inter-state mean (EU27)	18.4	564,710	30,192	31.0	43.6	69.6	9.6	1.1	46.2	51.2	51.1	47.6
Inter-state std. dev. (EU27)	23.2	794,102	13,206	4.3	6.6	6.0	0.8	0.7	12.0	20.3	10.5	12.6

SOURCES:

Pop'n: Population, in millions. Department of Economic and Social Affairs Population Division, 2009, World Population Prospects, Table A1, 2008 revision, United Nations.

GDP: Gross domestic product, at Purchasing Power Party, in US$ millions. International Monetary Fund, World Economic Outlook Database, data for 2008.

GDP/cap: GDP per capita, at Purchasing Power Parity (US$); column 3/column 2.

Income inequality (GINI): GINI index of income inequality, from Human Development Report 2007/08, United Nations Development Programme; except for Chinese Taipei, Cyprus, Luxembourg, Malta from CIA World Factbook.

Public spending as % GDP: Total government spending as a percentage of GDP; Heritage Foundation 2009, Government Size indicator (converted back to public spending), from various sources.

Economic freedom: Heritage Foundation 2009, Overall Economic Freedom Score; scale ranges from 0 (lowest) to 100 (highest).

Level of democracy: Polity IV "democracy" score, mean score 1998–2007; Polity IV Project: Political Regime Characteristics and Transitions, 1800–2007, http://www.systemicpeace.org/polity/polity4.htm; scale ranges from 0 (lowest level of democracy) to 10 (highest level of democracy).

Rule of law: Worldwide Governance VI rule of law, 2007, http://info.worldbank.org/governance/wgi/index.asp; scale ranges from −2.00 (least rule of law) to +2.00 (highest rule of law).

Citizen of EU/Asia: World Values Survey 2005, for Asian countries, with question for Thailand relating to ASEAN, percent who answered "agree strongly" or "strongly" to the question: "do you feel a citizen of Asean/Asia?"; Eurobarometer 68 (2008) for EU27, percent who said that they felt either "very attached" or "fairly attached" to the European Union.

Religion is important: World Values Survey, 2005 wave, except 2000 wave for Bangladesh, China, New Zealand, Philippines, Singapore, Vietnam; and European Values Survey, 1999 wave, for EU27 except Cyprus; percent of respondents who said that religion was either "very important" and "somewhat important" for them.

Environmental protection rather than growth: World Values Survey, 2005 wave, except 1999–2004 wave for Bangladesh, New Zealand, Philippines, and Singapore; percent who chose "protecting the environment" rather than "economic growth" as a priority.

Wealth accumulation is okay: World Values Survey, 2005 wave, except 1994–99 wave for New Zealand and Philippines, Czech Republic, Estonia, Hungary, Latvia, Lithuania, and Slovakia; 10 point scale, where 1 = People can only get rich at the expense of others and 10 = Wealth can grow so there is enough for everyone, reporting percentage of respondents who answered 7 or higher on the scale.

TABLE 2.2.

Preference heterogeneity in Asia

Country	Socio-Economic Characteristics					Political Indicators			Citizens' Values			
	Pop'n (mil.)	GDP, PPP (US$m)	GDP/cap, PPP (US$)	Income inequality (GINI)	Public spending as % GDP	Economic freedom	Level of democracy	Rule of law	Citizen of Asia	Religion is important	Environmental protection rather than growth	Wealth accumulation is okay
ASEAN												
Indonesia	230.0	908,242	3,949	34.3	20.0	53.4	6.7	-0.71	82.5	98.8	16.6	57.7
Philippines	92.0	320,384	3,482	44.5	17.5	56.8	8.0	-0.59		96.9	68.0	64.9
Vietnam	88.1	240,364	2,728	34.4	27.5	51.0	0.0	-0.53	91.0	33.6	85.9	69.6
Thailand	67.8	546,095	8,054	42.0	17.7	63.0	7.4	-0.06	73.6	94.2	27.1	47.7
Myanmar	50.0	68,203	1,364		7.1	37.7	0.0	-1.41				
Malaysia	27.5	384,119	13,968	49.2	24.9	64.6	4.0	0.53		96.0	51.5	54.9
Cambodia	14.8	28,239	1,908	41.7	13.5	56.6	3.0	-1.06				
Laos	6.3	13,792	2,189	34.6	18.5	50.4	0.0	-0.96				
Singapore	4.7	238,755	50,799	42.5	14.4	87.1	2.0	1.79		82.0	52.6	37.9
Brunei	0.4	19,683	49,208					0.30				

Others in EA Summit

China (incl. HK & Macao)	1,353.3	8,223,494	6,077	46.9	19.2	53.2	0.0	−0.45	82.0	9.4	61.0	68.6
India	1,198.0	3,288,345	2,745	36.8	27.2	54.4	9.0	0.10	63.5	80.7	38.0	60.0
Japan	127.2	4,354,368	34,232	24.9	36.0	72.8	10.0	1.39	77.6	19.5	3.3	60.9
South Korea	48.3	1,342,338	27,792	31.6	30.3	68.1	8.0	0.82	32.3	48.1	27.2	40.9
Australia	21.3	795,305	37,338	35.2	34.5	82.6	10.0	1.79		39.3	58.8	67.3
New Zealand	4.3	115,709	26,909	36.2	41.0	82.0	10.0	1.91		45.8	52.7	50.4
Inter-state mean (ASEAN)	58.2	276,788	13,765	40.4	17.9	57.8	3.5	−0.3	82.3	83.6	50.3	55.4
Inter-state std. dev. (ASEAN)	69.5	284,411	19,472	5.5	6.1	13.5	3.3	0.9	8.7	25.2	25.5	11.5
Inter-state mean (EA summit)	208.4	1,305,465	17,046	38.2	23.3	62.2	5.2	0.2	71.8	62.0	45.2	56.7
Inter-state std. dev. (EA summit)	421.8	2,222,216	17,823	6.6	9.4	14.0	4.1	1.1	19.4	32.8	23.4	10.6

NOTE: See note to Table 2.1 for the sources.

one hand, and Singapore, on the other, reflects the different economic policy preferences of these two groups of states: between more social-democratic frameworks on one side and more neo-liberal frameworks on the other. These differences in East Asia are also reflected in the different economic freedom scores of these states. These basic socio-economic policy differences will be difficult to reconcile in a common set of market regulations for the region, since despite similar levels of economic development, states like Japan, Australia, and New Zealand are likely to push for higher levels of environmental and social standards than a state like Singapore. On the other hand, such a conflict might not be so different to the battles that took place in building the EU single market, between the more deregulatory preferences of successive British governments and preferences for higher regulation of successive governments in France and Germany.

In terms of measures of democracy and the rule of law, the problem in East Asia may be less to do with the degree of heterogeneity than the fact that several states are not democratic, or do not have independent judicial institutions, or both. A democratic polity, in terms or free and fair elections and a free press, is a prerequisite for EU membership. This partly reflects some of the underlying political objectives of European integration, in terms of reinforcing democratic institutions against the former threats of Fascism and Stalinism. However, democratic practices and independent courts are also essential for the sustainability of economic integration, as they guarantee the equal treatment and protection of new market entrants, without which the commitment to economic integration is not credible. While there are some on-going issues relating to the independence of courts and the judiciary in Bulgaria and Romania, these states are under pressure from the EU to fix these problems, and all 27 EU states are considered to be stable functioning democracies. In contrast, in the East Asian Summit only 9 states can be considered to be "democratic": Australia, India, Indonesia, Japan, Malaysia, New Zealand, Philippines, South Korea, and Thailand. A ninth state, Singapore, could be added to this list, on the grounds that although elections are not as competitive or free and fair as in most democracies, the courts and judiciary in Singapore are probably independent enough to support regional economic integration. The remaining 6 states—Brunei, Cambodia, China, Laos, Myanmar, and Vietnam—are probably not democratic enough nor have sufficiently independent judiciaries to credibly commit to regional economic integration beyond a free trade area.

Turning to individual citizens' values, where data are available (from World Values Surveys), the variance in citizens' attitudes to some key issues that might arise as a result of regional integration are almost as great in the EU27 as they are in East Asia. There are some significant differences between Europe and Asia. For example, Europe is largely a "post-religious" society, which has enabled the EU to have common policies on a range of socio-political issues, such as equal treatment of women, the freedom to provide abortion services, and non-discrimination on the grounds of sexual orientation. Having said that, large sections of the publics in Poland, Romania, Cyprus, Ireland, Portugal, and Italy remain devout Christians, which has led to opposition to some EU social policies in these countries. Religious heterogeneity in Asia is far greater, however. On one side are the large populations of practicing Muslims, Hindus, Buddhists, or Christians in several countries, and on the other are the largely secular societies (such China, Japan, Australia, and New Zealand). This would suggest that common policies on something as basic as the equality treatment of women in the workplace would be much more difficult to achieve in East Asia than it has been in Europe.

Nevertheless, on attitudes toward protection of the environment and wealth accumulation, Europe and Asia look rather similar. On average, 51 percent of EU citizens compared to 45 percent of East Asians believe that protection of the environment should be prioritised over economic growth. Equally, while 48 percent of Europeans believe that wealth accumulation is socially acceptable, 57 percent of East Asians feel the same way, and the standard deviations around these averages is similar in Europe and Asia. These sets of attitudes suggest that there might be widespread support for common environmental standards in East Asia, as there has been in Europe, and that it would be reasonable to justify regional integration in Asia as a vehicle for economic growth and wealth creation.

Furthermore, significant populations in all East Asian countries reported in a survey in 2005 that they identified with a wider "Asian community." Of the countries included in the survey, Australians have, not surprisingly, the weakest Asian identity, but even in that country 32 percent of respondents declared that they felt a "citizen of Asia." These figures compare favourably with the latest data on identification with the EU amongst European citizens. On average, only 46 percent of citizens in an EU state say that they feel a "citizen of the EU." Also, there is significant variance across the EU, from over 60 percent of the public feeling a citizen of the EU in Poland, Belgium, Romania, Luxembourg, and Italy to less than 30 percent in the UK. This suggests that there is a potential reservoir of public support for economic integration in East Asia.

Overall, the level of political, economic, and ideological convergence is lower in East Asia than in Europe. Some of the huge differences in terms of scale between the states and economies in the region could be addressed through a careful institutional design of representation in some common institutions, as the next section will explain. Nevertheless, it is doubtful whether there is sufficient convergence in terms of political practices, judicial independence, or public and elite attitudes toward individual economic rights to underpin an ambitious economic integration project encompassing all the states in East Asia. However, this might not preclude a smaller group of states in the region, who share similar political preferences and economic integration incentives, to start a process of deeper market and financial integration (for example, with ASEAN or the ASEAN+3 states).

There is one important caveat to this conclusion. Although a basic level of common preferences (about the free market and some minimum social and environmental standards) might be a prerequisite for regional economic integration, convergence on a range of other issues and political practices might in fact be *endogenous* to regional integration. For example, it has been a conscious strategy in Europe to use EU enlargement to extend and strengthen democratic government, the rule of law, free markets, and liberal social values. The spread of democracy, the rule of law, free markets, and liberalism might be a product of, rather than a prerequisite for, economic integration in East Asia. But this would require a "core" group of states that share these characteristics to lead the integration effort, and China remains an obstacle to any process of economic and political integration amongst the democratic states in the region.

Rules for Adopting Policies: Weighted Council Voting and a Regional Parliament

Assuming that a group of states in East Asia could converge sufficiently around the goal of deeper economic integration, and decide to delegate certain agenda-setting powers to an independent agent to achieve this goal, how could a structure of decision-making be designed for such an organisation? Given the huge variance in the size of the states in East Asia, it may at first seem impossible to design a workable system of representation in a regional organisation. However, it *is* possible to design a system of weighted voting in a council of states which both balances equitable representation for all states and constrains China and India. Back in the 1940s Lionel Penrose, an English mathematician, came up with what many scientists still consider to be the fairest system of allocating voting power to states in an intergovernmental body. Penrose's starting assumption was that every citizen in every state should have an equal chance of being on the winning side in a vote. If votes are exercised en bloc, and coalitions between states are formed randomly, then Penrose proved mathematically that the only way to achieve true equality is if the "voting power" of each state is equal to some common divisor of the square-root of a state's population (Penrose 1946).

To understand the intuition behind this proposition, consider how powerful each state would be if each state had an allocation of votes in direct proportion to its population size. If this were the case, larger states would be far more likely to be on the winning side than their population share would warrant. For example, a state with just over 50 percent of the population would be on the winning side 100 percent of the time if a simple majority were required. So, Penrose proposed that voting weights should be allocated to states in proportion to their size, but in declining proportions: a system known in EU circles as "digressive proportionality." And the best way of applying a system of "digressive proportionality" is to use the square-root of each state's population.

Largely by chance, the EU founding fathers designed a system of qualified-majority voting in the EU Council which fits Penrose's logic almost perfectly. Under the QMV system, which applied to the EU15 between 1995 and 2003, each state had a certain number of block votes; there were 87 votes in total, and a majority of 62 votes (71 percent of the total) was required for a decision to pass. Assuming that coalitions formed randomly, this system of QMV meant that the largest states had an 11.2 percent chance of being pivotal while the smallest state (Luxembourg) had a 2.3 percent chance. Put another way, Germany, France, Italy, and the UK were about twice as "powerful" as the Netherlands, Greece, Portugal, or Belgium, and about five times as powerful Luxembourg (cf. Banzhaf 1965).

Another way of conceptualising the power of an actor in a decision-making body is to look at the proportion of all coalitions within which an actor would be on the winning side in a vote under a given set of rules. This is known as the "inclusiveness index" (König and Bräuninger 1998). The Rome Treaty design of QMV in the EU Council meant that the largest states could expect to be in 86 percent of all potential winning coalitions, the majority of states were likely to be in at least two-thirds of all winning coalitions, and the smallest state (Luxembourg) was likely to be in 50 percent of potential winning coalitions.

However, the EU has not kept the Rome model of voting in the Council. First, in the Nice Treaty, which entered into force in 2003, the member states changed the system in anticipation of EU enlargement in 2004. In return for losing one of their two Commissioners, and because most of the prospective new member states were small, the largest EU states insisted that a new system of voting should be used which would boost their power relative to the small states. The resulting system allocated 29 votes to the largest four states, and introduced a total of 345 votes and a QMV threshold of 255 votes. This system meant that the largest states were still approximately twice as powerful as the medium-sized states and five times as powerful as the very small states.

Then, in the process of negotiating a constitution for Europe and the resulting Lisbon Treaty, the issue of the voting weights in the Council was highly politicized. Germany felt that it was underrepresented, while many of the medium-sized states felt that Spain and Poland were overrepresented (as a result of the deal that Spain had secured in the Nice Treaty in return for giving up a Commissioner). The governments eventually agreed on a "double-majority" system, where to adopt a measure in the Council a majority must be composed of 55 percent of the states (15 out of the current 27) as well as 65 percent of total EU population.

At face value this sounds like a simple way of balancing a majority of states and a majority of populations. However, in reality such a system overrepresents the large states as well as the very small states. The majority based purely on population means that large states are more powerful than they should be (as Penrose discovered), and the majority based on one-state–one-vote means that tiny states have exactly the same power as all the other states. Realising this, during the EU treaty negotiations a large number of social and natural scientists supported a proposal by two Polish scientists, known as the Jagiellonian Compromise, to base the voting system in the Council on the ideas of Penrose. Sadly, the EU governments refused to listen to the scientists!

East Asia can learn a lot from the experience of the design of representation in the EU. Table 2.3 presents three possible representational designs for an "East Asian Economic Union": (1) with the 10 states in the Association of Southeast Asian Nations (ASEAN); (2) the 13 states in the ASEAN+3 arrangement (ASEAN plus China, Japan, and South Korea); and (3) the 16 members of the East Asian Summit. First off, an independent Executive should have representatives from every state, with perhaps an extra representative for the largest state or states in each organisation. Second, the number of block votes in a Council and seats in a Parliament should be allocated in proportion to the square-root of each state's population, following Penrose's logic. To keep things simple, each of these designs assumes a total of 100 votes in a Council, with a winning threshold of 67 votes (i.e., two-thirds), and 250 seats in a Parliament. In the table, the "voting power" of a state in the Council is the proportion of times a state would be pivotal in turning a losing coalition

TABLE 2.3.

Possible representation in an East Asian economic union

Country	Pop'n (m)	ASEAN Exec.	Parl.	Council	Voting power	Inclusiveness	ASEAN+3 Exec	Parl.	Council	Voting power	Inclusiveness	EAST ASIAN SUMMIT (ASEAN+6) Exec	Parl.	Council	Voting power	Inclusiveness
Indonesia	230.0	2	59	24	24.0	93.8	2	32	13	14.7	76.1	1	24	9	7.7	63.9
Philippines	92.0	1	38	15	15.2	77.7	1	20	8	8.2	64.6	1	15	6	5.3	59.6
Vietnam	88.1	1	37	15	15.2	77.7	1	20	8	8.2	64.6	1	15	6	5.3	59.6
Thailand	67.8	1	32	13	13.1	73.9	1	17	7	7.2	62.7	1	13	5	4.4	58.0
Myanmar	50.0	1	28	11	11.0	70.1	1	15	6	6.1	57.3	1	11	5	4.4	58.0
Malaysia	27.5	1	21	8	7.7	64.0	1	11	4	4.1	55.2	1	8	3	2.7	54.9
Cambodia	14.8	1	15	6	6.1	61.1	1	8	3	3.0	55.2	1	6	2	1.8	53.3
Laos	6.3	1	10	4	4.0	57.3	1	5	2	2.0	53.5	1	4	2	1.8	53.3
Singapore	4.7	1	8	3	2.7	55.0	1	5	2	2.0	53.5	1	3	1	0.9	51.6
Brunei	0.4	1	2	1	0.9	51.7	1	1	1	1.0	51.7	1	1	1	0.9	51.6
China (incl. HK & Macao)	1,353.3						2	77	31	28.1	99.8	2	57	23	26.0	97.2
Japan	127.2						2	24	9	9.3	66.5	1	18	7	6.1	61.1
South Korea	48.3						1	15	6	6.1	60.9	1	11	4	3.6	56.5
India	1,198.0											2	54	22	25.5	96.2
Australia	21.3											1	7	3	2.7	54.9
New Zealand	4.3											1	3	1	0.9	51.6
Total	3548.5	11	250	100	100.0	100.0	16	250	100	100.0	100.0	18	250	100	100.0	100.0

NOTE: "Voting power" is the normalised Banzhaf index, which calculates the proportion of times a state will be pivotal in a vote. "Inclusiveness" is a measure of the proportion of times a state is likely to be on the winning side in a vote. These indices are calculated using the voting weights in the Council in the table and the assumption that a two-thirds majority (67 votes) is required for a qualified-majority to be achieved. These indices were calculated using the IOP2.0.2 software (Banzhaf 1965; König and Bräuninger 1998; Bräuninger and König, 2005).

TABLE 2.4.

Representation under the Chiang Mai Initiative Multilateralization (CMIM)

	CMIM contributions (US$bn)	CMIM contributions (%)	Basic votes	Votes based on contributions	Total votes (no.)	Total votes (%)	Voting power	Inclusiveness
By country								
China								
Mainland China	34.20	28.50	1.60	34.20	35.80	25.43	24.49	72.86
Hong Kong	4.20	3.50	0.00	4.20	4.20	2.98	2.30	52.15
Japan	38.40	32.00	1.60	38.40	40.00	28.41	29.10	77.16
South Korea	19.20	16.00	1.60	19.20	20.80	14.77	22.07	70.60
Indonesia	4.77	3.98	1.60	4.77	6.37	4.52	3.49	53.26
Malaysia	4.77	3.98	1.60	4.77	6.37	4.52	3.49	53.26
Singapore	4.77	3.98	1.60	4.77	6.37	4.52	3.49	53.26
Thailand	4.77	3.98	1.60	4.77	6.37	4.52	3.49	53.26
Philippines	3.68	3.07	1.60	3.68	5.28	3.75	2.55	52.38
Vietnam	1.00	0.83	1.60	1.00	2.60	1.85	1.35	51.26
Cambodia	0.12	0.10	1.60	0.12	1.72	1.22	1.06	50.99
Myanmar	0.06	0.05	1.60	0.06	1.66	1.18	1.04	50.96
Brunei	0.03	0.03	1.60	0.03	1.63	1.16	1.03	50.96
Laos	0.03	0.03	1.60	0.03	1.63	1.16	1.03	50.96
By group								
ASEAN	24.00	20.00	16.00	24.00	40.00	28.41	33.33	75.00
China (incl. HK)	38.40	32.00	1.60	38.40	40.00	28.41	33.33	75.00
Japan	38.40	32.00	1.60	38.40	40.00	28.41	33.33	75.00
South Korea	19.20	16.00	1.60	19.20	20.80	14.77	0.00	50.00
Total	120.00	100.00	20.80	120.00	140.80	100.00	100.00	

into a winning coalition (Banzhaf 1965), and "inclusiveness" is the proportion of times a state would be on the winning side out of all potential coalitions that could form in the Council (König and Bräuninger 1998).

Regarding representation in a Council, the most important intuition to draw from Table 2.4 is that it would be possible to design a system of weighted block voting in East Asia which would both fairly represent each state and also prevent China and/or India from dominating the organisation. For example, in the scenario for an East Asian Summit organisation, China and India would have approximately five times more power than Japan, the Philippines, and Vietnam, but together China and India would need at least two other medium-sized states or all 8 of the smallest states to join them to reach the 62 vote threshold. At the other extreme, even the smallest states could expect to be on the winning side in about 50 percent of the coalitions that could form.

Finally, to maximise the degree of consensus in the adoption of policies, a regional organisation should also have a "parliament," perhaps based on delegations from national legislatures, as the European Parliament was before 1979. This might seem fanciful, but with a little creativity this might not be impossible to achieve in East Asia. This would create more checks and balances for the adoption of policies proposed by an independent executive. Such a Parliament would also be an important counterweight to a qualified majority in a Council. This is why the EU founding fathers set up an "assembly" at the European level, composed of delegates from the national parliaments (Rittberger 2005). The powers of the European Parliament were also extended in the mid 1980s at the same time as QMV was extended in the EU Council, as the states realised that increasing the power of the European Parliament would present a check on a Council majority and the new agenda-setting power of the Commission. Also, by establishing a supranational Parliament, it increases the probability that a section of the elite from a state would be on the winning side somewhere in the decision-making system. For example, if a centre-left government voted against a proposal to liberalise a particular market in a Council, the representatives from the opposition centre-right party from the same state would be likely to vote in favour of the proposal in a Parliament.

A Parliament broadly modelled on the pre-1979 European Parliament could be set up in East Asia, as a counterweight to a Council and an Executive, as Figure 2.1 illustrates. To produce this figure, I have assumed three things: (1) that each state has the allocation of seats listed in the Parliament column of the East Asian Summit representation design in Table 2.3; (2) that seats are allocated to national parties in proportion to their current

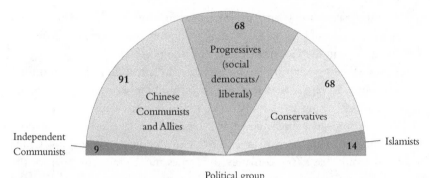

	Political group					
Country	Independent Communists	Chinese Communists and allies	Progressives	Conservatives	Islamists	Total
China		57				57
India	9		28	17		54
Indonesia			5	5	14	24
Japan			12	6		18
Philippines			3	12		15
Vietnam		15				15
Thailand			7	6		13
Myanmar		11				11
South Korea			3	8		11
Malaysia			3	5		8
Australia			4	3		7
Cambodia		4	1	1		6
Laos		4				4
Singapore			1	2		3
New Zealand			1	2		3
Brunei				1		1
Total Seats	9	91	68	68	14	250
Percent	3.6	36.4	27.2	27.2	5.6	

FIGURE 2.1 Make-up of a hypothetical East Asian parliament.

NOTE: The numbers of seats are calculated on the basis of the proportion of seats held by each political party in each national parliament of the states. The membership of the "political groups" is determined by the policy positions of national political parties and their membership of international party organisations (such as the Council of Asian Liberals and Democrats, the Socialist International, the International Democratic Union, or the Centrist Democratic Union).

representation in national parliaments; and (3) that these "national party delegations" choose to sit with like-minded politicians from other countries in "political groups." This last assumption is not inconceivable since many parties in East Asia are already members of one or other international party union, such as the Council of Asian Liberals and Democrats, the Socialist International, the International Democratic Union, or the Centrist Democratic Union.

To illustrate how this might work, the 54 Indian members of the parliament would comprise 28 from the Congress Party, who choose to sit in a group of "Progressives," 17 from the Bharatiya Janata Party, who choose to sit in a group of "Conservatives," and 9 members from the Communist Party of India, who choose to sit separately from the Chinese Communists and their allies. The overall result would be a fairly evenly balanced assembly, with three main groups—a centre-right group ("Conservatives"), a liberal/centre-left group ("Progressives"), and a group representing the Chinese Communist Party and its allied parties. There would also be several Islamists from Indonesia and the "independent Communists" from India. These political groups are unlikely to be as cohesive in their voting behaviour as the political groups in the European Parliament. Nevertheless, creating a Parliament which brings together elected representatives from across the region could play a critical role in facilitating the compromises and deals that would need to be made to move economic integration forward. One tricky issue would be where to locate such a Parliament!

Current Institutions in East Asia, and the
Chiang Mai Initiative Multilateralization

This discussion might seem rather abstract and unrealistic to policymakers in East Asia and economists and political scientists who are experts on the region. East Asia is one of the regions in the world with the least developed supranational institutions, compared to Europe, South America, or Central America, for example. ASEAN, ASEAN+3, and the East Asian Summit remain intergovernmental arrangements. Also, despite the goal of creating a European-style "economic community" in ASEAN by 2015, there has been little institutional progress toward this goal, in terms of the delegation of agenda-setting and enforcement to an independent body or the introduction of majority-voting between the governments to enable a body of legislation to be passed to facilitate the creation of a genuine single market. Many of the governments in ASEAN are clearly reluctant to take the next step. One possibility is that delegation and supranational decision-making, which inevitably involves the formalisation of rules and a degree of majoritarianism, is fundamentally incompatible with the highly consensual and informal nature of decision-making in ASEAN, and the ASEAN+3 and East Asian Summit frameworks.

Meanwhile, beyond these three multilateral intergovernmental structures a dense network of bilateral free trade agreements between ASEAN and third states, and between individual members of ASEAN and other states in the region and beyond, has developed rapidly in the last decade. These bilateral free trade agreements, if implemented, would further liberalise trade in the region, and perhaps make the need for a European-style "single market programme" redundant.

There are, however, several reasons to believe that these bilateral free trade deals are not a substitute for deeper economic integration in East Asia. First, the aggregate benefits from these agreements are likely to be limited given the low levels of tariffs and the exclusion of certain politically sensitive sectors in most bilateral trade arrangements in the region (esp. Ravenhill 2009). Second, even if these bilateral trade deals promote further trade liberalisation, removing barriers to the free movement of goods and services is likely to increase pressure for the adoption of some common standards, to prevent distortions in competition or to establish a level playing field in terms of social and environmental standards, as was the case in Europe. The pressure for common standards is likely to come from the states with the highest domestic standards, such as Japan, Australia, and New Zealand, who fear a race to the bottom.

Furthermore, the Chiang Mai Initiative Multilateralization (CMIM) demonstrates that with sufficient incentives, the states in East Asia *are* willing to allow the development of genuinely supranational institutional arrangements in the region. The CMIM is an initiative under the ASEAN+3 framework that establishes a system of bilateral swap arrangements. The Chiang Mai Initiative was set up after the 1997 Asian financial crisis, to manage short-term liquidity problems in the region and to facilitate the work of other international financial arrangements, such as the International Monetary Fund. In February 2009, the ASEAN+3 states agreed to pool $120 billion for this purpose. The states also introduced some new decision-making rules.

As the memo from the meeting of the ASEAN+3 Finance Ministers in May 2009 states: "On decision-making mechanism of the CMIM, the fundamental issues will be decided through consensus of members of ASEAN+3, while the lending issues will be decided through majority." The specific rules governing how this majority decision-making will operate are still unclear.

However, this is a historic agreement, as it is the first time that sovereign states in East Asia have allowed majoritarian decision-making rules to govern any aspect of their relations. Although the CMIM is in the area of financial integration, and although the majority decision-making aspect of the CMIM is restricted to currency lending issues, the establishment of this majority-based mechanism suggests that East Asian states might be willing to allow similar rules to be used on other technical aspects of economic integration, such as on the harmonisation of product standards, or packaging and labelling, or health and safety in the workplace.

Table 2.4 presents an analysis of representation and state power under the decision-making rules of the CMIM. Each country is allocated a number of votes, based on their contributions to the CMIM fund plus a number of "basic votes," and decision-making is by a simple majority (70.41 out of 140.80 total votes). With this vote allocation and the simple majority rule, the voting power of the three largest states (China, Japan, and South Korea) will be considerably greater than their proportional shares of the total CMIM fund. For example, South Korea contributes slightly more than four times what Indonesia has contributed, of $19.20 billion compared to $4.77 billion respectively, yet voting weights based on these amounts would mean that South Korea would be approximately 6 times more likely to be pivotal in decision-making than Indonesia.

However, the picture is very different if one assumes that the 10 ASEAN states vote as a single bloc. If this is the case, then South Korea would have zero power, as it would never be pivotal, since a coalition of ASEAN-China, ASEAN-Japan, or China-Japan would all be a majority without South Korea, and a coalition of South Korea with any other state would need a third actor to form a majority! Nevertheless, South Korea would be on the wining side in 50 percent of the coalitions that could be formed between these four actors.

Conclusion

In the early 1980s in Europe it would have been hard to imagine that in less than 25 years there would be a single market stretching from the Atlantic to the border of Russia and encompassing almost 500 million people. It would have been equally as difficult to predict that the European Commission would become a powerful supranational executive, that 27 governments would take most decisions by majority, and that the European Parliament would have equal power with the governments in the adoption of rules for Europe's single market.

Could something similar happen in East Asia in the next 25 years? In Europe in the mid 1980s there was a convergence of preferences amongst governments, businesses, and citizens around the goal of creating a single continental-scale market. This enabled the governments to unanimously agree to delegate agenda-setting power to the Commission, and to redesign decision-making in the Council and between the Council and the Parliament, to allow for more majority decisions but with new checks and balances. East Asia may be too heterogeneous in terms of population, economic size, wealth, democracy, the rules of law, and citizens' values, let alone the deep historical rivalries and suspicions in the region, for states to converge around a broad political integration project.

Nevertheless, there may be sufficient preference convergence amongst a smaller group of states—for example, amongst the ASEAN+3 states—to begin a process of deeper economic integration. If these states could agree on a common goal of a single market and deeper monetary cooperation, these states need not fear delegation to an independent agent (perhaps built on the current ASEAN Secretariat). Institutional rules could certainly be designed to limit autonomous action by the independent body, to ensure a high degree of consensus amongst the states, and to provide equitable representation between the states.

The basic elements of a new architecture for the region could be a two-tier structure. A first-tier could be a group of states (such as the ASEAN+3), who aim to achieve deeper economic integration, who establish an independent body, responsible for policy initiative and the oversight of policy implementation, and a set of mechanisms to limit the autonomous action of this body, such as unanimous agreement amongst the states before delegating to this body, and representation of all states in the body. The legislative authority of such a body could include a Council acting by a system of weighted block voting, based on the square-root of the populations of these states. This group of states might also consider establishing a supranational assembly (a "parliament"), composed of delegates from national parliaments and perhaps also representatives from civil society and economic actors. This would secure a broad intergovernmental and inter-societal coalition in favour of major integration steps.

A second tier could be a broader intergovernmental body (perhaps building on the current East Asian Summit), amongst the first-tier of states plus all the states who do not have sufficiently convergent preferences to aim for deeper economic integration at this stage, but who are likely to be concerned about possible "spillover" effects of greater economic integration amongst the first tier of states. This organisation could meet at the level of the heads of government, perhaps twice a year, and address the potential externalities of deeper integration amongst the first-tier as well as more general political issues facing the region, such as climate change, the trafficking of persons, cross-border crime, and Asian positions in the G20. In time, the two tiers might fuse into a single Asian regional organisation.

The experience of Europe in the past 25 years suggests that regional integration is at least partly endogenous to the institutional design of the project. When signing the Single European Act in the mid 1980s, most European governments could not have predicted how quickly the new institutional framework would get to work, or how far European integration would reach into other policy areas, or how attractive the EU would be for non-member states. If a group of states in East Asia could start the ball rolling, economic integration beyond a free trade area could be a genuine prospect for the region.

Notes

I would like to thank Giovanni Capannelli, Miles Kahler, and Stephan Haggard for their comments on the earlier versions of this chapter.

"Voting power" is the normalised Banzhaf index, which calculates the proportion of times a state will be pivotal in a vote. "Inclusiveness" is a measure of the proportion of times a state is likely to be on the winning side in a vote. These indices are calculated using the Dollar contributions as the voting weights and the assumption that decisions require a simple majority (70.41 out of 140.80 votes) to pass. These indices were calculated using the IOP2.0.2 software (Banzhaf 1965; König and Bräuninger 1998; Bräuninger and König, 2005).

Regional Judicial Institutions
and Economic Cooperation
Lessons for Asia?

ERIK VOETEN

The absence of regional judicial institutions in Asia is one of the most striking differences between its regional economic integration projects and those elsewhere.[1] While Asia has no active standing regional court, Europe, Latin America, and Africa each have at least four active regional courts that have issued thousands of legally binding judgments.[2] About 90% of these judgments have come since 1990 (Alter 2009). This increased usage stems not just from Europe but also from the Americas and even Africa. Effective regional judicial institutions resolve disputes in efficient and impartial ways and they coordinate the interpretation of laws and treaties. In so doing, they could also have broader effects on regional cooperation such as improving incentives for compliance, increasing the perceived commitment of parties to a regional integration project, and contributing to the implementation of agreements.

Why is Asia lagging behind other regions in this regard? And, what is Asian regional economic integration and cooperation missing by not partaking in this trend? A prevalent hypothesis among scholars and policymakers is that Asia has opted for a model of cooperation without legalization because Asian states are inherently averse to legalized dispute resolution for cultural or institutional reasons. I test this proposition using data and models from studies published in top peer-reviewed journals. I find no evidence that Asian states are less likely than other states to refer trade, investment, or territorial disputes to global judicial institutions. This also holds for inter-Asian disputes. A slightly different argument is that Asian regional cooperation projects have a distinct social logic that prescribe consensual as opposed to legalized forms of dispute resolution. This is, however, mostly based on a misconception about the nature of regional integration elsewhere. While regional inter-state dispute resolution mechanisms are ubiquitous, they are rarely used by states involved in a regional integration project. Resolving inter-state disputes is not and has not been the main contribution of regional judicial institutions.

Instead, the lessons from regional courts elsewhere suggest that they become active engines of integration if two conditions are present, which are largely absent in Asia.[3] First, there must be legally binding regional rules that create rights and obligations for private parties. This allows private parties to sue and be sued on the basis of international law. Second, there must be an institutional configuration that allows private parties access to a regional court.

While Asia has few regional treaties that create legal obligations and rights for private parties, there is a broad body of international trade and commercial law that is already relevant. I suggest that a judicial institution could be created that can, at the request of national courts or administrative agencies, offer advisory opinions on the interpretation of international rules, laws, and standards that are already applicable. The underlying assumption is that governments want to see those obligations implemented but that national administrative agencies or courts may not always be well equipped to do so. The new institution would allow Asian states to send a signal that they are committed to take their legal obligations seriously. Moreover, it would contribute to the uniform application (and thus harmonization) of commercial law while allowing each state to make new obligations at their own pace. The concluding sections offer some thoughts on political feasibility, issues of institutional design, and expected effects.

Are Asian States Less Likely to Resolve Disputes Through Legal Means?

Effective regional judicial institutions perform two core tasks: they resolve disputes in efficient and impartial ways and they coordinate the interpretation of laws and treaties. In so doing, they could have broader effects on regional cooperation such as improving incentives for compliance, increasing the perceived commitment of parties to a regional integration project, and contributing to the implementation of agreements. Why have Asian countries, in contrast to governments elsewhere, seemingly rejected these potential benefits?

Many accounts of why Asian countries prefer cooperation without legal-ization are based on the notion that Asian states share a preference for non-binding commitments and non-legalistic methods of dispute resolution. This is a central feature of the "ASEAN way" as well as the "Asia-Pacific" way of cooperation (e.g., Acharya 1997). To some, this stems from a distinct legal culture that is less adversarial and litigious than Western legal culture (e.g., Green 1994). Instead, Asian approaches to dispute resolution stress consen-sus and informality. Scholars have identified such differences in legal culture as one of the main challenges for Asian states to participate in global legal regimes, such as the WTO (Peng 2000). Others argue that Asian countries differ, not because they lack an adversarial legal culture, but because of their domestic political institutions and the sensitive nature of diplomatic relations between Asian states.[4] Again others maintain that Asian governments' unusu-ally strong concerns about sovereignty costs lie at the root of their unwilling-ness to use legalized forms of dispute settlement (Poon 2001).

These arguments are certainly not universally accepted. For example, scholars have pointed to the diversity in Asia's domestic political and legal institutions (Kahler 2000; Pryles 2006). Yet, as far as I am aware, there are no systematic tests in the literature of the proposition that Asian states are less likely than others to resolve disputes through legal means. Such a test is important for the purposes of this chapter. If Asian countries have unusually strong predispositions against using legal means to resolve disputes, then the lessons from other regions may not be applicable to the Asian context.

My empirical strategy for evaluating this question is to replicate recently published analyses of legalized dispute resolutions in three critical areas: trade, investment, and territory. I then add an indicator variable for whether a coun-try is Asian.[5] I checked for the robustness of the results by creating subgroups of Asian states (e.g., ASEAN states).

Trade Disputes

If Asian countries are averse to legalized dispute settlement, they should be less likely to initiate trade disputes at the GATT/WTO than are other coun-tries. In a study published in the *Journal of Politics*, Davis and Bermeo (2009) analyze why some developing countries are more likely than others to initiate disputes at the GATT/WTO. They argue that there are large start-up costs for using the dispute settlement process. Therefore, they hypothesize that past experience as a complainant or defendant makes states more likely to initiate disputes in the future.

I replicated their analysis (without problems) and added an indicator variable for whether a country is Asian. The sample includes 75 developing countries that were WTO members by 2003 (the end of the data), including 14 Asian countries. The analysis excludes 31 least developed countries who are beneficiaries of preferential market access and have less need to invoke WTO rights. Davis and Bermeo argue that the correlates that determine dispute initiation among developed countries are different and estimate a separate model for this group. The dependent variable is the number of cases a country initiated in a given year. The model is estimated using a negative binomial regression, with robust standard errors clustered on countries.

Table 3.1 offers the results of the specifications estimated by Davis and Bermeo. The indicator for Asia does not have an effect on either developing or developed country dispute initiation. This result also holds in the more extensive models with additional control variables and a model where the dependent variable is converted to a binary indicator, allowing for the use of a logit estimation. The result also holds for developing countries if the democracy variable is omitted from the regression model, indicating that it is not the scarcity of democracies in Asia that drives this result. Finally, the result is robust to the inclusion of a dummy for ASEAN countries: neither the ASEAN nor the non-ASEAN Asian states are any more or less likely than other states to seek legalized resolutions of their trade disputes.

Asian states have also used the WTO to resolve disputes among themselves. Of the 352 disputes initiated between the start of the WTO process in 1995 and October 2006, there have been 9 within-Asia disputes between Singapore

TABLE 3.1.

Trade dispute initiation (from: Davis and Bermeo, Tables 2 and 3)

Variable	Developing Countries	Developed Countries
Asia	.38 (.39)	−.16 (.37)
Previous initiations	.09 (.03)★★★	−.01 (.00)★★
Democracy	.19 (.09)★★	.50 (.22)★★
Log GDP	1.00 (.24)★★★	1.67 (.60)★★★
Log population	−.48 (−.22)★★	−.99 (.59)★
English	−.31 (.32)	1.31 (.41)★★★
WTO period	−.08 (.26)	.58 (.16)★★★
Constant	−18.80 (3.22)	−29.04 (6.55)
Dispersion parameter	.74 (.17)	.32 (.08)
N	1314	543

★p<.10, ★★p<.05, ★★★p<.01 (two-tailed).

and Malaysia, Korea and Japan (2), Japan and Indonesia (2), Korea and the Philippines, Bangladesh and India, Indonesia and Korea, and Taiwan and India.[6] This is more than the number of disputes filed among Latin American, European, African, or Central American states. There are different base-line probabilities for the filing of such within-region disputes, yet it is hard to maintain based on these data that Asian states have a deep regional cultural aversion against legalized resolutions of their trade disputes.

Investment Disputes

The regulation of foreign investment has long been a potent source for disputes, especially when foreign property is expropriated by host governments. In recent years, the regulation of foreign investment has increasingly taken the form of Bilateral Investment Treaties (BITs), which may or may not delegate authority to an international authority to resolve disputes between foreign firms and governments (e.g., Franck 2007). The most prominent international body that resolves the vast majority of investment disputes is the World Bank's International Centre for the Settlement of Investment Disputes (ICSID). ICSID rulings are public, are closely watched by investors, and are consequential for future foreign direct investments (FDI) streams (Allee and Peinhardt 2009b). Governments have much less control over ICSID dispute resolution mechanisms than if they delegated dispute resolution to ad hoc arbitral tribunals or domestic courts (e.g., Franck 2007).

If Asian countries indeed prefer cooperation without legalized dispute settlement, we would expect these countries to be less willing to delegate authority to ICSID when they agree on cooperation by signing a BIT. Allee and Peinhardt (2009a) coded all publicly archived BITs for their level of delegation to ICSID. They create an ordinal variable, coded 0 in the absence of any delegation, 1 if ICSID is one of the options for dispute resolutions, and 2 if ICSID is the only venue for international arbitration. They argue that this variable reflects the degree of delegation in an ordinal way because governments usually have some control over the venue of arbitration if ICSID is only one of more options. The negotiation of BITs tends to be asymmetric in that there is usually one "home" country (from which most of the investment originates) and a "host" country (toward which the investment is directed). Home countries typically (although not always) tend to prefer ICSID delegation, but the preferences of host countries vary.

Allee and Peinhardt identify a range of characteristics of host countries and home countries as well as of the relationship between them that would make it more or less likely that a BIT includes an ICSID provision. I refer the interested reader to their article for more details on the theoretical motivation for including these variables. The appendix lists the variables and precise data sources. I replicated their original results (without problems) and added to their model indicator variables for whether there is an Asian home or host country and an additional indicator variable for whether both countries are Asian.

Table 3.2 has the results from an ordinal probit model. Quite strikingly, an Asian home country makes it significantly more likely that a BIT delegates authority to ICSID. The same is true for an Asian host country, although this effect is only significant at the 10% level in a two-tailed test. The second column in Table 3.2 further explores the different dynamics between BITs that involve one Asian country and fully Asian BITs. The Asian region is split up between ASEAN and non-ASEAN countries. The results show

TABLE 3.2.

Ordered probit results for delegation to delegate dispute settlement to ICSID (based on Table 2, Allee and Peinhardt).

Variable	Coefficient (Robust S.E.)	Coefficient (Robust S.E.)
Asian Home Country	.48 (.17)★★★	–
Asian Host Country	.18 (.10)★	–
Both Asian Countries	−.18 (.29)	–
One ASEAN + non-Asian	–	.48 (.15)★★★
Non-ASEAN Asian + non-Asian	–	.08 (.11)
One ASEAN + other Asian	–	.61 (.32)★
Two non-ASEAN Asian Countries	–	−.04 (.36)
Two ASEAN Countries	–	−.52 (.53)
Presence of MNCs in Home	1.83 (.72)★★★	1.77 (.72)★★
Strength of Legal Institutions in Home	.13 (.04)★★★	.10 (.04)★★
Strength of Legal Institutions in Host	.03 (.04)	.01 (.04)
Durability of Host Regime	−.00 (.00)	−.00 (.00)
Political Constraints on Executive in Host	.38 (.19)★	.42 (.19)
Alliance Ties	−.05 (.08)	0.00 (.08)
Colonial Ties	−.12 (.12)	−.14 (.11)
Host Recently Independent	−.28 (.10)★★	−.25 (.10)★★
Domestic Economic Growth Host	−.00 (.00)	−.00 (.00)
Export Dependence Host	.00 (.00)	.00 (.00)
Reliance on External Financial Assistance Host	.77 (.39)★★	.81 (.39)★★
Right Wing Government Host	.02 (.08)	.03 (.08)
Ratio of Home to Host Economic Power	.66 (.16)★★★	.77 (.16)

N = 1032 Bilateral Investment Treaties, ★p<.10, ★★p<.05, ★★★p<.01 (two-tailed). Wald χ2 test (16df) = 97.12 (.00). MNC = Multinational corporations.

that the positive coefficients are due to BITs between ASEAN countries and non-ASEAN countries, both Asian and non-Asian. BITs among ASEAN countries are significantly less likely to include ICSID delegation than do BITS between ASEAN countries and other countries but not less likely than BITS between non-Asian countries. More generally, there is no evidence that BITs involving Asian countries are less likely to delegate authority to ICSID than BITs that involve no Asian country (the reference category in the regression).

It could be that Asian countries are less likely to sign BITs because they expect that a legalized commitment will be involved. There is, as far as I can tell, no evidence in the BIT literature of such a proposition. Moreover, coverage is broad. The data includes BITs with 16 different Asian home governments and 29 different Asian host governments. 112 (11%) of the BITs have home countries that are Asian and 251 (25%) have host countries that are Asian. This includes 65 BITs involving China, which only include exclusive ICSID clauses in 9% of its BITs and had no ICSID option in 59% of its treaties. In all, though, exclusive delegation to ICSID exists in 45% of BITs with an Asian home country, 36% of BITs with an Asian host country, 42% of BITs between two Asian states but only 29% of the total population of BITs. Moreover, countries that are threatening to leave the ICSID system appear to be from Latin America, not Asia (Franck 2009, p. 436–437). These data do not support a conclusion that Asian countries that have signed BITs are particularly averse to legalized dispute settlement (i.e., they do not prefer cooperation without legalization).

Territorial Disputes

Territory is another asset over which states frequently bargain and fight. Yet, territorial disputes can also be settled through legal dispute resolution, for example through the International Court of Justice (ICJ) or the Permanent Court of Arbitration (PCA). A characteristic of such legal solutions is that both countries generally need to agree to it. If Asian countries are averse to legalized solutions, then territorial disputes involving Asian countries should be less likely to be resolved by legal means than are other disputes.

In a study published in the *American Political Science Review*, Allee and Huth (2006) investigate what makes states more and less likely to choose legal dispute resolution over bilateral negotiations as a means for settling territorial disputes. They identify 1490 bilateral rounds of negotiations in 348 disputes over territory. They then code whether the negotiation round ended in a stalemate, compromise (bilateral concessions), or a legalized form of dispute resolution. Their core theoretical contribution is the argument that international legal rulings at least in some significant part provide political cover for leaders in need of making concessions.

I refer the interested reader to the Allee and Huth article for more detail on model specification. The appendix provides more detail on measurement. I successfully replicated their analyses (Table 2 in the article) and added two indicator variables: one for whether the dispute involved an Asian country (true for 350 [23%] of rounds of negotiations in the data) and one for whether both parties in the dispute were Asian (true for 199 [13%] of cases). The second variable is included to assess whether there is an additional effect if both parties are Asian and thus, presumably, unlikely to resort to legal solutions for their territorial disputes.

Table 3.3 shows that there is no significant effect of Asian involvement on the likelihood that a dispute has a legal resolution. Thus, the involvement of Asian countries makes it neither more or less likely that a dispute is resolved through legal means. Creating an exclusive category where one indicator variable measures whether only one Asian state is involved does not materially affect the result, nor does dropping the indicator for whether the conflict involves two Asian states.

TABLE 3.3.

Multinomial logit results for the outcomes of rounds of talks over disputed territory (Table 2 from Allee and Huth 2006)

	Legal Dispute Settlement vs. Bilateral Concessions	Legal Dispute Settlement vs. Stalemate
Asian involvement	−.27 (1.06)	−.55 (1.05)
Both countries Asian	.22 (1.24)	.40 (1.22)
Strong domestic political opposition	1.36 (.48)★★★	.95 (.47)★★★
Democratic dyad (accountability)	1.35 (.60)★★★	1.29 (.58)★★★
Ethnic ties with territory	.92 (.41)★★★	.89 (.46)★★
Enduring rivals	1.54 (.70)★★★	1.20 (.67)★
Hard-line stance in previous negotiations	.02 (.20)	−.47 (.19)★★★
Democratic dyad (norms)	−.70 (.65)	−.31 (61)
Military asymmetry	−3.64 (1.48)★★★	−4.60 (1.46)★★★
Common security ties	.60 (.43)	.62 (.42)
Strategic value of territory	−.64 (.58)	−.75 (.57)
Constant	−3.02 (.51)★★★	−3.36 (.50)★★★

NOTE: N = 1490. Robust standard errors in parentheses. *p<.10, **p<.05, ***p<.01 (two-tailed)

The Allee and Huth data only runs until 1995. Since then, there have been at least two other Asian territorial disputes that were submitted to the ICJ: the dispute over Pedra Branca/Pulau Batu Puteh, Middle Rocks and South Ledge between Malaysia and Singapore and the dispute over Pulau Ligitan and Pulau Sipadan between Indonesia and Malaysia. In all, there is no evidence that Asian countries are more reluctant than others to seek legalized dispute settlement for their territorial conflicts.

Regional Resolution of Inter-State Disputes

The preceding section demonstrates that Asian states are not less likely to resolve inter-state disputes through legal means in *global* institutions. Another plausible story is that Asian *regional* integration projects have a distinct social logic that warrants cooperation without legalization and that explicitly rejects European-style institutionalization. This is reflected in the "ASEAN" way of regional cooperation. As Acharya (1997, 329) puts it:

> [T]he "ASEAN way" is not so much about the substance or structure of multilateral interactions, but a claim about the *process* through which such interactions are carried out. This approach involves a high degree of discreetness, informality, pragmatism, expediency, consensus-building, and non-confrontational bargaining styles which are often contrasted with the adversarial posturing and legalistic decision-making procedures in Western multilateral negotiations.

The "ASEAN way" influenced Asia-Pacific regional cooperation and has also been termed the "Asian way" of regional cooperation (Acharya 1997). Indeed, there is no documented use of legalized regional mechanisms to settle disputes between states in Asia. Is this aversion to the use of regional legalized resolution of inter-state disputes unusual? As the following summary will show, while virtually all regional judicial institutions allow for such inter-state disputes (as does the ASEAN dispute settlement mechanism) they are rarely used for this purpose.

Inter-State Disputes in Regional Tribunals

There are four standing international courts[7] in Europe. The best known ones are the highest courts of the European Union: the European Court of Justice (ECJ) and the Court of First Instance (CFI). Under Article 227, EU member states could directly bring complaints to the ECJ against other member states. The article has been used only a handful of times and was described as "a virtual dead letter" in a recent overview of ECJ activity (Stone Sweet 2005, 25). The Court of Justice of the European Free Trade Association (EFTA) resolves disputes involving countries that are not part of the EU but that are part of the European Free Trade Area.[8] The agreement that establishes the EFTA Court grants the Court jurisdiction to settle disputes between two or more member states.[9] Yet, none of its 102 pending or decided cases are inter-state disputes.[10] The BENELUX Court of Justice interprets rules of law common to Belgium, the Netherlands, and Luxemburg. The BENELUX treaty established a College of Arbitrators to settle disputes between states, but it has not appointed new arbitrators since the first nomination in 1962 and has never been used.[11] Finally, the Council of Europe's European Court of Human Rights (ECtHR) has issued over 10,000 judgments on individual complaints but only 3 inter-state cases.[12] As of 2009, these courts have together allowed inter-state cases for 172 years. Yet, it is difficult to find even 10 examples of such cases. In short, European states have not settled their inter-state disputes by suing each other in regional courts.

In addition, the Economic Court of the Commonwealth of Independent States (ECCIS) was created in 1991 to resolve trade disputes among the countries belonging to the Commonwealth of Independent States (CIS) (Danilenko 1999).[13] Unlike the other European courts, the legal status of ECCIS decisions is in dispute and the court has weak enforcement capabilities, thus allowing losing states to ignore its rulings (Danilenko 1999; Dragneva and de Kort 2007). During its first decade, the court issued 65 decisions, 54 of which were advisory opinions and only 9 were disputes about non-performance of economic obligations (Dragneva and de Kort 2007, p. 260). While little information is available about these 9 cases, the perception is that they have been resolved through negotiation (Dragneva and de Kort 2007, fn. 112).

The evidence from Latin America is similar. The Court of Justice of the Andean Community (ATJ) is the third most active international court, with 1492 rulings (Helfer and Alter 2009; Helfer, Alter, and Guerzovich 2009). About 90% of these cases came from preliminary references by national courts. Almost all of the other cases were initiated by a treaty organ (the Secretary-General). I have been able to find only three pure inter-state cases.[14] Mercosur has had a formal arbitration system in place since 1991, which only allowed access to state parties. As of 2005, arbitration panels had issued only nine awards (Vervaele 2005). Institutional reforms to create more advanced forms of dispute resolution are under way.

The Central American Court of Justice (CACJ) was originally established in 1907 to maintain peace and resolve disagreements between Central American States. It was dissolved in 1918. Three of the court's ten decisions were inter-state cases.[15] Since its restart in 1990, the court has issued an additional 78 rulings, but it is unclear from the data how many are inter-state disputes (Alter 2009). The Caribbean Court of Justice (CCJ) was established in 2001[16] by the members of the Caribbean Community (CARICOM) to replace the Judicial Committee of the Privy Council and to interpret the Treaty Establishing the Caribbean Community. The court has issued 34 judgments, none of which were inter-state disputes.[17]

NAFTA does not have a standing court but does allow for ad hoc binational review panels, most notable those under chapter 19. This has led to concerns about strategic forum shopping with the WTO (Busch 2007) and to critiques that the NAFTA panels supersede conventional judicial review.[18] The chapter 19 procedure allows private parties to sue administrative agencies for their decisions on antidumping or countervailing duties. On at least 23 cases, government lawyers argued on behalf of these private parties, creating a perception of putting two state actors into conflict with each other.[19] Thus, NAFTA deals with more disputes that have the appearance of inter-state disputes than the other tribunals and thus is somewhat of an exception. It should be noted that NAFTA does not have a treaty organ in charge of enforcement, nor is it part of a deeper regional integration project.

Africa has four active international courts: Common Court of Justice and Arbitration of the Organization for the Harmonization of Business Law in Africa (OHADA, or OHBLA), the Court of Justice of the Common Market for Eastern and Southern Africa (COMESA), Court of Justice of the East African Community (EACJ), and the Court of Justice of the Economic Community of West African States (ECOWAS). OHADA aims to harmonize corporate law in 16 mostly francophone African states. Its Common Court of Justice and Arbitration had issued 274 judgments by 2007 (Alter 2009); none were inter-state cases. [20] COMESA established a common market between 19 states in Eastern and Southern Africa. Its court was established in 1994 and its first judges were appointed by 1998.[21] The Court had heard seven cases by 2007 (Alter 2009), none of which appear to be inter-state cases.[22] The EACJ and its predecessor have issued eight rulings, none of which appear to have been inter-state cases.[23] The ECOWAS court has received 33 cases, none inter-state disputes.[24]

There are also a number of courts that have been in existence for some time but that have never or rarely been used (Alter 2009). These include the Organization of Arab Petroleum Exporting Countries Tribunal (OAPEC) (1978), The West African Economic and Monetary Union Court (WAEMU) (1995), the Community of Central Africa Court of Justice (CEMAC) (2000), and the Tribunal of the Southern African Development Community (SADC) (2007).[25] Thus, the ASEAN dispute resolution mechanism is not the only existing Dispute Settlement Mechanism that has not been used.

Why So Little Use of Regional Mechanisms for Inter-State Disputes?

The number of standing regional courts is about equal to the total number of inter-state disputes that they have resolved. Why are there so few inter-state disputes submitted to regional courts? Part of the answer is that some regional agreements have supranational treaty bodies, such as the European Commission, that can file infringement suits against states and that can, to some extent, serve as substitutes for inter-state disputes. Some complaints about foreign practices may originate with other governments, yet be filtered through supranational bodies. Even so, the political externalities of a direct case between two states involved in a regional integration project may be greater. Moreover, the literature on the EU shows that the Commission often takes its own initiatives and is quite far from a simple tool that (powerful) member states can use to go after each other (e.g., Pollack 1997). Finally, DSMs in regions that lack a supranational body are also not frequently used, suggesting that this is not a simple substitution story.

Economic disputes between states are usually proxy disputes. Businesses are harmed or benefit from unfair trade practices. States are only hurt indirectly. There are many hurdles that may prevent states from filing suits against each other. Businesses must lobby governments to file suits on their behalves and pay the cost for this. This generally only works if they come from an influential or economically important sector. In such cases, it may be more useful to file at a global institution, such as the WTO, where the precedent will be broader. There are many other ways to resolve disputes between states and many issues that could be linked together in omnibus compromises. The patterns in the data also suggest that there are additional political costs to be paid when regional institutions are used to settler inter-state disputes. For example, the only regional tribunal that is used somewhat frequently to resolve (proxy) inter-state disputes is the NAFTA binational review panel, which exists in the absence of a broader political regional integration project, thus reducing political externalities.

At times, the existence of a regional inter-state DSM may be a useful option, if only as a potential outcome that all want to avoid. But there is little reason to believe that resolving inter-state disputes has been a major contribution of regional judicial institutions or that it will be in the Asian context.

What *Can* Be Learned from the Activity
of Regional Judicial Institutions?

The widespread perception that Asian states are unusual in their reluctance
to resolve their disputes through legal means is at least partially based on mis-
conceptions about the behavior of Asian states and about the logic of regional
integration elsewhere. Asian states are not generally less likely than are other
states to resolve their disputes through legal means. Moreover, regional integration in other parts of the world has not been driven by legal institutions
that resolve inter-state disputes. Indeed, European, Latin American, and African states are no more likely to sue each other in regional courts, preferring
to resolve their differences through other means.

   These findings are important because they suggest that there is potential
for learning from the experience of regional judicial institutions elsewhere.
But what are these potential lessons that could be valuable for Asian regional
cooperation projects? I review the evidence by answering the questions suggested in the theory section. What disputes do they resolve? What is their
interpretive authority? How does the exercise of their dispute resolution and
interpretive activities influence compliance, commitment, and checks and
balances? I then apply these lessons to the design of a potential new Asian judicial institution.

The Activities of Courts: Dispute Resolution and Interpretation

Most disputes examined by regional judicial institutions are of two kinds.
First, there are disputes between a treaty body, such as the European Commission, and a government, for example about whether a government has cor-
rectly implemented a treaty provision. Such cases constitute about one-fourth
of the ECJ's caseload and less than 10% of the ATJ caseload (Alter 2009). Second, and much more commonly, regional judicial institutions review disputes
between private actors and a government or a government agency. These
may be cases where a private party charges that a government has incorrectly
implemented regional law. More commonly, these are cases where the relevant law for a dispute over an administrative decision is regional rather than
national law.

   The activity of courts is not a simple function of institutional design. Allowing private actors access does not by itself ensure that a court becomes
active (Alter 2006), nor does granting a treaty body the authority to file infringement suits against governments mean that they will actually do so (see
Helfer and Alter 2009 for the Andean Community). For private access to

matter, two criteria need to be satisfied. First and most obvious, there must be legally binding regional rules that create rights and obligations for private parties. This allows private parties to sue and be sued on the basis of regional law. Second, if private access is indirect, as it is for virtually all cases other than the European Court of Human Rights, there must be national institutions that cooperate by referring cases to the regional court. In the case of the ECJ, it was crucially important that national courts started to see the ECJ as an ally that could help them advance their interests as opposed to an institution that encroached on their terrain (see Alter 1998, Weiler 1994). This is not (yet) the case for national courts in most OHADA member states (Dickerson 2005). In the case of the ATJ, the key national actors were national administrative agencies charged with protecting intellectual property rights (IP) that were the engines behind increased references to the regional court (Helfer and Alter 2009).

The ATJ illustrates these points well. Until recent research by Larry Helfer, Karen Alter, and Florencia Guerzovich, little was known about the world's third most active international court (Helfer et al. 2009; Helfer and Alter 2009). The ATJ had only a minimal caseload in the 1980s and early 1990s. Yet, references to the court started to increase in 1995. The Andean Community adopted IP rules that were broadly consistent with the TRIPS rules. These rules gave private actors rights and obligations under Andean law. At the same time, domestic administrative IP agencies were transformed or created. These agencies were in charge of reviewing trademark and patent registrations. Since the relevant IP law was regional law, they applied this law in those decisions. Consequentially, when dissatisfied businesses challenged these administrative decisions in courts, Andean law had to be interpreted by national courts. Initially most national courts were hesitant to refer such cases to the ATJ. Yet, through various forms of pressure by IP agencies, businesses, and lawyers, courts in three countries (Columbia, Ecuador, and Peru) started to refer IP cases to the ATJ.[26] Such cases make up about 90% of the nearly 1500 judgments the ATJ has issued.

Another interesting example of a regional regime that delegated authority in a limited issue area to a regional court is OHADA. OHADA (Organization for the Harmonization of Business Laws in Africa) is a system of business laws and implementing institutions adopted by sixteen mostly francophone West and Central African nations.[27] These countries adopted this regime in 1993 in order to stimulate (foreign) investments and promote growth (Mancuso 2007). The organization's Council of Ministers has the authority to adopt uniform acts that need not be implemented by national legislatures. Many of the acts are based on draft conventions and model laws created by other organizations, such as UNIDROIT, but they are adjusted to reflect Western Africa's realities. The Cour Commune de Justice et d'Arbitrage (CCJA) is an international court that ensures that OHADA laws are interpreted uniformly across the membership and to increase the credibility of the regional regime. Formally, the CCJA provides a forum for interstate arbitration as well as a court of last resort for disputes that were initiated under OHADA law within member states. Predictably, the first function remains undeveloped (Dickinson 2005, 56). The second function has led to at least 274 judgments, most coming from Côte d'Ivoire (the seat of the court), indicating that in reality national courts do not always refer OHADA cases to the CCJA.[28] Nevertheless, the regime is broadly perceived to be a remarkable success (Mancuso 2007).

Institutional Implications for Asia

What do these lessons mean for a potential judicial institution that could help stimulate transnational economic activity in Asia? It would be unwise to transplant one of the existing regional judicial institutions to Asia. Outright copying of formal institutional structure is common but rarely successful (Alter 2009). Yet, there are some lessons that could be learned. The most obvious negative one is that an institution that focuses solely on resolving inter-state disputes is unlikely to contribute much. There are few downsides to having a formal inter-state dispute settlement mechanism, such as ASEAN's, but it is not clear that such a mechanism will have significant effects either. A second negative conclusion is that given the present institutional structure, it would be unwise to create a court that primarily aims to reduce deliberate non-compliance by member states. Such courts can only function effectively in the presence of a strong supranational bureaucracy that can file infringement suits.

The most straightforward answer to the question of why there are no active standing Asian courts is that there are few if any regional rules that create rights and obligations for private parties. To some extent this is answering a question by positing a different one: why are such rules absent? I suggest three answers. First, heterogeneity within Asia is greater than in other regions. This is true even within the most developed sub-regional institution: ASEAN. This diversity makes it difficult to coordinate on regulations that are appropriate across a region or sub-region. Second, there are very few liberal democracies, thus reducing the space for binding human rights commitments or other regional law that focuses on the rights of individuals. Third, many Asian states have traditionally been "developmental states," which seek to exercise social and political control over business through informal means rather than through independent regulatory agencies that are delegated the authority to apply a well-defined body of formal law (e.g., Woo-Cumings 1999). Recently, scholars have argued that several Asian countries are moving towards a regulatory state model (e.g., Ginsburg and Chen 2008; Jayasurya 2007; Pearson 2005). This trend is at least partially a response to economic interdependence and membership in international regimes (Ginsburg and Chen 2008), as it was in Europe (Majone 1994). Such reforms create a demand for administrative review as both governments and private actors become increasingly concerned that agencies are unable to implement the new rules well or even that they might abuse their authority.

Although regional law plays a limited role in Asian administrative review, a regional court could aid national courts and administrative agencies in areas where global international legal obligations are already important. Asian countries are party to various multilateral treaties that create obligations vis-à-vis private parties. Although there are no regional rules on government procurement, several Asian states are part of the WTO's Government Procurement Agreement (Hsu 2006). The WTO's intellectual property rights regime (TRIPS) also has important implications for regulatory regimes. Moreover, many Asian states are actively seeking to bring their business law in accordance with international standards. All major Asian economies are members of UNIDROIT[29] and many are signatories to its conventions that seek to unify private law. Several Asian states are members of the Hague Conference on Private International Law (HccH) and are parties to its various conventions.[30] Asian states are also active in UNCITRAL, the UN body that seeks to harmonize and modernize international business law through conventions and model laws.

There is some evidence that Asian countries have increased such commitments in recent years. For example after long remaining outside the regime, South Korea (2005) and Japan (2009) are the latest major trading powers to join the 1980 *UN Convention on Contracts for the International Sale of Goods* (CISG),[31] leaving Brazil, India, the United Kingdom, and South Africa as the only major trading countries that have not signed what is arguably the most successful international contract treaty. Another example was discussed earlier in this paper: the frequency with which Asian countries are willing to delegate authority to ICSID to arbitrate in investment disputes between private parties and the government.

In short, several Asian states appear increasingly willing to make international legal commitments that create obligations vis-à-vis private parties.

Moreover, they have recognized that harmonization of commercial law is desirable. Even if this has not led to new regional law, a regional judicial institution could improve the uniform implementation of those existing international legal commitments, improve the perceived commitments by Asian states to those legal rules, and create further momentum toward harmonization. This role would not be unlike that of OHADA, which is based on regional law that was in turn strongly influenced by global conventions. One possibility, then, is to create a judicial institution that can, at the request of national courts or administrative agencies, offer advisory opinions on the interpretation of international rules, laws, and standards that are already applicable. The assumption is that governments want to see those obligations implemented but that national administrative agencies or courts may not always be well equipped to do so. Such an institution would issue advisory opinions on a well-defined set of treaties and conventions that countries have already ratified. It would leave the resolution of disputes to the national courts. This is appropriate as actual disputes often involve a mixture of domestic and international legal issues that can be better assessed by local courts. This may also alleviate some sovereignty concerns. It would specifically not be within the mandate of this institution to interpret domestic law or make judgments as to whether domestic law contradicts international legal obligations. Such determinations are left to the national review process.

The examples of the Andean Community and OHADA illustrate that it is possible to use a regional court to help harmonize narrow areas of law relevant for transnational economic activity without creating a powerful supranational bureaucracy. Moreover, these examples demonstrate that national institutions still play a major role in the extent to which such a regional court becomes active in a country, perhaps alleviating some concerns about sovereignty costs and that Asian states are too diverse to effectively harmonize laws.

While the benefits of such a judicial institution are potentially meaningful, there are some fundamental limits to the role a regional judicial institution could play in contemporary Asia. Simply put, the demand for an Asian regional judicial institution will remain weak until Asian states adopt regional legally binding treaties that create rights and obligations for private persons.

Notes

1. I thank Todd Allee, Karen Alter, Mely Caballero Anthony, Sarah Bermeo, Christina Davis, Barry Eichengreen, Stephen Haggard, Larry Helfer, Denis Hew, Locknie Hsu, Miles Kahler, Clint Peinhardt, and Tan See Seng for sharing data and suggestions that have helped to improve this chapter.

2. Alter (2009) finds evidence of almost 30,000 rulings issued by standing international courts until 2007. About 90% of these rulings come from regional courts. This number does not include rulings by arbitration panels or non-permanent courts.

3. For a similar argument, see Alter (2009).

4. For example, Davis and Shirato (2007) use such an account to explain Japan's restraint in initiating WTO trade disputes.

5. I rely on the ADB definitions http://www.adb.org/Countries/ (accessed June 30th, 2009). Japan is also included.

6. Based on the World Bank's WTO data: http://econ.worldbank.org/WBSITE/ EXTERNAL/EXTDEC/EXTRESEARCH/0,contentMDK:20804376~pagePK:64214825 ~piPK:64214943~theSitePK:469382,00.html (accessed July 13, 2009).

7. Information comes from the Project on International Courts and Tribunals: http:// www.pict-pcti.org (accessed July 7, 2009.)

8. Currently, these countries are Iceland, Liechtenstein, Norway, and Switzerland.

9. Article 32, see http://www.eftacourt.int/index.php/court/mission/esa_court_ agreement/(Accessed July 6, 2009).

10. http://www.eftacourt.int/index.php/cases (Accessed July 6, 2009).

11. http://www.pict-pcti.org/courts/beneluxCJ.html (Accessed July 7, 2009).

12. There were 17 inter-state complaints that were dealt with by the European Commission on Human Rights. Georgia has recently brought another inter-state complaint (against Russia): "Inter-State Application Brought by Georgia Against the Russian Federation" Press release by the Registrar of the European Court of Human Rights, march 27 2007) https://wcd.coe.int/ViewDoc.jsp?id=1111315&Site=COE (Accessed July 9, 2009).

13. It only became a formal judicial organ of CIS in 1993 (Danilenko 1999).

14. Article 24 of the Treaty Creating the Court of Justice of the Cartagena Agreement (http://www.comunidadandina.org/ingles/normativa/ande_trie2.htm) allows states to file non-compliance claims with the secretary-general. The ATJ website suggest that it has happened on only three occasions that a state was the originator of a non-compliance complaint (http://idatd.eclac.cl/controversias/can.htm?perform=estadisticas&numero=5). Yet, when reading cases it becomes clear that several of the cases brought by the secretary-general originated with state complaints (private communication with Karen Alter and Larry Helfer, July 7th, 2009).

15. http://www.worldcourts.com/cacj/eng/decisions.htm (accessed July 10, 2009).

16. The court was inaugurated in 2005.

17. http://www.caribbeancourtofjustice.org/judgments.html (accessed July 10, 2009).

18. Adam Liptak "Nafta Tribunals Stir U.S. Worries" *The New York Times*, Sunday, April 18, 2004.

19. Based on a reading of disputes at: http://www.sice.oas.org/DISPUTE/nafdispe.asp (Accessed July 7, 2009). In addition there were 25 disputes filed by private business where I did not find evidence of government involvement on both sides. Chapter 11 also gives private actors standing to sue governments for damages, a procedure that has been widely used. There has also been one inter-state dispute under Chapter 20.

20. http://www.ohada.com/jurisprudence.php (accessed July 13th, 2009).

21. http://about.comesa.int/lang-en/institutions/court-of-justice (accessed July 13, 2009).

22. I was able to find evidence of only five cases: http://www.aict-ctia.org/courts_subreg/ comesa/comesa_cases.html (accessed July 13, 2009).

23. Alter 2009 and http://www.aict-ctia.org/courts_subreg/eac/eac_home.html (Accessed July 13, 2009).

24. http://www.aict-ctia.org/courts_subreg/ecowas/ecowas_home.html (Accessed July 13, 2009).

25. Moreover, there are a number of courts that are not yet operational, including the Court of Justice for the Arab Magreb Union (AMU), the Court of Justice of the Economic Community of Central African States (ECCAS), and the African Court of Justice (ACJ).

26. See Helfer and Alter (2009) for the more precise story on the mechanisms in each country and also for a preliminary account of why the same trend has not happened in Bolivia and Venezuela.

27. The Western African members are Benin, Burkina Faso, Côte d'Ivoire, Guinea, Guinea-Bissau, Mali, Niger, Senegal, and Togo. The Central African members are Central African Republic, Chad, Cameroon, Comores, Congo, Equatorial Guinea, and Gabon.

28. Alter 2009. Private parties may also not always insist on this, given the expense of proceedings in a another country (Dickerson 2005). There are hundreds more rulings on OHADA law that are decided in national courts.

29. http://www.unidroit.org/english/members/main.htm

30. http://www.hcch.net/index_en.php?act=states.listing

31. They were the only major countries that signed in this period: http://www.uncitral.org/uncitral/en/uncitral_texts/sale_goods/1980CISG_status.html

Appendix: Data Sources

Variable	Description and Source
TABLE 3.1: *Trade Dispute Initiation (Davis and Bermeo 2009)*	
Democracy	Freedom House civil liberties
Log GDP	GDP in constant 2000 dollars, in purchasing power parity terms, World Bank's World Development Indicators
Log Population	World Bank's World Development Indicators
English	English language, which takes on the value of 1 if the CIA World Factbook listed English as "widely spoken" in a given country
TABLE 3.2: *Investment Dispute Delegation (Allee and Peinhardt 2009)*	
Presence of MNCs	percentage of world's largest MNCs located in the home country; data taken from various issues of *Forbes* magazine
Strength of Legal Institutions	International Country Risk Group measure of "law and order" ranges from 1 to 6
Durability of Host Regime	the number of consecutive years since a three-point change in the Polity score over a period of three years of less (see Marshall and Jaggers 2005)
Political Constraints on Executive in Host	Henisz's "POLCONIII" measure of political constraints on the executive in the host country; see Henisz 2002
Alliance Ties	equals 1 if the home and host country share any type of alliance tie and 0 otherwise; taken from the ATOP project (Leeds et al. 2002)

Variable	Description and Source
Colonial Ties	Equals 1 if the home and host country share any type of colonial tie and 0 otherwise; taken from the ICOW colonial history data set, version 0.4
Host Recently Independent	Equals1 if the host country achieved independence within the past 10 years and 0 otherwise; dates of independence are taken from the Correlates of War State System Membership List
Domestic Economic Growth Host	GDP growth in host country from last year to the current year; taken from World Development Indicators (WDI)
Export Dependence Host	Exports of goods and services as a % of GDP; taken from World Development Indicators
Reliance on External Financial Assistance Host	IBRD loans and IDA credits as a % of host country GDP (in current US$); taken from World Development Indicators
Right Wing Government Host	Equals 1 if the host country is governed by a right-wing executive and 0 otherwise; taken from the Database of Political Institutions' EXECRLC variable
Ratio of Home to Host Economic Power	The relative balance of home and host country GDP, calculated as home country GDP divided by the sum of home and host country GDP (all in current US$); data taken from World Development Indicators

TABLE 3.3: *Territorial Disputes (Allee and Huth 2006, more details on data in Huth and Allee 2002)*

Strong domestic political opposition	Equals 1 if in democratic countries are considered to face strong domestic political opposition, governing coalition of executive does not control a majority of seats in the primary legislative or parliamentary body, and if in nondemocratic countries there has been an attempted or actual coup within the country in the past year
Democratic dyad (accountability)	Those regimes that have a Polity net-democracy score of +6 or higher.
Ethnic ties with territory	Equals 1 if each state involved in the dispute has ethnic ties with a population living in the disputed territory
Enduring rivals	Equals 1 if the two disputants have experienced at least ten militarized conflicts during the past two decades
Hard-line stance in previous negotiations	Number of consecutive rounds of talks in the last five years have ended in stalemate
Democratic dyad (norms)	Equals 1 if both states possessed Polity net-democracy scores of +6 or greater for at least 16 of the past 20 years
Military asymmetry	Absolute difference in Correlates of War CINC scores.
Common security ties	Equals 1 if a formal security alliance exists.
Strategic value of territory	Equals 1 if the territory has strategic value as determined by Huth and Allee (2002)

4

The Potential for Organizational Membership Rules to Enhance Regional Cooperation

JUDITH G. KELLEY

Introduction

Regional organizations can pursue a wide array of membership rules ranging from "Convoy" rules that allow all regional states to participate unconditionally, to "club" rules that enforce strict criteria for admission and continued participation.[1] An organization may model its initial membership rules on other existing organizations, but the rules foremost reflect the preferences of the founding states: their ambitions for the organization, their willingness to make binding commitments to a common cause. However, even if membership rules merely reflect those preferences, they can still influence the organization's development, because the initial preferences contain uncertainty and imperfect information (Williamson 1985). States therefore cannot fully realize how the rules will play out over time; the rules can constrain future options, especially if the preferences of states change over time. Thus, states may not always comprehend the full implications of their choice of rules. And although states theoretically can change the rules to reflect their new preferences, the existing rules and institutional inertia often make that difficult to do. Membership rules therefore influence the ability of organizations to shape the behavior of states in the regions, and they may help or hinder the development of regional integration.

If all states in a region initially agreed on the nature of their cooperation and never developed incentives to defect from their agreements, then the membership rules would be unimportant. However, all regions are heterogenous:

States often prefer different policy solutions to their common problems, because they disagree about how to distribute the costs and benefits of cooperation among themselves (European Parliament 2001). Furthermore, in trade
and environmental issues, for example, most states would prefer to free ride
on the efforts of others (NDI 1994). Thus, even if states agree on their end
goals, reaching and enforcing agreements is challenging. States also vary in
their capacities to implement regional polices. Poorer states may have less administrative capacity, or their economic or political fundamentals may not be
conducive to stable coordination with other states in the region. Finally, states
vary in their information and belief systems. The more their norms about domestic governance, sovereignty, and interstate interaction differ, the harder it
will be for them to agree on and enforce joint policies. Thus, heterogeneous
preferences, capacities, and beliefs are the core challenges of intergovernmental cooperation and regional integration.

The choice of membership rules—whether organizations operate as convoys or clubs or some other design—can influence organizations' ability to
reduce or accommodate heterogeneity and forge successful regional integration. Figure 4.1 illustrates this "R-H-I" relationship between rules, heterogeneity, and integration. State heterogeneity in the region initially informs the
choice of membership rules. However, subsequently, the membership rules
shape the tools organizations can use to reduce state heterogeneity. Clubs can
leverage higher entry criteria to solicit changes prior to admission for late
joiners. However, convoys, with lower entry barriers, can take a less confron-
tational approach to outlier states by interacting with them within the organization rather than erecting barriers. Thus, these different membership rules
offer different mechanisms for reducing heterogeneity and forging integration. Furthermore, the membership and participation rules may also offer different ways to accommodate persistent heterogeneity by selectively deepening
integration among like-minded states.

Which membership rules best promote regional cooperation? This question continues to produce debate, particularly in regions such as Asia where
low entry requirements and consensus rules have dominated along with a
policy of non-interference in domestic matters (Acharya 1997). For example, as ASEAN has matured, its ambition for regional economic integration

Membership	$\longrightarrow$	State	$\longrightarrow$	Regional
Rules	$\longleftarrow$	Heterogeneity		Integration
(R)		(H)		(I)

FIGURE 4.1   The R-H-I relationship.

has grown and it has launched efforts such as the ASEAN Free Trade Area (AFTA) and the Trade in Services. But as more states have sought to join, the member states have disagreed over membership criteria and how heavily to weigh domestic conditions when admitting states. This was evident in the debate that arose in connection with the applications of Vietnam and Cambodia (Acharya 2001, 105). Uncertainty about how to respond to the coup in Cambodia led to a recognition that in the light of "growing interdependence" ASEAN needed to rethink some of its assumptions about non-interference (Acharya 2001, 118–119). ASEAN has also delayed observer status for Myanmar and vigorously debated the extent to which Myanmar's internal politics mattered for its entry. Some countries advocated demanding domestic policy changes before admission, others stressed the non-interference doctrine, and yet others argued that admitting Myanmar to ASEAN could help improve its domestic political situation (Acharya 2001, 112–114).

To understand how membership rules might influence regional cooperation, this chapter examines the roles of membership rules in light of the experiences of regional organizations, especially in Europe, and surveys insights from political science research. The central question is: How can organizations create or modify membership rules to deepen regional integration?

First, however, because membership rules influence the number of countries in an organization, it is important to consider whether the success of regional cooperation is really more about the number of member states than about membership rules. Perhaps restrictive rules lead to effective cooperation not because they are restrictive, but because they keep the number of participants lower. Scholars have argued that more participants increase enforcement problems and lower the benefits of cooperation (Olson 1965). Thus, mere size may make large organizations impractical, an argument that has resurfaced in the classic widening-versus-deepening debate in the European Union (EU). Indeed, the relative success of today's EU may rest partly on the initial decision of the "inner six," of Belgium, France, Germany, Italy, Luxembourg, and the Netherlands, to proceed with the European Coal and Steel Community (ECSC) in 1951, while the "outer seven," of Austria, Denmark, Norway, Portugal, Sweden, Switzerland, and the United Kingdom formed the European Free Trade Association (EFTA). However, although starting small may be advantageous, size need not impede strong cooperation. Institutional devices, such as voting rules, can ameliorate problems introduced by wider participation (Kahler 1992, 703), as both the Organization for Security and Cooperation in Europe (OSCE) and the EU have demonstrated. For example, the

OSCE adopted the "consensus minus one" rule in 1992 so that some decisions could be taken without the consent of the state concerned. The EU has also moved toward majority rules and other compromise-decision rules on several issues, and this has allowed it to deepen cooperation while also widening membership. The question of membership rules therefore relates to, but is distinct from, the question of the size of an organization. Larger organizations need not falter. Rather than size, the problems of cooperation among greater numbers of states likely stem from changes in other fundamentals as organizations expand (Keohane and Ostrom 1995, 22–23; Snidal, Duncan 1995). Most importantly, size likely relates to heterogeneity, which is the greatest obstacle to cooperation.

Indeed, heterogeneity has hindered cooperation in several regions. Thus, Sandholtz and Stone Sweet (1998, 11) argued that the main obstacles to European economic integration has been differences among national rules and norms. Venezuela's entrance into Mercosur also highlights the importance of shared norms. Oil-rich Venezuela's philosophical opposition to free trade and its nationalization of domestic industries has caused tensions as President Hugo Chávez advocated for a shift in the focus of the bloc. Cooperation benefits from shared information and beliefs (Keohane and Ostrom 1995), and it is useful if the participants share characteristics that define them as a community (Snidal 1995, 65). Thus, authors writing about regional integration in the 1960s not only emphasized economics, but also culture and geography (Russett 1967; Caparaso and Choi 2002, 482). More recently, scholars have found that democracies are more likely to enter regional integration arrangements and to choose arrangements of greater depth, although democracies with many veto players are less likely to enter deep integration arrangements than those with few veto players (Mansfield, Milner, and Pavehouse 2008).

Shared norms about sovereignty are especially important for building joint political institutions, which facilitate successful regional cooperation and economic integration (Haas and Schmitter 1964, 707; Pollack 2003) (Hix, this volume). Indeed, Hass defined regional integration as the "voluntary creation of larger political units" (Haas, Ernst B. 1970 608) and argued that in the process of regional integration, states cease to be wholly sovereign. Fear of intrusions on sovereignty therefore hamper regional integration, as has been observed, for example, in the AU and the League of Arab Nations (Barnett and Solingen 2007; Herbst 2007, 132). Asia's similar emphasis on sovereignty and non-interference (Caballero-Anthony, 2005) may also prevent ASEAN from strengthening the central secretariat to the degree necessary to carry out its goals (Severino 2009). In Europe, in contrast, the desire to avoid the rogue state behavior that spurred the rise of Nazi Germany softened the principles of sovereignty and non-interference and thus facilitated the creation of supranational structures (Krasner 2001). Thus, in Europe, the drive toward monetary unity has always been intertwined with ideas of political union (Henning, this volume), and even if monetary union was able to forge ahead, as monetary integration has increased, the EU has also discovered even greater pressures to create ever more centralized political governing structures—a point emphasized by the calls by German Chancellor Angela Merkel and others in 2011 for greater political cooperation amidst the Eurozone debt crisis.[2]

Divergent capacity among regional states also raises problems for cooperation. Research finds that states with a low rule of law or low administrative capacities are less likely to keep their international commitments (OAS 1996; Simmons 2000; Kelley 2007). Neofunctionalists also originally viewed similar economic development and societal structures as optimal for deepening economic integration (Haas and Schmitter 1964). Furthermore, regional economic integration depends on compatible domestic economic conditions (Russett 1967); differences in economic development hinders effective currency unions (Haas 1970, 619). Hass argued that such differences caused the failure of the Latin American Free Trade Association (LAFTA) in the 1960s. Others similarly attribute the failure of early regional integration in the Middle East to the economic differences between oil-poor and oil-rich (Coskun 2006). On economic cooperation especially, prospective members may simply not have the capacity or the economic fundamentals that make it optimal for the organization to invite them to join (Bayoumi and Eichengreen 1992). This is why the EU has spent so much on assisting candidate states through, for example, the EU Phare program. Furthermore, the European Commission has negotiated extensively with candidate countries to insure that they have the capacity to implement community law. Even with all these precautions, the EU has faced a deep crisis in 2010 as it learned of rising debt levels in Greece and other members of the single currency, the Euro. The instability in what was supposedly the most likely and supportive environment for monetary union illustrates just how volatile monetary union can be when domestic economic fundamentals diverge and countries operate their political systems independently.

Thus, heterogeneity of state preferences, norms, and capacities is the main obstacle to the creation and implementation of regional integration. A major concern of regional organizations therefore is how to mitigate the heterogeneity of states in their region so that they can cooperate more effectively. The next section discusses how membership rules provide opportunities for reducing heterogeneity, and the last section discusses ways that rules may be used to accommodate persistent heterogeneity.

Mechanisms for Reducing Heterogeneity and Shaping State Cooperation

Research suggests that organizations can influence the behavior of government and decision-making elites through at least two mechanisms. The first is the use of incentives. Sanctions and political conditionality can change the incentive structure of decision-making elites by altering their payoffs for different behaviors (Crawford 1997; Hufbauer, Schott, Elliott, and Oegg 2007). This mechanism rests on the rationalist assumption that actors are cost-benefit-calculating, utility-maximizing actors. This concept was illustrated well by Bulgarian Prime Minister Ivan Kostov's comment in April 2000 as Bulgaria was vying to join the EU: "With all my respect for the West, I am watching there only the opinion of the structures, which finance Bulgaria. All the others, whatever they say, are of no importance."[3] Because they yield benefits for their members, intergovernmental organizations may be able to alter the incentive structures of non-member and member states in a variety of ways, such as promising rewards or punishment for behavior, or by providing institutional assurances that help governments commit to certain policies.

The second mechanism seeks to change state behavior by changing the underlying preferences and beliefs of decision-making elites through socialization. Socialization does not link any material incentives to behavior, but relies on persuading or shaming actors in order to change their policies or simply to habituate them into new behavior. Socialization occurs though discourse, diplomacy, and frequent interactions with state actors. Intergovernmental organizations may function as "sites of socialization" (Checkel 2005, 806–808), because state agents are "exposed to alternative theories about the nature of world politics" (Johnston 2001, 508–509). Thus, constructivists scholars have argued that institutions can not only constrain states, but can actually change their interests (Checkel 1999, 2005; OAS 2008) and help diffuse norms between member states (COE 1994). The managerial approach within international law also suggests that international organizations may cause states to redefine their own interests. Participation in organizational discourse and activities is said to be able to realign domestic priorities and induce compliance with organizational norms (Chayes and Chayes 1995, 22). Convoy organizations, such as those in Asia, are argued to facilitate dialogue and socialization (Acharya, this volume).

Whether organizations can incentivize or socialize regional states depends on what tools they have available and how effective these tools are. This, in turn, may well depend on the membership rules: Some tools can be used *ex ante*, that is, before admitting a state, and others can be used better *ex post*, that is, after admitting a state. This chapter discusses the most common tools and asks: how does the ability of clubs and convoys to use these tools differ? How important is the ability of a club to use *ex ante* tools compared to a convoy's ability to use *ex post* tools? What advantages and disadvantages do the different organizational rules bring to each of the tools of influence?

Membership Conditionality

The strength of the club approach is its ability to set requirements for entry. The use of membership conditionality is, therefore, by definition restricted to clubs. Downs, Rocke, and Barsoom (1996) argue that if an organization uses club rules to manipulate the order and timing of entries, including promoting earlier entry for states that favor deeper cooperation, this allows it to reduce the negative consequences of increasing the breadth and depth of cooperation. They argue that starting out small with a club and then admitting more states, as they align their preferences with the organization, leads to organizations with greater depth than those based on a convoy model, because a club model with conditional enlargement can achieve both breadth and greater depth. Forming smaller clubs and then relying on strict admission criteria also allows the existing members to establish their preferred policies before inviting outsiders (Hausken, Mattli, and Plümper 2006, 2). Clubs can, therefore, be much more demanding of newcomers, offering asymmetrical benefits to the core founding states.

These claims align well with the experiences of the EU. The initial six member states were able to cooperate on a deeper level and in a manner closer to their preferences than would have been the case had a compromise been reached with the remaining states that chose instead to form EFTA. Only after EFTA's member states changed their preferences toward greater integration did they join the EU, and they did so on the EU's terms, adopting wholesale its existing policies and obligations (Winters 1997, 900).

Indeed, the European clubs have been quite effective at using membership conditionality to extract considerable concessions from applicant states.

This has been true even for the Council of Europe, although it does not offer benefits commensurate with those of the EU. However, because no state has ever joined the EU without first joining the Council of Europe, the Council has also been able to benefit from the leverage of the EU attraction on non-member states. Still, the Council of Europe has applied membership conditionality with mixed results, partly because its broad membership has sometimes made it difficult for the organization to be consistent in its enforcement of the membership criteria—a challenge that has only increased with the admittance of more members with lower standards. There are clear success cases, however. For example, since 1994, the Council of Europe has been effective at requiring the abolishment of the death penalty in any applicant states (EU 2002).

The particular success of the EU in using membership conditionality to solicit behavioral changes in candidate states is strongly established in the extensive literature on the subject. The assistance and incentives from the European organizations facilitated the tenuous transitions from post-communism, leading to greater convergence of preferences between the formerly divided halves of Europe and enabling broader and stronger regional integration. The EU ensured that candidate states adopted the required legislation and created needed capacity to address the economic commitments of their membership. Although candidate states could choose how to meet their obligations (Jacoby 2004), and sometimes obtain transition periods for obligations where they were not yet ready to meet, they could not reduce the content of their obligations as members (Grabbe 2002).

Some argue that the candidate states have adopted policies much faster than did current member states. Whereas Greece took over a decade to adapt to the EU's single market norms, the new Central and Eastern European members adapted before joining, in much less time, even though their starting point was more remote (Grabbe 2002, 4). This suggests that leverage is greater on countries outside the club than inside it and, therefore, all else being equal, the more behavioral adaptations an organization can extract prior to entry, the better.

Of course, the effectiveness of the club approach depends on whether the non-member states eventually wish to join. During the EU financial crises, for example, Turkey found the prospect of joining the EU less and less attractive. But the EU case suggests that to the extent that the club is able to achieve deep cooperation that yields highly valuable benefits, exclusion may become too costly for most non-member states, even if originally they preferred not to cooperate. Thus, strong regional clubs will likely present non-members with increasing incentives to meet the requirements to join the organization.

Associational Memberships

The EU has also made effective use of levels of membership by offering, for example, association agreements and pre-accession agreements. Advancing from one level of membership to the next has been a powerful incentive for candidate states, allowing the EU to use leverage at multiple points in time. The EU's accession process has evolved to include a multitude of steps and tools. The more arduous the process and the greater the number of evaluation points and stages of accession, the greater the opportunity for the organization to identify weaknesses, push for the adaptation of domestic laws and regulations, and create decision points that focus attention on applicant states. The danger, however, is that the process is so arduous that it appears unattainable, as it has perhaps at times in the case of Turkey in relationship to the EU. This may have the effect of lowering the organization's credibility and thus its leverage vis-à-vis a candidate state in the long run.

Again, club organizations are more likely to be able to use associational or other intermediate memberships as a tool of influence. Whereas convoys may use associational memberships, these are not considered halfway stations to full membership and, therefore, do not provide leverage as such. As noted, for example, Myanmar briefly had observer status in ASEAN, but this had no influence on Myanmar's behavior. That said, associational memberships or observer status can be used by any organization to bring countries into institutional forums, thus increasing the opportunity for socialization, as will be discussed further later.

Ex Ante Monitoring

Both the Council of Europe and the EU have used monitoring in conjunction with the accession process. The Council of Europe has extensive monitoring procedures and issues numerous political and legal recommendations before a country can enter the organization. The Council of Europe's *rapporteurs* visit applicant countries and bring reports to the Assembly, which then passes resolutions recommending policy changes that must be accomplished before admission. Sometimes however, the Council of Europe accepts a commitment from a state to change a controversial policy within a pre-set timeframe, most commonly 6 months. Although no systematic research exists comparing the pre-accession conditions with post-accession expectations, there is evidence that at least on some issues states are less likely to implement the changes if they are allowed to join the organization without having first implemented the changes (Kelley 2004b).

The EU has also monitored candidate states very effectively. The European Commission, which oversees enlargement, instituted annual reviews that contained recommendations as to the readiness of each candidate state according to the goals set out in various accession agreements. Candidate states know that their accession progress is closely tied to meeting the recommendations in the report and therefore work to address concerns.

Suspending Guest Status

The EU has also suspended intermediate agreements to pressure states. Because it uses an extensive graduated approach to membership, there are numerous stages at which the EU can suspend the association and accession process. After the overthrow of the democratically elected Greek government in 1967, the EU suspended Greece's Association Agreement. Some scholars argue that this pressure was important in Greece's 1973 transition to democracy, because it undermined the military regime financially and politically: "Exclusion from the rapidly integrating Community was a singularly dangerous prospect" (Buscaneanu 2006, 109). The EU has also suspended the associations of candidates and guest observers on several occasions with Turkey, Belarus, Croatia, and others. However, the EU's influence on Belarus appears minimal, and in Turkey's case, suspension may have only reinforced domestic beliefs that EU membership was unattainable.

The Council of Europe also suspended Belarus' Special Guest status in 1997 due to the lack of progress on democracy, human rights, and the rule of law; and froze Belarus' membership application the following year, albeit also to no avail.

Exchanges, Workshops, and Legal Advice

Both clubs and convoys may engage in various activities to educate non-member states. This may include academic or parliamentary exchanges, workshops or conferences. Results of such efforts are difficult to measure. However, research has shown that the North Atlantic Treaty Organization (NATO) was able to teach some new liberal-democratic norms to incoming East European actors (Gheciu 2005). Furthermore, the Council of Europe and the EU have both offered legal advice and often worked directly with national officials in candidate states to formulate draft legislation (ANFREL

2001; Kelley 2004a). The EU also offers support through "twinning"—a process whereby the EU sends a civil servant from a member state to advise candidate states on the implementation of EU policies.

Most of the examples of success with these programs are connected to clubs. Indeed, scholars have argued that monitoring and socialization of non-members may work only when used with states hoping to enter the organization (Johnston 2001). A convoy-structured organization can practice these tools just as much as clubs. For example, the OSCE has engaged extensively in providing legal advice on the protection of national minorities. However, the impact of OSCE efforts has been contingent on the EU stressing the importance of these efforts to candidate states (Kelley 2004a).

Socialization

Socialization refers to the process whereby actors, in this case state political elites, may come to adopt a set of behavioral norms purely through interaction with other state elites. Organizations may seek to socialize non-member states through monitoring, educational programs, and legal advice, as well as exposure to organizational discourse in meetings and communication of various kinds. After states join, these activities can continue and perhaps increase as the frequency and intensity of interaction increases.

Some scholars have found evidence of socialization within international organizations. Bearce and Bondanella (2007, 721) argue that membership in intergovernmental organizations promotes the convergence of voting records within the United Nations (UN) General Assembly. Interestingly, they find the strongest effect of this within Asia. Kent (2002) also documents several issue areas ranging from disarmament to labor rights, where the People's Republic of China (PRC) has redefined its interests via participation in international organizations. Sometimes this has been a pragmatic adjustment, but in other cases it has led to institutionalization of norms within the PRC. Acharya (2010, and this volume) also documents several instances of socialization with respect to the PRC, India, and Vietnam. Scholars also argue that the Conference on Cooperation and Security in Europe (CSCE), the OSCE precursor, changed human rights behavior within participant states. The participation of Mikhail Gorbachev and other high-level Soviet officials led to significant learning within the government, and, ultimately to changes in behavior (Thomas 2001, 2005). Similarly the UN Educational, Scientific and Cultural Organization (UNESCO) has also taught member states the importance of creating national scientific agencies (Finnemore 1993). Other research also finds some evidence of the socialization of domestic militaries after admission to NATO (Pevehouse 2003, 528–529; OSCE 2007, 167). Finally, several regional organizations—such as the Council of Europe, OSCE, and OAS—monitor elections in member states in an effort to teach electoral norms. Success has been mixed, but present (Kelley 2012).

In other cases, researchers have found little evidence of socialization within organizations. In a study of corruption, Pevehouse (2009) finds that that states are not socialized within organizations to root out their domestic corruption. Some researchers have found also that the views of EU officials remain largely determined by domestic factors (Beyers 2005; Hooghe 2005). Others also dispute that there are any effects of intergovernmental organizations more generally on member state preferences (Boehmer, Gartzke, and Nordstrom 2004, 2). Efforts by the Council of Europe and EU vis-à-vis the post-communists states, through a series of interactions and reprimands, tended only to work when domestic opposition to the proposed norms were weak, or when domestic actors favoring the norms held power within government coalitions, or when these socialization efforts were combined with powerful membership incentives from the EU (Kelley 2004b, 2004a). Furthermore, Myanmar has been a clear example that ASEAN's policy of constructive engagement, which rests entirely on a philosophy of socialization, is not working. Prior to admission, Myanmar made some minor concessions on the repatriation of Muslim refugees (Minzarari 2008b, 43), but has made no further concessions. On the contrary, after admission to ASEAN, Myanmar ratcheted up its oppression of the opposition, having seen its admission as a sign of legitimacy. Critics have noted that "expansion has not enhanced ASEAN bargaining power" (EU 2001, 50). Thus, the evidence that socialization may build trust and change beliefs and behavior is mixed, even within Asia, where scholars (Acharya, this volume) are most positive about the presence of socialization.

The deepened cooperation within the OAS over the last decades could be interpreted to show that the convoy structure of the organization indeed socialized member states. However, it is more likely the domestic changes in member states that drove recent reforms within the OAS. Many OAS activities to uphold democratic norms only emerged after the countries in the region established their democratic regimes (Cooper and Legler 2001). These national changes enabled the OAS to institutionalize organizational procedures such as the Santiago Declaration and the Unit for the Promotion of Democracy to help the countries in the region to "lock in" these domestic changes.

Thus, although the OAS has not changed its membership composition much, its membership rules have grown more club-like over time; the membership criteria have hardened, making suspension and interference more likely. Yet, these changes were gradual,[4] and only decades of changes in domestic conditions led to a move away from strict non-intervention.

Ironically, even if the OAS has been able to deepen political cooperation, it has still been unable to act as an effective vehicle for regional economic integration. Indeed, there is little research on whether socialization works with the economic issues that are so central to regional integration efforts. Theory suggests that to the extent that defection from economic commitments is important, building trust through interaction within organizations is equally important. However, given that organizations that deal with economic matters typically also have specific policy-related entry requirements, or have some enforcement mechanisms, it is difficult to establish whether states keep their requirement because they have been socialized into keeping such commitments or because of the enforcement mechanisms. For example, EU member states generally do keep their commitments, including economic commitments. EU member states now implement about 96% of their commitments satisfactorily (Tallberg 2003). Interestingly, in 90% of the cases where commitments were violated, the European Commission was able to gain compliance by naming and shaming violating states by publishing the violations. However, it is unlikely that this apparent socialization was really socialization at all, because states likely anticipated that the alternative to compliance would be court action, as discussed more below.

Furthermore, when France and Germany missed the targets of the Stability Pact in 2003 (Buti and Pench 2004), the EU was not willing to use socialization tools to shame these countries, let alone resort to the predetermined sanction measures. Thus, on such large economic matters and when dealing with powerful member states, membership in an organization does not appear to install a sense of obligation or appropriateness that automatically leads states to comply when other economic interests are at stake. The 2010 Greek debt crisis suggests a similar, albeit far more serious, failure of both enforcement and socialization.

To the extent that organizations can socialize states, are convoys better suited than clubs? Perhaps the more inclusive nature of a convoy-organization creates a better opportunity for constructive dialogue? On some issues that may be true. Consider the OSCE's predecessor, the CSCE, which was founded with the Helsinki Act in 1975 when the security preferences of European states diverged enormously. Indeed, some states were enemies.

Given that the purpose of the Act was "to improve and intensify their relations and to contribute in Europe to peace, security, justice and co-operation as well as to rapprochement among themselves,"[5] excluding potential member states through strict membership criteria would defeat the organization's very purpose to recognize "the indivisibility of security in Europe as well as their common interest in the development of co-operation throughout Europe and overcome differences."[6] A club approach would be more likely to increase hostilities, as demonstrated by the enlargement of North Atlantic Treaty Organization (NATO), which increased trust with new members but raised hostilities with the still excluded Russia (Kydd 2001). Thus, convoy rules appear to have an advantage over club rules when it comes to issues of reconciliation and security. This is important because regional integration efforts may not always begin with economic considerations. Indeed, as noted earlier, the EU, Mercosur, and ASEAN were motivated by political security considerations as well as economic goals.

On the other hand, if convoys are more diverse because of their lower admission criteria, perhaps when it comes to socialization on political issues other than security, their persuasive power is lower. Research has found that the ability of international organizations to influence the level of democracy in member states depends in part on how democratic the organization's general membership is (Pevehouse 2003).

Institutional Safeguards for Societal Elites

Another way regional organizations may influence member states is by influencing domestic stakeholders. This is particularly important on economic matters. Some research suggests that regional organizations make business interests more supportive of economic liberalization by helping to guarantee their economic interests (Pevehouse 2003, 526). Other research has found that regional trade arrangements help lock in commitments among states (OSCE 1994; COE 1998; OAS 2000).

Some research also suggests that regional organizations can decrease the domestic military's concerns that liberalization and regime openness will sideline the military. Southern European governments were able to internationalize the military's role through integration into NATO (Minzarari 2008a). By increasing resources for the military, membership in NATO's Partnerships for Peace program lowered military resistance to political opening and the completion of the democratic transition in Hungary (Carter Center 2007, 19). Thus, membership in regional organizations may increase the willingness of both economic and military stakeholders to liberalize.

Are clubs or convoys better able to reassure stakeholders? Importantly, however, it does not really seem to matter whether countries are actually full members of an organization. The stakeholder effect may even occur before a country becomes a full member of an organization. For example, Association Agreements between Spain and Portugal and the then-European Economic Community (ECC) helped assure the domestic elites that democratization would not lead to loss of property or hinder the free movement of goods (Dura and Vitu 2008, 271).

The types of guarantees required to convince stakeholders tend to be economic in character, and these guarantees can be rendered to countries just as well in intermediate associational membership arrangements as through full membership. This suggests that club organizations, which are more likely to have deep economic assurances to offer, are not hindered by their exclusionary structure in using these tools of influence. Theoretically, convoy organizations could also use these types of guarantees, but they have fewer guarantees to offer because they have not been able to develop deep economic integration.

Issue-linkage

Some scholars have argued that admitting countries to an organization can draw them into a set of interrelated bargains that influence the interests and negotiating positions of states (Sandholtz 1996). For example, research has found that in situations of asymmetric externalities, as in many environmental cooperation problems, welcoming states into an organization induces perpetrators to join and broadens the cooperative scope to take advantage of opportunities for issue-linkage (Mitchell and Keilbach 2001). No research, however, compares the ability of convoys and clubs in using issue-linkage. At first, it may seem that clubs are at a disadvantage, because it is harder to link issues with non-member states. This may be mitigated somewhat by giving non-members associational status, or by using membership conditionality, or by writing legal agreements with non-member states. Furthermore, if convoys tend to have shallower cooperation, then the linkage may not be very powerful. This is an area that requires more research.

Legal Enforcements

Organizations can also influence states through dispute resolution mechanisms ranging from informal ad hoc non-binding mechanisms to formal courts with binding authority that can serve as important compliance tools after admission. The Council of Europe and the EU have particularly strong courts. As noted earlier, the European Commission publishes violations before it uses its power to bring cases to court, and about 90% of cases are settled without court action. Thus, the threat of referral to the ECJ is a very important tool in achieving legal implementation of EU directives (Tallberg, Jonas 2002). In the Council of Europe, the European Court of Human Rights (ECHR) has been a strong tool for the Council's continued influence on member states after admission, although the level of compliance with court decisions is lower than in the EU.

Effective dispute resolution mechanisms and courts may be harder to acquire and use in organizations with more diverse membership and consensus-like rules. However, agreement might be reached even amidst diverse preferences. The Council of Europe's court was created at a time when some states were seeking ways to lock-in their preferences for human rights and democracy and thus had incentives to surrender some sovereignty to protect against domestic threats democracy (Moravcsik 2003). This played a big role in the creation of the court, which is one of the few cases where an organization that has considerably lower entry requirements than the EU still has a relatively effective compliance tool.

Despite a strong legal enforcement system, it is hard for regional organizations to sanction their own member states, especially if sanctions are costly to impost. When France and Germany missed the targets of the Stability Pact (Buti and Pench 2004), the European Commission took no formal action. It did start punitive proceedings against Portugal in 2002 and Greece in 2005, but never applied penalties. Nor did the member states of the Euro choose legal actions to address the 2010 debt crises in Greece and elsewhere. Thus, even strong legal tools may be useless in addressing fundamental economic issues that conflict with national interests.

Suspensions or Sanctions

Finally, organizations may be able to suspend or expel member states, as for example the suspension of Zimbabwe from the Commonwealth, Egypt from the Arab League, and Guinea from ECOWAS. Suspensions and expulsions are drastic measures, and they are difficult to execute because they require a high level of agreement among member states.

Suspension and expulsion are the most direct tools that convoy organizations have. Because they are so drastic, they are difficult for organizations to agree on, and even when they occur, they have been only mildly successful. In 1992, the OSCE suspended the Federal Republic of Yugoslavia (FYR), because the attacks on Bosnia and Herzegovina flagrantly violated the FYR's

OSCE commitments. The suspension of Serbia and Montenegro continued for 8 years, but it seemed to achieve little. There was great debate within the OSCE about the best course of action. Perry (1998) noted that keeping the FYR out of the forum of debates in the organization and being unable to send representatives to engage in dialogue was ineffective.

Both the African Union and the OAS have become increasingly willing to suspend member states, but often the target state merely shrugs off the act, as did Honduras after the 2009 coup. However, after the coup in Guatemala in May 1993, some argue that the OAS played a critical role by moving to sanction the regime. The military forced Serrano from office within 5 days and installed a civilian regime (Farer 1996; IFES 2007). Still, it is difficult to isolate the role of the OAS in these events.

The EU has only once sanctioned a member state by curbing relations. This occurred in the case of Austria in 2000, when the extremist Austrian Freedom Party led by the racist Jörg Haider entered the Austrian government. Virulent debate ensued within the EU, but the diplomatic sanctions had no effect on Austrian politics. Haider did step down from his party's leadership eventually, but remained influential in party politics.

In sum, although expulsions or suspensions may be useful on principled grounds, there is not much evidence that they increase cooperation.

Options for Modes of Integration to Accommodate and Reduce Heterogeneity

The existing rules of an organization were born out of the preferences of the founding states, and they continue to have repercussions for the organization as it evolves. However, within the existing rules, current member states have some scope to modify their participation and membership rules. Understanding the practical experiences of other regional organizations to date can provide insights about how to adapt rules to promote integration.

Table 4.1 summarizes some of the observations from the above discussion about the available research on the effectiveness of various tools for clubs and convoys toward non-member and member states. The research reviewed above does not exhaust all the possible tools, nor does it show clearly which membership rules best reduce heterogeneity among regional states. This is partly because membership rules cannot be assessed independently of the activities and context of specific organizations. For example, the power of a convoy organization may be greatly enhanced by close cooperation with other regional organizations that may be able to offer leverage. On the other hand, how effective any given tool is depends greatly on the vigor with which it is implemented. For example, when ASEAN leaders signed a charter to further economic integration and commit to creating a human rights body in November 2007, several ASEAN countries threatened to refuse to ratify the charter until Myanmar improved its human rights record. This effort was undermined, however, when within a year they had all ratified the agreement although Myanmar had showed no progress. Thus, all tools can lose force if implementation falters.

TABLE 4.1.

Summary of tools

	Clubs	Convoys
Membership conditionality	Extensively used. Strong effects, both political and economic	Not relevant
Associational memberships	Extensively used. Strong if used in conjunction with accession	No purpose, unlikely to have any effect
Ex ante monitoring	Extensively used. Strong if used in conjunction with accession	Not relevant
Suspending association status for non-members	Occasional use. Weak	Not relevant
Exchanges, workshops, legal advice	Weak, directly mostly at political issues	Weak. Any effects of CSCE/OSCE appear related to cooperation with EU
Socialization	Mixed results that appear contingent on the threat of enforcements or on the existence of inducements	May have advantages on broad issues concerning security and reconciliation. May be weaker on political issues due to greater organizational heterogeneity
Institutional safeguards for societal elites	Results uncertain. If it matters, it is likely to work best in trade areas and it is just as likely to work pre-accession, as long as trade occurs	Rare and uncertain
Issue-linkage	Common with both associational members and non-members through special agreements	Uncertain
Legal enforcements	Common. Effectiveness depends on enforcement	Rare and if it exists, likely weak
Suspensions/sanctions/expulsions	Weak	Weak

That said, the research does suggest that the inclusive nature of convoy organizations retains some advantages over clubs in promoting reconciliation, as shown by the OSCE and its predecessor the CSCE. Convoy organizations may also be able to deepen political cooperation, but the OAS example suggests that this depends on changes to first occur on the national level. By and large, however, clubs have more tools at their disposal, and at least in Europe these tools have been effective. Economic issues in particular seem to require the conditionality and ex ante approach of clubs, because of their practical complexity and the stronger distributional struggles that economic issues entail. Furthermore, convoys rarely have advantages that clubs cannot mimic. Whereas convoys often cannot use the tools that clubs can, simply because they have lost their leverage, clubs can often use the tools of convoys, because states need not have full membership before an organization can interact with them. Thus, clubs can extend various levels of inclusiveness that may offer opportunities for interaction akin to that of convoys.

Despite the advantages of clubs, the reality is that many regions launched their integration efforts through pan-regional convoy organizations either to protect national sovereignty or promote reconciliation. Thus, both the OSCE and ASEAN assumed a convoy form to build confidence and security in their respective regions. How, then, can regions and organizations navigate the membership rules to accommodate heterogeneity in ways that will still allow them to deepen regional integration? Clearly they cannot disinvite current members, and expulsion, as noted, is ineffective and would not be a positive step toward deepening regional integration. However, it may still be possible to modify current arrangements or create new ones that draw on the insights from the above analysis. And importantly: finding ways to *accommodate* heterogeneity may in the long run contribute to *reducing* heterogeneity, if those states that proceed with more intense cooperation can show results that entice the reticent states to join them.

Option 1: Use Levels of Membership

If all regional states are not already members, organizations can create new associational forms and employ different participation requirements for different levels. Observer states usually have few rights within the organization except to observe. Associate members, however, often have some rights and can obtain benefits from the organization. Observer states sometimes are states that do not have a prospect of full membership, whereas associate states may be members-in-waiting. In both cases, an organization may be able to bring countries into their institutional forums by granting them such intermediate levels of association. This may enable these states to be part of important debates within the organization, and it may enable the organization to set some conditions for granting association status. Thus, an organization may allow states to participate as observers or associate members, and these levels of membership can provide opportunities both for socialization as well as for continued leverage over prospective members.

Option 2: Change Entry Requirements

Organizations can introduce new entry requirements even if such have not traditionally existed. The Copenhagen Criteria introduced new requirements for joining the EU, with new member states having to meet requirements that the initial members were not asked to meet. New entry requirements can be necessary if the organization has evolved and requires a different level of preparation before members can join smoothly, but existing member states can also simply decide to impose new requirements. Furthermore, this need not mean that old member states will be scrutinized based on these new standards. The EU efforts at addressing ethnic minority problems in candidate states in the 1990s did not mean that the current members became subject to similar examination and requirements. This may seem unfair, but the reality is that the current members can set the rules.

Option 3: Create Multiple Institutions

Although a region might have created a convoy organization, all cooperation need not proceed within the frameworks of this organization. Instead, regions can take a layered approach to integration by creating multiple institutions to address different issues. Europe has been particularly successful at creating separate regional organizations to address security, human rights, economics, and political integration. This allows regions to apply different organizational membership rules to different issues. Yet, as in Europe, the organizations can work closely together. Thus, regional integration in Europe has emerged from a very diverse set of states through a network of interlocking organizations that were able to mix convoy and club rules to influence the states in the region.

Other regions may be able to emulate this model somewhat. It suggests, for example, that regional human rights or monetary organizations may not be best situated within the existing convoy structures created to address security issues, as is for example ASEAN's recent efforts to create an Inter-Governmental Commission on Human Rights. Rather, separate organizations, perhaps with fewer but more committed members, might be able to initiate deeper cooperation on human rights or on monetary issues if they are not held to the lowest common denominator of the existing convoy structure.

Whereas it may be beneficial to have multiple regional organizations that address different issues, it may be less constructive to have multiple sub-regional organizations pursuing the same objectives. Africa, for example, has multiple Regional Economic Communities (RECs) that have been formed among sub-groups of states in the region. These RECs are nested within the African Economic Community (AEC), but they often have overlapping membership. In addition, there are RECs that are not organized within the AEC. Such parallel organizations, however, create a very fragmented structure of regional organizations that progress at very different speeds while not following similar standards and procedures. In Africa, this has complicated the attainment of the AECs goals of a single market and a central bank.[7] Sub-groups may also present inter-organizational conflicts. For example, Mercosur members cannot join the Andean Community of Nations (CAN), because Mercosur's charter prohibits its members from forging an FTA with nonmember nations. Thus, to join Mercosur, Venezuela had to leave CAN. However, Bolivia, which also aims to join Mercosur, refuses to leave CAN. To address the problem, CAN and Mercosur have sought to form a third organization, Unasur, which could eventually replace both organizations.[8]

Asia faces these similar risks, because several regional organizations now have overlapping membership and overlapping agendas. As Dent (2010) notes, there is a risk that organizations such as ASEAN+3 or the East Asia Summit (EAS) will have competing goals and duplicate efforts on issues such as free trade and energy security. The Australian Chamber of Commerce and Industry has warned that "less can be more [because] while ASEAN, ASEAN+3, APEC, ARF, and the EAS are all potentially useful regional bodies, their mutual existence has the real potential to result in duplication of effort and dilute outcomes for both businesses and countries in our region."[9] Similarly, Haggard (this volume) argues that the proliferation of free trade agreements in Asia may encumber future coordination.

Option 4: Differentiate Integration

Organizations can also use differentiated integration to overcome the challenges of heterogeneity. Differentiated integration refers to how an organization's existing member states may pursue future integration *within* the organization. Here again lessons are best drawn from the EU, where three modes of differentiated integration have occurred and where significant debate continues about which of these is the best approach to apply to future cooperation.

Multi-speed integration is when "the pursuit of common objectives is driven by a core group of member states which are both able and willing to go further, the underlying assumption being that the others will follow later" (Stubb 1996, 287). It is exemplified by the harmonization of value-added taxes (VAT), as well as by the accession agreements and transition periods given to states. Multi-speed integration has also been used vis-à-vis new member states in the EU by allowing new member states transition periods to adjust (Winters 1997, 910). In political areas, however, transition periods can be detrimental to achieving eventual compliance. As discussed, the Council of Europe has often allowed new member states a fixed period to comply with certain democratic standards. Once admitted, however, states have been likely to ignore these requirements (Kelley 2004a).

Even within large organizations, smaller groups of states can also enhance their cooperation, as demonstrated by the EU's use of so-called "variable geometry," a prominent example being the monetary union (Alesina and Grilli 1993). As opposed to multi-speed integration, where the intent is that all members join eventually, variable geometry is "a mode of differentiated integration which admits to unattainable differences within the main integrative structure by allowing permanent or irreversible separation between a core of countries and lesser developed integrative units" (Stubb 1996, 287). Thus, variable geometry allows more stable separation between the hard core and periphery, permitting a core group of states to advance their cooperation without the rest. The term is most often used to describe efforts such as include Airbus, the European Operational Rapid Force (EUROFOR), Schengen, and the European Monetary System (EMS) (Stubb 1996). Whether Britain's December 2011 veto of a new EU treaty to address the debt crises ultimately produces yet another example remains to be seen. More recent examples can also be found in Africa. For example, the five initial Organization of African Unity (OAU) states formed the New Partnership for Africa's Development (NEPAD) in July 2001. In March 2007, NEPAD leaders decided to integrate the partnership into the AU structures.[10]

Lastly, à la carte integration is when member states can choose what policy areas to participate in while sharing only a minimum number of common objectives. Rather than a group of states advancing with integration on a certain issue, à la carte integration occurs when individual states opt out of cooperation that is proceeding among the rest of the organization. Examples include Denmark and the UK with the euro, Denmark with defense, the UK with social policy, and Ireland on abortion (Smith 2004, 286). À la carte integration is the least visionary mode of integration and it has so far been used mostly as emergency options when single countries have been unable to agree to further integration steps. As such, it is an important tool to circumvent consensus-based decision-making procedures, although it is not a way to promote comprehensive regional integration.

Whether policies are described as à la carte, multi-speed, or variable geometry may at times be hard to decipher. The point, however, is that by differentiating integration, organizations can promote deeper cooperation without waiting until all states are ready to undertake the commitments of cooperation. Existing convoy organizations can include all member states in the visionary discussions of future integration, and then the prepared states can commence without excluding the other states, because these states are already on course to join the cooperation when they are ready and they have had some voice in creating the institutional structures and rules. Thus, the non-participants remain outside, but are not excluded. Although differentiated integration falls short of deep and comprehensive integration, it offers alternatives to the paralysis that heterogeneous convoys might otherwise produce. Over decades, these differentiated developments may turn out to be important stepping-stones to fuller integration.

Furthermore, using differentiated forms of integration may allow organizations to make better use of the tools of clubs, even if the overarching organization is a convoy. By having states that remain outside one form of cooperation, even if still a member of the main organization, entry requirements can be made for states wishing to join the more specialized cooperation. Such requirements are often already built into multi-speed integration, where they benefit from an inclusionary process of debate, such that late joiners have had a voice in the rules from the start. When organizations use variable geometry, the states that opt for deeper cooperation may eventually display such benefits from their cooperation that the other states wish to join. In that case, the core group is able to use the tools of conditionality to ensure that states only join when they are committed to and capable of cooperating.

Possible Implications for Asia

Although Asia's large economies have engaged successfully with global organizations, the lack of progress on a new trading round within the WTO and the Asian disenchantment with global institutions after the Asian Financial crises makes regional organizations increasingly attractive for Asian countries (Kahler, this volume). But Asia remains a highly heterogeneous region on a number of key dimensions (Haggard, this volume; Hix, this volume) that include preferences, capacities, and beliefs, and such heterogeneity is the greatest obstacle to regional integration. Unlike in Europe, market forces, not political forces, have driven economic integration in Asia. The result has been several sub-regional arrangements, and the absence of a pan-Asian umbrella organization. This has left less room for grand political planning (Capannelli and Filippini 2009). The region's strong antipathy toward delegation of authority to region-wide supra-national institutions further weakens the foundation for integration in Asia (Baldwin 2010, 64–65).

As countries in the region continue to consider how to expand existing regional organizations or create new ones, these challenges make it important for Asia to consider the role that membership rules can play in both widening and deepening of regional cooperation. Regarding widening of membership, debates in organizations such as ASEAN+3 (APT) or various regional FTAs (See Haggard, this volume) need not focus narrowly on which countries can join, but can also be about types of membership and conditions for joining. Thus, organizations in Asia can take greater advantage of tiers of membership, thus avoiding outright exclusion, yet reserving some leverage. They can even change their existing membership rules for new members.

Existing Asian organizations can also use differential integration to break deadlocks about future deepening of cooperation. Some Asian organizations already grant transitional periods for new members, but this concept of multi-speed integration can also be used when a set of existing states within an organization wishes to proceed. Haggard (this volume) argues that current APT does not have full membership for all as the goal. Nevertheless, such variable geometry arrangements can be useful even when member states differ on the end goals, and some states simply want to opt out of cooperation on particular issue areas in the long run. The caveat with both multi-speed integration and variable geometry is that non-core countries may try to free ride off the greater sovereignty costs paid by the core countries, as the non-core countries take a wait-and-see approach. On the other hand, later joiners may have less influence of the rules. Therefore, as long as the core states benefit from their cooperation, this outcome may still be preferable to allowing a complete lowest denominator approach where any current member state essentially vetoes future cooperation.

Asia may also be able to benefit from layering integration rather than bundling multiple issues in existing convoy structures. Layering integration allows for different membership structures for different issue areas. As has been seen in Europe, creating more autonomous and specialized organizations for security and human rights may be more effective. The EU has been effective at leveraging membership to press for better human rights in candidate states, but it has done so largely in cooperation with the Council of Europe and the OSCE, rather than by institutionalizing such specialized organs within the EU. Such topical subdivision makes it easier to maintain autonomy and credibility for each organization. In Asia, this means that a Human Rights Commission, for example, may be better situated outside ASEAN's framework.

Ultimately membership rules are endogenous to the preferences of the founding members. However, the fact that the rules merely reflect what states want does not mean that only one set of rules is possible. When states are deciding on the rules of membership of new organizations, they need to consider more than what the rules mean for the immediate outcome of who participates. First, they need to consider the benefits and costs of the rules themselves in terms of their value as tools of influence on other states in the region over time. As this chapter has discussed, different membership rules provide different types of opportunities for influencing states in the region over time. Second, states need to consider the implication of membership rules for their ability to pursue deeper cooperation within the organization. Thus, as Asia moves toward greater pan-regional cooperation, states should consider membership rules as a potent tool for both deepening cooperation when that is most desirable, and widening it when that is better.

Once membership rules are established, they can be hard to change, especially in regions such as Asia, which is characterized by a combination of consensus decision-making and heterogeneity among states. To the extent that the rules can be designed to help accommodate and reduce divergent state preferences, capacities, and beliefs, regional integration will be more likely to succeed.

Notes

1. Here "club" is not used to denote that the organization is providing a traditional economic "club good"—that is, some private benefit that derives value partly from the exclusion of some actors—but merely to denote organizations that have high entry requirements.

2. Nicholas Kulish, "Merkel Urges More Unified Continent to Save Euro," *New York Times*, November 14, 2011. Available online at http://www.nytimes.com/2011/11/15/world/europe/angela-merkel-urges-political-integration-to-stabilize-euro.html?scp=1&sq=political%20integration&st=cse. Last accessed December 12, 2011.

3. Reuters Wire Service, 14 April 2000.

4. For a good overview of the history of the many events that led to a deeper and more formalized OAS commitment to democracy, see NDI 1990.

5. Helsinki Final Act. 1975. Introduction.

6. Helsinki Final Act. 1975. Questions Relating to Security in Europe.

7. AFP, October 22, 2008. African leaders agree to form single market, http://afp.google.com/article/ALeqM5ioGmLiOhihzyOZ4WZrjTghlGPosQ

8. See Council on Foreign Relations, Backgrounder: Mercosur: South America's Fractious Trade Bloc. Available online at http://www.cfr.org/trade/mercosur-south-americas-fractious-trade-bloc/p12762. Last accessed December 12, 11.

9. Australian Chamber of Commerce and Industry. February 2006. Asian Regionalism: Less can be More. Press Release.

10. See PRlog, United States of Africa—African Economic Community, available at http://www.prlog.org/10132837-united-states-of-africa-african-economic-community.html. Last accessed December 12, 11.

THREE

REGIONAL COMPARISONS: LATIN AMERICA AND EUROPE

Regional Economic Institutions in Latin America
Politics, Profits, and Peace

JORGE I. DOMÍNGUEZ

Why, when, and how have Latin American states endeavored to create regional economic institutions, and what explains the results of those efforts?[1]
My analysis asks two questions: Do regional economic associations in Latin
America foster trade within the association's region? Does regional economic
integration increase the likelihood of generating positive public-good exter-
nalities such as interstate peace and does such peace increase the likelihood
of better economic results? I examine seven cases: the Latin American Free
Trade Association (LAFTA), the Southern Common Market (MERCOSUR;
MERCOSUL, in Portuguese), the North American Free Trade Agreement
(NAFTA), the Central American Common Market (CACM) in the 1960s
and 70s, the Central American Common Market since 1990, the Andean
Community in the 1970s, and the Andean Community since 1990.

Four outcomes are noteworthy. First, each region achieved substantial
trade liberalization; the value of trade grew within each region and between
the countries of each region and countries outside the region, especially after
1990, notwithstanding some severe economic crises and various militarized
interstate disputes in the 1990s and 2000s. In 2008, the value of trade in each
region was the highest in their respective histories (International Monetary
Fund 2009). Second, the level of trade within each region varied greatly. In
2009, within-NAFTA trade was 48 percent of the total trade of its member
countries but within-region trade was just 9.3 percent for the Andean Community, 15.2 percent for MERCOSUR, and 22.3 percent for CACM. (By
the same measures, the peak years and amounts for trade integration were

56.6 percent in 2002 for NAFTA; 12.8 percent in 1998 for the Andean Community; 25 percent in 1998 for MERCOSUR; and 24.8 percent in 2008 for CACM.) Third, NAFTA and MERCOSUR were built on, and the latter contributed to, pluralistic security communities to ensure inter-state peace, whereas the CACM and the Andean Community still suffer from militarized inter-state disputes. Fourth, no region achieved a common market. And in practice none established supranational entities that had a significant impact on trade liberalization, growth, inter-state peace, or advancing much beyond a trade liberalization agreement.

What explains these outcomes and the variation across cases? I formulate three arguments about the establishment of these regional associations. Domestic politics mattered in two senses. The inter-presidential level explains the start and the founding design of these institutions and also the common benign economic outcomes. And, in the late 1980s and early 1990s, domestic political economy coalitions succeeded in all regions at unilaterally lowering trade barriers in advance of the new regional arrangements. Second, businesses responded to the profit opportunities created by unilateral trade liberalization. In the late 1980s, intra-zonal value and shares of trade grew across the cases, preceding the new or renewed inter-state agreements. Third, where inter-state peace had been established before creating a regional economic association (NAFTA), or where such an association was an outcome of a process simultaneous with peace building (MERCOSUR), the resulting economic arrangements proved more effective at both peace and trade. Where governments paid less attention to securing inter-state peace (Andean Community, CACM), the regional economic associations could not prevent militarized interstate disputes and regional trade suffered.

After the regional associations had been launched, two arguments address the variation in performance. The more "automatic" the trade liberalization rules are, the more comprehensive and effective the trade liberalization will be. By "automatic," I mean a high level of precision and obligation, with extremely limited delegation to supranational bodies and comparably limited room for inter-presidential or inter-governmental discretion (Abbott 2001). Precision and obligation matter not just to undertake the original commitments but also with regard to the timetable of implementation (see O'Rourke's chapter, for the European Economic Community). Second, domestic inter-presidential politics matter as well after an association has been established. The ongoing role of presidents as decision makers in NAFTA was minimal, limited to a handful of contentious issues. In MERCOSUR, in

TABLE 5.1.

Economic asymmetries in the Americas

MERCOSUR	GDP/cap 1960	GDP 1960	GNP/cap 1988	GDP 1988
Argentina	1167	24055	2520	79440
Brazil	506	35815	2160	323610
Paraguay	352	602	1180	6040
Uruguay	1188	2949	2470	6680
CACM				
Costa Rica	656	823	1690	4650
El Salvador	431	1049	940	5470
Guatemala	536	2124	900	8100
Honduras	366	694	860	3860
Nicaragua	487	692	NA	3200
CAN				
Bolivia	283	938	570	4310
Chile	1065	8201	1510	22080
Colombia	398	6131	1180	39070
Ecuador	312	1355	1120	10320
Peru	635	6362	1300	25670
Venezuela	1377	10123	3250	63750
NAFTA				
Mexico	672	23451	1760	176700
Canada			9976	435860
USA			9373	4847310
Maximum/minimum				
MERCOSUR	3.375	59.49336	2.135593	53.57781
CACM	1.79235	3.069364	1.965116	2.53125
CAN	4.865724	10.79211	5.701754	14.79118
LAFTA	3.375	59.49336	5.701754	75.08353
NAFTA			5.668182	27.43243

SOURCE: Inter-American Development Bank, Economic and Social Progress in Latin America, 1978 (Washington: Inter-American Development Bank), 420; The World Bank, World Development Report, 1990 (Oxford: Oxford University Press, 1990), 178–181.

NOTES: For 1960, gross domestic product (GDP) is in 1976 US dollars. For 1988, gross national product (GNP) and GDP are in 1988 dollars. MERCOSUR is the Southern Common Market; CACM is the Central American Common Market; CAN is the Andean Group, later Andean Community; LAFTA is the Latin American Free Trade Association, which by the 1980s became the Latin American Integration Association; NAFTA is the North American Free Trade Association. Maximum/minimum is the ratio of the largest to the smallest member country on each indicator. In 1988, CAN excluded Chile. In 1960, LAFTA excluded Venezuela.

contrast, presidents were the only significant decision makers, at times stopping the enforcement of some of the automatic rules.

By "institutions," I mean shared norms, rules, and obligations whose adoption within each region is fostered by formal agreements, though they may be supplemented by informal understandings. Institutions vary depending on their organizational content. Institutions with precise and binding legal rules are at one end of the spectrum; they do not include inter-governmental or supranational regional organizations with substantial delegated authority. At the other end are those that include both rules and supranational or inter-governmental organizations, where these organizations have substantial authority, as in the European Union.

Other factors play some role in the analysis that follows. Liberal economic regimes and benign hegemons are helpful background factors. Supranational organizations matter but as secondary elements. Changing association membership had disruptive but also secondary effects. The political regime homogeneity or heterogeneity and various structural asymmetries (see Table 5.1) did not account for variation between the cases.

Over the past half century, Latin American integration efforts have been much less successful than those of the European Union. Moreover, Latin America's growth record has markedly lagged East Asia's. In 1950, Latin American countries looked successful in comparison to East Asian countries: as a proportion of the per capita GDP of the United States, Argentina's per capita GDP was 52 percent, Brazil's 17 percent, and Mexico's 25 percent—South Korea's and Taiwan's were 8 and 10 percent, respectively. By 2000, Argentina's GDP per capita had fallen to 30 percent of that of the United States; Mexico held at 26 percent, while Brazil rose to 20 percent. In contrast, by 2000 South Korea's GDP per capita as a proportion of the similar statistic for the United States had risen to 51 percent and Taiwan's to 59 percent (computed from Maddison 2003, tables 2c, 4c, and 5c). Readers beware! There is much in the Latin American story that should not be emulated. Domestic politics and policy errors may trump gains from regional economic integration.

The Latin American Free Trade Association (LAFTA)

In 1960, through the Treaty of Montevideo, Argentina, Brazil, Chile, Mexico, Paraguay, Peru, and Uruguay founded LAFTA; Ecuador and Colombia joined in 1961, Venezuela in 1966, and Bolivia in 1967. Their governments responded principally to technical and economic considerations, although the signing of the Treaty of Rome in Europe was a background factor and some individual Latin American leaders thought about the political utility of economic integration as a means to cope with the United States. The United Nations Economic Commission for Latin America (ECLA) was the driving force for the establishment of LAFTA in order to create sufficient economic scale for more effective import-substituting industrialization (Prebisch 1959, 18, 378). In 1960, ECLA's fundamental proposition was that Latin America would be unable to develop economically unless it established capital goods industries, for which it "need[ed] a common market" (quoted in Wionczek 1970, 52). LAFTA was founded to decouple Latin America from the world economy.

Emulating early European integration processes, LAFTA privileged inter-governmental negotiations as its chief means of operation. It envisaged only the elimination of barriers to intra-regional trade. The 1960 Treaty of Montevideo contained no provisions to coordinate external commercial policies, nor rules to harmonize the domestic economic policies of member countries.

Intergovernmental negotiations would proceed through the adoption of lists of products. National lists would contain those products for which an individual member country agreed to reduce its tariff level by at least 8 percent after each round of negotiations. The common lists would include all items for which the members agreed to eliminate all trade restrictions over a twelve-year period via product-by-product negotiations. The "most-favored-nation" clause from the General Agreements on Tariffs and Trade was modified to enable the more successful countries to compensate those that gained less from trade (Blejer 1984, 15–19).

LAFTA failed. Even in the early 1960s, governments scarcely mentioned it in their development programs. Only one common list was ever approved (in 1964) and it never went into effect; national lists had little practical importance and were abandoned by the end of the 1960s. No attempt was made to coordinate investments, or to provide special benefits for the lesser-developed members. LAFTA also lacked the funds to finance projects of regional importance and scale (Griffin and Ffrench-Davis 1965).

In the face of such unsatisfactory early results, ECLA, the Inter-American Development Bank (founded in 1959), and the presidents of several countries attempted a rescue, establishing LAFTA's Council of Ministers; the inter-American conference held in 1967 called for the establishment of a Latin American common market by 1985. Nothing of the sort happened and, instead, meeting in Caracas in 1969 the LAFTA governments postponed their goal for establishing a free trade area, slowed down the pace of tariff negotiations, and suspended the implementation of the common list of products. LAFTA for practical purposes ceased to matter (Wionczek 1970, 58–59).

LAFTA experienced increased political heterogeneity during the 1960s. Coups led to military governments in Brazil in 1964, Argentina in 1966, and Peru in 1968. At LAFTA's founding, these three along with Chile and Uruguay had been governed by civilians. The Argentine and Brazilian military governments had a significant interest in industrialization, however, thus mitigating the impact of this greater heterogeneity.

Intra–LAFTA trade did increase. The share of intra–LAFTA trade in total trade of LAFTA members hovered about 10 percent in the early 1960s and it rose to about 20 percent twenty years later, but LAFTA deserves little credit. Intra-regional imports not subject to LAFTA agreements grew faster than those imports governed by some LAFTA agreement (Blejer 1984, 17)! Twenty years after the Montevideo Treaty, imports subject to LAFTA agreements were no more than 6 percent of the total imports of the region from the rest of the world.

In 1980, the Latin American Integration Association (LAIA), an even looser association with more limited scope, replaced LAFTA just before the outbreak of the Latin American debt crisis in 1982, which started the region's decade-long economic collapse. Regional integration had thus failed before the debt crisis, though the subsequent deep recession delayed the recovery of intra-regional economic relations. The new LAIA had no better success than LAFTA (French-Davis, Muñoz, and Palma 1994, 223) but it still exists as a broad framework for bilateral trade agreements.

In the late 1970s, war and its threat made regional integration less likely. In 1978, Argentina and Chile came to the brink of war over the disputed Beagle Channel islands; Argentina prepared a declaration of war, stopped only by the Pope's mediation (Mares 2001, 138). Also in 1978, Bolivia broke diplomatic relations with Chile over the continued impasse in negotiations to give Bolivia some access to the Pacific Ocean—access that Bolivia lost a century earlier, following war with Chile. In 1981, Ecuador and Peru went to war over territory that Ecuador had lost in 1942. Argentina and Brazil faced deteriorating relations over the management of the Paraná River system waters until an agreement in 1979. These factors better explain LAFTA's failure at the time than its institutional design flaws, technical reasons, or economic concerns. One may have supposed that the political homogeneity of dictatorships in Argentina, Bolivia, Brazil, Chile, Paraguay, and Uruguay may have led to collaboration. They did collaborate through Operation Condor (McSherry

1999) to murder some adversaries but otherwise remained hostile toward each other. This milieu impeded deepened economic integration in South America.

The LAFTA failure illustrates that economic integration is a political endeavor; a multilateral agency like ECLA could not make it work. It requires the active engagement of presidents, without whom there was also no proactive peace-building intergovernmental work. After the founding, intergovernmental product-by-product negotiations were unwieldy and ineffective; middle-level bureaucrats lacked sufficient political support. Business incentives were few or absent. These were serious design flaws.

Alternative explanations are unpersuasive. LAFTA's mandate was limited; its scope does not explain the failure. LAFTA never progressed enough for structural asymmetries between big and small countries or distributive disputes to account for its failure. Intra-LAFTA Latin American trade increased but despite LAFTA, not because of it. Businesses traded with each other within the region when it was economically profitable, not because of LAFTA inducements.

The Andean Group, 1969-1985

In 1969, Bolivia, Chile, Colombia, Ecuador, and Peru signed the Cartagena Agreement to create the Andean Group in response to LAFTA's perceived failures (Peña 1973). Chile's President Eduardo Frei and Colombia's President Carlos Lleras Restrepo launched the Andean Group and led it during the first couple of years. There was also some ideological convergence: all five countries had left-of-center presidents with statist preferences, yet Bolivia's and Peru's presidents were military men. In 1970, the Andean Group enacted its Decision 24 to regulate foreign direct investment in member countries, prohibiting foreigners from investing in activities that competed with existing firms and mandating compulsory divestment of majority control by international companies twelve to fifteen years after entry—at the time the only such scheme worldwide to set joint restrictions on international firms within a common market area (Vernon 1971, 246).

The Andean governments created an executive body with significant powers, set out a schedule for trade liberalization and the gradual establishment of a common external tariff, agreed upon a system of preferences to benefit the least developed members (Bolivia and Ecuador), and proposed to harmonize many economic policies. Internal tariffs were to be phased out entirely by 1981. Once within-area tariffs and other barriers to trade were removed, these would become irrevocable decisions. The Andean Group also established an automatic mechanism for tariff dismantling but it covered only about half of all tariff lines. By 1981, the average intra-regional tariff had dropped to 14 percent, which was one-third of the 1969 value. The share of intra-Andean exports in all exports from the Andean countries rose from 8 percent in 1970 to 15 percent in 1980 (Ffrench-Davis, Muñoz, and Palma 1994, 217–219; Inter-American Development Bank 1984, 51). A common external tariff was never completed (Devlin and Estevadeordal 2001, 23–27).

The Andean Group incorporated Venezuela in 1973 but Chile defected in 1976; President Augusto Pinochet's Chile found the Andean Group too statist. In 1979, in response to perceived poor outcomes, the Andean Group created the Andean Parliament, whose members are elected by the legislative organs of each member country; the Andean Council of Foreign Ministers, designed to foster the coordination of foreign policies; and the Andean Court of Justice, composed of five judges from the five member countries.

Notwithstanding, during the economic crisis of the early 1980s, Andean country trade with the "rest of the world" dropped less than Andean country trade with each other. Alas, just two years after the creation of these Andean regional entities, in 1981 two member states—Ecuador and Peru—went to war. Six years after the creation of these supranational organizations, intra-Andean Group trade had dropped to 3 percent. The Andean Group's adoption of greater institutional complexity at the end of the 1970s was an act of desperation that failed to stop the Group's weakening. Decision 24 regarding foreign investment was also repealed. The Andean Group achieved neither trade integration nor peace.

In short, engagement by Andean presidents enabled the Group to achieve at the outset very high economic policy coordination, notably regulating foreign investment (Avery and Cochrane 1973). Other initial conditions were less propitious. There was no prior trade liberalization; the statist bias provided disincentives for business. There was no simultaneous peace-building work. After the launch, trade liberalization implementation was in the hands of middle-level bureaucrats with insufficient authority. The trade liberalization design, more agile than LAFTA's, was still cumbersome. Design obstacles impeded integration.

Political homogeneity among members facilitated the Group's launch; increased political heterogeneity generated difficulties by the 1970s. Other alternative explanations mattered little. Structural asymmetries were modest and the lesser-developed economies benefited; distributive disputes were not serious obstacles. The Andean Group's agenda was very ambitious from the start yet agenda complexity was not why the Group stumbled. Intra-Andean trade grew in response to the Andean Group's policies but the achieved level of trade integration always remained modest.

The Central American Common Market (CACM), 1960–1985

Between 1951 and 1961, Guatemala, Honduras, El Salvador, Costa Rica, and Nicaragua launched several compartmentalized integrative processes. In 1951, ECLA created the Central American Committee for Economic Cooperation to foster economic integration, and the Foreign Ministers of the five countries created the Organization of Central American States (ODECA) to engineer their political unity. In 1961, the War Ministers of the five countries independently formed the Central American Defense Council. In 1951, those responsible for economic policy stopped the diplomats from subordinating them to ODECA. That enabled the Economy Ministers to fashion the plans to sign the General Treaty for Central American Integration, which established the CACM in 1960 (Costa Rica joined in 1963) (Schmitter 1970, 1–4; Nye 1968).

The CACM's General Treaty automatically removed tariffs on 75 percent of the items listed in the Uniform Central American Customs Nomenclature and set a five-year clock to liberalize 95 percent of all traded goods items. By mid-1966, 94 percent of all items accounting for 95 percent of total intra-regional trade were subject to intra-regional free trade; a common external tariff covered nearly 98 percent of all import items for all five countries, amounting to three-quarters to four-fifths of the region's imports (Cochrane and Sloan 1973, 23–24).

The governments created complementary organizations, such as the Central American Bank of Economic Integration (1961), the Central American Clearing House and Monetary Council (1961), and others. By 1966, cooperation between Central American had led to 97.5 percent of all inter-regional trade and transactions being registered through the Clearing House, with 71.3 percent clearing automatically, almost totally replacing the former system of utilizing U.S. banks for those purposes (Inter-American Development Bank 1984, 57; Schmitter 1970, 19).

In 1969, Honduras and El Salvador went to war. Honduras formally pulled out from CACM agreements. The underlying cause of the war was directly related to issues of regional integration. Capital movements had long been rather free across Central America and the CACM freed nearly all regional trade, but there was no free movement of labor. Demographic pressures in El

Salvador had stimulated Salvadoran migration to Honduras; in 1969, Honduras began to deport some of these Salvadorans. In July, El Salvador's army attacked Honduras.

By 1970, intra-CACM exports reached 28 percent of total exports and 96 percent of total manufactured exports—this 28 percent level still held in 1980 (Ffrench-Davis, Muñoz, and Palma 1994, 222). In 1980, the regional central bank Clearing House registered nearly all intra-regional trade transactions and automatically cleared 84 percent of such transactions (Inter-American Development Bank 1984, 57). CACM agreements remained effective notwithstanding the Honduras-El Salvador war.

Central America's integrative success had limitations. The intra-regional trade increase resulted almost exclusively from intra-industry specialization in textiles and shoes; CACM's greater scale induced this import-substituting industrialization but it was also its only significant example (Balassa 1971, 72). Only about one-seventh of the regional economic growth rate during the 1960s was attributable to the CACM. Moreover, the common external tariff was set higher for a number of industrial products than the previous tariffs on those products in the individual countries (Wionczek 1970, 55). On balance the CACM of the 1960s and 1970s was mainly a trade-diverting customs union for non-durable consumer goods (Willmore 1976).

In the 1980s, domestic and international warfare gripped Nicaragua, El Salvador, and Guatemala, affecting indirectly also Costa Rica and Honduras. This war nearly killed the CACM. Central America suffered as well from a general economic crisis. Intra-regional trade fell to 14 percent in 1986 when the value of intra-CACM exports was about a third of what it had been in 1980, declining three times faster than the overall decline of Central American exports to all parts of the world. Registration of transactions with the Clearing House fell to 76 percent in 1983, with only 59 percent of those transactions being cleared automatically (Ffrench-Davis, Muñoz, and Palma 1994, 222; Inter-American Development Bank 1984, 57).

In short, CACM Economy Ministers and technocrats insulated integration to launch in the 1960s, helped by multilateral organizations and CACM governments. Thus CACM's success was political at its birth. However, there was no prior unilateral trade liberalization and few business regional incentives outside the textiles and shoes sector. Governments did not undertake simultaneous peace-building efforts; CACM's agreements were de-linked from foreign policy and military coordination. CACM integration withstood the effects of the 1969 Honduras-El Salvador war but not the prolonged war in the 1980s.

After birth, the most successful design feature was the rule of automaticity for intra-regional trade and intra-regional payments via the Clearing House. The treaty commitments as well as the timetable for their implementation were precise and binding. They were not delegated to supranational organizations or to inter-governmental or inter-presidential processes.

Alternative explanations matter little. Structural asymmetries between CACM members were small, perhaps contributing to success. On the other hand, Honduras and Nicaragua—the smallest economies in 1960—bore asymmetrical burdens during the 1960s (Cochrane and Sloan 1973, 27) and this was one factor that led Honduras to pull out from CACM institutions after the 1969 war. Distributive disputes thus were a secondary explanation.

CACM's integration agenda was ambitious. CACM was most successful in creating a free trade area and facilitating financial transactions—even poor countries with limited technical capacities in the 1960s integrated successfully.

The Andean Group, 1985–Present

The first of the integrative schemes to be reborn from the 1980s Latin American economic catastrophe was the Andean Group as part of the wider effort to reactivate Andean economies. Andean states were also undergoing tumultuous domestic changes. In the 1980s, incumbent political parties lost every presidential election in Bolivia, Ecuador, and Peru, while the new presidents in Colombia and Venezuela brought to office economic teams with much stronger market-oriented views. A frenzy of nine summits occurred from 1989 to 1991 between the new heads of state. Peru remained an outlier—facing high levels of domestic violence, wrenching economic policy changes, and a more authoritarian regime than its neighbors; between 1992 and 1997 Peru withdrew from Andean trade negotiations.

By 1995–1997, domestic political conditions had stabilized, intra-regional trade had recovered, new Andean political institutions were created, and the Andean Group became the Andean Community. The new design emphasized intergovernmental processes (the Andean Council of Foreign Ministers created in 1979, the Andean Presidential Council founded in 1990), but the Community retained the Andean secretariat, parliament (a deliberative, not a legislative body), and court. Andean governments seemed to have been influenced by the 1986 Single European Act and the views of the United Kingdom regarding European integration (Casas Gragea 2002).

As was the case in the 1950s leading to the Treaty of Rome and as it would be in North America preceding the start of the NAFTA, so too with the

Andean Community: the prior growth of trade between businesses generated the incentives for governments to adopt measures to consolidate the new economic behavior and to lock in their own policies against the risk of future reversal (see also Baldwin 2009). Intra-Andean exports, which had plummeted to 3.2 percent of the total exports of the five Andean Group members in 1985, rose to 4.1 percent in 1990 and 12 percent in 1995.[2]

This trade growth responded to the redesign of domestic economic policies in the five Andean countries in the early 1990s (in Bolivia since 1985), which included impressive unilateral trade liberalization, contributing to a burst of economic growth. In 1988 average tariffs in Colombia, Ecuador, and Venezuela ranged between 42 and 46 percent; Peru's average tariff exceeded 70 percent. In 1991, all four countries had reduced average tariffs to between 15 and 17 percent—Bolivia's average tariff had fallen to 9.2 percent (Devlin, Estevadeordal, and Garay 2000, 157). The flurry of Andean presidential summitry and proliferation of integration-friendly talk led enterprises to anticipate measures to lock in these gains from tariff reduction. Thus the jump in intra-regional trade responded to the business cycle of recovery from the 1980s, the market-oriented domestic policy shifts, and inter-state presidential summitry, all in the context of worldwide economic liberalization (Banco Interamericano de Desarrollo 2002, 27-28). All this intra-regional trade growth (reaching 12 percent in 1995) preceded the institutional redesign during 1995–97—that redesign did not cause the growth in intra-regional trade. Intra-Andean trade peaked at 12.8 percent in 1998 and stabilized at between 8–10 percent in the 2000s.

Peru's non-participation in the processes of trade negotiation and Andean supranational organization rebuilding had negligible impact on Peru's de facto trade integration with its neighbors, which implies that the supranational organizations mattered little. Peru had liberalized its trade regime unilaterally. Its exports to the Andean Community hovered between 6 percent and 8 percent of its total exports throughout the 1990s, as during the 2000s. In 1997, Peru rejoined the formal institutions of the Andean Community, with little impact on the direction of its trade with its neighbors.

Nor did the new Andean Community institutions sustain inter-state peace and contain inter-state conflict. Ecuador and Peru went to war in 1995 in the midst of the relaunching of the Andean Community; their trade had not engineered peace. In the 2000s, severe disagreements emerged between Colombia's President Álvaro Uribe and Venezuela's President Hugo Chávez, with the latter occasionally expressing sympathy for the FARC—the Revolutionary

Armed Forces of Colombia. In March 2008, Colombia's troops crossed into Ecuador in chase of FARC guerrillas. Ecuador and Venezuela broke diplomatic relations with Colombia and rushed troops to the Colombian border; mediation by Latin American presidents and diplomats persuaded the three countries to stand down (Mares 2008; Kahhat 2008). The Andean Community neither prevented this escalation to near-war nor had a discernible impact on its de-escalation.

Increased domestic political heterogeneity weakened the prospects for the Andean Community and worsened inter-state disputes. The consolidation of the Hugo Chávez presidency upon surviving a failed coup attempt in 2002, and the forced departures from office of Bolivia's president in 2003 and Ecuador's in 2005, left the three countries with market-unfriendly governments. Colombia and Peru retained market-oriented economic policies and signed bilateral free trade agreements with the United States. In April 2006, President Hugo Chávez invoked the signing of these two agreements with the United States as reason for Venezuela to withdraw from the Andean Community.

Chávez had a point: the Community failed to coordinate the foreign economic policies of member countries as two of them bargained with the United States. U.S.-Colombian and U.S.-Peruvian free trade agreements are not easily reconciled with an Andean Community common market with a still-in-the-works common external tariff. However, Venezuela's withdrawal from the Community had little impact upon its trade with its former partners. During the 2000s, Venezuela's proportion of exports to Andean Community countries trended down; as the price of petroleum rose during the decade, the value of Venezuela's exports to the industrialized countries rose accordingly. Yet, the absolute worth of Venezuelan trade with its former partners increased as well. The Andean Community's relative share of Venezuelan trade was lower as the decade unfolded, but between 2006 and 2008 the value of Venezuelan exports to Bolivia, Colombia, Ecuador, and Peru increased every year (International Monetary Fund 2009). Andean Community institutions had done little to foster such trade, and Venezuela's withdrawal from them did little to hinder it.

Venezuela and Colombia had developed trade that preceded the institutionalization of the Andean Community in the mid-1990s and survived the Venezuelan withdrawal therefrom. During the 1990s, Colombia and Venezuela became each other's principal destination for their non-traditional exports. Bilateral investment flows picked up as well. Notwithstanding Venezuela's

Andean Community withdrawal in 2006, the year 2008 was the best ever for the absolute value of Venezuelan exports to Colombia and Colombian exports to Venezuela (International Monetary Fund 2009).

Some Andean Community's supranational organizations merit comment. The rulings of the Andean Court on intellectual property issues matter for Colombia, Ecuador, and Peru (see Voeten's chapter) but Court rulings do not bear on inter-state peace nor have they been effective on most trade disputes (Banco Interamericano de Desarrollo 2002, 105). The Andean Development Corporation (CAF) predates the Andean Group. By the end of 2008, its paid-in capital was about $2.2 billion (Corporación Andina de Fomento 2009). It finances infrastructure projects effectively; its wider impact on intra-region trade or peace is harder to discern. The Latin American Reserves Fund (*Fondo Latinoamericano de Reservas*—FLAR) involves all Andean Community members, including Venezuela, plus Costa Rica and Uruguay. It is a regional financial swap agreement; participating countries may borrow on short notice for a limited time. It is akin to the Chiang Mai Initiative (CMI) or the North American Framework Agreement. From its foundation in 1978 through 2008, it disbursed cumulatively over $8.7 billion, principally during financial crises (Fondo Latinoamericano de Reservas 2008, and Henning's chapter). The FLAR and the CAF raise funds in international markets at interest rates below the costs each member country would pay individually, thereby lowering costs thanks to these regional risk pooling arrangements (Borensztein, Levy, and Panizza 2006, 267–269). The salience of the FLAR remains modest, however. Consider Ecuador, hit hard by financial crises between 1997 and 2002 and an uprising in 2000 to overthrow the president. At the end of 2001, Ecuador's debt to the FLAR amounted to 3 percent of Ecuador's external debt; by early 2003, the FLAR amounted to just 1 percent of the 38 percent of external debt that Ecuador owed to multilateral institutions (Inter-American Development Bank 2001, 2004).

In short, domestic political and economic policy changes defined the renamed Andean Community. Presidential summitry facilitated the rebirth of intra-Andean trade. Domestic policy changes, including unilateral anticipatory trade liberalization prior to re-launching Andean integration, explain the growth of trade. Businesses responded quickly, boosting intra-regional trade. Intra-regional trade levels were nearly three times higher by the end of the 2000s than they were when the Andean Group unraveled in the early 1980s. Andean Community institutions and their redesign followed the new spurt in inter-regional trade and, therefore, could not have caused it.

The withdrawal (Peru, Venezuela) and reincorporation (Peru) of states as Community members had no discernible impact on intra-regional trade. The Andean Community institutions did not prevent war (Ecuador-Peru) or severe conflict (Colombia and its neighbors). Nor did these conflicts depress trade. Andean supranational entities resolved intellectual property disputes and provided modest support for members in financial crises and financed development projects. Political homogeneity among member states facilitated the Andean relaunch in the early to mid-1990s while the increased political heterogeneity weakened it in the 2000s. Structural economic asymmetries widened slightly from 1960 to the 1988 eve of the Andean re-launch, to little effect.

The Central American Common Market, 1985–Present

Under the impact of domestic and international war and economic crisis, intra-regional Central American trade plummeted to 10.5 percent in 1986. The regional payments system broke down as governments defaulted on commitments to each other. As with the Andean countries, intra-regional trade recovered as the economic depression abated, reaching 15.3 percent in 1990 when a war settlement was finally reached in Nicaragua. Serious negotiations to end the war in El Salvador got under way during 1991, when intra-regional trade reached 17.6 percent. As peace was secured (El Salvador 1992, Guatemala 1996), the economies and intra-zonal trade recovered, unleashing a torrent of inter-governmental negotiations. The newly relaunched CACM would build on the accomplishments of the 1960s, in particular intra-regional trade virtually free of tariffs outside agricultural products (Banco Interamericano de Desarrollo 2002, 32).

In December 1991, the Protocol of Tegucigalpa amended the charter of the long-existing Organization of Central American States (ODECA) to give rise to the Central American Integration System (SICA), bringing the economic integration process under government control to avoid the compartmentalized regional institutions of the 1960s. Decision making would be by consensus; each member state thus had a veto. The SICA's institutions include presidential summits, a council of ministers, an executive committee, and a general secretariat—the latter two for technical and support services. The Central American Parliament and the Central American Court of Justice are supranational entities (Sánchez Sánchez 2003).

The born-again CACM looked better on paper than in reality. By the end of the 1990s, only three of the five CACM countries had ratified the agreement that established the Central American Court of Justice. Even those that ratified it made little use of the Court. Of the sixteen trade disputes that broke out formally between CACM members from 1993 to 2001, in only one case did the parties resort to the Central American Court. Moreover, trade in agriculture and services had not yet become a part of Central American free trade. In 1995, the newly vigorous common external tariff covered 95 percent of the tariff universe, but coverage fell to 50 percent by the end of the decade, Nicaragua being the main but not the only culprit (Devlin and Estevadeordal 2001, 19; Granados 2001; Banco Interamericano de Desarrollo 2002, 32, 98–99, 104–105).

Compliance with CACM rules and institutions was spotty. Central American intra-regional trade grew at the same rate before and after the 1993 Guatemala Protocol until 1996, when it reached 22.6 percent, dropping to 13.6 percent in 1999, rising to 24 percent in 2001, remaining thereafter above 20 percent, and reaching its peak at 24.8 percent in 2008. CACM rules and institutions, and the associated political processes, thus fostered intra-CACM trade but subject to oscillation.

Costa Rica helps us to assess the impact of CACM institutions. It refused to ratify the 1991 Tegucigalpa Protocol; it rejoined CACM institutions only with the signing of the 1993 Guatemala Protocol. Yet the value of Costa Rican exports to the other Central American countries grew significantly between 1991 and 1993, though the proportion of its exports to Central American countries fell from 11 to 9 percent.

Central American governments exhibited higher levels of foreign economic policy coordination than had the Andean Community. They negotiated agreements as a trade block with the United States, the European Union, Mexico, and Venezuela. In 2006, the U.S.-Central American Free Trade Agreement (CAFTA) went into effect for all but Costa Rica (where it did in 2009). In 2006-2009, CAFTA had no adverse effect on intra-CACM trade. But Central American governments have also made individual deals. In the early 1990s, each Central American government reached a separate trade deal with the United States. Between 1994 and 2000, Mexico signed separate bilateral free trade agreements with Costa Rica and Nicaragua and another jointly with El Salvador, Guatemala, and Honduras (Devlin and Estevadeordal 2001, 29).

War and peace issues affected the prospects for the CACM. Central American integration probably could not advance further after 1991 because the CACM and associated institutions could not prevent the threat of war. Disputes involving some use of force broke out between Honduras and Nicaragua in 1991, 1995, 1996, 1997, 1998, and 2000; between Nicaragua and El Salvador in 1996 and 2000; and between El Salvador and Honduras also in 1996 and 2000. In the 2000s, each of the five CACM members was involved in at least one militarized inter-state dispute with a neighboring country (Mares 2001, 43; 2008, 5). The reactivation of intra-CACM trade did not make these disputes go away, while the threat of war probably made regional integration deepening more difficult.

In the end, the CACM succeeded not as a common market but as a trade liberalization area. The absolute value of Central American exports to neighboring CACM members increased dramatically for each and every Central American country between the signing of the Protocol of Tegucigalpa in 1991 and 2008. By dollar value, varying by country of destination, Guatemalan exports to the CACM more than quadrupled, Costa Rican exports to the CACM more than quintupled, Nicaraguan exports increased by a factor of six, Salvadoran exports grew between three and ten times (with a 23-fold increase of exports to Honduras), and Honduran exports to the neighbors grew between 19 and 135 times. From 2000 to 2008, the exports of each CACM member to the region more than doubled, increasing from each and every member to each and every member (computed from International Monetary Fund 2009). Business firms led the revival of the CACM in the late 1980s, taking advantage of the still-enduring 1960s CACM trade liberalization. Politicians followed business initiatives and restarted the CACM. CACM trade liberalization and central bank clearing would be the region's most lasting economic integration accomplishments.

In short, the CACM was reborn in the early 1990s lush with parchment institutions, but the rules that worked were just those that had ever worked, namely, trade liberalization and central bank payments clearing, which were the most automatic and depended least on ongoing decision making by politicians or CACM institutions. Presidential initiative was a key reason for the flourishing of parchment institutions, and lack thereof for their weak institutional consolidation. CACM countries had a mixed record of foreign economic policy coordination. No inter-state war broke out in the CACM after 1990 but militarized inter-state disputes were frequent. The CACM provided incentives to sustain inter-state peace but not enough to consolidate it; this failure hindered the deepening of regional economic integration.

Structural asymmetries between CACM members remained the smallest in the Americas. For most of the 1990s and the 2000s, right-of-center parties governed throughout the CACM region. This political and economic homogeneity sustained market-oriented economic policies but did not prevent militarized inter-state disputes between like-minded governments. CACM dealt with its much more ambitious institutional agenda in the 1990s and 2000s by failing to ratify those most ambitious agreements or failing to implement them if ratified—the common external tariff was porous, the justices of the Central American Court were not busy.

The Southern Common Market (MERCOSUR)

The Southern Common Market (MERCOSUR) had an impressive start and lasting results because it emerged from a slow process of bargaining between Argentina and Brazil, with time for correction and maturation. Argentina and Brazil have not been at war with each other since the 1820s but in the 1970s each feared that the other was developing nuclear weapons, although that perception would prove inaccurate (Hymans 2001). In November 1979, the dictatorships of Argentina, Brazil, and Paraguay signed the Itaipú-Corpus Treaty to govern the Paraná rivers system waters and permit the construction of two hydroelectric projects, This treaty would be a turning point in their bilateral relations; in the 1980s and 1990s Argentina and Brazil would sign agreements over multiple topics to consolidate the peace and foster a shared prosperity (Escudé and Fontana 1998; Hirst 1998).

Economic integration accords, signed in 1986, liberalized trade sector by sector; in two years, 24 sectoral agreements were signed (Bouzas and Fanelli 2002, 119). In 1985, exports to each other from the four countries that would go on to found MERCOSUR—Argentina, Brazil, Paraguay, and Uruguay— were only 5.5 percent of their combined total exports, rising to 11.1 percent in 1991. Thus, as with reactivation of intra-zonal trade in the CACM and the Andean group and in Western Europe before 1958, within-region integration accelerated prior to the signing of the Treaty of Asunción in 1991, which founded the MERCOSUR. Business firms used the new opportunities that governments had provided.

The deepening of this Southern Cone integration cannot be explained simply as a result of these economic agreements, however. Three other factors intervened. First, in 1990 and 1991, Argentina and Brazil undertook dramatic domestic economic policy changes, including unilateral trade liberalization, before signing the Treaty of Asunción. Market-oriented economic policy convergence helped the negotiations toward that treaty (Devlin, Estevadeordal, and Garay 2000, 157). From 1988 to 1991, Argentina and Brazil cut their respective average tariff rates in half: Argentina, from 31 percent to 14 percent; Brazil, from 42 percent to 20 percent. Paraguay and Uruguay also brought them down to similar levels. The results were instantaneous, most notably for Brazil, whose exports to Argentina more than doubled from $645 million in 1990 to $1476 in 1991 (International Monetary Fund 2009).

Second, in 1985 dictatorships ended in Brazil and Uruguay and, in 1989, in Paraguay; Argentina's had ended in 1983. The greater democratic political homogeneity of MERCOSUR countries paved the way to the Treaty of Asunción. (The structural economic asymmetry between MERCOSUR countries was not an obstacle to the treaty signing or its early success.) This treaty did not include a "democracy clause," as the European Community had, but the MERCOSUR behaved as if it did, acting to block a military coup attempt in Paraguay in 1996. Thereupon, the MERCOSUR agreements were modified to include such a democracy clause. MERCOSUR governments would rally repeatedly and automatically to prop up civilian rule in Paraguay.

Third, there was intense peace-making. In November 1990, Argentina and Brazil agreed to forego nuclear weapons and signed a nuclear safeguards agreement under the auspices of the International Atomic Energy Agency. In 1991, they established a bilateral institution to monitor their nuclear energy endeavors intrusively and systematically (Sotomayor Velázquez 2004). They had the scientific and economic capacity to build nuclear weapons, for a time hostile bilateral relations that could have led to a nuclear weapons arms race, and yet on their own they stepped back from nuclear weapons proliferation to found an effective bilateral nuclear safeguards regime.

These combined elements buttressed MERCOSUR and generated continuing incentives for policy coordination. Two decades after the birth of the MERCOSUR integrative processes, the peace-sustaining effects of the wider political relationship would be the most important legacy. They were not a formal part of any MERCOSUR agreement; rather, these were parallel political processes. The *process* of integration, rather than MERCOSUR parchment institutions, was the more important explanatory factor, and it led to the longest-lasting effect.

The Treaty of Asunción discarded the old product-by-product (LAFTA) or sector-by-sector (1986 Argentine-Brazilian agreement) approach to trade liberalization. Instead, it adopted a tariff phase-out program based on preprogrammed liberalization schedules that were easily calculable and transparent (see Bouzas and Fanelli 2002). By 1996, 99.4 percent of all trade items had been liberalized between Argentina and Brazil (Devlin and Estevadeordal 2001, 9, 30; Peña 1992, 101). The commitments and the timetable were precise, obligatory, nearly universal, and not delegated to supranational organizations or inter-governmental or inter-presidential processes—what I have called "automatic."

As a result, trade boomed. From 1991 to 1996, the proportions of Argentina's, Brazil's, and Paraguay's exports to their MERCOSUR partners doubled. In the mid-1980s, Paraguay sent a quarter of its exports within the Southern Cone; from 1994 onwards, it never shipped less than 46 percent of its exports to MERCOSUR countries. Paraguay's peak year of exports to MERCOSUR was 1996, at 63.2 percent. In 1985, Argentina delivered 8 percent of its exports within the Southern Cone; in 1998, on the eve of the 1999 Brazilian financial panic, Argentina sent 35.2 percent of its total exports within MERCOSUR (its peak year had been 1997, at 35.5 percent). In 1998, this statistic for Uruguay peaked at 55 percent. In absolute terms, between 1991 and 1996 Brazilian exports to Argentina more than tripled; Argentine exports to Brazil more than quadrupled (International Monetary Fund 2009). Brazil's peak year of exports to MERCOSUR was 1997, at 17.7 percent. At the end of the 1990s Argentines and Brazilians thought well of MERCOSUR and the parallel political and peace-building accomplishments (Campbell 1999). Indeed, the 1990s were good for MERCOSUR; the 2000s would be much less so, as these statistics imply.

During its first decade, MERCOSUR members also coordinated their foreign economic policies, negotiating trade agreements with other states only as a block. MERCOSUR in the 1990s avoided the proliferation of uncoordinated trade agreements that characterized both the CACM and NAFTA and, in the 2000s, the Andean Community. Thus, in 1996 the MERCOSUR as a bloc signed separate association agreements with Bolivia and Chile, neither of which became a formal MERCOSUR member. MERCOSUR also launched still-inconclusive negotiations with the European Union; even absent a MERCOSUR-EU agreement, the Southern Cone has long traded extensively with European countries.

The association agreement between MERCOSUR and Chile was also part of the dense development of relations between Chile and Argentina. During the 1990s, they settled the remaining two dozen distinct territorial disputes that had survived since their independence in the 1810s. Thus this process, parallel to MERCOSUR expansion, furthered the peace agenda in the Southern Cone, thereby facilitating trade and investment (Domínguez 2003).

What went wrong with MERCOSUR? Intra-MERCOSUR exports peaked at 25 percent of all exports in 1998. In January 1999, Brazil's financial panic threw its economy into recession and contributed to Argentina's deep economic crisis in 2001-2002, which culminated in the resignation of its president. By 2002, intra-MERCOSUR exports plummeted to 11.5 percent of the total; member countries turned to export to economies not engulfed in such crises. Intra-regional trade would recover but just to 15.2 percent in 2009.

MERCOSUR also weakened as a result of its mid-2000s choice of widening over deepening. Brazilian President Lula's government took the lead to establish, in December 2004, the South American Community of Nations, renamed in 2008 the Union of South American Nations (UNASUR). Also in 2004, MERCOSUR granted associate member status to Colombia, Ecuador, and Venezuela. In December 2005, MERCOSUR accepted Venezuela as a full member, a decision ratified only in 2012 after years of doubt regarding Venezuela's commitments to democratic and common market's rules. In December 2005 as well, Evo Morales was elected president of Bolivia. Chávez backed the Morales government when, on 1 May 2006, it nationalized Bolivia's natural gas sector (including Brazil's Petrobras) and doubled the price for its natural gas exports to Argentina. Argentina and Brazil accepted the Bolivian nationalization but their enthusiasm for Chávez cooled (Turcotte 2008, 801-802). The inclusion of statist Venezuela created greater economic heterogeneity within MERCOSUR and its associates; Chávez's ongoing autocratic practices weakened the MERCOSUR's democratic credentials.

A bad turn in Argentine-Uruguayan relations further punctured intra-MERCOSUR relations. In 2006, Uruguay allowed the construction of two pulp mills on its bank of the Uruguay River—its border with Argentina. With the support of Argentine President Néstor Kirchner, Argentines blocked a busy border bridge to compel Uruguay to discontinue the mills; tourism and trade suffered. Argentina and Uruguay sued each other before the International Court of Justice at The Hague (International Court of Justice 2009). The governments eventually backed off but the experience soured Uruguayan ardor for MERCOSUR (Caetano 2007, 167-168).

MERCOSUR has been "light" on institutionalization. Implementation has depended on relations between presidents, not on supranational organizations, nor does MERCOSUR have an inter-governmental process. MERCOSUR's presidents have been the decision makers and the dispute settlers, often changing the rules to accommodate a partner country. Presidents carved out "special" procedures within MERCOSUR to deal with politically important and economically sensitive sectors, such as automobiles and sugar, and have agreed to peremptory waivers of free trade rules during economic crises, especially between 1999 and 2003. The presidents of Argentina and Brazil came to see the MERCOSUR as a strategic alliance; economic matters that got in the way would thus be set aside (Malamud 2005; Gomez Mera 2005). Phillips (2004, 96, 99) put it well: "The governance structures of the Mercosur have always been rather informal than rule-based . . . which left ample space for political whim, unilateral action and non-observance of agreed-upon policy commitments."

Of the 283 trade disputes that surfaced in MEROCOSUR in its golden years (1995–1997), none was settled through rule-oriented institutional mechanisms; of the 201 such disputes during the period of economic crisis (1998–2003), only 9 were settled through rule-oriented institutional mechanisms. MERCOSUR generally failed to use its formal institutions to settle disputes (Delich 2006, 14, 20). The only significant rules-based approach to trade dispute resolution in the Southern Cone side-stepped the MERCOSUR and resorted to the World Trade Organization (WTO). Between 1987 and 2003, Argentina sued Brazil before the WTO 47 times, mainly over dumping allegations. That is more often than Argentina sued China and four times more often than it sued the United States (Sanguinetti and Bianchi 2006, 160). In the 2010s, Argentina remained the most protectionist original MERCOSUR member.

MERCOSUR has had a Common Market Council, a Common Market Group, and a Trade Commission as venues for decisions, though always subject to presidential deals; their officials are not appointed on a permanent basis. There are no MERCOSUR purely technical institutions (Floreal González 1999, 84). The only permanent administrative body in MERCOSUR has been its Secretariat, which staffs member governments but does not make decisions. The MERCOSUR Court (2004) and Parliament (2005) have yet to function properly. MERCOSUR's Permanent Commission reaches out to civil society but its work is at most symbolic (Grandi and Bizzózero 1997).

MERCOSUR suffered from lax implementation of its rules. In the mid-2000s, its common external tariff covered only 35 percent of the value of MERCOSUR imports. MERCOSUR subjects to rules of origin all goods that received preferential treatment, but it lacks a common code to govern customs procedures (Bouzas, Veiga, and Ríos 2008, 321). Between 1991 and 2002, the MERCOSUR Council approved 149 decisions that required their incorporation to the domestic legal system of each member country, of which 70 percent remained unenforced in 2002. The MERCOSUR's Common Market Group approved 604 resolutions for those same years, of which 63 percent remained unenforced in 2002 (Peña 2003).There has been little harmonization of macro- and micro-economic policies, little coordination of policy toward foreign direct investment, no competition policy, and no co-ordination of social policy (Phillips 2004). MERCOSUR sponsors no monetary cooperation and ranks well below the multilateral financial relationships evident in the Association of Southeast Asian Nations.

In short, South America's most successful economic integration agreement emerged from a multi-year multi-faceted, self-reinforcing process of confidence- and peace-building in the Southern Cone. MERCOSUR was built atop prior convergent domestic economic policy changes—unilateral albeit concurrent trade liberalization—and convergent transitions from dictatorship to democracy. Domestic economic and political changes before the signing of the Treaty of Asunción facilitated the agreements. Presidents played a key role over three decades. Businesses responded to regional integration incentives.

The two most successful MERCOSUR design features provided for automatic responses. Governments mandated and upheld the automatic removal of trade barriers—precise and legally binding with regard to both commitments and timetable, without delegation to other entities—and members rallied to the defense of democracy when threatened in some other member state.

The inter-presidentialist MERCOSUR decision making and problem solving procedures, the delayed establishment and ineffectiveness of a MERCOSUR parliament and court, and the lack of delegation of powers from the presidents to MERCOSUR institutions were sources of vulnerability. When economic crisis hit in the late 1990s, the presidents solved problems by exempting whole sectors from trade liberalization rules. When political crisis hit in the 2000s, the presidents backed away from democracy criteria for membership. The inter-presidential decision in the 2000s to choose expansion over deepening weakened MERCOSUR. MERCOSUR admitted Chávez's Venezuela without negotiating the technical trade details, overlooking both democratic and economic criteria for membership, and ignoring Venezuela's near total lack of implementation of any of MERCOSUR's formal economic decisions.

At its founding, the MERCOSUR integration agenda was not ambitious. It eschewed institution building. The MERCOSUR responded to its troubles, starting in 1999, by creating more supranational organizational machinery and adopting more formal mandates: the more the MERCOSUR weakened, the more it resorted to parchment institutions and rhetoric as a substitute for effectiveness and deepening. Structural economic asymmetries were just as severe in MERCOSUR as in LAFTA (Table 5.1). Such asymmetries did not impede MERCOSUR nor do they account for its debilitation.

Despite flaws, MERCOSUR successfully constructed a much-liberalized trade area within the founding core group of four states. Its trade integration success weakened from the 1990s to the 2000s, but even during the 2000s the proportion of exports from MERCOSUR countries to each other was twice higher than in the late 1980s before signing the Treaty of Asunción. This successful trade liberalization has survived many crises. Comparing 1998 (the year before the Brazilian financial panic) when intra-zonal trade integration was at its highest, to 2008, the value of exports from MERCOSUR member countries to each other—$43.5 billion in 2008—grew. For Uruguay, such exports increased by 18 percent; for Paraguay, between 2.3 and 3.4 times. Argentina saw its intra-zonal exports jump between 1.5 and 2.8 times, while for Brazil, by factors of 1.5 to 2.5 (International Monetary Fund 2009).

The MERCOSUR's most lasting achievement is not in its charter, namely, its contribution to a process of confidence- and peace-building, creating a "pluralistic security community" where war seemed plausible as recently as the 1970s (Deutsch et al. 1957; Hurrell 1998). In the 1990s and the 2000s, the Southern Cone countries built a secure peace and liberalized and expanded trade significantly—worthy achievements.

The North American Free Trade Agreement (NAFTA)

NAFTA had it easy, although few thought so on the eve of its establishment. War had become unthinkable between the United States and Canada in the late nineteenth century and between the United States and Mexico in the 1940s. The prior construction of peace facilitated the construction of NAFTA. (I emphasize U.S.-Mexican relations in this section.) NAFTA would facilitate security cooperation between Mexico and the United States to counter drug trafficking, albeit this relationship remained fraught with difficulty (Domínguez and Fernández de Castro 2009).

Structural asymmetries between members were not daunting. As Table 5.1 shows, the GDP gap on the eve of NAFTA's foundation was lower in North America than in MERCOSUR on the eve of the Treaty of Asunción or in LAFTA before the signing of the Treaty of Montevideo. NAFTA's GDP per capita gap was about the same as for the Andean Community and LAFTA. There was economic policy and political regime heterogeneity but it had been narrowing.

In the second half of the 1980s, Mexico sharply reoriented its economic policy. It reduced average tariff levels unilaterally from 34 percent in 1985 to 10 percent in 1988; Mexico's tariff peak came down from 106 percent in 1985 to 20 percent in 1988 (Devlin, Estevadeordal, and Garay 2000, 157). On the eve of NAFTA, Mexico was governed by an authoritarian regime, yet the president was a civilian and levels of repression were low. Mexico's transition to a competitive, democratic political system coincided with NAFTA's consolidation; NAFTA contributed, albeit moderately, to this political regime transition (Domínguez and Fernández de Castro 2009, 106-111).

NAFTA could declare victory even before its birth. In 1989, before its creation was proposed, the exports of the three would-be North American partners to each other were 40.8 percent of their total exports to the world. As in the run-up to the Treaties of Rome, Asunción, and Tegucigalpa, so too with NAFTA: from the start of negotiations (1990) to the year before NAFTA came into effect (1993), U.S. exports to Mexico jumped 46 percent and Mexican exports to the United States more than doubled (computed from International Monetary Fund 2009). The Canadian-U.S. Free Trade Agreement (CUSFTA) had already gone into effect; CUSFTA provided design features to guide the NAFTA negotiations and contributed directly to the NAFTA text.

NAFTA's negotiations and eventual ratification actively engaged the heads of government. The CUSFTA and then NAFTA depended crucially on Canada's prime minister and the presidents of the United States (two Republicans, one Democrat) and Mexico (Golob 2003). Ratification by the U.S. Congress in 1993 was a bipartisan undertaking to commit the country (Domínguez and Fernández de Castro 2009). Similarly, the three leading Mexican political parties converged to support NAFTA by the 1994 presidential election. And Mulroney's Conservative Party won the 1988 national parliamentary election by emphasizing its achievement of CUSFTA (Johnston, Blais, Brady, and Crête 1992).

Two design decisions made the construction of NAFTA easier. One was to agree on what to exclude. There would be no NAFTA free movement of labor and no NAFTA energy policy; the United States cared about the first and Mexico about the second. The second founding design decision was to omit a "democracy clause"; the United States and Canada would become partners of authoritarian Mexico. NAFTA would become a club of democracies in the 2000s but it was not so at birth; NAFTA still lacks a democracy clause akin to those in the European Union and MERCOSUR.

NAFTA's signal design feature is a specific form of legalization that emphasizes high levels of precision and obligation, with extremely limited delegation to supranational bodies and comparably limited room for inter-presidential deal-making or inter-governmental discretion. NAFTA's precision seeks to reduce the transaction costs inherent in inter-governmental bargaining and to constrain government strategic behavior. NAFTA's precision and obligation seek to make its trade liberalization procedures automatic and self-implementing. The NAFTA text typically and unambiguously mandates or prohibits behavior, leaving little room for delegation, interpretation, discretion, or continuing bargaining. NAFTA's dispute settlement procedures are rules-based (Abbott 2001).

NAFTA incorporated dispute settlement processes on investment, financial services, antidumping and countervailing duties, the functioning of the agreement, labor, and the environment. The dispute settlement process has worked well where NAFTA obligations were precise. NAFTA has worked less well on three big cases where domestic political forces blocked treaty compliance—U.S.-Mexico trucking, U.S.-Mexico sugar and high fructose corn syrup, and U.S.-Canada softwood lumber. (The WTO has been no more effective at settling these three disputes.) In instances with intentionally cumbersome procedures and reliant on consultation (the side agreements on labor and the environment were not automatic or self-enforcing), NAFTA-related actions have been hortatory (Hufbauer and Schott 2005).

NAFTA achieved what it sought to accomplish. From its first year of implementation in 1994, intra-NAFTA trade has consistently exceeded its levels in prior years. From 1998 through 2007, intra-NAFTA exports exceeded 50 percent of the worldwide exports of the three members, reaching a high of 56.6 percent in 2002, dropping to 48 percent in 2009.

NAFTA did not prohibit its members from signing free trade agreements with other countries and from the start all three members negotiated with other governments to create bilateral or minilateral free trade agreements. NAFTA itself was born, of course, from the U.S.-Canadian free trade agreement.

NAFTA's founders would also consider the agreement successful in prohibiting certain behaviors that other observers may have found desirable. NAFTA permits little executive or legislative interference with its precise obligations on member states, except for the three disputes just noted. NAFTA did not open up rounds of inter-governmental bargaining. NAFTA entities, other than the dispute settlement panels, have minimal mandates and, in the case of the North American Development Bank (NADBank), minimal funding. NAFTA was designed to impede or make difficult the creation of new supranational organizations or to foster state-led NAFTA-wide initiatives. NAFTA was designed to eliminate barriers to cross-border trade and investment in North America and to constrain its states from getting in the way of transactions between private actors. From the perspective of its founders, NAFTA succeeded because its organizations did not "deepen." It was not to be a "European Union wannabe."

Nevertheless, NAFTA has resulted in wholesale legal changes to the domestic Mexican trade regime, spurred as well by the WTO and internal pressures within Mexico. And three NAFTA supranational processes—the Free Trade Commission and the institutions created by the side agreements on environment and labor—have had some effects that surprised initial proponents and critics alike (Aspinwall 2008; Clarkson 2007).

NAFTA did not obligate national governments or central banks to come to each other's rescue in the event of a financial panic. Yet, since 1936 the U.S. Treasury's Exchange Stabilization Fund (ESF) had provided a swap line to Mexico to help it manage short-term financial crises. From 1972 to NAFTA's eve, the ESF provided a swap line to Mexico on average once every five quarters; from 1994 to 2002, the ESF did on average once every three quarters. In April 1994, the United States, Canada, and Mexico signed the North American Framework Agreement, which incorporated this U.S.-Mexico swap-line (U.S. Department of the Treasury 2009). In early 1995, the U.S. government responded to the Mexican financial panic as if it were the lender of last resort; Mexico resumed growth within two years.

In short, NAFTA was the most circumscribed integration agreement attempted in the Americas. It focused on trade and investment, eschewing a more ambitious agenda. It built upon the prior construction of peace in North America and ongoing high levels of intra-regional trade and investment. Economic policy convergence through prior unilateral trade liberalization explains why it became possible. Business firms responded enthusiastically even during NAFTA's negotiation. Political regime differences and wide structural economic asymmetries were not obstacles to its establishment. At its origin, NAFTA required the leadership of the heads of government of the three states. Upon enactment, however, the role of heads of government in its operations has been minimal. NAFTA's design excluded democracy, movement of peoples, and energy from its agenda. It featured very high precision and obligation in order to become automatic and self-enforcing, leaving little room for delegation or interpretation by supranational entities.

NAFTA generated positive externalities. It fostered high central bank and finance ministry coordination across North America, most evident during the Mexican financial panic in 1995 and the worldwide financial crisis of 2008–2009. And it contributed to Mexico's democratization in the 1990s.

NAFTA achieved what it set out to do. Between 1994 and 2008, Canada's exports to the United States and Mexico nearly tripled, Mexico's to its partners about quadrupled, and those of the United States to the neighbors doubled. Even comparing 2008 to the year of highest within-NAFTA trade integration (2002), the three member countries exported about 50 percent more to their NAFTA partners in 2008 than in 2002.

Analysis

Politics, profits, and peace are the key factors to explain the establishment of regional economic organizations in the Americas and the variation in the likelihood of their success.

To launch regional economic integration agreements, politics mattered in two respects. Common to all the reactivations or foundings in the late 1980s and early 1990s, governments unilaterally lowered trade barriers in advance of signing or reactivating the integration schemes, thus participating in the worldwide trade liberalization during the decade that preceded the enactment of the WTO. These decisions anticipated and paved the way for the regional economic associations, enabling them to "declare victory" on their respective birthdays. There were no such unilateral decisions in the 1960s and 1970s, which explains in part LAFTA's failure.

Politics also mattered because presidents mattered. Presidents created the Andean Group in the late 1960s and resuscitated it in the early 1990s. Presidents were keys for the establishment of MERCOSUR and NAFTA and the reactivation of the CACM in the 1990s. Presidents mattered little in the establishment of LAFTA and CACM in 1960. As a result, from its start LAFTA lacked a political underpinning and was doomed. The CACM had a successful founding decade but it lacked the political wherewithal to withstand the impact of later wars.

Profits provided a decisive incentive. Firms responded to the new incentives created through unilateral trade liberalization, increasing intra-regional trade in North America, Central America, the Andean region, and the Southern Cone prior to the respective foundational agreements from the late 1980s or early 1990s. Businesses sustained Colombian-Venezuelan trade even after Venezuela withdrew from the Andean Community in 2006. Businesses engaged Costa Rica, typically a latecomer, in Central American integrative schemes, and they sustained Peru's involvement with the Andean Group even when Peru suspended its Andean Group participation in the mid-1990s. In contrast, LAFTA's failure is explained in part because business firms found fewer opportunities within its framework.

Peace was the handmaiden of politics and profits to construct regional economic associations. The prior provision of inter-state peace as an international public good explains why NAFTA could be negotiated, signed, ratified, and implemented over what seemed difficult odds. The hard work to provide the same public good in the Southern Cone, in advance of and simultaneous with the founding of MERCOSUR, explains why MERCOSUR survived crises and misguided decisions that might have killed it. Over three decades, MERCOSUR countries fashioned state practices to carry the new sub-regional work forward. This process became path-creating and eventually path-dependent: NAFTA and MERCOSUR went on to facilitate subsequent political relations and further consolidate the peace. In MERCOSUR, the new regional integration agreement also helped to strengthen the peace in its region.

The absence of a secure inter-state peace prior to a regional economic integration agreement distinguished those two more successful cases from all other less successful cases. Threats of war contributed to the Andean Community's troubles in the 1990s and 2000s and the CACM's in 1969 and since the 1980s. Regional economic integration runs aground when war or threats of war lurk. Just as importantly, a regional integration agreement by itself, absent parallel successful peace-promoting agreements, does not generate inter-state peace; militarized inter-state disputes persisted in the CACM and Andean Community areas notwithstanding the regional economic integration agreement.

The initial conditions, therefore, sort the empirical cases into three sets. Institutions mattered as norm- and rule-setting agreements that set obligations. The anticipation of the agreements and their design explain the outcomes and the variation. First, NAFTA and MERCOSUR liberalized and increased trade and fostered and sustained regional peace. Second, the Central American and Andean countries at various times were unsuccessful at using regional integration to sustain peace and thereby foster further economic integration, but they liberalized trade and made it grow for periods of time as long as a decade. There is in Central America and the Andes, therefore, a close match in the middling achievements with regard to both peace and regional economic integration. Third, LAFTA did not succeed.

Past the founding moment, automatic self-implementing designs (precise and legally binding regarding commitments and timetable for implementation) work better than either inter-presidential or intergovernmental processes or the delegation of decision making and implementation to supranational organizations. NAFTA featured automatic procedures. MERCOSUR worked best when its automatic trade liberalization schedules were in effect. MERCOSUR was equally impressive as member states leapt automatically to defend constitutional democracy to stop coup attempts in Paraguay. CACM automatic rules in trade and finance, dating from the 1960s, have been its best performing features. Automatic rules provided clear incentives to business firms, which made trade and the economy grow, thereby providing "quick and easy wins" for politicians and businesses.

Inter-presidential bargaining past the founding moment characteristically blocked the operation of automatic trade rules. On balance, it weakened MERCOSUR. NAFTA trade failures exist in those few areas where political processes blocked the application of the automatic rules. Inter-presidential politics also weakened the functioning of the Andean Community. The more automatic the rules were in the foundational agreement, the more adverse for the integrative scheme is ad hoc presidential intervention to block the application of such rules.

Two background factors were helpful: economic regime convergence and the behavior of the regional hegemon. Convergence or divergence in economic regime better explains integration outcomes than convergence or divergence in political regimes. Authoritarian and democratic regimes cooperated in both LAFTA and NAFTA (the first failed, the second succeeded) and in CACM and the Andean Group (both with mixed results); thus political regime factors do not explain the difference between them in economic outcomes. LAFTA lacked member convergence on economic regime; NAFTA converged on a liberal economic regime. Difference in economic regime better explains why LAFTA failed and NAFTA succeeded.

Liberal economic regimes succeeded best: NAFTA, and the 1990s for MERCOSUR, the Andean Community, and CACM. As less-liberal economic regimes appeared, divergence is associated with setbacks for the Andean Group in the 1970s and 1980s and the Andean Community in the 2000s. The CACM worked poorly in the 1980s when economic regime divergence prevailed but better in the 1990s with liberal economic regime convergence. Liberal economic regimes start unilateral trade liberalization and adopt benign attitudes toward business and profit growth, which are the more proximate explanations to the launch of economic integration schemes.

Regional hegemons also matter. The United States signed NAFTA expecting Mexico to reap disproportionate gains and, except in three high-visibility disputes, the United States has complied with adverse NAFTA dispute resolution panel decisions. The process that would become MERCOSUR began in 1979 thanks to Brazilian concessions to Argentina and Paraguay. MERCOSUR was sustained in the 2000s, as Argentina ran into economic head winds, because Brazil made further economic concessions. These benign hegemons in North and South America promoted and sustained subregional economic integration, incurring near-term losses for the sake of wider systemic gain. From this optic, LAFTA failed because Brazil was not yet able to behave in that way, and the Andean Community fails because it lacks a benign hegemon. However, this hegemonic behavior has been sporadic, not a dominant explanation.

In contrast, other potential explanations matter less. The presence or absence of supranational organizations explains little with regard to the prospects of peace or trade. ECLA was the midwife for LAFTA, which failed, and the CACM, which could not address war and peace issues effectively. The Andean Community's and the CACM's splendid supranational entities did not much promote intra-zonal trade or curb militarized inter-state disputes between members, notwithstanding in the Andes some other positive results regarding crisis and development finance and intellectual property issues. The CACM outperformed the Andean Community as a free trade area and in coordinating some foreign economic policies. Andean Community delegation of trade liberalization to supranational organizations failed; its trade liberalization design was most effective when it relied on automatic procedures. Automatic rules served the CACM well in the 1960s and helped its revival in the 1990s. In the 2000s, MERCOSUR created new supranational entities that remained without much effect. NAFTA is thin on supranationality, yet highly successful regarding trade and peace.

Disputes were settled through informal inter-presidential bargaining, as in MERCOSUR, or in other ad hoc ways. Rules-based dispute settlement was the exception outside NAFTA, which possessed the least elaborate supranational organizations. The formal establishment of integration courts in Central America, the Andean region, and MERCOSUR also had little impact on trade or peace.

A strong supranational secretariat bears no relationship to regional integration outcomes. NAFTA has succeeded without one. The Andean Community has had an excellent secretariat, albeit powerless to fix the Community. MERCOSUR has a weaker secretariat than CACM or the Andean Community—all three fostered intra-zonal trade liberalization through automatic rules, not their secretariats. Purely technical inter-state processes have at most temporary benefits. ECLA at its moment of glory could not make LAFTA work and could not save the CACM in its first incarnation. Technical virtuosity in the Andean Community supranational entities could not address the organization's weaknesses. Technocrats in the CACM cannot stop militarized interstate disputes.

Even the changing membership in various associations had few effects on the relationship between those entities and trade. Countries became members or stopped being members of regional economic associations without much apparent benefit or cost to membership.

Other explanations were even less important. Defensive responses to European integration lurked in the background in the late 1950s and the late 1980s. Concern over the United States was also a secondary factor in the late 1950s, but in the 1990s and the 2000s, the United States was neither lure nor fear. Similarly, integration worked approximately the same where structural asymmetries are very wide (MERCOSUR) and very small (CACM); very wide asymmetries existed in both LAFTA and MERCOSUR but the outcomes of these two differ greatly. Distributive concerns are important and a constant across all integration schemes, with groups lobbying to protect or to gain privileges; therefore, they cannot explain the variation in outcomes. The international political economy milieu grew more liberal by the late 1950s, facilitating regional economic integration, but that does not explain why the CACM was more successful than LAFTA, both founded in 1960. This milieu grew even more liberal by the start of the 1990s; that does not explain the variation between the four regional economic associations created or relaunched at that time. Nevertheless, the international liberal milieu did promote regional integration much more in the 1990s than in the 1960s.

The existence of several overlapping regional integration groups may have weakened pre-existing groups. The Andean Group justified its founding as a response of LAFTA's ineffectiveness, yet the Andean Group's founding helped to kill LAFTA (for similar examples, see O'Rourke's chapter). Venezuela withdrew from the Andean Community in 2006 on the grounds that the U.S. free trade agreements with Colombia and Peru had altered the content of the Community. The MERCOSUR's conscious choice of widening over deepening in the 2000s, taking in Venezuela as a member and signing association agreements with the Andean Community and its member countries, may have diluted MERCOSUR. The effect of relations between regional and subregional integration groups seems secondary, however; relationships between such groups mainly accelerated processes of unraveling that had already begun.

Implications for Asia

Latin America's experience with regional economic integration has implications for other countries, specifically in Asia. It is more important to have good policies than integration agreements. In the 1960s and 1970s, Latin America's use of integration schemes (LAFTA, Andean Group) to minimize its engagement with world trade and investment was a mistake, on top of other bad domestic economic policy decisions. On the other hand, the lack of a formal integration agreement did not prevent the impressive development of trade and investment in North America along with the construction of a pluralistic security community between Canada, Mexico, and the United States. Good policies work even without a formal integration agreement. Moreover, there is no need for alarm if a member leaves the association for a while; so long as the economic relationship continues, trade levels may be sustained, and the member may return—as Costa Rica, Peru, and Venezuela in different ways demonstrated.

Two background factors are likely to improve collective outcomes. A benign regional hegemon helps. The United States engineered peace with Mexico, and Brazil with Argentina and Paraguay, by ceding small bits of territory for the sake of a grand strategy to foster peace and prosperity. In both regions, peace preceded the boom in economic relations, though much higher trade and investment did follow. China's role in the South China Sea is a good parallel: instead of threats over rocks and islets, China could lead a shared growth and security in Southeast Asia. Peace in South and North America was not a prerequisite for trade, but once achieved peace was a secure platform for trade growth.

Economic regime homogeneity also facilitates economic integration, and many countries in East and South Asia have been moving in such convergent directions. Political regime heterogeneity did not prevent economic integration. Authoritarian and democratic regimes cooperate. In this respect, Latin America's experience may be more relevant to Asia than is Europe's. Very wide structural asymmetries did not derail integration schemes in Latin America. Severe distributive disputes are to be expected but, though often costly, they need not impede generally successful integration—and, yes, they are a constant across agreements.

Supranational organizations may help. They work best in specialized realms, such as the Inter-American Development Bank, the Andean Development Corporation, and the Asian Development Bank, or for swaps in financial crises (FLAR, the Chiang Mai Initiative, or the North American agreement). But regional parliaments, courts, and secretariats are powerless in the face of larger political and economic processes even when excellent professionals staff them (as in the Andean Court and Secretariat). Negotiations through such organizations are often cumbersome and may contribute to setbacks.

Latin America's more successful integration processes were inter-presidential at their founding (NAFTA, MERCOSUR, the relaunching of CACM and the Andean Community). The role of key leaders may be pertinent in Asia. In contrast to Europe, intergovernmental processes mattered little in MERCOSUR and have been deliberately curtailed in NAFTA. Presidents must also anchor the domestic political economy coalitions that may enact unilateral trade liberalizations and implement integration agreements.

The process of negotiating agreements would increase the likelihood that the agreement would be implemented if there are clear incentives for businesses to reshape their operations in anticipation that the agreement would become a reality. The economic boom that results enables the integration agreement to proclaim victory on its birthday, rewarding and encouraging politicians to undertake the more difficult tasks of implementation.

Where militarized interstate disputes persist, as is the case along Asia's eastern rim and has been part of the Latin American experience, the parallel effort to resolve such military and political disputes fosters economic growth and cooperation. That was a key lesson of MERCOSUR. Integration schemes may endure even in the presence of those disputes (CACM, Andean Community) but they are less likely to realize their potential.

Institutional design matters. The more automatic the rules, the more effective the agreement will be. That is the lesson from NAFTA, MERCOSUR, CACM, and the Andean Community. When automatic rules coexist with rules that require negotiation, the former process is more effective. The automatic rule applies also to parallel political processes, for example, instantly stop a militarized interstate dispute (Ecuador-Peru war, CACM disputes), instantly prevent an unconstitutional government overthrow (MERCOSUR with regard to Paraguay). And, remove presidents—essential at the founding—from quotidian trade dispute-resolution processes because they are likely to be disruptive.

Ultimately, the Latin American experience implies that the institutions for regional integration should appeal to Asian countries. Yes, trade may exist without regional integration, but trade growth is likely to fare even better with integration. Yes, trade does not ensure peace, but improving security and securing peace may propel trade growth and may make easier the resolution of political and military disputes.

Conclusion

The Latin American regional economic integration schemes have a key outcome in common: Each contributed to significant trade liberalization. In NAFTA, that was the predominant goal. The Latin American regional experience suggests skepticism that economic integration on topics other than trade liberalization may succeed. The Andean Community, the CACM, and MERCOSUR attempted but failed to become common markets. Trade liberalization worked, mainly thanks to automatic rules buttressed by responsive business firms that rewarded their firms, politicians, and their countries. Automatic rules have low transaction costs and near-term gains. More complex integrative schemes on other topics are challenging and costly.

Success went to international cooperation efforts that built both peace and trade liberalization. Trade liberalization works best when it interacts positively with peace. NAFTA and MERCOSUR approximate this outcome. They liberalized trade within the respective regions and built or developed pluralistic security communities in which inter-state war becomes unthinkable. A lesson for other countries is to be distracted less by supranational organizational tinkering and focus more, systematically and consistently, on peace-building and growth through trade liberalization.

Notes

1. I am grateful to the Asian Development Bank for support; Etel Solingen, Barry Eichengreen, Alisha Holland, and especially Miles Kahler for comments; and Lena Bae for research assistance. All errors are mine alone.

2. In this and other sections, all percentage statistics regarding the direction and value of trade (1985–2010) were calculated from International Monetary Fund, *Direction of Trade Statistics*, various years.

6

Why the EU Won

KEVIN H. O'ROURKE

Introduction

Why did European regional integration take on a supranational form, rather than involving looser intergovernmental structures, such as a free trade area? During the 1950s, only a minority of European countries—just six—were willing to go down the supranational route, the majority preferring inter-governmental cooperation. Why was the situation in which the minority pursued their preferred option, and the majority pursued theirs, not a stable equilibrium? Why was most of the European Free Trade Association (EFTA), and the rest of Europe, eventually incorporated into what is now the European Union? And what, if any, are the lessons for Asia today?

At a broad level, one can divide the question of "Why the EU Won" into two sub-questions. First, why did the EU-6 choose to go down a supranational route? And second, why did the rest of Europe eventually join them? The answer to the second question is largely to be found in the domino mechanism described by Baldwin (2011), and so I will deal more with the first, as well as with the issue of why the UK decided to apply for European Economic Community (EEC) membership in the early 1960s. That decision was crucial in making the already considerable gravitational pull of the EEC irresistible. The chapter will therefore focus on the 1950s and 1960s, and only deal briefly with the later decades which are covered in detail elsewhere. For the same reason, I will not dwell on the "deepening" of European integration since the 1980s (see chapter 2), although I briefly mention it later in this chapter.

Answers as to why Europe adopted a supranational approach to integration can be found at three levels. First, there are deep structural factors relating to European geography and history, which increased the demand for European integration, expressed in supranational institutions of various kinds. These include Europe's political fragmentation, its relative cultural homogeneity, and the legacies of the Industrial Revolution and the industrial warfare which it ultimately spawned. Second, there are the geopolitical and economic interests of national governments who had to decide whether to meet this demand, or instead adopt a more intergovernmental framework for regional cooperation. These interests included fears of diminished status on the world political stage, and the important role which agricultural trade had to play in any comprehensive European free trade bargain. Third, there is the role of chance and contingency, in the form of the negotiating skills (or lack thereof) of particular governments at particular times, and the political composition of these governments. When comparing the European and Asian experiences, the main focus presumably ought to be on structural and mid-level factors. However, when asking whether the victory of European supranationalism was inevitable or not, one has to take contingent factors into account as well.

Structural Factors: History, Geography and Culture

Size and Diversity

Europe is much smaller than Asia, and is in consequence much less diverse. This matters, since political integration across historical cultural divides can be problematic. Findlay and O'Rourke (2007) distinguish between Western Europe (defined by the influence of the Roman Catholic Church and the Latin script) and Eastern Europe (defined as those regions whose major formative cultural influences were the Byzantine Empire and the Greek Orthodox Church). The distinction is still relevant, as was tragically demonstrated during the Balkan wars of the early 1990s. When several parts of Western Europe were forcibly incorporated into Soviet-dominated "Eastern Europe" after 1945, Soviet rule was challenged there on several occasions, and the election of a Polish Pope in 1978 marked the beginning of the end of the Soviet empire. Even today, the EU only incorporates four member states from Eastern Europe: Greece, Cyprus, Bulgaria, and Romania. The experience of EU membership has been difficult in all four cases. An even clearer demonstration of the importance of history and culture is the reluctance to admit Turkey to the EU. Despite the linguistic diversity of the EU, and the large number of states included in it, this impressive experience of integration has in fact taken place within a relatively small and homogenous region.

Geography, Fragmentation, and War

Geography is crucial in understanding the different historical trajectories experienced by Europe and Asia. For example, there are a sufficient number of natural barriers within the region, such as the Alps, the Pyrenees, and the English Channel, that would-be conquerors of Europe, from Charlemagne to Hitler, have found it impossible to unify the continent by military means. For Eric Jones (2003), this political fragmentation was a crucial advantage for Europe over Asia, largely because of the political and military competition which it implied, and which gave the continent a "comparative advantage in violence." It was also more difficult to suppress inconvenient ideas, since a Voltaire could always move to Geneva, and the common European culture then ensured that ideas could move across frontiers even when their originators could not.

By contrast, China has been a unified country, more or less, for over two millennia. There have been many other large empires in Asian history: the early Islamic empire, the Ottoman Empire, the Safavid Empire, the Mughal Empire, the Russian Empire, and the Mongol Empire being some of the most famous. One could argue that the current Indian and Chinese states represent more impressive examples of political integration, within comparable regions, than the European Union is ever likely to achieve within Europe. There are two points here. First, European integration can seem impressive precisely because there was so much fragmentation to begin with. Second, Asian integration would by definition have to take place across very different "world regions," since within several of the Asian world regions there has already been an impressive degree of integration.

The backdrop to postwar European integration is the conflicts of 1914–1945. The political fragmentation which *had* traditionally been a source of competitive strength for Europe became more and more costly with the onset of modern industrial warfare. During the First World War, deaths of military personnel amounted to 1.6% of the total population in Britain, 3.4% in France, and 3% in Germany (Broadberry and Harrison 2005, 27). World War II was even more destructive, since it was no longer concentrated along a more or less static front and involved very heavy aerial bombardment across the continent. In addition, the Nazis directly targeted civilian populations. Over half a million Frenchmen were killed, over 350,000 Britons, almost 300,000 Americans, and over 4 million Germans.

The timing of moves toward greater European unity is thus hardly surprising, nor is strong US support for the process. This history also explains the importance of the Franco-German relationship as a driver of European integration. One could speculate that a *rapprochement* between China and Japan might someday play a similar catalyzing role in the context of East Asian integration, and the participation of both these powers in the Six-Party Talks, ASEAN+3 (APT), East Asian Summit (EAS), and most recently the Trilateral Summits, may augur well in this regard for the future. However, the contrasts between the post-war Franco-German and Sino-Japanese relationships remain striking.

Also striking is the strong US encouragement of European integration after 1945. In contrast, the US has tended to prefer bilateralism in its relationships with Asia, Southeast Asian Treaty Organization (SEATO) notwithstanding. US opposition to Japan's Asian Monetary Fund proposal in 1997 led to the withdrawal of that proposal (even though something very similar emerged twelve years later, with the multilateralizing of the Chiang Mai Initiative).[1] The Cold War is key to understanding why the Americans were so keen to promote political integration in Western Europe after 1945. It is not clear that they would have similar interests in the context of 21st century Asia, even if political integration were ever to become a realistic possibility there.

The Aftermath of the Industrial Revolution: Relative Decline

Europe was the first continent to experience the Industrial Revolution. As such, it enjoyed an enormous increase in its relative economic, military, and political power, symbolized by the European empires of the 19th century. In the long run, however, the spread of industry across the globe was inevitable, and the relative decline of Europe with it. Europe's primacy was already ending at the beginning of the 20th century, as the US emerged as the world's largest industrial power. The two world wars hastened the transition from a Western European–dominated world, and by 1945 the two dominant military powers in the world were clearly the US and USSR. A key question for European statesmen was then how to avoid being overwhelmed by the Soviet Union and ignored or condescended to by the US. Greater unity seemed an obvious solution.

Europe's diminished status was more obvious on the Continent than in Britain. France, Germany, Italy, and the Benelux countries had all been defeated in one way or another during the war. By contrast, the UK had remained undefeated throughout the war and retained a large overseas empire: it is probably not surprising that the UK was more reluctant to move beyond intergovernmental cooperation than other countries.

The contrast with 21st century Asia is obvious and will be stressed later: Asia is not a declining power, but a rising one. Furthermore, while the experience of decolonization led to former colonizers seeking security by banding together, it also produced post-colonial states intent on preserving their national sovereignty. These differences are crucial in assessing the prospects for Asian supranational integration today.

The Aftermath of the Industrial Revolution: The Role of the State

Industrial warfare required the mobilization of large conscript armies. A logical consequence was that the state needed to compensate its citizens by providing them with services which would increase their identification with the state and ensure their loyalty. The result was a gradual growth of state education and other public services. Globalization also led to a demand for state regulation and social insurance policies which would protect workers against the insecurities, real or perceived, associated with open international markets. The late 19th and early 20th centuries thus saw the introduction of a wide range of labor market regulations across Western Europe, as well as old-age pensions, and sickness and unemployment insurance.

The world wars gave a further impetus to the growing involvement of the state in domestic economies, and to the development of social welfare systems. The aftermath of World War I saw a significant extension of the franchise, as well as an increase in the influence of trade unions and Socialist parties. The defeat of Churchill in 1945, and the election of a Labour government, was similarly a reflection of the desire of ordinary workers who had suffered greatly during the war to see their lives improve in its wake. Given the experience of the Great Depression, they were hardly going to be willing to leave it to the market: "embedded liberalism" was a logical consequence.

As Alan Milward (2000) points out, these heightened expectations on the part of ordinary people coincided in most of Europe with the widespread feeling that traditional nation states had failed their people—in providing economic security during the interwar period, and in providing physical security after 1939. According to Milward, the three crucial constituencies which had to be placated were agricultural voters, whose disillusionment had led them to support extremist parties during the interwar period in many countries, workers, and those dependent on the welfare state. The solution was to provide workers with rising wages and full employment, to ensure rising living standards for the agricultural sector, and to establish modern welfare states.

Accomplishing all three goals required an extension of government intervention in the economy. So did the economic growth strategies pursued by governments at the time, which relied on high investment facilitated by complex corporatist bargains keeping a lid on wage growth (Eichengreen 2007): the extension of the welfare state was a key part of these bargains. As Milward says, "in the long run of history there has surely never been a period when national government in Europe has exercised more effective power and more extensive control over its citizens than that since the Second World War, nor one in which its ambitions expanded so rapidly. Its laws, officials, policemen, spies, statisticians, revenue collectors, and social workers have penetrated into a far wider range of human activities than they were earlier able or encouraged to do" (Milward 2000,18).

This in turn provided both direct and indirect reasons for governments to cooperate with each other. One direct reason can be found in the fears of governments during the 1950s that their industries would be placed at a competitive disadvantage vis-à-vis industries in other countries whose social welfare systems were less well developed. A logical response to this fear was to argue, as the French did, that a common market required common social policies. In order to develop such policies, a deeper institutional framework would be required than would be the case under a simple free trade area. Indirectly, Milward argues that governments pooled sovereignty, since this was essential if they were to achieve the economic growth they needed. I will return to this argument in the concluding section.

Clearly the state has been an important actor in many Asian economies since 1945. However, to date this has not produced the same pressures for supranational integration as it did in Europe. Asian economies were able to grow by exporting to Western markets, which were relatively open: they did not need to carve out a large enough regional market via regional integration to promote export-oriented investment. Nor would the defensive motive of protecting firms from being undercut by foreign competition, given generous domestic social welfare provisions, have been much of a consideration in countries who were undercutting, rather than being undercut.

The Aftermath of the Industrial Revolution: The Role of Agriculture

A third consequence of Western Europe's industrial history is that the region had become a large net importer of agricultural goods. The "grain invasion" of the late 1870s and 1880s sparked agricultural protection across much of the continent, which would become a permanent feature of the European landscape. What the grain invasion failed to achieve, the Great Depression accomplished in such traditionally free-trading countries as the UK and the Netherlands. In 1932, it was agreed at Ottawa that while Empire agricultural goods would continue to be admitted into the UK duty-free, new duties on non-Empire goods such as wheat would be introduced in Britain. This did not provide British farmers with much protection, since Canadian and Australian farmers were so much more productive; they were thus guaranteed a minimum price for their output. However, the UK's historical commitment to cheap food for consumers meant that the government did not wish to raise the market price. British farmers therefore obtained their guaranteed prices by means of a subsidy, known as a deficiency payment, equal to the difference between the average market price and the guaranteed price.

After World War II, all European governments wished to achieve food self-sufficiency for strategic reasons, and widespread agricultural intervention became the norm across Europe (Tracy 1989, chapter 11). Governments promoted agricultural production by a variety of means: guaranteeing farm incomes and encouraging agricultural investment and better farming practices. They also guaranteed prices for farmers. This meant raising domestic prices above world levels and insulating domestic agricultural markets from world markets by means of strict import controls. In the UK, on the other hand, deficiency payments remained the policy tool of choice, allowing farmers to benefit from higher prices while maintaining the advantages of cheap food, and allowing Commonwealth countries access to British markets. (This of course increased the direct cost to the British Exchequer.)

By the early to mid-1950s, food shortages were becoming less of a problem, and food surpluses started to emerge as a result of the guaranteed prices. At the same time, low farm incomes remained a problem, with rising productivity and outmigration being insufficient to bridge the gap between agricultural and non-agricultural incomes. Faced with the inherent contradictions of the situation, agricultural policy in Europe became "increasingly complicated" (Tracy 1989, 219) and more intrusive.

No European government of the 1950s could have contemplated a liberalization of agricultural production. There were therefore two logical choices facing politicians wishing to liberalize European trade. The first was to liberalize trade in industrial products alone, maintaining existing national agricultural policies. The second was to liberalize intra-European trade in agricultural products, but to replicate national agricultural policies at the European level—in other words, to develop some sort of common agricultural policy. Such a policy would require a lot more intergovernmental cooperation than a mere free trade area: for example, decision-making rules on setting minimum agricultural prices and rules for financing the consequences of surplus production.

The initial British desire to limit intra-European integration to an industrial free trade area was rational, given these choices. First, there was Britain's relationship with the Commonwealth to be considered. Second, Britain's preferred deficiency payment system was very different from the policy of raising domestic consumer as well as producer prices favored by countries such as France and Germany. Economic considerations can also help to understand why the EU-6 opted for an agreement covering agriculture as well as industry. Europe as a whole was a food importer, but within Europe there were regions which relied heavily on food exports. German industries stood to gain from industrial free trade since Germany was an industrial exporter. However, agricultural exports were very important for France and crucial for the Netherlands, so any sensible bargain involving these three countries would have to incorporate agriculture as well as industry. A common agricultural policy of some sort was thus inevitable.

The argument is not that agriculture made regional integration easier, since agriculture has been an obstacle to European free trade for nearly a century and a half. Rather, it is that, given that agriculture had to be a part of the new Common Market for political reasons, a logical implication was the development of institutions to organize Europe-wide government activity in this sector. In Asia, agriculture has hindered moves toward free trade; for example, agricultural considerations prompted the Japanese government not to support the Early Voluntary Sectored Liberalization (EVSL) approach to meeting APEC's Bogor Goals, with the tacit approval of other East Asian nations (Dent 2010). Indeed, Asian countries have tended to adopt the favored approach of the British, limiting free trade agreements to industrial products. Such a policy would have been anathema to the French and Dutch.

The World Economic Context

In 1945, the world was emerging from three appalling decades which had seen two world wars and the Great Depression. All three catastrophes led to widespread restrictions on trade, which tended to become locked in as a result of the political process. The result was a highly fragmented world economy, characterized by inconvertible currencies, high tariffs, and widespread quotas. To be sure, 23 states signed the General Agreement on Tariffs and Trade (GATT) in 1947, with the purpose of encouraging "reciprocal and mutually advantageous arrangements directed to the substantial reduction of tariffs and other barriers to trade." However, by the 1950s the GATT process had stalled, in part as a result of the free rider problems associated with the Most-Favored Nation (MFN) clause (Irwin 1995). The high investment growth strategy of the period was premised on firms being able to sell their output, abroad if necessary: the net result was that regional trade agreements were desirable for export-oriented economies, such as the Netherlands, who wanted to see trade liberalized more rapidly than could be achieved at the global level. German industrialists might have preferred a wider free trade area, but the EEC could be seen by them as a second best solution. (Even more important in the German context, however, was the opportunity afforded by the EEC for re-establishing the Federal Republic as a normal country.)

In contrast, today's world economy is highly globalized. Asian export sectors do not have the same interest in regional trade agreements as their European colleagues did fifty years ago, given that they can already export to markets worldwide. It is perhaps not surprising, then, that finance rather than trade has been the focus of Asian regional initiatives in recent years. Even if the Chiang Mai Initiative evolves into an Asian Monetary Fund, however, this will not require the supranational political institutions of the EU, any more than does the International Monetary Fund (IMF).

European Integration: A Brief Narrative

I now provide a brief narrative of some of the key turning points in the history of postwar European integration. The purpose is to pick out key episodes which can help us understand what the main impulses were behind European supranationalism, and at what points in time history might plausibly have evolved differently. In achieving the former, the emphasis will be on structural and mid-level factors, while in achieving the latter the emphasis will be more on contingency and chance.

Britain at the Heart of Europe

The late 1940s saw a burst of institutional innovation in Western Europe.[2] By the end of the decade three major international organizations had been created, in the economic, security, and political spheres. All three included the UK as a leading founder member, and all three operated on essentially intergovernmental lines. At the same time, future battle lines were already being drawn between federalists and "intergovernmentalists."

The origins of the Organisation for European Economic Co-Operation (OEEC) are largely American. When the US decided in 1947 to provide Marshall Aid to Europe, one of the things that it insisted on was that the European Recovery Programme be administered by the Europeans themselves. The OEEC was set up for this purpose in 1948, and involved 17 European countries who would be the key players in the maneuvers and counter-maneuvers of the succeeding decade. It is helpful to classify these countries into three groups. First, there were "the Six": the three Benelux countries, France, Germany and Italy.[3] Second, there were the "Other Six": the three Scandinavians (Denmark, Norway, and Sweden), the two neutral alpine states (Austria and Switzerland), and the UK. Third, there were five peripheral and less industrial countries: Greece, Iceland, Ireland, Portugal, and Turkey.

The OEEC also had a remit to advance European economic integration. In accordance with the wishes not just of Britain, but of the Scandinavians and the Low Countries (Urwin 1995, 20), the organization was strictly inter-governmental in nature—contrary to the wishes of France. Decisions were taken by the Council of Ministers, and required unanimity. It was largely successful in achieving its objectives. Notably, the establishment of the European Payments Union in 1950 greatly facilitated the establishment of a multilateral trade system and the eventual resumption of convertible currencies, without which the adoption of more ambitious free trade proposals would have been impossible. The OEEC also made considerable progress in removing non-tariff barriers to trade amongst its members.

NATO was another organization where American input was crucial by definition. In 1948 the three Benelux countries joined France and Britain in signing the Treaty of Brussels, a 50 year collective security agreement which also called for "collaboration in economic, social and cultural matters" (Urwin 1995, 32). The Brussels Treaty soon became redundant, due to Western European weakness and fears about the Soviet Union. The result was the signature of the Atlantic Pact in 1949, establishing NATO, by 12 countries: the five Brussels Treaty countries, three Nordics (Denmark, Iceland, and Norway), Italy and Portugal, and Canada and the US. Greece and Turkey were admitted three years later.

Thirdly, in 1949 the Council of Europe was established as a two-tier structure, involving both a European assembly, meeting in public, which is what the federalists wanted, and a ministerial committee meeting in private, and making decisions on the basis of unanimity, which is what the British wanted. The Consultative Assembly, as it was called, and which met in Strasbourg, became a focal point for pro-federalist politics during the 1950s. However, the structure of the Committee of Ministers ensured that the Council of Europe would become an organization based on intergovernmental cooperation. Its major contribution was in the area of human rights, with the European Convention for the Protection of Human Rights and Fundamental Freedoms being signed in 1950, and European Court of Human Rights established in 1959.

A British politician surveying the European scene in 1950 would probably have felt quite pleased. Western European was being stabilized, economically and politically, with the active support of the US. A web of interlocking institutions had been created in order to facilitate this, in particular the OEEC and NATO, with Britain a leading member of both. And while the federalists had obtained a European assembly, the organizational framework that had been erected to date was intergovernmental rather than supranational.

The Path to Rome

Events were soon to take a new and very different turn. In May 1950 Robert Schuman announced a proposal to pool Western Europe's coal and steel industries, and have them administered by a new supranational authority. His declaration also stated that "Europe must be organized on a federal basis." All European countries were invited to participate in the venture, but only "the Six" did so. The result was the Treaty of Paris, establishing the European Coal and Steel Community (ECSC), signed in 1951. Ratification was completed the following year. The ECSC was committed to establishing a common market in coal and steel, without tariffs, quotas, restrictive practices, discriminatory subsidies, or other measures, and with a common tariff on imports from the rest of the world. It also took on functions in areas not directly related to trade, such as investment, research, health and safety, and the housing and resettlement of workers.

The ECSC established an ambitious supranational institutional framework. Four institutions were created: the High Authority, the Council of Ministers, the Court of Justice, and the Common Assembly. The High Authority administered the Community and had decision-making power. In addition, it had the power to fine firms in breach of the treaty and to collect production levies. The Authority had nine members, and decisions were made by simple majority voting. It was thus a clearly supranational institution. The purpose of the Council was to coordinate the actions of the High Authority and of member states. It was made up of one minister representing each state. In some matters its consent was needed, and it made decisions on the basis of either unanimity or weighted majority voting. The Court of Justice was charged with making sure that the treaty was respected, and had the power to annul the actions of the other institutions. Finally, the Common Assembly was a purely advisory body, which did however have the power to dismiss the High Authority.

Recent historical scholarship has not been particularly kind to the ECSC (Gillingham 1995). One of Monnet's major aims was the decartelization of German heavy industry, and the High Authority was given widespread powers to bring this about. The attempt proved a failure, partly because the needs of the Korean War implied that a costly reorganization of German industry could not be contemplated. Nor did the ECSC succeed in creating a single market for coal and steel. Domestic coal subsidies and price controls remained, given the importance of coal prices for ordinary families as well as industry, while steel tariffs were not eliminated. German exports to non-ECSC European countries grew more rapidly than exports to the ECSC (Eichengreen and Boltho 2010).

The ECSC did provide the institutional blueprint for future European institutional development, if only superficially. The four institutions it established—the High Authority, Council of Ministers, Court of Justice, and Common Assembly—correspond well to the Commission, Council, Court of Justice, and European Parliament of our own day. Indeed, the Court of Justice and Assembly became institutions of all three Communities (ECSC, EEC, and EURATOM) in 1958. The Court of Justice in particular has played a crucial role, ensuring that the Communities developed on the basis of the rule of law. It was thus essential in maintaining the supranational character of the Communities, although obviously it would not have had the influence that it did had the member states not agreed to be bound by its rulings. (The fact that they did was crucial for subsequent developments, but ex ante they might not have.) Similarly, the High Authority and Council were merged with the corresponding bodies of the EEC and EURATOM in 1967, becoming the Commission and Council of the European Communities. However, as we will see, the EC would eventually develop into a much less supranational, and much more intergovernmental, organization than the ECSC.

Nevertheless, the ECSC was an important development. For Gillingham, its crucial contributions were, first, to permit the reintegration of Germany into Europe, as a state which could sign treaties with others on the basis of equality; and second, to provide politicians and negotiators with valuable lessons on the process of negotiating and implementing experiments in integration. It also provided the political framework within which German heavy industry could be allowed to revive without threatening Germany's neighbors—although Eichengreen and Boltho (2010) speculate that the importance of achieving this was so great for the West that some other means would have been found to accomplish the same goal in the absence of the ECSC.

The second major development during this period had Asian and American origins. The outbreak of war in Korea in June 1950 prompted an increasingly overstretched US to call for West German rearmament within NATO. This prospect horrified the French and other victims of Nazi aggression. The solution, proposed by the French government in October, and known as the Pleven Plan, was to set up a common European army, so that Germany could contribute to NATO without doing so under a separate German command. This was to be done within a European Defense Community, which was to involve similar supranational institutional structures as the ECSC. The Americans were supportive, while the British refused to become involved; the Germans only did so on the basis that the Western allies end their occupation of Germany and return it to full sovereignty (Urwin 1995, 62).

In turn, the EDC sparked negotiations on an over-arching European Political Community to which both the EDC and ECSC were to be subordinate. However, the French had always viewed the Pleven Plan as the lesser of several evils and remained opposed to German rearmament. Eventually, in August 1954, the French National Assembly rejected the EDC treaty, and with it the EPC fell as well. The problem of how to handle German rearmament was therefore solved in the manner that the British had always wished: the expansion of the 1948 Brussels Treaty to include Germany and Italy while removing the anti-German language of the original. The treaty establishing the resultant organization, the Western European Union (WEU), was signed in October 1954. The WEU came into being, and Germany joined NATO, in May of the following year.

For federalists, this sequence of events must have seemed a debacle. However, the debates surrounding the EDC led fairly directly to the Messina process and the EEC (Milward 2000). The Netherlands, as a low tariff country, were not particularly happy with the trade liberalization program of the OEEC. The removal of quota restrictions disproportionately liberalized Dutch trade, while leaving the trade of such high tariff countries as Britain and France relatively unaffected. As a result, it was difficult for the Dutch to expand their manufactured exports, while agricultural exports, which were important to the country, were excluded from the ongoing liberalization efforts.

The solution was to engineer a reduction in tariffs in the Netherland's major export markets. It seemed difficult to envisage progress being made within the context of either the OEEC or GATT. On the other hand, the Dutch had found that their interests had been well protected in the negotiations leading to the formation of the ECSC, two of whose members (Belgium and Germany) were, by a happy coincidence, the Netherland's largest export markets, and two of which were large high-tariff countries (France and Italy). It was therefore logical for the Netherlands to propose, in 1952, that the EDC and EPC should form a customs union. Discussion of the Beyen Plan, named after the Dutch foreign minister who proposed it, was wide-ranging and covered many of the issues that would eventually be tackled in later negotiations. One notable feature of the plan, on which the Dutch insisted, is that there would be no scope for national governments to determine the pace of trade liberalization—rather, a precisely defined schedule would be written into the treaty. This would become a central part of the Treaty of Rome bargain.

Two points are relevant here in the Asian context. First, Asian exporters are operating in a world that is already largely globalized. They therefore do not have the same incentives as did European export interests during the 1950s to push for regional free trade, especially since the ultimate consumers of what is produced in "Factory Asia" are largely outside the region. Second, Dutch doubts regarding whether their partners could be relied upon to deliver on their promises did not lead to a breakdown of negotiations, but rather to the development of supranational institutions designed to lock in mutual concessions. In turn, those supranational institutions were valued by other participants in the negotiating process for their own sake. If the latter is not true in the Asian context, one wonders how easy it would be to negotiate regional trade arrangements there, which would of necessity (given that industrial trade is already largely liberalized) have to focus on sensitive sectors such as agriculture.

As soon as the Mendès-France government which had been responsible for the defeat of the EDC fell from power in France, in February 1955, Beyen revived his customs union proposal. In June 1955 the foreign ministers of the Six met at Messina and agreed to set up a committee, headed by Paul-Henri Spaak, to study the establishment of a common market and a nuclear energy community. The Spaak Committee became a treaty drafting committee in May 1956, and in March 1957 the Treaty of Rome was signed, establishing the EEC and EURATOM. As Baldwin (2011) points out, the economic ambitions of the treaty were considerable: not just to establish a customs union, but also inter alia a Common Agricultural Policy (which, as suggested above, was a logical consequence of the former), the free movement of capital and labor, common competition rules, and the harmonization of social policies.

The institutional structure of the EEC differed in one crucial respect, however, from that of the ECSC. In the ECSC, the supranational High Authority made the decisions, although it had to consult with the Council on certain issues. In the EEC, it was the Council—that is, the intergovernmental body representing the member states—which had the power to make decisions, while the Commission could formulate proposals which the Council of Ministers then discussed. The Treaty of Rome thus established two new Communities which were far less supranational than the ECSC, although it retained the Court of Justice. On the other hand, the treaty also envisaged a gradual transition from unanimity or weighted majority voting to simple majority voting by 1966. No sooner did that date arrive, however, than the Luxembourg Compromise reinstated unanimity as the basic decision rule, as a result of the Empty Chair crisis of the previous year. The treaty was seen at the time as a victory for those governments who believed in an intergovernmental, rather than a supranational, vision of Europe, and de Gaulle's subsequent actions further strengthened that intergovernmental reality.

From Plan G to de Gaulle's First Veto

Despite all this drama, the OEEC remained the basic building bloc of Western European economic integration—even though it had become much less important after the ending of the Marshall Plan in 1952, and was becoming a victim of its own success in dismantling quantitative restrictions on trade and moving European currencies toward convertibility. Moreover, Britain remained a leading European power, and the hope remained among several members of the ECSC that Britain might join with them in moving toward a customs union and common nuclear community. Indeed, Britain had signed an association agreement with the ECSC in 1954. The Six therefore invited Britain to participate in the work of the Spaak Committee, and the British accepted the invitation. They were present at the first meeting of the Committee in July 1955, and participated for the next five months.

There were two main differences between the British position and that of the Six (Camps 1964, chap. II). The first, and most important, was the British preference for a free trade area rather than a customs union. The Six opposed a free trade area on the grounds that it would require the maintenance of internal border controls to monitor compliance with the rules of origin, something which they wish to avoid "for psychological and political as well as for practical and economic reasons." The common external tariff would also have a "unifying effect," and "be useful in GATT negotiations" (Camp 1964, 39). For the British, on the other hand, a customs union was problematic precisely because of the common external tariff, with the difficulties that this implied for maintaining Britain's traditional preferences vis-à-vis the Commonwealth. The second difference had to do with institutions. Following the collapse of the EDC, there was skepticism among several continental countries regarding the desirability of new supranational institutions, and indeed the word "supranational" was scrupulously avoided by Spaak in the course of the negotiations (Camp 1964, 41). On the other hand, the Six agreed that some new institutional structure was required, whereas the British favored continuing to work within the framework of the OEEC.

Eventually, in November 1955 the British withdrew from the Spaak Committee, and for the next two or three months displayed a hostile attitude toward the work of the Six. Telegrams were sent in November to both Germany and the US, attempting to dissuade them from supporting the common market project on the grounds that it would be both economically and politically divisive. Similar arguments were made at an informal meeting of OEEC delegates which had been convened by the British for the purpose—angering the governments of the Six (Schaad 1998, 44–45). The US made it clear to Britain that it did not approve of this attitude, and supported the creation of both EURATOM and a European common market. By January or February 1956, initial hostility was being replaced by a realization that the Six might well succeed in forming a customs union, and that Britain needed to find a way to work with it. However, Macmillan's attempts to sabotage the customs union project, and the fact that these had been abandoned largely because of US pressure, helped to create a climate of suspicion among the Six regarding British intentions, which made it much more difficult for Britain to achieve her subsequent objectives (Kaiser 1996, 91–92).

By the spring of 1956, concerns about the customs union project started to become more widespread within the OEEC, since it would be discriminatory. Furthermore, the success of the organization in dismantling quantitative restrictions on trade left low-tariff countries such as Denmark, Sweden, and Switzerland (as well as the Benelux countries) feeling that they were now at a competitive disadvantage vis-à-vis those countries that retained higher tariffs. This meant that they had an interest in securing lower tariffs independent of whatever the Six might agree amongst themselves. A Europe-wide free trade area was appealing to such countries. The notion of an OEEC-wide free trade area, incorporating the EEC, eventually became government policy in Britain in early 1956, where it was known as "Plan G."

Some British officials seem to have hoped that Plan G might undermine the customs union project by providing a more desirable means of expanding industrial exports to opponents of supranationalism in Germany, such as Ludwig Erhard, whose liberal instincts led him to favor as wide a free trade arrangement as possible. Whether this was the main motivation for the Plan G, or whether it was a reactive attempt to deal with the consequences of the customs union project in a way that minimized the negative consequences for British industry, and her relationships with the Commonwealth, is a matter of controversy (Kaiser 1996, Moravcsik 1998, Schaad 1998, Ellison 2000). The truth may have varied over time, but what mattered were European perceptions of British motivations, and here Macmillan's original hostility to the Messina process meant that key actors such as Spaak remained deeply suspicious of Plan G, even after the British government had come around to the view that it would be a complement to, rather than a substitute for, the EEC.

This British debate, however, should not obscure the fact that when the Spaak Committee reported in March, it also suggested that a customs union involving the Six could establish a free trade area with the other OEEC countries, and that other countries were also keen on a free trade area. In July 1956 the OEEC Council of Ministers therefore decided to set up a working party to study the possibility of an OEEC-wide free trade area including a customs union involving the Six. Among the issues which the working party had to consider was whether agriculture should be included in the proposed free trade area. Britain objected to this, given its ties with the Commonwealth, while other countries such as Denmark and the Netherlands strongly favored the inclusion of agriculture. Another interested party was Ireland, which would have benefited from being able to export agricultural goods to the rest of Western Europe. However, the Irish Department of Agriculture took a realistic view: "The deliberations of the Six have shown that if agriculture is to be included in a free trade area it would be preferable that this should be done on the basis of a Common Market under which essential safeguards such as harmonisation of agricultural policies, market organisation, etc, could be extended to meet the special problems of farmers" (Maher 1986, 55). Given that there was little prospect of Britain accepting such common policies, the Irish conclusion was that any European free trade area would necessarily involve industry only.

The British initially hoped that the European free trade area negotiations would take place simultaneously with those establishing the Common Market. Crucially, it soon became clear that the Six would push ahead with the negotiation and ratification of the Treaty of Rome, leaving serious discussion of a free trade area to later. This was due to the fear that the prospect of a European free trade area might undermine support for a common market, particularly in France and Germany (Camps 1964, 102).

Following the publication of the working party report in January 1957, the OEEC Council of Ministers decided in February to enter into negotiations regarding the establishment of a European Free Trade Area. Again, the British hoped for speedy negotiations so that the free trade area and the customs union might come into effect simultaneously, thus avoiding any trade discrimination within the OEEC. Again, the Six resisted any attempt to slow down the Treaty of Rome negotiations, or to change any of its provisions in order to accommodate the free trade area negotiations—despite the objections of Ludwig Erhard. The following month the Treaty of Rome was signed, and it was ratified by the French Assembly in July.

Trade liberalization within the EEC was now due to begin on 1 January 1959, which added a sense of urgency to the free trade area negotiations. In October 1957, the OEEC Council decided to establish the Maudling Committee in order to "secure the establishment of a European Free Trade Area which would comprise all Member countries of the Organisation; which would associate, on a multi-lateral basis, the European Economic Community with the other Member countries; and which, taking fully into consideration the objectives of the European Economic Community, would in practice take effect parallel with the Treaty of Rome" (Camps 1964, 135). This objective had the strong support not only of the "Other Six" but of Germany and the Benelux countries as well.

This placed France in a dilemma (Lynch 2000, Warlouzet 2008). From 1956 onward, the Algerian war had placed its government finances and balance of payments under pressure. France had not been particularly keen on trade liberalization to begin with, and these developments made it even less keen. On the other hand, it seemed clear that pressure for trade liberalization would grow in the years ahead, and in that context the EEC offered important economic as well as political advantages. Trade liberalization would be gradual; regard would be taken for the French concern that its industries would not be competing on an unfairly tilted playing field; and important side payments would be put in place, notably the Common Agricultural Policy and the European Development Fund which would provide money for French overseas territories. Crucially, the bargain involved trade liberalization first, and side payments later, which was one way of making sure that France would comply with its side of the bargain.

The free trade area contained all of the costs associated with trade liberalization, and none of the benefits. It thus had very little to offer the French government. Even worse, by providing German industry with an alternative way of expanding its exports, it might undercut German willingness to deliver on those aspects of the EEC bargain which were of particular interest to

France. The French were therefore hostile to the proposal from the beginning, but could not initially afford to torpedo it for fear of the international opprobrium, inside and outside the EEC, which this would entail.

However, from January 1958, the new EEC Commission, which had strong federalist sympathies, and wanted to avoid the EEC becoming a mere free trade area, emerged to become another force strongly opposed to the free trade area proposals. Even more importantly, a history of British diplomatic ineptness meant that France was not as isolated as it otherwise would have been. For example, the initial British insistence on excluding agriculture from the negotiations left it completely isolated among the 17. For Kaiser (1996), British diplomatic mistakes were crucial in explaining the failure of the free trade area negotiations. According to Ellison (2000), a key error was to not take sufficient account of other countries' interests in designing Plan G, with British policymakers being more focused on what was required in order to achieve domestic consensus. For Camps (1964), the key to explaining the eventual outcome was a determination among the Six to preserve their political unity. The accounts in Lynch (2000) and Warlouzet (2008), on the other hand, suggest a more fluid bargaining situation, in which the outcome might have been different almost until the very end. In October 1958, the EEC Council of Ministers agreed to a common approach on the free trade area, suggesting that free trade area participants agree to limit their external tariffs within a band on either side of the EEC's common external tariff. It took some adroit French diplomatic maneuvering, combined with a direct challenge by de Gaulle to Adenauer to demonstrate his commitment to the EEC by rejecting the free trade area, before the French were able to effectively veto it. Even still, the price they had to pay for German acquiescence was the restoration of French franc convertibility, which in turn required a rigorous French austerity plan, and a devaluation of the franc.

This, then, is one potential turning point in the history of European integration. If Britain had played its cards differently, might an OEEC-wide free trade area have come into being, and if so, might this have undermined the political consensus within the Six in favor of the EEC bargain?

EFTA and EC Enlargement

Almost immediately, discussions began in Geneva to see if it would be possible to salvage a smaller free trade area from the wreckage of the Maudling negotiations. The countries concerned were the "Other Six" and Portugal.[4] Formal negotiations began in June 1959, and the Stockholm Convention establishing the European Free Trade Area was signed in January 1960.

The Stockholm Convention committed member states to establish an industrial free trade area by 1970. It contained no commitments regarding trade barriers erected against third parties. It was and remains a purely intergovernmental organization, whose sole institution was a Council of Ministers which would meet only rarely, supported by a small secretariat. It thus reflected British preferences. The result was that the OEEC was now divided into three groups: the EEC, EFTA, and the rest (Greece, Iceland, Ireland, and Turkey). Greece and Turkey would soon seek associate membership of the EEC, while Ireland would establish a bilateral free trade agreement with the UK in 1965. Iceland joined EFTA in 1970.

The purpose of EFTA in the eyes of the British was not to serve as a permanent alternative to the EEC, but as a temporary bridge to it (Kaiser 1996, 101–107). On the one hand, the British hoped that by presenting a united front, the "Other Six" might maintain some cohesion, and avoid being "eaten up, one by one, by the Six," as Macmillan put it (101–2). Denmark in particular, with its heavy reliance on German as well as British markets, was seen as being potentially vulnerable to falling within the EEC orbit. Less defensively, the hope was also that the continuing importance of EFTA markets for German industry would lead that country to put pressure on its partners (that is, France) to agree to a trade agreement between the two blocs. EFTA was thus conceived of as a new tactic to achieve the British objective of a Europe-wide free trade area.

In the first year of its existence, therefore, EFTA was largely concerned with trying to relaunch Europe-wide discussions on free trade. These efforts came to naught, however. There followed one of the most startling reversals of policy in postwar European diplomatic history: Harold Macmillan's decision in July 1961 to apply for EEC membership. There were several reasons for this, and there is considerable debate as to which were most important. Urwin (1995, 117–120) lists three economic considerations. First, the UK traded more with the EEC than with EFTA, and in the absence of a wider free trade agreement EEC membership might be required in order to protect Britain's export trade there. Second, Commonwealth trade was becoming less important for the UK, as colonies achieved independence and opted to pursue inward-looking trade and development policies. Third, the EEC was at this stage experiencing a golden age of economic growth, which heightened the importance of its markets to Britain, and strengthened worries about British economic performance. The hope was that industrial competition with Germany would serve to improve productivity at home.

There were also important political considerations. Particularly important was the attitude of the US (Camps 1964, Kaiser 1996). Regional trade arrangements in Europe imposed a direct economic cost on the US, which the US was willing to pay if this were necessary in order to obtain moves toward European political integration. On the other hand, a European free trade area which did not involve supranational political elements offered economic costs, with no political benefits, and the same was true of EFTA. The US was therefore hostile to EFTA, while remaining strongly supportive of the EEC. Gradually, British policymakers began to realize that if they wished to retain a special relationship with the US, they would need to join the Common Market, rather than remaining aloof from it. For Camps this was "a very important—perhaps the controlling—element in Mr. Macmillan's own decision that the right course for the United Kingdom was to apply for membership" (Camps 1964, 336).

While the British may have been motivated by a mixture of economic and political considerations, Macmillan's decision to apply for EEC membership triggered three other applications that were clearly economically motivated. The British market was sufficiently important to Denmark, Ireland, and Norway that all three lodged membership applications to Brussels. As had been the case during the discussions about a European free trade area, there was a division of opinion between France and the other five EEC member states regarding the merits of these applications, and once again de Gaulle eventually vetoed the applications, in January 1963. The result was a sharp deterioration in relationships between France and her partners, and an equally sharp improvement in the functioning of EFTA, which decided to speed up the abolition of internal tariffs by three years. Britain's image in both Europe and the US improved sharply, and the independent nuclear deterrent was saved. As Kaiser (1996, 203) puts it, "At the diplomatic level . . . the failed application was a full success for the British government."

Why did de Gaulle veto British entry? As in the case of why the British decided to enter, and consistent with France's status as a former imperial power with aspirations to preserve its status on the world political scene, there is a debate about whether political or economic motivations dominated. On the face of it, the French decision seems surprising, since the Gaullists shared Britain's traditional skepticism regarding supranational institutions: the British would have been useful allies for them in that regard. Indeed, one factor which suggested to the British that 1961 was a good time to try to enter the EEC was precisely the fact that they might be able to work with de Gaulle and shape the evolution of the Community in a manner that would be to their liking.

Politically, the General was not anxious to see French influence within the EEC diminished in favor of Britain. On the contrary, viewing Europe as "a lever with which France could move the world," he had (unsuccessfully) attempted to negotiate an intergovernmental "union of European states" involving the Six, which would have been headquartered in Paris and promoted the development of a more independent European foreign and defense policy. Furthermore, de Gaulle shared Macmillan's view that the UK might serve as a Trojan horse representing US interests within the Community. Needless to say, he was as negative about this prospect as Macmillan was positive.

Moravcsik (1998, 2000) argues, to the contrary, that economic motives are key to understanding de Gaulle's veto. Crucial for French acceptance of the Treaty of Rome was the assurance that a Common Agricultural Policy would be set up providing French farmers with markets in Germany, as well as high prices. However, the precise details of this policy had not yet been settled, in particular the question of how it would be financed. De Gaulle's fear was that if the British entered the EEC before the final details of the CAP had been negotiated, France would not succeed in obtaining the favorable terms which she required. If France later relaxed its views on British entry, this was not just because the General was forced to resign in 1969, but because the CAP as we know it today had already been "locked in."

For whatever reason, the EC opened membership negotiations with Denmark, Ireland, Norway, and the UK in 1970.[5] The negotiations were concluded in January 1972, and the first enlargement of the EC took place a year later. However, it did not involve Norway, since that country's voters rejected EC membership in a referendum. Strikingly, the initial hopes that EFTA would facilitate the negotiation of a free trade area between the Six and the rest of Europe were realized at precisely the same time that Denmark and the UK quit the organization. By this stage EFTA was a fully functioning industrial free trade area, and it was generally accepted that the UK's former partners could not find themselves facing tariff barriers in Britain as a result of that country's joining the EC. The EC therefore negotiated separate free trade agreements, involving most industrial goods, with the remaining EFTA countries (Austria, Iceland, Norway, Portugal, Sweden, and Switzerland, as well as Finland). In this manner, EFTA fulfilled its historical purpose.

The focus of this chapter is on the early decades of the EC, so I will now be brief. Greece joined the Community in 1981, after two decades as an associate member. Five years later, Portugal and Spain followed suit. On the other hand, Greenland left the EC in 1985, following a referendum in 1982.

However, 1985 also saw a major breakthrough with the adoption of the Single European Act, which envisaged the creation of a true single market by the end of 1992. The SEA marked an important shift toward supranational decision-making, since it extended the scope of qualified majority voting within the Council of Ministers, thus speeding up decision-making. There followed a major burst of activity by the Commission and the member states, sweeping away many obstacles to a single market. This soon prompted a reaction by EFTA member states, which feared being left at a competitive disadvantage in the new single European market. In 1989, Austria applied for EC member-ship, and officials from the two blocs started negotiating a European Economic Area which would enable EFTA member states to benefit from the EC single market while remaining outside the Community. In this way, the EC could be deepened without the difficulties of enlargement.

The ploy was not successful. In order to benefit from the single market, EFTA countries had to accept EC legislation affecting it, with the EC Court of Justice providing legal arbitration. What had been designed as an alterna-tive to EC membership became a waiting room: of the six EFTA members in 1986, Austria, Norway, Sweden, and Finland all decided that EC membership was preferable. (The issue became moot in Switzerland when a referendum rejected EEA membership in 1992.) If it had not been for Liechtenstein join-ing in 1991, and Norway's voters rejecting EC membership for a second time the following year, EFTA would have been reduced to a rump of just two countries.

The next wave of accessions came as a result of the collapse of the Iron Curtain. Once again, the attractions of the EC's single market, its regional policies, and the promise of political stability which EC membership held out were irresistible for the newly liberated countries of Eastern Europe. Despite great hesitation among the more federal-minded Western Europeans, they were eventually admitted, along with Malta and Cyprus, in 2004 and 2007.

Why the EU Won, and Lessons for Asia

There was nothing inevitable about the development of supranational institu-tions in Europe. Any complete account of the history of postwar European integration would have to consider the role of chance and contingency, as well as the governments and individuals who were involved in the negotiations at the time. For example, it was surely significant that Christian Democrats were in government in all six founding member states during 1950-1952. This transnational network "fulfilled multiple functions, not least creating political trust, deliberating policy, especially on European integration, marginalising internal dissent within the national parties, socialising new members into an existing policy consensus, coordinating government policy-making and facilitating Parliamentary ratification of integration treaties. These and other functions together provided crucial guarantees for the exercise of what political scientists have called entrepreneurial leadership by politicians like Robert Schuman and Konrad Adenauer, for example, by limiting their domestic political risks in a decisive way to facilitate bold and at times extremely controversial policy choices." In turn, these choices reflected a common project of middle-class Catholic elites "for creating an integrated Europe based on a curious mélange of traditional confessional notions of occidental culture and anti-communism and broadly liberal economic ideas" (Kaiser 2007, 9-10).

One can also speculate about whether France would really have signed up to the EEC had de Gaulle been in power between 1955 and 1957—given his statements at the time, one would have to doubt this. Nor would the EEC project have passed in France if the Mendès-France government had not fallen in 1955, to be replaced by a government which included more "pro-European" members such as Robert Schuman. There was a crucial window of opportunity, which was exploited to the full.

Nonetheless, various structural features of postwar Europe help explain the supranational choices that were made during the 1950s. Trade was an essential component of postwar European growth strategies, and regional trade agreements were a way of speeding liberalization in the context of a fragmented world economy. In devising such agreements, politicians had to wrestle with a number of difficulties.

First, agriculture would have to be included in any free trade agreement, if the agreement were to be of interest to countries such as France and the Netherlands. This required a European agricultural policy which would replicate the extremely interventionist policies which already existed at the national level. Institutions would need to be devised, therefore, which would set minimum prices, organize the disposal of surplus output, insulate Community markets from those of the outside world, and so on. The small secretariat which EFTA established in Geneva would not have been sufficient for this purpose. Even more importantly, decision-making rules would be required to reach agreement on what were bound to be divisive issues, or alternatively decision-making authority would have to be delegated to some supranational body such as the Commission.

Second, in developing free trade arrangements it was essential that the domestic social welfare systems which underpinned governments' political legitimacy as well as their economic growth strategies not be undermined by the development of Europe-wide free trade. Would firms in high tax jurisdictions be placed at an unfair disadvantage vis-à-vis their competitors in more liberal jurisdictions? As Milward puts it (2000, 216), "The problem genuinely was how to construct a commercial framework which would not endanger the levels of social welfare which had been reached. . . . The Treaties of Rome had to be also an external buttress to the welfare state."

Third, as we have seen, the Dutch insisted that the Treaties incorporate a built-in and irreversible schedule of tariff reductions, since as Beyen argued "tariffs would not be lowered except by a supranational authority which had been set up to enforce a preordained, irrevocable course of action" (ibid., 187). The experience of EFTA suggests that this was not in fact the case, a point which EFTA's supporters made frequently during the 1960s. On the other hand, getting the Nordics and Britain to liberalize was one thing, getting the French to liberalize was perhaps another. The difficulties in achieving APEC's Bogor Goals suggest that in certain circumstances, ex ante commitments to achieving regional free trade are not sufficient to guarantee its realization. In any event, what mattered was that key policymakers in the Six agreed with Beyen's assessment.

Fourth, the fact that the commitment to free trade had to be irreversibly locked in had further consequences for the negotiations: "had it been possible for France to commit itself only to the first four-year stage (of tariff cuts) and then, if it wished, withdraw, the fears that the tax, social security and wage burden on French manufacturing costs would remain much higher than in Germany would not have had to be translated into demands for prior harmonisation and these into the beginnings of a European Community social policy" (ibid., 210). Even more important, perhaps, since we are still waiting for such a social policy, were the side payments made to France in exchange for her agreeing to an irreversible schedule of tariff liberalization, notably the Common Agricultural Policy. A big problem from a French point of view was that whereas the liberalization schedule was explicit, the clauses in the Treaty relating to the CAP were vague. The key French focus in EC negotiations during the 1960s was thus to secure access to German and other markets for her farmers, on favorable financial terms.

For Moravcsik (1998, 2000) this was why the French eventually supported delegating agricultural policies to the supranational Commission in Brussels. This would lock in the benefits of the CAP, preventing German or eventually British policymakers from diluting it. This is one example of his more general thesis that the purpose of supranational political institutions was to prevent countries from later reneging on those parts of international agreements which they found most unappealing. Whereas earlier theories of European integration suggested that policymakers were not always fully aware of the long-run consequences of their actions, such as the decision to set up a supranational Court of Justice answerable to no one but itself, for Moravcsik the irreversible nature of such decisions was the whole point. Thus, in negotiating the Treaty of Rome, countries attempted to pool or delegate sovereignty, that is to render decision-making supranational, where they had vital interests that were not necessarily shared by their partners.

Such an economistic account can help to explain the supranational choices made by the Six, and economics can also help explain why the EC eventually sucked in most of the rest of Europe, despite the instinctive dislike of supranational institutions across much of the continent (Baldwin 2003, 2004). The EEC accounted for no less than 59% of Western European GDP in 1957 (Maddison 2003), and economic growth was more rapid among the Six than in Britain. As soon as the Six started to liberalize internally, British manufacturers feared that they would be left at a disadvantage. When the initial preferred solution of a Europe-wide free trade area failed, Britain eventually decided to apply. This inevitably led to the applications of Denmark, Ireland, and Norway, which could not afford to find themselves discriminated against in the British market. The other EFTA members had always wished to achieve a free trade agreement with the Six, again for reasons of trade discrimination (this was particularly true of Austria), and were able to finally achieve this with the enlargement of the EC in the early 1970s, by pointing to their pre-existing EFTA relationship with the UK. Fear of trade discrimination was clearly important in motivating Austrian and Nordic applications to the EC in the late 1980s and early 1990s, with the Single European Act providing the spur which initial moves to cut tariffs had done in the British case in the early 1960s. This domino effect, as Baldwin terms it, clearly does well in explaining the motivations of the smaller countries, where the low politics of commercial advantage were predominant.

As we have seen, there is a debate about whether commercial considerations also fully explain the motivations of Britain, which along with France maintained the aspiration to play a leading role on the world stage, and did not have the luxury of regarding Europe's security architecture as exogenous. A considerable literature argues that the primary purpose of European supranational institutions was to permit the re-emergence of German heavy industry and military power, both of which were essential to the West as it waged the Cold War, without this threatening the security of Germany's European neighbors. The ECSC and abortive EDC can both be seen in this light, as well as EURATOM: according to Adenauer, "A German attempt at a national nuclear production would be met with the greatest mistrust abroad."[6] Even the EEC could be rationalized as a way of tying an increasingly economically powerful Germany into a common European framework.

While social scientists enjoy such stark oppositions as "economics versus geopolitics," historians are probably more comfortable inhabiting a world in which multiple motivations may matter at different levels of the political process. Fortunately, the purpose of this paper is not to adjudicate between such alternatives, but to see what, if any, are the lessons for Asia. The lessons all seem to point in the same direction.

As pointed out in the introduction, Asia is a vastly bigger and more diverse continent than Europe. This of itself would seem to rule out European-style supranational institutions for the immediate future, at least for the continent as a whole. But the historical context is also completely different. Asia is not a declining giant which feels the need to unite against rising threats from the rest of the world, but home to the two undisputed rising giants of the 21st century, China and India. It is hard to see either of these surrendering much sovereignty, except in the context of tightly defined economic bargains bringing benefits to both parties.

Furthermore, the economic context is completely different today. Countries like China do not have modern European style welfare states, and the question of how to reconcile these welfare states with increasing levels of trade is hardly going to prompt a search for pan-Asian social policies. Nor is it going to be necessary, one supposes, to develop an Asian Common Agricultural Policy in order to deepen regional trade integration. Even more importantly, regional trade integration has already occurred, in the industrial sphere, with the development of "Factory Asia" exporting into a largely liberalized global economy. No need for supranational institutions there.

Initiatives such as the Chiang Mai Initiative may prove very beneficial to the region but do not require much in the way of supranational institutions. As noted earlier, international financial cooperation via the IMF has not required global supranational institutions either. The reason that trade integration required such institutions in Europe, it has been argued here, is that the decision to liberalize trade required a series of inter-related bargains, on such sensitive subjects as agricultural policy, which would have broken down in the absence of such institutions. Even more fundamentally, issues like agricultural or social or regional policy could not be delegated to independent bodies like the European Central Bank—these are political issues, requiring European political decision-making structures.

The discussion thus far has been positive rather than normative. European supranationalism was facilitated by a set of unique historical, geographical, and economic circumstances. Their absence in the Asian context may indeed mean that similar developments are unlikely there. However, geopolitical and security considerations suggest that closer political cooperation in the region would be extremely beneficial. Asia and the world as a whole have a mutual interest in avoiding the type of international struggle that has typically taken place in the transition from one geopolitical equilibrium to another. Regional institutions, however modest, encouraging dialogue and cooperation have a valuable role to play in this regard.

Notes

1. Dent (2010).

2. In discussing postwar European history, I will tend to use "Western Europe" to refer to those parts of Europe west of the Iron Curtain, as is common practice—despite the fact that as alluded to earlier, "Western Europe" is in a long-run historical perspective a rather broader concept.

3. Initially, Germany was represented at the OEEC by two delegations representing the Anglo-American Bizone, as well as the French occupied zone. There were thus 18 participants, rather than 17, in the original OEEC. In 1949, the British, French, and American occupation zones were merged to form the Federal Republic of Germany, henceforth referred to for simplicity as "Germany." In addition, that portion of the Free Territory of Trieste which was under Anglo-American control also participated in the organization, until it was handed back to Italy in 1954.

4. Finland was also involved in the discussions. However, the latter state was not even a member of the OEEC, and given its relationship with the Soviet Union would have to content itself with associate membership of EFTA, beginning in 1961.

5. The four countries had submitted membership applications in 1967, and had again been vetoed by de Gaulle. On this occasion, however, their applications had remained dormant, rather than being withdrawn.

6. Cited in Eilstrup-Sangiovanni and Verdier (2005, 108).

7

Economic Crises and Regional Institutions

C. RANDALL HENNING

Introduction

Regionalist movements are intimately connected to economic and financial crises. Most of the financial crises of the last four decades have had a strong regional dimension. We identify them as the "Latin American debt crisis," the "European currency crisis," and the "Asian financial crisis" because their impact has been geographically concentrated. Crises call into question the adequacy of multilateral arrangements for prevention and stabilization and, under certain circumstances, galvanize support for proposals to strengthen regional agreements and institutions. Once in place, regional arrangements can shield countries against the adverse effects of global financial turbulence, if they are well designed.

Our understanding of regionalism would benefit from more systematic analysis of its relationship to crises. This chapter examines the extent to which economic crises help or hinder the development of more effective regional institutions and addresses the determinants of institutional evolution and design in the Asian region. First, it conducts a structured comparison of the most important region-wide crises over the last four decades and their impact on regional institutions. By asking similar questions in each case, we can draw generalizations about the conditions that are conducive and averse to institutional building. Second, the chapter elaborates on aspects of cases that speak to key points in the present Asian discourse on regional institutions. While considering a common set of factors, the treatment here will sometimes explore instructive aspects of cases even when they might not fit with a common template.

After comparing these crises, the chapter concludes that five conditions are especially important in facilitating a constructive regional response to a crisis: a significant degree of regional economic interdependence (market integration); an independent secretariat or intergovernmental body charged with cooperation; webs of interlocking economic agreements; and, as elements of the multilateral context, conflict with the relevant international organization (such as the IMF) and acceptance by the United States of regional integration. These findings are further supported by the European sovereign debt crisis more recently. The chapter does not argue that regional movements can only be generated by crises, but that these conditions are conducive to institution building in response to them. Asian regionalism would be favored in the future by shocks that are external to the region, rather than coming from a member state, and responses from multilateral institutions that are averse to Asian preferences. Asian regionalists would be well served by using crises to ratchet up governments' commitments to secretariats and intergovernmental bodies, establishing linkages among economic issue areas, and forging cooperation with multilateral institutions.

The following section discusses the nature and definition of "crisis" and "institution," central concepts in this study. The third section addresses the causal links between crises and institution building, as well as the factors that condition regions' responses to crises. The fourth section presents five crisis cases. The fifth section draws conclusions from the comparison of cases and identifies conditions favoring further institution-building in Asia and strategies that advocates of Asian regionalism might adopt.

Defining the Concepts

The Oxford English Dictionary's first definition of "crisis" is "a time of intense difficulty or danger." Original usage in English meant "a time of decision" and has evolved toward "an emergency requiring decision." The concept is employed widely, though inconsistently, in comparative politics, international relations, and political science generally. (See, for example, Allison and Zelikow 1999, as well as Phillips and Rimkunas 1978; Svensson 1986; Goertz 2006.) General modern English usage coincides with our current use with respect to economics and finance: *an economic or financial emergency that requires a rapid policy response.*

In practice, this label applies to major declines in the value of national currencies and financial assets, the bankruptcy of financial institutions, collapse of financial markets, and macroeconomic recessions or depressions. The Latin

American debt crisis of the 1980s, European exchange rate crisis of 1992–93, Mexican peso crisis of 1994–95, Asian financial crisis of 1997–98 fall under this definition. Also falling under this definition are major shifts in currency values and conflicts over payments balances and macroeconomic adjustment, such as the "Nixon shock" of 1971, and major shifts in commodity prices and supply, such as the "oil shocks" of the last four decades. Each of these events forced decisions by governments that had ramifications for international cooperation, including cooperation on a regional basis.

Crises are characterized by phases. First, crises are preceded by periods of normality, an equilibrium during which economies and the political relationships among actors and institutions are relatively stable. Tranquility nonetheless masks the gradual buildup of debt, for example, that becomes ultimately unsustainable. Second, the acute phase is initiated by a spark that triggers a cascading series of events, such as collapse in financial markets. Third, policymakers struggle to respond, during which time they might broker or be subject to realignments in international and domestic politics. Fourth, the crisis is resolved and the political economy returns to a new and usually different equilibrium—until the next crisis occurs. (Compare to Gourevitch's [1983] staging of crises, pp, 21–22, and Frieden's [1991] stylized evolution of crisis politics, pp. 35–38.) Construction of regional institutions could occur during the response phase or in the new equilibrium.

Consider now the concept of "institutions" somewhat more carefully. The notion is defined differently across the various subfields of political science and economics.[1] The definition chosen for this chapter, guided by the overall purpose of the book, is broad but not all encompassing. The term "institution" is employed here to include *(a) explicit, formal commitments and organizations and (b) common processes and informal networks among governments that facilitate cooperation*. The term can thus refer to ASEAN+3, the Chiang Mai Initiative, or Economic and Monetary Union, as well as regular official meetings, peer review, and surveillance processes. The concept is broader than simply a formal regional bureaucracy but not so broad as to include norms and expectations. Nor does the term include private-sector networks and transnational political and technocratic alliances.

Crises as Catalyst for Regional Institutions

Consider next the reasons we might expect crises to stimulate national governments to construct regional institutions and the background conditions that explain why some regions respond to crises in this way while other regions do not.

Causal Links

If crises are exceptional moments of political realignment and policy shift that can be institutionalized in bargains and arrangements that define a new, durable equilibrium, what, precisely, are the *mechanisms* of the change with respect to regional institutions? In principle, we can posit several causal channels.

1. Political demand. Crises give rise to demands for state action to protect corporations, banks, private sector groups, and social groups from economic dislocation. These demands operate through domestic politics, but satisfying them is sometimes more effective when coordinated regionally, which regional institutions facilitate.

2. Preference reshuffling. Crises can change the material bases of domestic coalitions; destruction of wealth and shifts in competitiveness empower some firms and sectors and weaken others. When these shifts motivate or empower transregional groups, they promote cooperation. When crises affect states within a region similarly—which is not always the case—that can foster cooperation through the convergence of preferences. Crises can raise regional cooperation higher on the political agenda of national leaders.

3. Political realignment and regime transformation. Crises can stimulate the realignment of domestic social groups (Gourevitch 1983) and transform domestic political regimes. Sometimes, such changes can make governments more predisposed to trade off national autonomy for the benefits of regional cooperation. Crises sometimes stimulate transitions to democracy (Haggard 2000), and democracies might be more inclined to international cooperation.

4. Network reinforcement. Crises stimulate communication, discourse, and negotiation among government officials and international civil servants within a region, reinforcing elite intergovernmental networks that can support regional integration in a subsequent stage (Calder and Ye 2010).

5. Leader agency. Whereas in normal circumstances, heads of government and their ministers will often be beholden to important constituencies and pressure groups, crises alter the constraints upon them. Crises typically impose strong financial and economic constraints that limit the policy options of governments. By discrediting some ministries and agencies and by forcing quick, unpleasant choices, however, crises can liberate leaders from interest-group and bureaucratic politics-as-usual, temporarily giving them more political room for maneuver.[2]

Two frequent candidates have not been included in this list: ideational convergence and power shift. One might be tempted to argue that crises stimulate reassessment of policies and institutions leading to a convergence of analytical beliefs and frameworks that facilitate institutionalization. More often, in my observation, crises generate vigorous debate over causes and widen, rather than narrow, the range of alternative views.

One might also hypothesize that, when they affect countries differently, crises can alter the relative power position of states within a region. The Asian financial crisis of 1997–1998 shifted influence within East Asia away from Japan and toward China, for example (Pempel 1999: 228–232). However, this effect is almost always a temporary acceleration or retardation of an underlying structural trend. Rapid changes in relative power positions can discourage institutionalization because the ascendant state will anticipate a more favorable institutional bargain if it defers agreement.

Background Conditions

Crises are not the only or necessarily even primary determinants of regional institution building. They occur against the background of existing circumstances which configure a region's predilection toward regionalism. Moreover, crises cannot stimulate institution building directly; instead, national officials, international civil servants and pre-existing regional forums construct them. These officials in turn exercise partially independent choice, agency. Whether any given crisis generates institution building thus depends on a set of third variables.

The various approaches to regional integration—neofunctionalism, institutionalism, realism, constructivism, and domestic politics and epistemic approaches—would each advance candidates for this set.[3] Those candidates include pre-existing regional institutions, intergovernmental and transnational networks, norms, ideas, regional dominance, intra-regional rivalry, linkages to political integration, security externalities, and geopolitics. In previous work, I have stressed the role of institutions and preferences in the context of multilateral arrangements. The source of the shock (whether internal or external to the region) and the response of the multilateral regime strongly condition the regional response to crisis and conflict.[4]

Drawing on several of these theoretical perspectives, we can expect that a crisis will stimulate the building of common institutions within a region in the presence of:

1. a secretariat that is charged with fostering cooperation;
2. substantially integrated markets for goods, services and capital;[5]

3. functional linkages to pre-existing agreements in related economic areas;[6]

4. a single dominant country within the region;

5. preferences that conflict with the relevant multilateral institution; and

6. a benign posture toward regionalism on the part of the United States.

Conversely, in the absence of these background conditions, we would not expect crises to produce institution building.

Alternative Outcomes

There is no a priori reason to expect that crises cannot also weaken or destroy regional institutions, just as they might national or multilateral institutions. The 1992–1993 crisis in the Exchange-Rate Mechanism of the European Monetary System witnessed the ejection of the British pound and the Italian lira from the regime and a formal widening of the bands of exchange rate fluctuation. A constructive response by European governments, though ultimately forthcoming, was by no means inevitable. In the absence of these background conditions, counterfactually, we might have observed subsequent institutional *decay*.

To list the set of possible outcomes comprehensively, we must acknowledge that it is also possible in principle that a crisis might have *no effect* on regional institutions. One variation on this outcome would be an apparent effect that proves transitory, leaving the degree of institutionalization unchanged in the long term. "No effect" can be treated as the null hypothesis and the cases of crises can be used to test whether outcomes differ substantially from it and, if so, in which direction.

Finally, in cases where crises contribute to the creation or strengthening of regional institutions, we would expect this to apply primarily to a specific set of institutions—those that provide defenses against crises or the means to manage them. In response to a balance-of-payments crisis, for example, we might expect states to create balance-of-payments financing facilities and bodies and processes to activate them—not free trade areas, customs unions, or other regional arrangements unrelated to the crisis. We expect the functional form of the crisis to dictate the type of institutional response.

Cases of Crises and Regional Responses

Consider now the prominent cases of economic and financial crisis in the last four decades. We begin with the treatment of Europe and the process of monetary integration, which was punctuated by a number of crises over the span of several decades. We then consider specific crises and responses, beginning with the Latin American debt crisis of the 1980s, then the Mexican peso crisis of 1994–1995, the Asian financial crisis of 1997–1998, and the Asian dimension of the 2007–2009 crisis.

European Monetary Integration

A substantial literature addresses the political economy of exchange-rate stabilization, macroeconomic convergence, and the creation of the euro. Authors emphasize various factors as the driving force for European monetary integration: integration of markets, German dominance, domestic politics, intergovernmentalism, linkage politics, institutions, economic ideology, geopolitics and political integration.[7] My own contribution emphasizes the international monetary system and disturbances transmitted through it as the context for monetary integration. This approach gives pride of place to conflicts between Europe and the United States over exchange rates, the balance of payments and macroeconomic adjustment as incentives for European cooperation (Henning 1998). Because several of these episodes were full-blown crises, a review of that approach is suitable here.

International monetary conflict and turbulence provides strong incentives for groupings of vulnerable states to consider regional monetary cooperation in order to create an "island of monetary stability." Regional arrangements help countries limit the shifts in intra-regional exchange rates, deflect pressure for policy adjustments, and perhaps even exercise countervailing pressure on a dominant state outside the region. Beginning in the 1960s, the United States ran large current account deficits during several episodes, pressured the governments of surplus countries to stimulate their economies, and encouraged depreciation of the dollar in order to persuade them to comply and otherwise achieve adjustment. Confronted by the appreciation of their currencies, the surplus countries, which frequently included Germany, could expect a drop in exports, growth, and employment—which reinforced U.S. demands for macroeconomic stimulus.[8]

In the teeth of the conflict, European governments parried, deflected, but ultimately often accommodated U.S. pressures for macroeconomic adjustment. The recurrence of U.S. pressures and international monetary instability sustained the interest on the part of targets, which often included Germany, in developing regional arrangements as defensive mechanisms. After periods of transatlantic monetary conflict, therefore, Europe responded with initiatives for currency cooperation. Conversely, during periods of transatlantic monetary tranquility, the impetus for monetary integration tended to flag.

The historical narrative, in brief, begins with the Bretton Woods regime, the context for the origins of the European Community. Because that regime stabilized European cross rates at the same time that it stabilized European currencies against the dollar, monetary matters were virtually off the agenda of early European integration. As the Bretton Woods regime experienced a succession of currency crises in the 1960s and then collapsed altogether in the early 1970s, however, the Europeans developed plans for currency cooperation. If the Bretton Woods regime had remained intact, European governments would not have sought regional exchange rate stabilization.

As much of the rest of the world went to flexible exchange rates during the 1970s, Europe experimented with the "snake." Conflict with the Carter administration during 1977–78 persuaded German Chancellor Helmut Schmidt and French President Valéry Giscard d'Estaing of the benefits of tightening the European monetary regime. They thus created the European Monetary System (EMS) in 1979. Conflicts with the United States during the Plaza and Louvre accords in the mid-1980s and during 1990 and 1991 helped to reinforce the process leading to the Maastricht treaty.[9] (We consider subsequent episodes in the sections below.) Exchange rate and balance of payments crises were thus integral to the process of European monetary integration.

There were large and sometimes heated conflicts among countries within the region, of course. Member states exhibited considerable variation in their macroeconomic preferences and disagreements over the direction and design of common monetary arrangements. Germany was famously devoted to monetary orthodoxy and fiscal conservatism to restrain inflation while benefiting from external demand and export-led growth. France and Italy pursued monetary and fiscal activism in efforts to sustain domestic demand and employment. Conflicts with the United States served to highlight the benefits to macroeconomic convergence in Europe as a route to monetary integration.[10] U.S.-generated disturbances did not extinguish intra-European disputes, but they increased the payoff to intra-European accommodation.

Conflict and crises were not the only important factors, of course. Three background conditions were particularly important also. First, Europe had a substantial degree of intra-regional market integration. In the mid-1970s, intra-European exports were about 45 percent of total European exports and about 8 to 9 percent of European GDP. Cross-rate shifts could therefore disrupt a significant amount of trade and investment. Second, Europe had a set of common policies with respect to agriculture, trade, competition, development, and structural cohesion and was almost continuously negotiating enlargement of its membership. Political and institutional linkages among these policies facilitated a regional response to crises. Third, the institutional structure of the European Community had established forums for ministers and heads of government, regularized meetings among them, a committee of central bank officials responsible for operating currency arrangements, and a Commission with strong bureaucratic incentives to further integration.

For crises to have a sustained effect on regional integration, member states must not abandon post-crisis monetary arrangements during periods of tranquility. By creating organizational actors and political bargains, governments institutionalize the lessons of earlier conflicts regionally. With institutions in place, and the analytical capacity and institutional memory they provide, each successive external shock raises the expectation on the part of vulnerable states that similar shocks will occur in the future. Defensive arrangements set in place after previous episodes, moreover, alter the set of choices available to small states when responding to subsequent episodes, creating path dependency. Within a semi-institutionalized region, states have a better platform on which to bolster cooperation after each international monetary crisis, as opposed to allowing it to decay between disturbances. Over successive crises, this can produce an upward ratcheting of regional integration.

Aspirations for political union, by contrast, were not decisive in producing monetary union in Europe. This link is widely asserted in public commentary and some parts of the literature on the European economic integration. EMU, in particular, is frequently cited as the product of widely shared political ambition for something akin to a United States of Europe. (See, for example, Eichengreen 1992.) Because this argument carries negative implications for the possibility of integration in other regions, it deserves brief attention here. While commitment to political integration played a role, however, it has been substantially over-rated by some analysts.

Over the course of postwar history, first of all, economic projects for European integration have consistently received greater support than projects for political and security cooperation. Proposals for European Defense Community and European Political Community failed in the 1950s, for example, while the European Economic Community succeeded. (See, for example, Dinan 2004.) To choose a contemporary example, the constitutional treaty would have gone some distance toward political integration, but it failed to secure support in critical referenda in France and the Netherlands. The

Lisbon treaty preserves many of its institutional provisions but falls decidedly short of constituting a political union (Reh 2009).

Second, while it is true that war in Western Europe has become "unthinkable," it has been "unthinkable" for quite some time, at least the 1960s and 1970s if not before. European integration has continued far beyond the point where interstate violence was a conceivable threat. Finally, ambitions for political union do not easily explain the successive enlargements of the membership. Britain, Ireland, and Denmark did not join the European Community because they wanted to participate in an ever closer political union. Many of the nineteen countries that have been inducted into the European Union in successive enlargements since then are similarly reticent. Indeed, the greater number and diversity of member states spawned by enlargements have created substantial barriers to political deepening. For these reasons among others, many political scientists conclude that the political-unity motive is a contributing but distinctly secondary motivation for European integration.[11]

Latin American Debt Crisis of the 1980s

At the outset of the Latin American crisis, in August 1982, an analyst might have been forgiven for anticipating a shock of that magnitude to provoke a substantial regional response. Latin America had many of the qualities that might have been expected to favor regionalism. Relative to other regions, including Europe, it had cultural and linguistic homogeneity. Its members largely shared the state-led development strategy of import-substitution industrialization. The Economic Commission for Latin America and the Caribbean (ECLAC), based in Santiago, Chile, had established itself as an informal regional secretariat. Structural economics, developed by Raúl Prebisch as ECLAC's director in the late 1940s and early 1950s, and then dependency theory was widely shared as an economic ideology, one that fostered regional integration as an alternative to market-friendly multilateral trade liberalization. The debt crisis struck nearly all of the members of the region—their interests converged as debtors—and most were similarly antagonized by the policies of the United States and the International Monetary Fund. Yet, the region's response was less integrative, not more, than the responses of Europe and East Asia to their crises.

A broad range of regional, subregional, and cross-regional institutions underpinned Latin America's tradition of regionalism prior to the crisis. At the broadest level, the Organization of American States (OAS) and the Inter-American Development Bank (IDB) were both headquartered in Washington,

D.C. At the subregional level, the Central American Common Market, Andean Community, and Caribbean Community, among others, predated the debt crisis.[12] Each subregional group created a development bank to supplement the work of the IDB and World Bank. These supplemented clearing and settlement systems that had been created to facilitate intraregional trade. For liquidity and balance of payments support, the least developed area of regional financial cooperation, the Central American Monetary Stabilization Fund and the Andean Reserve Fund had been established.

As Titelman (2006) reports, the crisis undermined most of these regional institutions, hitting clearing and settlement systems hardest and the subregional development banks as well. The Andean Reserve Fund (ARF) lent substantially more to the Andean countries during 1983–1989 than the IMF lent under exceptional financing arrangements. The ARF, which became the Latin American Reserve Fund (LARF) with the accession of Costa Rica in 1989, thus later inspired proposals for its expansion (Agosin 2001 and Ocampo 2002). While its financing might have been significant among its particular members, the ARF was a small player in the larger debt crisis and in the event did not leverage the crisis into greater capital commitments or institutional strengthening. The debt crisis also weakened most of the subregional trade agreements, with the exception of the creation of an agreement between Brazil and Argentina that laid the basis for Mercosur's establishment in 1991.[13]

A small literature inspired by the prospect of a "debtors cartel" was an exception to the general absence of political economy studies of the regional response to the debt crisis. The logic behind a debtors' cartel was clear: the crisis was not simply a matter of illiquidity; some degree of debt reduction was also necessary. Individually, countries would not opt for or demand debt reduction, as this would place them at a disadvantage in capital markets; but together debtors could have greater bargaining leverage vis à vis creditors and would be less likely to be blacklisted from future borrowing. In the event, most debtors did not make true transfers of resources back to creditors; with the exception of Mexico, Venezuela, and Ecuador, debtors made repayments from loan rollovers (Lindert 1989 in Eichengreen and Lindert 1989). But each debtor chose to negotiate individually with creditors rather than collectively; debt reduction was effectively accomplished in an ad hoc, uncoordinated, non-transparent fashion across the region.

The failure of the debtors' cartel was due to several factors. First, despite being similarly affected by the crisis, the economic situations of the debtors differed enough to lead some to conclude that they could get better terms by negotiating directly rather than through a cartel. Second, the international banks were implacably hostile to any arrangement that accepted transparent, ex ante debt reduction. Third, low rates of domestic savings and low foreign exchange reserve holdings rendered Latin American debtors crucially dependent on capital inflows and thus on appeasing the banks. Fourth, U.S. policymakers, concerned most for the stability of the banking system, sided firmly with the banks—at least until the threat to systemic stability had passed. (On the failure of the debtors' cartel, see Hojman 1987; Kugler 1987; and Lissakers 1991: 198–204. On U.S. policy, see Cohen 1992.)

The debtors' cartel concept was a narrow regional proposal, one with clear zero-sum distributional consequences. What explains the failure of other regional initiatives, ones that would not have so obviously harmed the interests of powerful private actors, to emerge? There are several plausible answers. First, regional and subregional institutions, which antedated the crisis, did not have the staff, financial resources, or legal mandate that would have enabled them to leverage the crisis into greater delegation from member states. Second, regional trade agreements were not developed to the point where their disruption could inflict major economic pain in member countries. Regional exports relative to total exports dropped from above 22 percent in 1980 to less than 12 percent in 1985—the largest five-year decline in any of the major regions of the postwar period. But these numbers represented only 3.6 and 1.7 percent of regional GDP, respectively, apparently below the threshold for provoking a regional response. Third, more influential in this region than any other, the United States was not particularly inclined toward Latin American regionalism. "U.S. governments have felt deep ambivalence about supporting a more fully institutionalized regionalism that other states might use as a shield against the United States," Katzenstein (2005, 226–227) writes. "The inter-American system was never based on a congruence of interests that might have supported the growth of regional political institutions."

NAFTA and the Mexican Peso Crisis of 1994–1995

The North American Free Trade Agreement (NAFTA) and the peso crisis of 1994–95 were intimately connected. In anticipation of entering into force of the agreement, multinational corporations and institutional fund managers invested more into Mexico than any other emerging market country in the early 1990s. But NAFTA did not provide for the policy adjustments that would have been necessary to prevent the crisis nor the financial facilities necessary to deal with it once it occurred. The United States responded instead with a large bilateral ad hoc package through the Exchange Stabilization Fund in concert with financing from the International Monetary Fund (IMF) in early 1995.[14] This case is an instance in which a crisis certainly failed to strengthen regional institutions and, if anything, probably weakened the prospects for creating robust ones.

NAFTA is in essence a free trade agreement coupled with some liberalizing investment provisions. It is not a customs union or single market and contains little in the way of regulatory cooperation. It has no provision for currency stabilization, monetary cooperation, fiscal coordination, or development assistance. The Federal Reserve negotiated a currency swap agreement with the Bank of Mexico in conjunction with the Bank of Canada as an adjunct to NAFTA that was quickly overwhelmed during the 1994–95 crisis. NAFTA contained side agreements on labor and environment, of course, as well as established processes for settling dispute in various issue areas. The agreement also created the North American Development Bank, a NAFTA Commission, and a NAFTA Secretariat. But these institutions exist in name only; they are underfunded and nearly invisible in policymaking surrounding trade and investment in North America.[15] Instead, as Hufbauer and Schott (2005) observe, NAFTA and the European Union are "polar opposites" in institutional terms.

NAFTA therefore lacked the surveillance capacity at the regional level to anticipate and head off the financial crisis. There was growing consternation with the U.S. Treasury department over the overvaluation of the Mexican peso and efforts to persuade the Mexican finance ministry to address it. But NAFTA placed Mexico under no obligation in this respect and provided no institutional "hook" for the US administration vis à vis the Mexican government. In political terms, this lacuna was important. NAFTA presented the most serious and long-fought debate in the United States over trade policy since the Second World War. Though currency matters were missing from the debate, the bilateral exchange rate bore directly on the issues that were discussed: trade, outsourcing, and employment. The depreciation of the peso to half its former value within fifteen months of the agreement's coming into force fundamentally changed the terms of competition between the two countries. As a partial consequence, to this day NAFTA remains controversial in U.S. politics, especially within the Democratic Party, and exercises a restraining effect on trade liberalization generally and, for present purposes, regional institution building.[16]

Asian Financial Crisis of 1997–98 and the Chiang Mai Initiative

If the Mexican peso crisis was the "first crisis of the twenty-first century," as Michel Camdessus declared, the Asian financial crisis of 1997–98 was the second. Beginning with Thailand in July 1997, the crisis quickly spread to most of the rest of Southeast Asia and South Korea, before infecting Russia and Brazil, among other places, and eventually the United States through the collapse of LTCM. Stabilizing financial markets involved commitments from the international community summing to hundreds of billions of dollars. Chastened by the Mexican crisis and wary of indulging moral hazard, however, the United States and IMF were relatively slow to respond.

Shortly after the onset of the Thai financial crisis in July 1997, the Japanese Ministry of Finance famously proposed the creation of an Asian Monetary Fund. The Chinese government failed to endorse it, however, and the US government opposed it outright, offering to create instead a forum in which East Asian concerns could be addressed, the Manila Framework Agreement. Japan provided significant bilateral financing to its Asian neighbors instead through the New Miyazawa Initiative. The greater share of balance of payments support for Southeast Asian countries and South Korea during the crisis nonetheless came from the IMF, which imposed policy conditions that cut deeply into the political economy of borrowing countries. Such conditionality became the center of controversy within the domestic politics and regional discourse in East Asia. The literature on the political economy of Asian regionalism is virtually united in the assessment that these countries were profoundly alienated from the IMF and that this alienation was principally responsible for their creating the Chiang Mai Initiative.[17]

The CMI was launched at a meeting of ASEAN+3 finance ministers in Thailand in May 2000. They announced a broad set of objectives for financial cooperation, involving policy dialogue, monitoring of capital flows, and reform of international financial institutions. The finance ministers would also later add bond-market initiatives and regional bond funds to their agenda for regional cooperation. But at Chiang Mai, their core objective was to establish a network of bilateral swap arrangements (BSAs) between Northeast and Southeast Asian members. As these BSAs were negotiated and concluded over the subsequent years, their number grew to sixteen.

There were several noteworthy things about these arrangements. First, in principle, Thailand, Malaysia, Indonesia, the Philippines, and Indonesia could borrow several multiples of their IMF quotas through their CMI BSAs.

Second, however, their access was linked to their negotiating a program with the IMF with its attendant policy conditionality—except for the first 20 percent of their allotment. Conceived as such, the CMI was largely a "second" or "parallel line of defense" to IMF financing. The "IMF link," as this provision is called, helped to secure the accession of the Chinese government to the CMI and mollify the U.S. government. Third, ASEAN+3 finance ministries and central banks also launched a regional surveillance mechanism called the Economic Review and Policy Dialogue (EPRD). Many officials within the region hoped to develop the EPRD to the point where it could define regional conditionality in a crisis and thereby permit a diminution, and perhaps eventually elimination, of the IMF link.[18] Finally, partly owing to the IMF link, none of the BSAs were activated, even during the 2007–2009 crisis.

The ASEAN+3 process has been almost entirely intergovernmental. The leaders of the ASEAN states invited their counterparts from China, Japan, and South Korea to join them for the first time in the heat of the crisis, November 1997, and have been meeting at least annually since then. The CMI was developed by the ASEAN+3 finance ministries, with their central banks, in meetings of deputy ministers and working groups. The ERPD is conducted through the ASEAN+3 finance deputies meeting, which central bank deputies attend, twice each a year. The Asian Development Bank and the ASEAN Secretariat provide input to the ERPD discussions, as well as the IMF staff. But much of the surveillance discussion and all of the negotiations surrounding the establishment of the CMI and the individual BSAs took place without the benefit of a collectively appointed secretariat.

Member states of the region are also engaged in negotiating multiple, cross-cutting bilateral, subregional, and cross-regional preferential trade agreements.[19] While the pattern of trade liberalization is broadly consistent with regional financial cooperation, there is little or no linkage between the regional initiatives in the trade and financial areas. Measures of the degree of integration of markets in East Asia are sensitive to the choice of group. For the seventeen economies,[20] intra-regional trade has exceeded half of their total trade since 2000. But for ASEAN+3 alone, this figure is only about 34 percent, roughly comparable to the current figure for the six original members of the European Community.

Tension between Japan and China over the pace, direction, and institutionalization of these arrangements has pervaded regional negotiations. Prospective shift in relative influence within the region toward China as its economic growth outpaces that of Japan by a wide margin counsels officials in Beijing to bide their time until they might bargain from a more favorable position.

Meanwhile, regional initiatives have benefited from the tendency of the two countries to compete for the favor of ASEAN with cooperative measures (Grimes 2009). But more robust institutional arrangements will require transcending or suspending the rivalry. Agreement between the two is a necessary but not sufficient condition for deepening institutionalization.

The posture of the United States has evolved substantially over the twelve years since the Asian financial crisis. After scuttling the AMF proposal in 1997, the U.S. Treasury accepted the creation of the CMI in 2000 but reserved judgment on its merits.[21] Comforted by the IMF link, however, the administration of George W. Bush did not oppose the further development of the CMI, the other regional financial initiatives, or the surveillance mechanism.[22] Equally importantly, the U.S. Treasury supported reforms in the IMF that were advocated by many Asian governments, including redistribution of quotas and voting shares, the introduction of quick-disbursing, low-conditionality financial facilities, and reconsideration of policy conditionality on standby loans. Substantial progress was made on this agenda when the IMF was enlarged and refitted to combat the 2007–2009 crisis.

2007–2009 Crisis and CMIM

The crisis that began in the subprime mortgage market in the United States in 2007 and became global over the course of 2008 had two substantial consequences for East Asian financial regionalism. In the first instance, it revealed some of the limitations of the CMI. South Korea, which was most affected among ASEAN+3, declined to activate the CMI, the IMF link having made this option politically unattractive for the government. Instead, the U.S. Federal Reserve extended currency swap arrangements to fourteen countries in autumn 2008, including South Korea and Singapore, in the amount of $30 billion, and for Japan, in unlimited amounts.[23] Korea drew large amounts from this facility to provide dollar liquidity to banks in a successful crisis response. These swap facilities provided an alternative to both regional and multilateral financial cooperation for some, but not all, of the ASEAN+3 members.

Over the following year, by contrast, the crisis also prodded ASEAN+3 to re-energize negotiations to transform the CMI, a network of bilateral swaps, into a commonly activated arrangement. The credibility of ASEAN+3 hinged substantially on demonstrating progress toward their previously declared objective of CMI "multilateralisation," or CMIM. The most difficult matter, in addition to several important technical ones, was the relative shares of the three Northeast Asian states in the new arrangement, those of Japan and China in particular.

Meeting in Bali, Indonesia, on the margin of the Asian Development Bank meetings in May 2009, the ASEAN+3 finance ministers announced agreement on the main features of the CMIM. Members earmarked a total of $120 billion in their reserves and placed them at the disposal of the arrangement; the contribution of Japan would be equal to that of China and Hong Kong together, 32 percent each; borrowing limits were defined as multiples of quota; membership and lending terms would be decided by consensus while lending would be decided by two-thirds majority.[24] The CMIM retained the link to the IMF, but the linked proportion was subject to review. Reducing it would continue to hinge on development of a robust regional surveillance mechanism. The CMIM became operational in March 2010 and ASEAN+3 agreed to create a relatively modest-sized surveillance secretariat.[25] That secretariat, the ASEAN+3 Macroeconomic Research Office (AMRO), was established in Singapore in May 2011. AMRO's mandate is to collect and analyse information on the economic and financial conditions and policies of members and present its findings to the deputies' and ministers' meetings, including with respect to any activation of CMIM.[26] Meeting in Manila in May 2012, ASEAN+3 finance ministers and central bank governors agreed to double the size of the CMIM to $240 billion, increase the portion that is delinked from the IMF to 30 percent, and make financing available on a precautionary basis.[27]

The progression from the CMI, a network of bilateral swap arrangements, to the CMIM, a common institution, is a potentially profound movement. As a common regional facility, the ASEAN+3 partners in the CMIM commit themselves to a joint decision-making process. Moreover, the majority rule for lending decisions provides in theory for individual members, even Japan or China, to be overruled. This shift, in principle, is akin to the transition from a free trade area to a customs union—which requires a common decision on external tariffs and a governing body or process for making decisions. If ASEAN+3 were to implement common decision-making fully, this would represent a substantial change in regional politics. The establishment of a secretariat for surveillance and backstopping the CMIM, AMRO, crosses a similarly novel threshold for the region.

East Asian governments are hedging their move to the CMIM, however, in three ways. ASEAN+3 members have also embraced self-insurance in the form of unilateral reserve accumulation, expanded some of the bilateral swap arrangements, within and outside the region, and continued to support the IMF. Thus, East Asian governments have not placed all of their crisis-defense "eggs" in one regional "basket"; they have diversified.

Taken together, the 1997–98 and 2007–09 episodes nonetheless highlight the importance of crises as generators of regional institutions. Skeptics might argue about the significance of the CMIM, given that it has not been used, but few would argue that the 1997–98 crisis was not a direct motivation for its creation. Moreover, the impetus toward regional surveillance and a commonly administered arrangement flagged during the liquidity boom years, when the threat of crises was small, and then accelerated when crisis loomed again in 2008. Crises were more than mere accelerators of some hypothetical underlying trend toward regionalism; it is hard to imagine a plausible counterfactual scenario without them that could have brought East Asia to implement the CMIM.

Comparison and Conclusion

The review of these cases generates several observations and insights about the effect of crises on institution building within regions. We would not logically expect all crises to generate a regional response. When a *crisis originates* within the region and when the *extra-regional response* is supportive, then regional institution building is not likely. But, when a crisis originates outside the region and the extra-regional response is inadequate or adversarial, regional institution building is a logical response, and we can sensibly ask analytical questions about the sources of variation in the regional reaction. In these instances, several background conditions emerge from this comparison as favorable for institution building in the wake of a crisis.

First, the presence of a *secretariat* with a mandate to defend and advance regional integration appears to be important, as it characterizes the most successful case, that of Europe. Intergovernmental cooperation through the Committee of Central Bank Governors and Ecofin was sometimes more important than the activism of the Commission, in that case, and the CMI case suggests that substantial institution building can take place without a secretariat. We can conclude that, while neither strictly necessary nor sufficient, a secretariat facilitates further institution building.

Second, a significant degree of *market integration* appears to be necessary but not sufficient for post-crisis institution building. The two cases of substantial institution building, Europe and East Asia, exhibit moderate to high levels of intra-regional trade; but so does North America, which produced little or no institutionalization beyond NAFTA after the 1994–95 crisis.

Third, functional spillovers among regional arrangements that are related to trade, money, and finance appear to be necessary conditions for an institution-building response. Crises must threaten the interests vested in political agreements on related economic matters in order to provoke institution-building. But the Mexican peso crisis case suggests that such linkages are not sufficient.

Fourth, the presence of a dominant state appears to have ambivalent effects on regional institution building. Germany had greater influence than France over the construction of the monetary union in Europe, but that influence fell well short of regional hegemony. U.S. dominance of North America contributed to the creation of NAFTA, but probably prevented the development of supranational bodies within it. A regional rivalry, as seen in East Asia, on the other hand, appears to constrain the depth and form of institutions.

Fifth, the multilateral context matters a great deal: when the international monetary system or international financial institutions clash with the preferences of member states, these states will seek to build regional institutions that better serve their aspirations. Because a challenging multilateral environment was present in both the European and East Asian cases, this condition appears to be necessary.[28] Also present in the debt crisis of the 1980s and the Mexican crisis of 1994–95, this condition is clearly not sufficient to produce institution building. Conversely, if the multilateral system is benign or supportive, the construction of regional institutions is not a high priority and possibly redundant.

Sixth, the position of the United States on institution building within a region appears to be a powerful determinant. No regional institution was constructed over the opposition of the United States. European monetary integration benefited from a benign stance in Washington,[29] Treasury officials opposed the AMF proposal, and East Asian financial cooperation progressed after establishing the IMF link and thereby shifting the U.S. stance toward "neutral." That said, U.S. support for regional institutions is certainly not sufficient; some organizations with U.S. sponsorship have failed.

One might question the importance of the American position for the future of regionalism in Asia in light of long-term projections of the relative decline of the economic size of the United States. It is indeed possible that the posture of the United States will be less influential in the future than it was during the second half of the twentieth century. However, U.S. influence is not likely to vanish altogether and the degree of the structural shift toward Asian influence is uncertain. Given the robustness of this finding historically, advocates of regionalism would be unwise to dismiss its relevance for institution building.

Finally, this chapter has argued that aspirations for political integration or political union were neither necessary nor sufficient for substantial progress on regional institution building in economic areas. Analysis of political motivation should carefully distinguish between (a) ambitions for political union, (b) desire to avoid security conflict and war, and (c) political agreement on economic measures and the institutions necessary to implement them. Regional integration obviously cannot take place in the face of sharp security threats or interstate violence. Ambitions for political integration and a peace community can certainly reinforce regional integration, but they are not necessary. Political agreements on common economic measures and the institutions to monitor them are indeed necessary, but pose considerably lesser hurdles than agreements on political integration. Significant political integration is out of reach in East Asia, and probably in North America, whereas agreement on economic cooperation has been achieved and can be deepened in both regions.

The turmoil within Europe's monetary union that began with Greece during early 2010 presents a new case of the relationship between crisis and institution building. The euro crisis demonstrates that, while a monetary union might insulate member states from currency crises, it does not inoculate them from payments, banking, or sovereign debt crises. Whether the member states of the euro area succumb to or surmount this threat to the monetary union remains to be seen. European institutions and national governments were consistently "behind the curve" during the first two years of this episode, creating doubts about whether the monetary union would navigate the crisis successfully. At the same time, nonetheless, the Eurogroup created new financial facilities on a scale virtually no one envisioned prior to the crisis, the euro area member states tightened fiscal rules and procedures with a new treaty, and the European Council advanced reforms that could permanently strengthen the institutional architecture of the euro area and redefine its relationship to the rest of the European Union. This episode also suggests however that a monetary union requires a more robust banking and fiscal union, and the political arrangements to support it, than originally envisaged in the Maastricht treaty.

With respect to Asia in particular, our review of crises over the last four decades shows that they can provide a strong boost for regional institution building. But, as in other regions, the magnitude of this boosting effect depends on the source of the shock, response of multilateral institutions, and prior circumstances. When the source of crises is external to Asia and the response of multilateral institutions conflicts with the preferences of ASEAN+3 governments, regionalism is likely to be reinforced. Conversely, when the crisis is indigenous to the region and the response of the international financial institutions is aligned with Asian preferences, regional institution-building is not likely to accelerate.

Regional intergovernmental bodies can be as conducive to further institution building as supranational ones; both can be reinforced by regular summits of heads of governments. A fruitful strategy for advocates of Asian regionalism, therefore, would be to first lay the institutional groundwork for integrative responses (as ASEAN+3 has done with CMIM and AMRO) and then exploit it opportunistically when crises open new possibilities for cooperation. By designing such institutions well, Asia could ratchet regional cooperation upward over successive iterations of crises—following the European pattern even while declining to adopt the European institutional form.

Kahler emphasizes the segmentation of Asian institutions by issue area in the introduction to this volume; indeed, this applies to trade, development, and finance as well as to economic and security issues more broadly. Because interlocking agreements, secured with cross-issue bargains, can be a strong inducement for institution building—our finding here—there are likely to be substantial unexploited gains from cross-issue bargains in Asia, which regionalists will want to foster.

Finally, the importance of the multilateral environment and outside states, such as the United States, suggests that Asia should advance cooperation between its regional institutions and those at the global level. Although accommodation of regional preferences by multilateral institutions might weaken the case for regional institutions, cooperation with global institutions will help to soften the objection of outsiders and bridge differences among states within the region over the path along which regional institutions evolve, as witnessed in the creation of the CMIM. Such cooperation can also help assuage possible concerns on the part of the candidates that are next in line in the membership convoy.

Notes

This chapter has benefited from feedback conveyed through the "Institutions for Regionalism" project sponsored by the Asian Development Bank, including project workshops in Honolulu, Hawaii, August 10–11, 2009, and Shanghai, People's Republic of China, December 2–3, 2009. For comments on preliminary versions, the author wishes to specifically acknowledge the editors, Andrew MacIntyre and Miles Kahler, as well as Jenny Corbett, Barry Eichengreen, Giovanni Capannelli, members of the staff of the Office of

Regional Economic Integration at the ADB, two anonymous reviewers, and the other contributors to the project.

1. See, for example, Krasner (1983, 1); Goldstein, Kahler, Keohane, and Slaughter (2001, 387); Koremenos, Lipson, and Snidal (2001, 762); Milner (1998, 761); and Eichengreen (1998, 996).

2. Quoting Gourevitch (1983, 240), "The moments of greatest freedom are crisis points."

3. For reviews, see, Wallace, Wallace, and Pollack 2005; Caporaso 2007; Eichengreen 2006; Henning 2005; and a special issue of the *Journal of European Public Policy* (April 2005).

4. Henning 1998, 2002, and 2008.

5. Defined as the inter-penetration of national markets, as opposed to common regional rules and frameworks, and thus measurable by trade relative to GDP, capital flows relative to domestic market capitalization, and price convergence across borders.

6. Defined as consequences in one sphere of regional cooperation that are generated by disturbances in another sector. Drastic shifts in the exchange rates among European currencies severely complicated the Common Agricultural Policy, for example, to which European officials responded by stabilizing currencies. Distinct from economic transmission effects, this process evokes "spillover" from the neofunctionalist literature.

7. For examples of these approaches, see Eichengreen 1996, esp. 3–12; Padoa-Schioppa 2004; Giavazzi and Pagano 1988; Gros and Thygesen 1992, 100–60; Willett and Andrews 1997; Frieden 2002; Moravcsik 1998; Cohen 1993; Pauly 1997; McNamara 1998; Sandholtz 1993; and Eichengreen and Frieden 1994.

8. Elsewhere (Henning 2006), I have referred to the use of the exchange rate in this way as the "dollar weapon" and discussed its analytical underpinnings.

9. Treatments of these episodes can be found in Putnam and Henning 1989, Destler and Henning 1989, and Henning 1994, among a number of other places.

10. Henning 1998, esp. 547.

11. See, for example, Moravcsik 1998. O'Rourke's chapter for this volume gives similarly little credence to this motive.

12. Jorge Dominguez reviews these, emphasizing the trade and political features, in his chapter for this volume.

13. For an assessment of the impact at the time of the crisis, see Gauhar 1985.

14. Lustig 1998, Henning 1999, and Pastor 2001.

15. Dominguez's chapter in this volume is somewhat more generous.

16. On prospects for currency union, see Helleiner 2006.

17. The development of the CMI and associated policy issues are debated in Henning (2002, 2009), Eichengreen (2002b), Bergsten and Park (2002), de Brouwer (2004), Kuroda and Kawai (2004), Katada (2001, 2004), Rajan and Sirigar (2004), Amyx (2008), Lee (2006), and Grimes (2009), among others.

18. Contributions on ASEAN+3 surveillance include Kawai and Houser (2007) and Institute for International Monetary Affairs (2005).

19. See Ravenhill (2009), Baldwin (2004, 2008), and Solis, Stallings, and Katada (2009).

20. Australia, New Zealand, Hong Kong, and Taipei, China in addition to ASEAN+3.

21. Arran Scott and James T. Areddy, "U.S., IMF Cautiously Welcome Asia Currency Swap Plan," *Dow Jones International News*, May 8, 2000.

22. US Treasury Department, "Remarks by Under Secretary for International Affairs Timothy D. Adams at the World Economic Forum—East Asia Panel on Asia's Financial Integration: A Miracle in the Making?," Tokyo, June 15, 2006.

23. U.S. Federal Reserve Board press release, Washington, D.C., October 29, 2008, available at http://www.federalreserve.gov/newsevents/press/monetary/20081029b.htm.

24. ASEAN+3 finance ministers' statement, Bali, Indonesia, May 3, 2009, paragraphs 7-9 and Annex; Capannelli (2009).

25. ASEAN+3 finance minister's statement, Tashkent, Uzbekistan, May 1, 2010. The surveillance unit is named the ASEAN+3 Macroeconomic Research Office (AMRO).

26. ASEAN+3 Finance Ministers, Joint Media Statement of the 14th Meeting, Nha Trang, Vietnam, April 8, 2010.

27. ASEAN+3 Finance Ministers and Central Bank Governors, Joint Statement of the 15th Meeting, Manila, the Philippines, May 3, 2012.

28. Henning 1998 and 2008.

29. Similarly, O'Rourke's chapter for this volume stresses the importance of the U.S. support for European supranationalism in the 1950s.

FOUR

ASIAN REGIONAL INSTITUTIONS: FUTURE CONVERGENCE?

8

The Organizational Architecture of the Asia-Pacific
Insights from the New Institutionalism

STEPHAN HAGGARD

The weakness of international institutions in the Asia-Pacific has long been treated as a stylized fact, whether compared to Europe (for example, Kahler 2001, Katzenstein 2005) or even the Western Hemisphere (Haggard 1997, Ravenhill 2007). This characterization has become less and less accurate over time. At the present, we can distinguish at least five significant institutional "complexes" in the region[1]:

- The ASEAN proper, including the ASEAN Free Trade Area (AFTA) and the recent commitment to create an ASEAN Economic Community (AEC);
- The ASEAN+3 (APT) and its associated institutions, most notably the Chiang Mai Initiative (CMI) and the collateral development of the Trilateral Summits among China, Korea and Japan;
- The East Asian Summit, initially consisting of the APT plus India, Australia and New Zealand (the ASEAN +6), bur adding the United States and Russia in 2010;
- Asia Pacific Economic Cooperation (APEC), which remains a significant trans-Pacific institution;
- The multiplicity of overlapping regional trade arrangements (Aggarwal and Urata 2006; Dent 2006; Suominen 2009; Ravenhill 2009), mostly bilateral but including several multilateral agreements with wider significance (most notably the China-ASEAN FTA and the Trans-Pacific Strategic Economic Partnership Agreement [TPP]).

Despite the proliferation of institutions, a second stylized fact seems more accurate: that these institutions are "shallow" or "thin," and in several senses:

- The agendas of regional institutions are expansive, but the range of issues on which they are capable of forging joint action is limited.

- Institutions operate on the basis of consensus decision-making procedures that push toward modest "lowest common denominator" agreements.

- Commitments are non-binding, voluntary, and in some cases simply imprecise.

- The extent of delegation to standing international secretariats or bureaucracies is limited.

This characterization is at least partly misleading. The region has seen ongoing efforts to finesse consensus decision rules, strengthen commitments, and expand delegation. The global economic crisis of 2008–2009 spurred new initiatives with respect to financial cooperation (Henning, this volume).

But skeptics have more than a grain of truth in their favor. Despite the obvious economic success of the region, the proliferation of institutions has not been matched by formalized economic cooperation. This chapter explains why by looking at Asian institution-building through the lens of the new institutionalist literature in political science. The first section provides an overview of simple models of cooperation and delegation. A key finding in the literature is the tradeoff between the "widening" of institutions through inclusion of new members and "deepening" through more robust forms of economic cooperation (Kelley, this volume).

The second section takes these models to the historical record, showing how the heterogeneity of the region and the push to widen institutions has had an adverse effect on institutional deepening. ASEAN has played a crucial role in the development of region-wide institutions, and its preferences for loose forms of organization have thus had significant effect. China—clearly the most economically significant country in the region—has been content to let ASEAN play this leadership role, in part because early institutional designs were Asia-only and thus provided China significant clout. Over time, however, and partly in response to concerns about Chinese heft regional, institutions have continued to widen. But the effect has been to compound the very problems of heterogeneity that have blocked more robust cooperation.

The drawbacks of the "ASEAN way" are recognized in the region, and a number of strategies have been pursued to finesse it. These include empowering smaller groups, either inside existing institutions ("variable speed geometries") or through creation of altogether new institutions ("convergence clubs"). The third section addresses these strategies. Variable-speed geometries have had difficulty generating commitments that are both variable and precise. The creation of smaller "convergence clubs," particularly FTAs, is more effective in advancing deeper integration. The TPP has recently emerged as an important focal point in that regard. But these organizations ultimately reflect the diverse interests of the countries negotiating them as well, making them difficult to negotiate, expand, or subsume under a more encompassing organization. The result has been increasing institutional fragmentation.

Efforts to change the design of regional institutions must ultimately look at two key questions: how interests will be represented, including through voting rules (Hix, this volume); and the extent to which tasks are delegated. These questions are addressed in the next two sections, respectively.

There is some evidence of efforts to finesse the constraints of consensus decision-making, particularly when redistributive transfers or lending is involved. Nonetheless, domestic political constraints make it highly unlikely that the institutions in the region will move from consensus procedures toward either weighted voting, more majoritarian decision-making rules, or direct representation of citizens through regional parliaments.[2] At best there is some scope for greater participation by non-governmental actors, most notably for the private sector and academics.

The last section explores the logic of delegation. Two core problems are apparent, one having to do with the principals, the other with the agents. First, there is a mismatch between the stated economic objectives of many of the core institutions in the region and the dominant influence exercised by foreign ministries in the conduct of what might be called "institutional diplomacy." A crucial reform is to strengthen the role of inter-governmental bodies made up of ministers of finance, the economy, and trade as well as central bankers. The second problem is that the extent of delegation to standing secretariats remains limited, with little delegation for the purposes of surveillance, monitoring of compliance, dispute resolution, and other judicial functions.

What is the scope for reform? First, there is need for more independent information that will support monitoring, surveillance, and assessment of what both individual countries and institutions have done. Second, regional integration efforts, whether bilateral (as in many FTAs) or multilateral (for example through the AFTA or TPP), need robust dispute settlement procedures that will incentivize firms to push regional integration at the policy level.

Finally, more attention needs to be paid to the use of transfers or sidepayments as a means of securing more flexible decision-making processes, more binding commitments, and greater delegation.

Institutional innovation along the lines described here is possible at all levels, from FTAs through ASEAN up to the most encompassing regional institutions, such as APEC and the EAS. Region-wide cooperation would obviously yield the largest gains. But the efforts to negotiate it either through existing institutions or through expansion of "high quality" FTAs such as the TPP will be hamstrung by the region's very heterogeneity. The existing multiplicity of institutions is thus likely to persist into the future.

A Simple Model of Cooperation and Delegation through International Institutions

The range of explanations for the "stylized fact" of relatively weak institutions range from culture (Acharya 2000, 2009), to historical animosities and nationalism (Rozman 2004; Shin and Sneider 2007), the legacies of the Cold War (Ikenberry and Moon 2008; Aggarwal and Koo 2008), and geostrategic rivalries among the United States, China, and Japan (Green and Gill 2009). Others have argued that the very economic success of the region has mitigated the demand for inter-governmental institutions (Katzenstein 2005).

Yet in the simple analytic framework of the new institutionalism, the most general constraint on institutionalization is the heterogeneity of the countries of the Pacific Rim. The effects of divergent preferences can be clarified by considering a simple spatial model of cooperation.[3] Countries join international organizations because they provide public goods with positive externalities. These externalities might take the form of mutual security assurances, access to pooled financial resources, free trade, or harmonization of regulatory policies. These network externalities exhibit increasing returns; the more members of an institution, the greater the benefits it can confer. At the same time, membership entails *sovereignty costs*: the extent to which members have to adjust policies on entry into the institution. Institutions may place little demands on their members. Alternatively, entry into the institution may require members to move policy very dramatically or make substantial contributions in support of public goods (Kelley, this volume).

When countries consider creating or entering an institution, they calculate the anticipated network externalities from the organization, which are contingent on the number of other parties joining, and weigh them against the sovereignty costs of adjusting the policy status quo. It can be shown formally that the propensity of organizations to form is endogenous to a number of parameters, including the benefits derived from the public good, the number of issues on which countries seek to cooperate, and the decision-making rules.

But organizations are clearly more likely to form among countries with similar or contiguous preferences (Kelley, this volume). Countries with similar preferences can create an institution without having to move policies far from their stand-alone ideal points. Those who want either more cooperation ("high-demanders") or less ("low-demanders"), by contrast, pay high sovereignty costs and will therefore face more daunting domestic political tradeoffs from joining.

These distributional conflicts can be seen more clearly if we think about an institution that includes some but not all of the countries in a given region. Bringing in more countries is presumably good since expanded membership increases the provision of the relevant public goods. However, it is easier to bring in countries with contiguous preferences than countries that are either high- or low-demanders. High-demanders will threaten insiders with further policy adjustments if they are granted any decision-making influence after entry. There are only three obvious ways for insiders to avoid this eventuality:

- stipulate ex ante that cooperation will be limited to the issues on which insiders agree;
- create decision-making rules that give insiders either veto power over new entrants or agenda control once they enter;
- change the nature of commitments themselves so that they are either non-binding or are "variable-speed."

Note that the very institutional arrangements designed to assure that insiders will exercise agenda control have the effect of making the institution less attractive to "high-demanders." As Epstein and O'Halloran (2008) put it, the limits of cooperation are determined by the organization's "biggest weakest link": the lowest-demand country in the organization (see also Berglof et al. 2008).

The admission of low-demanders, by contrast, poses the opposite problem of threatening to dilute the gains from the organization. This can only be managed in the context of a "common rule" institution by:

- stipulating strict accession rules that require up-front policy adjustments;
- strong monitoring, compliance and dispute-settlement mechanisms, including the threat of expulsion;
- decision-making processes that guarantee insiders agenda control.

These simple ideas provide insight into the tradeoffs between widening and deepening (Hausken, Mattli and Plumper 2006). Insiders are likely to choose deepening (on the issues of interest to them) when the number of regulations and policies awaiting harmonization is relatively high in comparison to the number already harmonized. Insiders are more likely to opt for deepening—again, on the issues of common interest—the more the mean preference of insiders deviates from the mean preference of outsiders in areas likely to become harmonized in the future. Again, insiders seek to avoid circumstances in which the admission of new entrants will shift the focus of the organization away from their (mean) preferences.

As Hix (this volume) argues, preference convergence was key to European integration. Among the more salient differences across countries in Asia have been divergent alliance commitments; level of development; the nature of economic systems, and development strategies and regime type. Table 8.1 outlines some of these differences and notes their predicted effects and examples from the region's institutional history. In the following section, we trace out the consequences of some of these differences by considering the evolution of the four main "institutional complexes" noted in the introduction, setting aside the FTAs for the moment. A central theme is path-dependence: the substantial power wielded by the ASEAN incumbents on the regional architecture.

The Stylized Facts Revisited: Path Dependence in Asian Regionalism

The US did not opt for a multilateral approach to the provision of security in Northeast Asia, on top of which multilateral economic institutions such as the OECD might be built (see Calder and Ye 2004; Cha 2009/10). As a result, the most significant international institutions in the region were initially the bilateral alliance arrangements of the so-called "San Francisco system," which included a substantial economic component (Ikenberry 2001, 2003).[4] Cold War cleavages blocked even the consideration of multilateral institutions among the major powers of Northeast Asia (China, the Soviet Union/Russia, the two Koreas, Japan, and the United States) until Gorbachev's Vladivostock speech of 1986 and the gradual embrace of multilateralism on the part of China since the mid-1990s (Goldstein 2005). Not until 1999 did a thin multilateral structure emerge linking China, South Korea, and Japan in the form of the Trilateral Summits, and as will be seen this was a spinoff of an ASEAN initiative.[5]

TABLE 8.1.

Structural and preference heterogeneity:
Consequences for cooperation

Dimension	Predicted effects	Salient examples of institutional and policy consequences
Alliance arrangements	• Alliance commitments limit the significance of multilateral security arrangements • Tendency for multilateral security institutions to mirror alliance commitments	• Persistence of "San Francisco system" • Creation of SEATO, Shanghai Cooperation Organization, and "expansive bilateralism" such as TCOG and TSD • Limited institutionalization of Northeast Asia • "Lowest-common denominator" quality of multilateral security arrangements, including ARF, Six Party Talks
Level of development	• Conflicts over financing of institutional initiatives • Divergent expectations about extent and terms of redistribution through international institutions • Conflicts over provision, access to, and rules governing pooled liquidity	• Limited funding for trade facilitation and Ecotech through APEC • Continued link of CMI to IMF conditionality and move toward weighted voting in "mutilateralized" CMI
Differences in economic system, and in preferences over "deepening"	• Conflicts over scope and pace of liberalization • Conflict over mechanisms for assuring compliance	• Variable speed geometry of ASEAN FTA • FTAs not conforming with GATT/WTO Article XXIV commitments • Difficulty in enforcing and monitoring APEC Bogor commitments; "Individual Action Plan" approach • Failure of EVSL
Regime type	• Limits on direct representation (regional parliament) or representation for NGOs • Limited role for multilateral or regional courts • Conflicts over democracy and human rights agendas	• Delay in China's entry into APEC following Tiananmen • Intra-ASEAN conflicts over Myanmar • Ongoing difficulties in integrating North Korea into regional institutions

In Southeast Asia, similar Cold War cleavages limited the scope of regional cooperation. The Southeast Asian Treaty Organization (SEATO) did not provide the foundation for trans-Pacific multilateral economic cooperation between the United States and Southeast Asia. As a result, ASEAN (1967)— and ASEAN procedures—came to exercise a very important influence over subsequent developments. Until some adjustments in the ASEAN Charter (2007), these included:

- an overwhelming emphasis on inter-governmental as opposed to supranational bodies, with a weak Secretary-General (nominated by member states in alphabetical order and serving a five-year term) and Secretariat (only created in 1976, initially with a staff of only seven);
- consensus decision-making procedures;
- strong norms of "non-intervention" or "non-interference," which were typically interpreted to mean that compliance with joint initiatives was voluntary and non-binding.

Acharya (2009) shows how these rules reflected very particular concerns about sovereignty costs, particularly given the newness of the countries in the region. But these procedures also reflected the substantial heterogeneity within ASEAN itself, a problem that became more acute with the accession of Vietnam, Laos, Cambodia, and Burma (Ravenhill 2007; Jones and Smith 2007).

Because of the weak institutionalization of Northeast Asia and the first-mover advantages enjoyed by ASEAN, much institutional development in Asia has constituted either a "widening" of the "ASEAN complex" or a response by "high-demanders" to the institutional deficiencies of it. ASEAN's influence was first revealed in the creation of APEC. After a very long negotiation, ASEAN conceded to the formation of the new, trans-Pacific institution but insisted that it operate according to ASEAN rules. In addition, the so-called Kuching Consensus (1990) on ASEAN's participation in APEC stipulated that APEC would not engage in formal negotiations that would lead to binding commitments on its members, a perfect example of agenda control. The APEC Secretariat, created in 1992, was even weaker than ASEAN's.

The Bogor Declaration (1994) subsequently stated that "in order to facilitate and accelerate our cooperation, we agree that APEC economies that are ready to initiate and implement a cooperative arrangement may proceed to do so while those that are not yet ready to participate may join at a later date" (Para. 9). This statement of principle became the core of the Osaka Action Agenda approach from 1995. However, this approach does not commit those who are "not ready" to subsequently join in any common undertaking. Not until 2001 was there an effort to clarify a process through which even the "ready" could initiate and implement joint actions in the context of the institution.

Consensus rules set in train a predictable set of conflicts within APEC between high- and low-demanders (Ravenhill 2001).[6] The Bogor Declaration of 1994 defied expectations by committing the organization to the ambitious—if temporally distant and "two speed"—goal of "free and open trade and investment" by 2010 for industrialized countries and 2020 for developing ones. Yet subsequent developments revealed that the differences in preferences were too large to maintain the organization as a "single undertaking." The Osaka Action Plan (1995) sought to finesse these differences with voluntary and non-binding Individual Action Plans ("concerted unilateral liberalization") and weak Collective Action Plans, but these reflected rather than overcame divergent preferences within APEC. The failure of the Early Voluntary Sectoral Liberalization (EVSL) initiative made the same point even more forcefully (Krauss 2004).

The next round of institutional innovation—the formation of the ASEAN+3 (APT) structures—is often attributed to the "critical juncture" of the Asian financial crisis. The leaders of China, Japan, and Korea were invited to an informal ASEAN leaders' meeting in December 1997, just as the US was being criticized for not responding to the crisis in a robust way (Stubbs 2002; Calder and Ye 2004; Aggarwal and Koo 2008). However, the origins of the APT are in fact much earlier, and can be found in a succession of ad hoc mechanisms through which ASEAN sought to bring non-ASEAN members into its orbit.[7] Moreover, the "founding documents" of the APT—from the Joint Statement on East Asian Cooperation (1999) to the Second Joint Statement on East Asia Cooperation (2007)—are clear that APT procedures would essentially mirror ASEAN's. Accession rules retained significant discretion on the part of ASEAN,[8] and only ASEAN members could host APT meetings.

At the third APT summit in 1999, the organization appointed a group of scholars to flesh out what a deeper East Asian Community might look like (the East Asia Vision Group, or EAVG), followed by an inter-governmental East Asia Study Group (2002). The Study Group outlined an ambitious array of 17 short-term measures through which the APT process could be deepened. Over a longer time horizon, it called for an East Asian Summit and the creation of an "East Asian community." In November 2004, ASEAN agreed to convene an East Asian Summit (EAS), adding India, Australia, and New Zealand to the ASEAN+3 structure in what was widely seen as an effort to balance Chinese influence.

The vision documents saw the East Asian community as "an evolutionary process that builds on the substantive comfort level of the existing ASEAN+3 framework" (East Asia Study Group 2002, 59). But the creation of the EAS immediately raised delicate issues of membership. Would the EAS come to subsume the APT? Would this further "widening" of the ASEAN complex ultimately reach across the Pacific to a membership closer to APEC's? Or would ASEAN and APT incumbents favor a more narrow membership that did not have to accommodate new entrants?

It quickly became clear that China preferred the membership of the APT to that of the EAS. As Wu Xinbo (2009) points out, China believed that the purpose of including non-East Asian countries was to dilute Chinese influence, possibly at the behest of the United States. By contrast, Japan and particularly Australia openly favored a more inclusive regional organization including the United States and floated competing proposals at the 4th East Asian Summit in 2009. Again partly in response to concerns about Chinese influence, and its behavior in the South China Sea, ASEAN chose to invite Russia and the United States to join the EAS in 2010.

These conflicting preferences with respect to the core regional institutions were mirrored in competing proposals with respect to the membership in a region-wide FTA. The East Asia Study Group vetted the idea of an East Asia Free Trade Area and an East Asian Investment Area presumably based on the APT membership. In 2006, Japan proposed a Comprehensive Economic Partnership for East Asia (CEPEA) that would mirror EAS membership. At the 2004 APEC meeting in Santiago, the APEC Business Advisory Council (ABAC) proposed study of a Free Trade Area of the Asia Pacific (FTAAP), an idea that was formally proposed by the Bush administration (Dent 2008, 219-221). In 2011, a group of nine countries coalesced around a potential FTA with an open accession clause: the Trans-Pacific Strategic Economic Partnership Agreement (TPP).[9] However, it is unlikely that the countries in the region will easily coalesce around any of these options. By default, the most overarching regional institutions—the ASEAN Plus Three institutions and the East Asia Summit—remain wedded to "the ASEAN way."

In the 2000s, however, criticisms started to mount that these rules were retarding cooperation. The result has been a succession of institutional efforts seeking to finesse or circumvent them.

Making Credible Commitments in a "Soft Law" Context: Variable Speed Geometries, Convergence Clubs, and Sidepayments

Before continuing, it is important to ask whether the critique of the "ASEAN way" is warranted. Consider, for example, the following passage from the first ASEAN Concord of 1976 (3, ii): "member states shall progress towards the establishment of preferential trading arrangements as a long term objective on a basis deemed to be at any particular time appropriate through rounds of negotiations subject to the unanimous agreement of member states." This is a somewhat extreme case of ambiguity about basic objectives. Nonetheless, ASEAN did commit in 1992 to an AFTA process that subsequently made progress toward the freeing of inter-regional trade (Nesadurai 2003). Are the limitations of "the ASEAN way" overstated?

Proponents of "hard law" argue that both the *precision* of commitments and their *binding status* are crucial for those commitments to be credible, for adjudication and third-party enforcement to evolve, and for reputational effects to operate. In recent years, however, there has been a resurgence of interest in the possible benefits of "soft law." Abbot and Snidal (1998) argue that soft law lowers sovereignty costs and therefore increases the prospects for reaching agreements. Gersen and Posner (2008) note that non-binding statements have effect by working their way into customary international law or by providing the framework for informal cooperation. The passage of soft law resolutions can signal future intent. Even non-binding resolutions can signal the future direction of policy to important domestic audiences.

However, there are good reasons for skepticism with respect to the merits of "soft law" in the Asia-Pacific context. The positive effects of "soft law" depend heavily on the credibility of the institutions generating it. The proliferation of multiple "soft law" resolutions—most notably in the Osaka Action Agenda and the ASEAN AEC—ultimately served to dilute the institutions' credibility as states proved unwilling to abide by their commitments. These problems can be seen by considering some of the dilemmas inherent in variable-speed geometries.

Variable Speed Geometries

One way of introducing discipline in "soft law" agreements is to permit tiered commitments that conform more closely to the preferences of the actors. At least in principle, a variable-speed geometry approach can entail precise commitments; they are simply differential. Nesadurai (2003) outlines an example from the AFTA. In the mid-1990s, governments began to backtrack on commitments to liberalization, which were not initially binding. Negotiations relaxed initial targets to accommodate the interests of critical sectors, thus securing political support for the larger project. But the negotiations also produced quite precise, though variable-speed targets.

The new ASEAN Charter institutionalizes the "ASEAN-x" concept, but this concept is decidedly looser. Under "ASEAN-x," "flexible" participation in economic agreements is allowed "if there is a consensus to do so" (ASEAN

Charter Art. 21 para. 2); note the ambiguity over whether such flexible participation would ultimately include binding, even if variable, commitments. The Singapore-Thailand Enhanced Economic Relationship (STEER) framework, launched formally in 2003, rested on a similar logic (labeled by Singapore's Minister for Trade and Industry "2 plus x."). Within APEC, the 2001 Shanghai Leaders' meeting formally endorsed the "pathfinder" approach, which also permits initiatives to move forward among clubs of interested parties.

But there is some reason to doubt whether these various formulae should be considered "variable-speed geometries" at all. Under a variable-speed geometry, countries undertake a common commitment but implement it at different speeds. The formulae discussed above entail commitments on the part of some that will not necessarily be undertaken by others at all. At least in principle, the limited success of these efforts was not a function of the variable-speed nature of the commitments per se, but the broader problem that commitments were not seen as binding. But this failure may be a function of allowing variability in the first place. Low-demanders will have incentives to overestimate the difficulty in meeting stipulated goals, particularly if there are benefits from free-riding on high-demanders.

In principle, institutions could also be created to monitor compliance with variable speed commitments. Within ASEAN, for example, the recommendations of the High Level Task Force on ASEAN Economic Integration argued for flexibility but proposed that commitments be more precise and transparent. The Task Force also called for the creation of an ASEAN Compliance Body and a strengthened Dispute Settlement Mechanism to "ensure expeditious and legally binding decision in resolving trade disputes." But low-demanders have incentives to weaken ex post monitoring as well, for example by opposing independent information-gathering, monitoring, and dispute-settlement or judicial functions.

Convergence Clubs: Misreading the FTAs

An alternative solution to the lowest-common-denominator problem is to forge overlapping agreements among countries whose preferences are more closely aligned. Such "convergence clubs" are presumably characterized not only by higher levels of cooperation but more robust institutional arrangements as well. One strategic reason for the formation of such clubs is that the revealed benefits of cooperation and delegation will induce low-demanders to reassess their stand-alone or alternative-institutional ideal points, thus creating cascading agreements pushing toward freer trade (Baldwin 1997, 2011). This might occur "positively," as the benefits of membership are revealed, leading states to learn the benefits of cooperation. Cascades might also be created "negatively" if the formation of the convergence club lowers the welfare of non-members through discrimination. The Bush administration's strategy of competitive liberalization through the pursuit of "high-quality FTAs" and the Obama administration's interest in the TPP self-consciously pursued this logic.

Given weak multilateral disciplines on the formation of FTAs, however, clubs need not converge on higher levels of cooperation. Club rules need only constitute an equilibrium for their members, and may in fact lock-in more limited commitments. This more cautious assessment seems to more accurately capture the diversity of recent FTAs in the region. National initiatives followed national templates and accommodated the interests of the parties (Dent 2006; Aggarwal and Urata 2006; Hufbauer and Schott 2007; Ravenhill 2009). For example, Japan has had ongoing difficulties committing to FTAs because of political constraints with respect to agriculture, and China seems content to exploit its market position to create its own hub-and-spoke system of agreements, most notably with ASEAN.

Nor is it plausible that institutions that are incapable of generating common agendas and institutions in the first place will be able to reconcile or incorporate these divergent clubs once they have formed; to the contrary, the existence of path dependencies is amply apparent. At the APEC Ministerial Meeting in Santiago, Chile, in 2004, member countries agreed to develop a set of non-binding "best practice" guidelines for FTAs, and the Committee on Trade and Investment (CTI) subsequently produced several model chapters. However, the APEC standards mirrored US agreements, and some core suggestions, such as simplified rules of origin and open accession rules, would undermine the very political foundations of existing agreements. As Hufbauer and Schott (2007, 33) put it succinctly, "member countries almost always resist gratuitous entry by 'outsiders,' mainly because that would reduce the implicit protection provided by the original deal."

Sidepayments

An alternative to variable-speed geometries and separate convergence clubs is to maintain the insistence on a common undertaking (for example, with respect to trade liberalization or regulatory harmonization) but to offset the sovereignty costs of the low-demanders with sidepayments. The most direct way of doing this is through transfers or joint policies with a redistributive component. Redistributive bargains, including in the form of direct transfers (regional policy, agricultural supports), have been pivotal to maintaining the European common market as a single undertaking. This solution requires a willingness and ability of the high-demanders to undertake such transfers, in part on the self-interested grounds that they will benefit from concessions from the low-demanders.

The use of sidepayments to achieve cooperation and delegation appears to be underappreciated in East Asia. The Initiative for Asian Integration (IAI, 2000), aimed primarily at the new entrants (Cambodia, Laos, Myanmar, and Vietnam or CLMV), represents a modest redistributive program tied loosely to the AFTA. The entirety of ECOTECH constitutes a channel for such redistribution through APEC, and is repeatedly justified as a necessary complement to the TILF agenda.

There are several reasons why such transfers have been limited in the Asia-Pacific. The first is a classic sequencing or chicken-and-egg problem; the incentives to redistribute for the purpose of securing binding commitments is diminished in institutions that have not managed to make binding commitments. Yet governance issues also matter; those financing such transfers—namely the richer countries—will be more comfortable in making transfers only if they can influence decision-making and implementation.

Decision-Making: Forms of Representation in Asian Institutions

Voting rules can influence outcomes by enfranchising different coalitions of actors and thus changing the choices international organizations make (Hix, this volume). But since members are forward-looking, voting rules are endogenous; they are dependent on the composition and preferences of the membership. As a result, there are good reasons to be skeptical that formal changes in rules are likely to resolve the problems outlined in the previous section because of the problem of endogeneity: such reforms are unlikely to be undertaken in the first place. This can be seen by considering some of the institutional choices on offer with respect to both inter-governmental and individual representation and how they have fared in fact.

The most inclusive inter-governmental voting rule is a requirement for unanimity or consensus, often called a unit veto system; as Hix argues in this volume, such a system has been instrumental for the success of European institutions. However, such a system does not require unanimous support—in effect, a "yes" vote by all—to undertake an initiative. All that is required is that the proposal avoids a veto. Former ASEAN Secretary General Severino is worth quoting at length on this point:

Consensus on a proposal is reached when enough members support it—six, seven, eight or nine, no document specifies how many—even when one or more have misgivings about it, but do not feel strongly enough about the issue to block action on it. Not all need to agree explicitly. A consensus is blocked only when one or more members perceive the proposal to be sufficiently injurious to their national interests for them to oppose it outright. (Severino 2006:34.)

As we have seen, the formal (or typically the informal) structure of most multilateral institutions in East Asia conforms to this procedure.

If unit vetoes are both cause and effect of shallower cooperation, the opposite is not necessarily the case; that more majoritarian voting systems would be associated with higher levels of cooperation. Powerful (and richer) states are not likely to submit themselves to binding decisions taken by simple majority rule because weaker and poorer states would engage in excessive redistribution. The rich and powerful will either limit the agenda on which majority decision-making takes place, insist on voting rules that preserve their influence, or exit into convergence clubs that do not face such risks.

There are a variety of ways to split the difference between consensus rules and simple majority rule; these include qualified majority or supermajority rules, weighted voting, and granting vetoes to powerful members outright. The most interesting efforts in this direction is the case of the multilateralization of the CMI, which involves a weighted voting scheme in which the major powers—China, Japan, and Korea—have preponderant influence (Kawai and Houser 2007; Grimes 2009; Henning 2009 and this volume). It is noteworthy that such weighted voting has emerged in the same sort of institutions in which it prevails elsewhere, namely, those in which it is important to accommodate the interests of creditors.[10]

What are the prospects for direct representation (Hix, this volume)? If there is a "democratic deficit" in Europe, it is a yawning chasm in Asia. To date, there has been relatively little discussion of direct voter input or control over international institutions through elected regional parliaments. Again, the reason for strong inter-governmental bias is fairly obvious. The persistence of authoritarian rule in a number of significant countries in the region, most notably China, is likely to block the evolution of direct voter representation at the multilateral level. It is also likely to block the creation of courts in which individuals would have direct standing (Voeten, this volume).

The potential for a more active NGO or private advisory role in international institutions is a more intriguing possibility. But for reasons already noted, institutionalized representation of many civil society groups in Asia is likely to be blocked for political reasons or tightly circumscribed. For example, tripartism would have to accommodate official unions. The groups most likely to gain representation are business groups, such as the APEC Business Advisory Council (ABAC). The Pacific Economic Cooperation Council (PECC, 1980) is an even earlier progenitor. We return in more detail below to how the incorporation of such interests might serve to deepen regional cooperation, but we turn first to the evolution of delegation in the region.

The Varieties of Delegation: Theory and the Asian Case

Delegation is a conditional grant of authority to an independent body to make decisions and take actions (following Lake 2007 and Bradley and Kelly 2008). If we take the peak council of country members—the inter-governmental structure—as the principal, we typically think of an executive, secretariat, commission or bureaucracy as the key agent; the extent of delegation to secretariats defines the extent of delegation within a given international institution. However, secretariats are only one body to which principals can delegate. Adjudicative bodies—courts, panels, arbitration committees—can play a crucial role in resolving disputes and enforcing compliance (Voeten, this volume). Moreover, principals can delegate to a variety of other entities as well, including outside experts, other international institutions (as has been the case in the CMI's reliance on the IMF) and sub-groupings of the principals themselves.

This last form of delegation—from one inter-governmental body to another—is by far the most significant form of delegation in Asia's international institutions. Inter-governmental structures can range in composition from the highly political summits among heads of state, which have been an enduring feature of both ASEAN and APEC, to meetings of foreign ministers and their subordinates (i.e., "high level officials" or "ministerial" meetings), to meetings of trade, finance, and other functional ministers, down through various working-level inter-governmental bodies.

Before turning to a more detailed review of delegation in Asia, it is first important to underscore that the composition of the principals also acts as a crucial constraint. There is a very important mismatch in Asia between the composition of the controlling bodies of key regional institutions and their stated objectives. Ministries of foreign affairs do not have influence over economic policy. Nor do they have the connections with interested private sector parties required to make credible commitments with respect to policy. A crucial institutional innovation in the region may lie as much in the creation of new bodies of principals as in proposals for new bureaucratic agents.

Two examples make the point. First, the influence of the APT structure over economic cooperation in the region rests heavily on the APT Finance Ministers meetings, beginning in 2000 (Henning, this volume). This pivotal body bears responsibility for a number of significant initiatives, including the CMI, the Asian Bond Markets Initiative, and the APT Economic Review and Policy Dialogue. A core institutional reform in the ASEAN Charter is the delegation of responsibility for implementation of the ASEAN Economic Community (AEC) blueprints to the ASEAN Economic Ministers (AEM), through the newly established Council of ASEAN Economic Community. This body in turn has authority to delegate further to relevant functional ministerial bodies as well as to the Secretariat. A core institutional test of the AEC is whether these newly formed bodies will prove as innovative for ASEAN as the meetings of finance ministers have proven for the APT.

Information Gathering and Agenda Setting

Probably the least risky form of delegation is a grant of research and advice authority. A specialized body or committee is granted the resources to conduct research and gather information on a topic and thus to set an agenda. Principals may delegate in this way not only because they lack expertise, but precisely because they recognize they are incapable of reaching decisions.[11] In East Asia, the question of leadership can also be sensitive. The countries that are natural agenda-setters, including China, Japan, and the US, face risks of backlash if they assume that role.

East Asian institutions have undertaken a lot of "research, advice and agenda-setting" delegation, and it is precisely for this reason that these institutions are frequently derided as mere "talk shops." The array of bodies that take this form runs into the hundreds, from working-level intergovernmental meetings to highly specialized consultative bodies of experts; many of these operate on an ad hoc basis. Bodies of highly visible policy intellectuals have also played important agenda-setting roles in all of the core bodies outlined here, including ASEAN, the APT, EAS, and APEC. Recent efforts to build more enduring research and analytic capacities include the Economic Research Institute for ASEAN and East Asia (ERIA) and its flagship Deepening Economic Integration (DEI) project.

Grants of authority for information and research or agenda-setting are by definition non-binding. However, the logic of such delegation is much more complex than it appears. Lake (2007) explains why. In his simple model, the advisory body proposes policies that the principals can then either accept or reject. Recall that in the simple model of cooperation, states make choices about the extent of cooperation based on assessment of the net benefits. Research and information gathering could change those cost-benefit calculations, for example, by revealing the extent of negative externalities (transborder effects of pollution, such as acid rain) or positive ones (the precise extent of gains from trade or financial cooperation).

For such delegation to lead to increased cooperation, however, the agents must make proposals that are superior to the status quo and the principals must act on them. Satisfying this condition can be tricky in settings where preferences of the principals are heterogeneous. High-powered advisory bodies often do little more than recreate the heterogeneity among the principals. The most famous regional example of this sort was the well-known disagreements among APEC's Eminent Persons Group on "open regionalism."[12]

To date, there has been virtually no research on whether such delegation has had effect in the Asia-Pacific. More importantly, there has been little delegation for the purpose of independent assessment of cooperative initiatives. ASEAN does not devote resources to serious study of the AFTA and its effects. APEC does not study whether commitments reported under its trade and investment facilitation initiatives are additional to what countries were already doing. And although the signing of FTAs is typically proceeded by quite detailed analytic work, there is much less research ex post on whether these agreements have had effect.

Implementation: Do Things Get Done in Asian Institutions?

A major reason why Asia is seen as thinly institutionalized centers on the absence of standing secretariats engaged in the direct implementation of projects. In theory, such delegation is most likely in issue areas in which there are informational and organizational economies of scale and tasks are frequent, repetitive, and require specific expertise. The most obvious example of this sort of delegation is the international financial institutions, which exhibit both organizational and political advantages over national agencies in extending and monitoring conditional lending and aid. The emergence of the CMI suggests that it is precisely in this area where the most substantial capacity to implement is emerging (Henning, this volume).

Outside of the ADB, however, there is little delegation of this sort in the Asia-Pacific, and the ADB itself has only recently been exploited as a possible implementing body for decisions taken in other forums. The reasons for this reticence appear to be both financial and programmatic. ASEAN was founded as an organization of developing countries, and its capacity to pool and redistribute resources was initially limited. Since that time, ASEAN has been hamstrung by budget rules that require equal contributions from all members, despite the fact that per capita incomes have diverged immensely (partly as a result of the accessions of the 1990s). The ASEAN Secretariat has a staff of only 60.

Within the institutions that encompass both developed and developing countries, such as APEC, the developed countries have been reluctant to commit financial resources. The result has been a fragmented and ad hoc implementation process. Donors finance initiatives they deem of interest but do not commit resources to the organization as a whole. In addition to the financial constraints on delegation, principals may feel that they would lose control if too much power is delegated. As Hix (this volume) shows for the European case, however, this concern is exaggerated. Important decisions with respect to delegation are typically taken by intergovernmental bodies through consensus procedures. Although the Commission has primary responsibility for the implementation of Community initiatives, it is assisted by a dense network of committees made up of representatives from member states.

Regulation

Regulation constitutes a higher level of delegation since it grants authority to standing institutions that "create administrative rules to implement, fill gaps in, or interpret preexisting international obligations (Bradley and Kelly 2008, 14). The extent of such delegation is a function of binding and uniform rules, which are largely absent in East Asia. Some of the more purely advisory and ad hoc bodies that currently exist in organizations such as ASEAN could lead a process of regulatory development were the decision taken to develop a more permanent secretariat or commission structure; the development of common standards provides an important example. The AEC currently constitutes the most likely test of this proposition, but similar regulatory functions could emerge out of the current APT projects, which include areas as narrow as the harmonization of industrial statistics up through the Asian Bond Market Initiative; the latter already has its own complex working group structure.[13]

Dispute Settlement

An important reason for delegating to international institutions is to increase the credibility of commitments and to "lock-in" cooperative policy positions in the national arena (Voeten, this volume, for a review). Compliance can be enhanced in two main ways: by granting parties the right to take violations of commitments to an independent third-party dispute-settlement mechanism; or by allowing the international institution to play a more direct monitoring and enforcement role.

Formal dispute settlement in the four main regional institutions appears weak; this reticence with respect to formal dispute resolution has been identified as a key feature of the ASEAN way and of Asian culture more generally. But this is highly misleading. As Voeten shows in this volume, Asian states are no more or less likely to use multilateral dispute settlement mechanisms than other countries. Nor do regional dispute-settlement mechanisms elsewhere work any better than ASEAN, at least for managing inter-state disputes. ASEAN adopted a dispute settlement protocol in 1996 and an "enhanced" dispute settlement mechanism in 2004. An important feature of recent FTAs has been the inclusion of dispute settlement mechanisms as well.

To date, however, it is true that the use of these mechanisms appears to be limited. The strength of dispute settlement depends in the first instance on the extent of uniform, precise, and binding law. The existence of clear statute has the benefit of increasing the probability of detection and bringing national law into conformity with international obligations. "Soft" law weakens both precision and the binding nature of commitments, and thus also has the effect of weakening possible means of enforcement.

Smith (2000) provides a useful introduction to the menu of choices with respect to dispute settlement mechanisms, and shows that the extent of delegation to DSMs can be "harder" or "softer" as well.

- Disputes can be handled by consultation, mediation, and arbitration, or recourse to an independent third party in the form of a panel or court.
- If there is third-party review, rulings can be binding or subject to effective ex post revision or even veto by further formal or informal political processes.
- Judicial bodies can be ad hoc, and arguably weaker as a result, or standing bodies with independence guaranteed through standard mechanisms (terms of appointment, independent budgets).
- Standing can be granted only to states, or direct legal standing can be granted to aggrieved parties—firms or individuals. Direct legal standing strengthens the force of law because of the high-powered incentives to seek redress.
- Finally, remedies may range from measures that are legally binding in national law to those that are negotiable ex post.

If we set aside the FTAs, the most important institutional innovations have taken place in ASEAN. As envisioned by the High Level Task Force on Economic Integration (HLTF), the new system was to be comprised of an advisory, consultative, and adjudicatory mechanism in addition to a revised ASEAN DSM. The HLTF proposed the creation of an ASEAN Legal Unit, the ASEAN Consultation to Solve Trade and Investment Issues (ACT), the ASEAN Compliance Monitoring Body (ACMB) or ASEAN Compliance Board (ACB), as well as an enhanced ASEAN DSM.

The actual Protocol on the Enhanced DSM (2004) proved a surprisingly weak instrument, however. On the surface, the new DSM looked very similar to the WTO mechanism. But on closer inspection, the Senior Economic Officials Meeting (SEOM)—a key inter-governmental body—plays a central role in the process. Like the WTO dispute settlement process, the 2004 Protocol adopted the negative consensus rule. Panels for disputes are convened upon the request by the complainant party unless there is a consensus finding by the SEOM not to do so. Since the complainant parties are unlikely ever to vote against a panel's establishment, the process should be virtually automatic. However the SEOM's rules of procedure are consensual. Firms do not have independent standing, and national level procedures for them to bring cases do not appear to be well elaborated and functioning. As a result, governments socialized to a highly consensual inter-governmental process would have to confront one another in an arena where other forms of cooperation are continually being sought. Not surprisingly, the process has gotten little use.

Credibility and Lock-In: Delegation for Monitoring and Enforcement

In principal, members of an international institution can allow the international body not only to monitor commitments but to enforce them as well. The European Commission has the authority to initiate proceedings before the European Court if it has reason to believe that a member state is failing to fulfill an obligation under EU law (such proceedings may also be started by another EU country).

Such measures are still a long way from consideration in East Asia. However, there have been marginal steps to strengthen monitoring and surveillance. Two examples can be mentioned. The first is the evolution of the peer review process in APEC. The core of the Osaka process is the Individual Action Plan, but there has been no mechanism to guarantee that the IAPs are additional to what countries are already doing. In conjunction with the mid-term stock review of the Bogor Goals in 2005, APEC strengthened the peer review process. These changes included the establishment of a timetable for the review of all 21 member economies. Prior peer reviews, which began at the second Senior Officials Meeting in 1997, were voluntary and ad hoc with no fixed schedule. The new peer review process also allows the review team to explore issues not listed explicitly in the IAPs, albeit with agreement of the reviewed party. The new peer review also adds a second outside expert and has been scheduled to coincide with the Senior Officials Meeting (SOM).

A second example of monitoring and surveillance are the emergent institutions of the APT. ASEAN+3 finance and central bank deputies hold two-day meetings semiannually (Henning, this volume). At the Economic Review and Policy Dialogue, ministers exchange views. At present, external experts and ADB staff provide general input, but assessment and evaluation of performance and policy in any given country appear to be the domain of the country's minister. There is no peer review process. But given the consensus-driven culture of APT organizations, even the introduction of inter-governmental peer review would be less compelling than introducing formal participation from outside parties, whether from the ADB, independent economists, the private sector, or even independent panels.

Conclusion

The political and economic heterogeneity of the countries of the Pacific Rim has posed challenges to the governance of regional institutions. Until the 2000s, the dominant institutions in the region—initially ASEAN and APEC—managed this diversity through consensus decision-making. Binding commitments were limited and monitoring and adjudicative functions correspondingly weak. Governments were also reluctant to delegate any significant authority to standing secretariats. In combination, these institutional arrangements fundamentally limited what institutions could achieve. It has been hard to demonstrate that regional institutions—rather than multilateral ones or the unilateral choices of governments—have contributed substantially to the tremendous growth and economic integration of the region.

Since these initial institutions were set in place, there have been several efforts at institutional reform of existing institutions. Variable speed geometries have been made explicit, but these have not generated commitments that were simultaneously both variable and "hard." More fundamental institutional reforms of existing institutions, such as qualified majority voting, did not even come up for discussion. The most important institutional reforms have come not in the decision-making rules but with respect to the composition of inter-governmental bodies. The creation of the APT Finance

Ministers meeting, and hopefully the new structures for the ASEAN Economic Community, empower ministries that are more capable of making binding decisions.

Rather than reform of existing institutions, institutional innovation in the region has come largely through the creation of altogether new institutions. The adjustment of *memberships* has proved more significant than the adjustment of *rules* (Kelley, this volume). Two developments have proven noteworthy; the multiplication of FTAs; and the ongoing battles over whether the APT or the EAS would be the institutional core of the regional integration process.

The proliferation of FTAs may well reflect the domino theory of liberalization advanced by Baldwin (1997, 2011). But from a governance perspective this institutional proliferation creates numerous coordination problems. Some of these new organizations reflect the disaffection of "high demanders" with existing institutions; the TPP is the most significant example. It is revealing that a number of APEC and ASEAN members are willing to make concessions that go far beyond what APEC and ASEAN have managed to achieve (Ravenhill 2009). But FTAs may be formed among "low demanders" as well; the China-ASEAN agreement and Japan's economic cooperation agreements constitute examples.

Can these efforts be reconciled through a more encompassing agreement? To date, the proposals for a more overarching FTA—whether a Free Trade Area of the Asia-Pacific, a Comprehensive Economic Partnership for East Asia, or an APT-led East Asian FTA—have foundered on debates over membership (Yamazawa 2008). The TPP has attracted the interest of the US and Japan, and has an open accession clause that might permit it to grow. But path dependencies are having potentially adverse effects. With the conclusion of FTA projects between ASEAN and China, Japan, and South Korea, much of the region's trade will be covered by FTAs. But specific features of these agreements pit the interests of insiders against outsiders, including the structure of phase-in of commitments, rules of origin, and accession rules. Rather than paving the way for an overarching agreement, the variety of memberships, rules, and decision-making procedures make these FTAs harder rather than easier to reconcile over time.

If the evolution of FTAs has resulted in institutional fragmentation, there is also ongoing debate about the very definition of the region. The geostrategic stakes are large. From a purely economic perspective, coordination through APEC or a trans-Pacific organization would yield greater gains. The ascent of the APT posed the question of whether the exclusion of the United States (and of the Western Hemisphere more generally) was a temporary development or an enduring feature of a new, China-centered East Asian order. The United States accession to ASEAN's Treaty of Amity and Cooperation and US (and Russian) entry into the EAS shows that the both the US and other countries in the region are concerned about such an outcome. But the widening of these institutions simply compounds the issue of structural and preference heterogeneity which is the core theme of this chapter.

With respect to core decision-making structures, it is highly doubtful that consensus rules would be changed within any of the core institutions in the region (ASEAN, APT, EAS, and APEC). The multilateralization of the CMI shows that the APT is capable of delegating to bodies that are governed by qualified majority or weighted voting. But it is not clear what if any other policy areas would be appropriate for this model.

As a result, more emphasis should be focused on the structure and process of delegation in existing institutions: means through which inter-governmental bodies can increase the power of supranational ones to generate more robust cooperation. Three modest suggestions provide examples of the issues.

A common complaint is that regional institutions have suffered from a deficit of independent information. ASEAN's High Level Task Force on Economic Integration recommended the creation of a Compliance Board modeled on the WTO Textile Monitoring Body.[14] The advantage of this structure is that it overcomes the problem of self-dealing: the board has a mandate to focus on violations of rules—areas where countries are not in compliance with obligations—rather than areas where they are. The disadvantage of this model is that it replicates the inter-governmental structure of existing regional arrangements and consensus rules. One way of getting around this would be to constitute Compliance Boards that are tripartite, including government, academic, and business representatives. This structure would generate more independent policy assessments.

A related problem is the absence of independent research on whether institutions are having any effect. Are FTAs leading to trade diversion? Have trade and investment facilitation agreements reduced transactions costs? This sort of research goes on within the academic community, of course, but there is no means of transmitting it into the deliberations of existing institutions. At all levels, from the ASEAN to the APEC, there is a need for independent assessment and evaluation. This can be accomplished in three ways: through economic research divisions or units within secretariats (where they exist) or the ADB; by commissioning ad hoc assessment studies; or through some mix of the two. Equally if not more important are assuring that this work is regularly summarized and presented before decision-making bodies within organizations: the ASEAN Economic Ministers, the APT Finance Ministers, perhaps through the EBRD process, and the Senior Officials or Finance Ministers meetings in APEC.

A second issue has to do with dispute settlement. A broad DSM model has emerged from the innovations in the WTO process and its modifications. However, governments continue to act as gatekeepers over the initiation of cases, and inter-governmental processes with consensus biases subsequently influence their disposition. A very simple remedy to this problem exists: grant private standing. Private agents have high-powered incentives that are missing in existing arrangements. Given the multiplicity of FTAs that currently exist, a first step would be to commission a study of the modalities of introducing private standing into them.

A third innovation would be to create more direct linkage between institutional commitments and sidepayments to "low-demanding" states. ECOTECH seeks to build capacity in the region, but does not link capacity building to commitments. Within ASEAN, lending to poorer countries is broadly linked to the integrity of ASEAN, but is not tied to particular commitments. One way of doing this at the ASEAN level would be the creation of dedicated Regional Integration Funds that would undertake lending in the context of voluntary—but monitored—commitments.

It is important to close with a reminder of the fundamental limitations of institutional fixes. Actors in regional institutions reach agreements not only on substance, but on the rules that govern their interactions. Weak rules may well reflect underlying preferences. In the absence of a willingness to undertake binding commitments, it is misguided to think that changing institutions will matter much; to the contrary, institutions might even weaken if expectations are raised only to be dashed, as has happened so frequently in ASEAN and APEC already.

However, preferences are not fixed. We have already seen an important, if gradual, evolution on the part of ASEAN and China toward greater interest in regional cooperation. Providing better information and incentives for making compromises is exactly what institutions are designed to do.

Notes

My thanks to Giovanni Capannelli, Jenny Corbett, Richard Feinberg, Stuart Harris, Simon Hix, Miles Kahler, Andrew MacIntyre, T.J Pempel, Eric Voeten, and the late Hadi Soesastro for their comments. Thanks as well to a very thorough anonymous reviewer for the ADB and the participants at workshops in Canberra, Honolulu, and Shanghai.

1. I do not address the growing number of institutions forged by subnational governments, such as "growth triangles" and "growth corridors," nor the myriad of specialized functional bodies in the region (such as the Mekong River Commission, Executives' Meeting of East Asia and Pacific Central Banks, Asian-Pacific Postal Union).

2. See the more hopeful arguments in Hix, this volume.

3. Political scientists tend to model cooperation as a mutual adjustment of policies. See Nielson and Tierney 2003; Lyne, Nielson, and Tierney 2006; Hawkins et. al. 2006; Epstein and O'Halloran 2008. Economists consider centralized provision of public goods financed by contributions from the members. See Alesina, Angeloni, and Etro 2005; Hausken, Mattli, and Plumper 2006; Berglof et al. 2008. The basic insights emanating from the two literatures are quite similar.

4. These were with Australia (1951); New Zealand (1951); the Philippines (1951); South Korea (1953); Japan (1954); Thailand (1954); and the Republic of China (1954). A multilateral economic initiative by South Korea in 1966 to join these countries as well as Malaysia and Vietnam was disbanded in 1975.

5. The Six Party Talks, first convened in 2003, were an ad hoc arrangement designed to address the nuclear crisis on the peninsula; as of this writing in January 2012 they remain in abeyance.

6. These did not fall precisely along lines of level of development, as Japan sometimes occupied an ambiguous position. But "Western" (and essentially Anglo-Saxon) countries wanted to place greater priority on trade liberalization through binding agreements.

7. These mechanisms included joint committees, "dialogue partnerships," and the Post-Ministerial Conferences. The ASEAN + 3 Foreign Ministers met informally as early as 1994. The first joint meeting between ASEAN, China, Japan, and Korea took place in the context of preparing for the ASEM.

8. Accession rules included close ties to ASEAN, signature of the ASEAN Treaty of Amity and Cooperation, and status as an ASEAN dialogue partner.

9. Initially created by the most liberal states in the region—Singapore, Chile, and New Zealand—the framework agreement of November 2011 was signed by Australia, Brunei, Chile, Malaysia, New Zealand, Peru, Singapore, Vietnam, and the United States. Japan also formally expressed an interest in joining.

10. The "pathfinder" approach within APEC might also be seen as an alternative voting rule. Pathfinder initiatives require a full consensus for initial approval but permit initiatives to move forward with support from only 25 percent of the membership. Pathfinder initiatives have been launched in such diverse areas as food mutual recognition arrangements (MRA), data privacy, and corporate governance, with all but one spearheaded by the advanced industrial states in APEC (including Singapore). Yet this interpretation of the pathfinder language in the Shanghai Declaration would technically still allow a veto over the initiative even if parties chose to abstain from joining (Feinberg 2003, 13). Since the pathfinder initiatives do not commit other parties to join ("these initiatives should . . . encourage the broadest participation by other APEC members when they are ready to join"), they really do not constitute a form of qualified majority voting.

11. For example, as a result of socially intransitive preferences or cycling.

12. The differences centered on the American representative's preference for a more standard FTA vs. the concept of "open regionalism," under which concessions extended under the APEC process would be extended unilaterally beyond the region on an MFN basis.

13. Working Group 1 (WG1) has responsibility for research on ways to increase the supply of local currency denominated bonds; WG2 studies the business model of a new credit guarantee and investment mechanism for the region; WG3 focuses on a possible regional clearing and settlement mechanism and impediments to cross-border bond investment and issuance; and WG4 prepares Asian credit rating agencies for Basel II implementation fundamentals. Each of these could result in joint bodies focusing on greater intraregional regulatory harmonization. See Henning, this volume.

14. The Textiles Monitoring Body is a quasi-judicial, standing body which consists of a Chairman and ten members, discharging their function on an ad personam basis and taking all decisions by consensus. The ten members are appointed by WTO Member governments according to an agreed grouping of WTO Members into constituencies but with rotation allowed within the constituencies. The purpose of the body is to supervise the implementation of the WTO Agreement on Textiles and Clothing by examining all measures taken under it and ensuring that they are in conformity with the rules.

9

Contingent Socialization in Asian Regionalism
Possibilities and Limits

AMITAV ACHARYA

This chapter examines the "socializing effect" of Asian regional institutions, using the theoretical and conceptual prism of constructivist approaches to international relations. The concept of socialisation is constructivism's foremost theoretical tool in explaining change in world politics. (Johnston 2001, 2008, Checkel 2005). Constructivists hold that international (including regional) institutions, as key agents and sites of socialization, not only regulate the behavior of states, but also reconstitute their interests and identities. In this analysis, I examine the extent to which Asian regional institutions have socialised their member states, and to what extent the motivations and conditions of socialisation as specified by constructivist theory have played out in the region and shaped its regional institutions. A key contribution of this essay is the identification of a dynamic which I call Type III socialisation, or "contingent socialisation," which is an important function of Asian regional institutions, and is the key reason why they "matter."

Why turn to constructivism and especially to the concept of "socialization" to understand Asian regionalism? The distinctive contributions of constructivist approaches to Asian regional institutions, as opposed to the rationalist institutionalist approaches (best exemplified in this volume by the contributions by Haggard, O'Rourke, and Hix) include the following.

First, while rationalist theories tend to adopt a fixed, geographic and geopolitical view of regions, constructivists stress the politics of regional definition and identification. There can be no preordained, permanent, or changeless regions. Regions, whether Southeast Asia (Acharya 2000), or East

Asia (Evans 1999, Pempel 2005) or the Asia-Pacific (Dirlik 1992), are social constructs, whose boundaries are subject to negotiation and change. The effectiveness of regional institutions thus depends on the identity. Moreover this identity is not culturally preordained, but socially constructed. Constructivists do not necessarily agree on all the question about identity, especially whether regions are constructed from *within* or from *without*. But unlike realists who often think of regions as extensions of great power geopolitics, constructivism makes greater allowance for the bottom-up construction of regions.

A second distinctive contribution of the constructivist approach to Asian regionalism concerns the question: why do they differ from the European variety. While Europe's regionalism is older, much more institutionalized, and legalized and marked by supranational governance, Asia's is late, sovereignty bound, informal, and non-legalistic. Katzenstein (2005) argues that the reason for this has to do not only with differing domestic structures (which will be consistent with liberal perpsectives) such as Asia's non-Weberian polities versus Europe's Weberian ones, but also with international norms, such as Asia's adherence to the norm of "open regionalism," and variations in mutual identification among the actors that comprise the two regionalism. Identity also addresses one of the key puzzles of Asian regional institutionalism: why did post-War Asia not develop a multilateral institution? While realists explain the puzzle by pointing to American's "extreme hegemony" in the early postwar period as a factor inhibiting multilateralism, and liberals do so by pointing to the region's initial lack of economic interdependence, constructivists point not to the role of identity and norms. For Katzenstein (2005; Hemmer and Katzenstein, 2001), US perceptions of a greater collective identity with its European partners as a community of equals led it to encourage NATO-like multilateralism in Europe; the absence of such identification and the perception of Asia an inferior community led it to shun multilateralism there. Another constructivist explanation looks beyond the US-Asia identity dissonance and argues that the late development of Asian multilateralism could be explained in terms of the normative beliefs and preferences of Asian actors against great power led security multilateralism (Acharya 2009).

Third, constructivism has much to say about the issue of institutional design. For example, the literature on ASEAN authored by constructivist scholars were among the first to theorize about the distinctive features of Asian institutions, including their informal, non-legalistic, consensus-based, and process-driven approach to coordination and collaboration (Acharya 1997; Haacke 2003). These design features of ASEAN have also been grafted onto the wider Asia Pacific institutions such as APEC and ARF. While rationalist theories consider these features in a negative light, as barriers to cooperation, constructivists tend to see them on a positive light, in bringing about accommodation and cooperation in a acutely sovereignty conscious and bound region.

Fourth and most fundamentally, the constructivist approach redefines and broadens our understanding of the conditions for the success of regional institutions and the criteria for measuring their "effectiveness." For example, rationalist neoliberal perspectives (such as Hix and Haggard in this volume) stress "preference convergence" as a key condition to the success of regional institutions (in this volume, Hix uses it to explain the success of the EU, whereas for Haggard, the absence of preference convergence explains the weaknesses of Asian institutions). Constructivists on the other hand stress normative convergence as key to the success of institutions. This focus on normative convergence and agency also distinguishes constructivism from rationalist explanations of institutions which revolve around geopolitical and economic interests (seen in the contribution to this volume by O'Rourke, who also stresses chance and contingency in explaining the EU's progress). Moreover, it is commonplace for rationalist and materialist theories to argue that institutions matter only if they provide collective security or defence (stressed by realists), or free trade (stressed by neoliberals). Constructivists on the other hand argue that the contribution of regional institutions are fundamentally social and normative, meaning it cannot be understood without taking into consideration their role in inducing rule-governed behavior. In other words, institutions encourage actors to act from a logic of appropriateness, rather than purely from a logic of consequences.

To elaborate, constructivists (Acharya 1997; Johnston 1999; Acharya 2003, 2009a, 2009b; Ba 2009) believe that the major contribution of Asian institutions is ideational, social and normative. For example, the constructive literature on ASEAN highlights the role of ideational forces—norms, identity, community, and strategic culture—in the origin and evolution of ASEAN (Acharya 2005; Haacke 2003; Ba 2009). Subsequent constructivist studies have highlighted ASEAN's constraining impact on inter-state conflicts and great power behavior, and the strengths and limits of ASEAN's informal regionalism, including the extension of the ASEAN model to East Asia and Asia-Pacific. Asian institutions act as sites of normative contestation, creation—"norm breweries" to use Katsumata's (2006) term—and localization. While Asian regionalism is influenced by global norms, these norms are not imported wholesale, but are "localized" by regional actors to suit their own context and need and in accordance with their prior beliefs and practices. Thus, the usefulness and relevance of these normative discourses carried through regional institutions is enhanced by such "constitutive localization" (Acharya 2004). A related subsequent line of investigation concerns the socialising effects of security institutions, particularly the ASEAN Regional Forum. Johnston (2008) cautiously argues in support of the ARF's influence in inducing a more cooperative behavior by China. This challenges Leifer's (1996) skeptical view of the ARF which pointed to its 'structural flaw" as a group of weak states (ASEAN) aspiring to manage a security institution whose membership includes practically all the great powers of the international system.

Yet, socialization theory offers perhaps the most powerful challenge to realist skepticism that generally dismisses international institutions as mere adjuncts to great power preferences and balance of power dynamics. Below, I discuss why and how.

Socialisation and Asian Regional Institutions

Socialisation means getting new actors to adopt the rules and norms of a community on a long-term basis without the use of force or coercion. There are four key aspects to this definition. First and foremost, socialisation's key ingredient is norms. Socialisation implies norm transmission by socialisers resulting in pro-norm behavior by the socialisee. Risse (1997,16) emphasises processes "resulting in the internalisation of norms so that they assume their 'taken-for-granted' nature" as the core aspect of socialisation; while Ikenberry and Kupchan (1990,289–90) define socialisation as a process of learning in which the norms and ideals are transmitted by one party to another. Second, for constructivists, such norm transmission that underlies socialisation is pacific and non-coercive. There is no socialisation through force or conquest; the key mechanism of socialisation is persuasion. Third, socialisation is directed at newcomers, or novices. Fourth, socialisation leads to long-term and stable change in behavior, rather than short-term adaptation. Checkel's definition of socialisation which draws upon previous writings on the subject, including sociological perspectives, is useful to borrow. Socialisation is:

> defined as a process of inducting actors into the norms and rules of a given community. Its outcome is sustained compliance based on the norms and rules of a given community. In adopting community rules, socialisation implies that an agent switches from following a logic of consequences to a logic of appropriateness; this adoption is sustained over time and is quite independent from a particular structure of material incentives or sanctions. (Checkel 2005,804, reference marks deleted)

The insights of the constructivist literature on socialisation can be summarized as follows:

1. Whereas previous works on socialisation focused more on the motivations and role of "socialisers," more recent works (especially Johnston,
   2008; Acharya, 2004, 2009) investigate it from the perspective of
   the "socialisee" or the norm-taker. In other words, in understanding
   socialisation, it is more important to understanding the domestic and
   external conditions of the socialisee/persuade/norm taker as that of
   socialiser/persuader/norm giver.

2. International institutions play a vital role in socialisation, whether
   as promoters of socialisation from outside or as sites of socialisation
   (when the socialisee is a member of the institution).

3. There is no one pathway to socialisation. Mechanisms of socialisation
   can include strategic calculation (whereby the target actor calculates
   that the benefits of socialisation exceeds its costs) and bargaining, as
   well as persuasion, teaching, mimicking, social influence, argumen-
   tation, "role playing," or normative suasion. The shift to a logic of
   appropriateness is not necessarily a shift to what is morally appropriate, but to what is socially appropriate, from a calculation of what is
   instrumentally beneficial to the socialisee (logic of consequences).

The dependent variable of socialisation (when we know socialisation has
taken place) is internalisation of "the values, roles, and understandings held by
a group that constitutes the society of which the actor becomes a member.
Internalisation implies, further, that these values, roles, and understandings
take on the character of "taken-for-grantedness" (Johnston 2007,21). The
degree of internalisation may vary, however. Socialisation may or may not
involve a fundamental redefinition of the interests and identities of the target;
sometimes, the target may agree to play by the rules of the group it is being
inducted to without developing a "we feeing." Checkel distinguishes between
Type I socialisation, where the socialisee has accepted new roles out of instrumental calculations (incentive-based) in order to conform to the expectations
of a community it seeks to belong to, but does not necessarily like it or agrees
with it, and Type II socialisation, where genuine and long-term (taken for
granted) changes to the interests and values of the socialisee have occurred,
and where new roles and behavioral changes reflect a new normative conception that "it's the right thing to do" (Checkel 2005, 808, 813).

Socialisation depends on a number of conditions. Zurn and Checkel's
(2005, 1055) list of scope conditions of socialisation includes properties of the

international institutions that trigger socialisation, properties of the political systems and agents that become socialised, properties of the issues or norms regarding which socialisation takes place, and properties of the interaction between socializing and socialised agents (e.g., intensity of contact, style of discourse). A more selective and specific set of hypotheses about socialisation may be derived from the literature on persuasion, an important mechanism or "micro process" of socialisation (Checkel and Moravcsik, 2001; Checkel 2005). According to this literature, persuasion is more likely to succeed if (a) the target actors are in a new and uncertain environment, (b) if the prior and ingrained beliefs of the persuade does not clash with the beliefs and messages of the persuader, (c) if the persuader is an authoritative member of the in-group to which persuade wishes to belong, (d) if the persuader itself sets the example and acts out the principles of deliberative argument and, (e) if the interaction occurs in setting that is relatively less politicized or more insulated from public opinion and pressure (in-camera setting). (For a more extensive list of the 'scope conditions' but generalized out of European cases, see Checkel 2005, 813; Zurn and Checkel 2005.) Other determinants of socialisation include group size, intensity and frequency of contact, and shared identity among the persuader and the persuade.

How do these conditions apply to Asian regionalism? To investigate this question, I focus on three main cases of socialisation through regional institutions in Asia: Vietnam, China, and India. (One might plausibly include the US here, but I have kept America out on grounds of regional belonging and identity.) I discuss below these three cases in terms of the insights of the socialisation literature outlined above.

The first area to look at concerns the socialisee's imperative. In each of these cases, the changing domestic conditions (including regime legitimacy

TABLE 9.1.

Key norms of Asian regional institutions

Institutions	ASEAN	APEC	ARF
Norms (substantive)	Non-interference; Pacific settlement of disputes; Primacy of regional solutions; Avoidance of multilateral military pacts reflecting great power rivalry; One Southeast Asia concept	Open regionalism; market-driven regionalisation	Common/cooperative security, Inclusiveness; non-interference, avoidance of NATO-style military cooperation
Norms (procedural)	Consensus; Informalism; Voluntary compliance	Flexible consensus; Concerted unilateralism; Soft institutionalism	Consensus; ASEAN leadership; Voluntary Compliance

and survival) of the target have been critical. Deng Xiaoping's reforms in China (inspired by domestic economic pressure, ideological shift, regime insecurity, and a desire to restore China's standing in the world) beginning in the late 1970s, Vietnam's withdrawal from Cambodia (induced by domestic economic failure earlier in the 1980s created by the burden of its occupation of Cambodia), and India's crisis-induced (a severe balance of payments crisis and near default on foreign debt) liberalization in the early 1990s paved the way for critical foreign policy shifts leading to their eventual membership in regional institutions. External conditions, especially the end of the Cold War, have also been a critical factor, but not sufficient by itself to explain why these countries chose to be socialised, since the end of the Cold War did not generate similar responses from North Korea. Moreover, the socialisation of the three states did not begin simultaneously, Vietnam's was first and perhaps most advanced, China's was second in sequence, followed by India. And the socialisation of China and India has not progressed to the same extent. Hence domestic conditions and the preferences of the *socialisee* are the more important variables here than the singular external event, the end of the Cold War.

The second area is the role of institutions, especially regional ones. There is little doubt that regional institutions have been critical in the socialisation process, both before and after the target states became formal members. While ASEAN has been the most important institution for Vietnam, the ARF has been especially important for China. For India, the prospect of becoming an ASEAN dialogue partner and a member of ARF and the East Asian Summit has been similarly important. Once they have become members, regional institutions have become sites of dialogues, rule-making, and creation of new mechanisms of cooperation.

The third, the issue of strategic calculation, versus persuasion/argumentation/social influence, is especially important. No one can exclude strategic calculation on the part of the three states in engaging and being engaged by these institutions. For Vietnam, membership in ASEAN offered an opportunity to attract foreign investment, even before the AFTA and ASEAN Investment Area, and a platform to cushion its reentry into the international system after a decade of isolation due to its occupation of Cambodia. It also meant diplomatic support (albeit implicit and limited) for its territorial claim (Spratlys and Paracels Islands) against China (in the sense that its bilateral dispute with China now became a China-ASEAN issue). For China, the strategic calculation in joining the ARF, despite substantial misgivings, would have been the opportunity afforded by ARF as a platform to launch a "charm offensive" and reduce the perceptions of the "China threat." Neutralizing Taiwan's influence-seeking in Southeast Asia through trade and investment was also important. For India, improving its then dismal economic condition, having ASEAN as its bridge with the prosperous East Asian neighbours, and strategic competition with China were important motivations that a rationalist framework would easily recognize.

But as noted, constructivists accept that norm compliance and socialisation is not inconsistent with self-interested behavior. The key is whether what we are witnessing is pacific, long-term, and transformative (in the sense that they involve a redefinition of interests and identities, and not simply short-term adaptation and reluctant role-playing). The jury is still out on this question. But certain important indicators of internalisation are visible in each cases, in which regional institutions have played an important role, whether as external promoters or sites of socialisation.

Turning to Vietnam first, there is considerable evidence that Vietnam has accepted and internalised ASEAN's non-intervention norm, in contrast to its past disregard and violation of the norm, evident in its support for communist movements in neighbouring Southeast Asian states, its grand scheme of an Indochinese federation dominated by itself, and its invasion and occupation of Cambodia. In the case of China, the key change has been the shift from an exclusively bilateral approach to conflict management to a multilateral approach. This is evident in its acceptance of multilateral talks with ASEAN on the South China Sea dispute leading to a Declaration on the Code of Conduct in the South China Sea (not yet a full-fledged legal instrument or code, but an important step toward it; further progress toward such a code will be a key test of its internalisation of multilateralism norm). China's growing support for the ARF despite earlier misgivings about it is also important. My research offers a graphic account of the conceptual shift in Chinese thinking on multilateralism in the 1990s. Johnston (2007) provides considerable evidence of changes to Chinese bureaucratic and decision-making structures that support the internalisation of new norms of multilateralism. As for India, the key change is in the economic arena: it's evident in India's gradual shift from economic nationalism and protectionism to trade liberalization and openness to foreign direct investment. Again, this shift is occurring (albeit haltingly) not just because of regional institutions, but regional institutions have provided key sites for the change, including the negotiations over the ASEAN-India Free Trade Agreement and India's own interest in developing an Asian Free Trade Area (as well as prospective membership in APEC, as yet unrealized but an incentive for accepting free trade liberalization norms). What is striking about India's membership in ASEAN, ARF, and EAS is that unlike the 1940s and 1950s, when India was the leading provider of Asian regionalist ideas and a key force behind Asian multilateral conferences (such as the Asian Relations Conference of 1947 and 1949 and the Asia-Africa Conference of 1955), it is now following someone else's (ASEAN's) lead in regionalism.

These instances of internalisation (as indicator of socialisation) have their limits. China does not accept a preventive diplomacy role (signifying deeper multilateralism) for the ARF, or resorting to multilateralism in addressing the Taiwan issue, and India is not yet a full convert to free trading with East Asian countries, or to multilateralism in resolving the Kashmir conflict. But while not comprehensive, in my judgment, their normative and behavioral shifts are irreversible. There is no going back to the Indochinese federation for Vietnam, exclusive bilateralism for China and the Nehruvian socialism for India. And it is fair to say that these shifts are induced by socialisation through regional institutions, although not exclusively by them. Regional institutions have helped to create and reinforce the convergence between domestic interests, strategic calculation, and international behavior.

The evidence seen thus far suggests the possibility of a Type III internalisation, in addition to Checkel's Type I (states acting in accordance with group expectations "irrespective of whether they like the role or agree with it"), and Type II in which there is real value and interest change leading agents to "adopt the interests, or even possibly the identity, of the community of which they are a part" (Checkel 2005,804). In either case, instrumental calculation, which may be initially present as a mechanism of socialisation, has been replaced by a logic of appropriateness. Although Checkel calls for a "double interpretation" of every instance of socialisation, once from the perspective of constructivism and once from the perspective of rational choice, he is quite clear on what socialisation entails; in order to be socialised, whether into a Type I or a Type II outcome, states must discard instrumental calculation (logic of consequences) in favour of logic of appropriateness (Checkel 2005,804). By contrast, I suggest a Type III internalisation to refer to a condition in which agents act both instrumentally and normatively, concurrently, and on a more or less permanent basis. Moreover, in Type III internalisation a key factor in determining the outcome may be the logic of expediency. Creating a room for states to determine their own pace within regional institutions/agreements is an important enabler for Type III internalisation, in which states act both instrumentally and normatively, concurrently, to support regional cooperation and integration. In this situation, states tend to pursue new initiatives or new directions at a pace comfortable to all stakeholders. Yet this is no short-term shift from purely instrumental calculation and behavior, the shift is irreversible, even though it may or may not lead to Type II internalisation, in which values and interests change permanently.

I call this Type III internalisation as "contingent socialization." Contingent socialization best describes the effects of Asian institutions today on newcomers. While the socialisees (China, India, Vietnam) are not in the danger of backtracking, they need more time and convincing before fully committing to the new norms and roles to an extent where interest and identity transformation becomes discernable. And they may never get to that stage. In other words, Type III internalisation may or may not be an intermediary stage or the tipping point between Type I and Type II. Moreover, Type III internalisation may not be comprehensive in terms of issue areas. Vietnam, China, and India have all committed to non-interference, multilateralism, and trade regionalism, respectively and irrevocably, but they each have not embraced all the three areas, at least to the same degree. Uneven socialisation and internalisation is thus a feature of Type III socialisation.

Let me offer three examples which illustrate the differences between the three types of socialization at work in Asian regional institutions.[1] The first example concerns the ASEAN Regional Forum. The key goal of the ARF, set up in 1994, was to induce Chinese acceptance of multilateral security, which would "constrain" its rising power. China, after initially being skeptical of the ARF, warmed to closer engagement in what some would regard as Asia's first truly multilateral cooperative security institution (Acharya 2009a, 2009b). Type I internalization would expect that China agreed to join the ARF and participate in its activities simply to satisfy the expectations of its neighbours, principally ASEAN (and to a lesser extent Australia and Canada), and learning to be multilateral despite having misgivings that multilateralism

TABLE 9.2.
Types of socialisation / internalisation

	Type I	Type II	Type III
Agent's (Socialisee) motivation	To be socially accepted by satisfying group expectations	Because "it's the right thing to do"	To be socially accepted by finding the best fit between self-interest and group purpose
Indicator of internalisation	Learning and playing new roles even when the agent may not like it or agree with it	Changes in interests and identities that can be "taken for granted"	Learning new roles that it agrees with, with some redefinition of its interests and identities
Logic of action	Logic of appropriateness	Logic of appropriateness	Logic of consequences and logic of appropriateness

might give the weaker ASEAN countries an opportunity to gang up against Chinese power. There is some truth to it, certainly more than the evidence that there is of China's participation in the ARF being guided by a purely normative concern, that it was the "right thing to do." And nearly two decades after China's joining in the ARF, one can hardly take its interest and level of support for the ARF for granted, as would be consistent with Type II internalization.

But in my view, China's decision to participate in the ARF and the extent and limits of this participation to date are more consistent with Type III internalization. For China, joining the ARF was partly due to *strategic calculation:* dampen the "China threat" perception among its neighbours, ensure peaceful regional environment conducive to its own economic development and hence national empowerment; enhance China's international status and demonstrate China's "peaceful rise"; use ASEAN's support to influence US position toward China, especially any US approach toward "containing" China. At the same time, China could also relate positively to the "group purpose" of the ARF, as defined by ASEAN, which was in the "driver's seat" of the grouping. ASEAN had made it clear that the purpose of the ARF was not collective defense, but cooperative security, that it would be an inclusive grouping which would also respect the sovereignty and national interests of all members, big or small. In the end, China's participation in the ARF reflected this "mixed motive." It accepted the confidence-building role of the ARF (especially as a forum for dialogue) but opposed or stymied more intrusive measures planned by some members of the grouping, including intrusive measures and binding agreements on security cooperation. It would only agree to a limited and minimal role of the grouping in preventive diplomacy and conflict definition. Overall, the outcome of socializing China through the ARF is consistent with Type III internalization, guided by scope conditions such as the reputation of the socializer (ASEAN), sustained and intense contact, and consistency with socializee's prior norms.

The outcome of APEC's Trade Liberalization (circa 1993–1997) offers another example of Type III socialization. During this period, APEC featured a contest between the objectives of the US (as the socializer) and those of ASEAN (as the socializee). The US wanted to use ASEAN and APEC as a counter to EU single market, introduce reciprocity into APEC's trade agenda, and introduce and secure adherence to the so-called "Washington Consensus" principles. As the socialize, ASEAN wanted to use the US as a counter to EU's single market, keep the US engaged as a regional security guarantor, and prevent its marginalization in APEC. In the end, ASEAN remained within

APEC not wanting to wreck this Australian-inspired forum, but succeeded in ensuring the location of the APEC secretariat in Southeast Asia (Singapore) and diluting strict reciprocity in trade agreements. It was able to promote its own preferred norms, such as developmental regionalism, flexible consensus, and concerted unilateralism within APEC. Here too, the outcome is consistent with Type III internalisation. The key scope conditions which shaped this outcome were the persuader's lack of reputation as a socialiser, insufficient intensity and duration of contact, and clash between the persuader's norms and the prior norms of socializee.

A third example of Type III internalization can be found in the ASEAN-India FTA (2004–2009). The signing of this initiative reflected strategic and normative concerns on the part of both the socializer (ASEAN) and the socializee (India). The goals of ASEAN, as the socializer, in pushing for this FTA were partly based in instrumental calculation: to use India as a balancer against China in Southeast Asia; to exploit trade and investment opportunities in India. Other goals included gaining access to India's large domestic market without granting it too many exceptions and to enhance ASEAN's reputation and status as a regional integrator and driver of wider Asian regionalism. ASEAN also wanted to utilize its Treaty of Amity and Cooperation, and open regionalism norms as basis for engaging India. The motivations of India similarly included strategic calculation: to use ASEAN as a stepping stone to regional influence in East Asia and balance China. It also involved an element of bargaining: to protect elements of India's domestic sector from competition while gaining access to ASEAN's markets. But not to be ignored were cultural and historical factors which were conducive to normative suasion, such as India's historic cultural and demographic links with Southeast Asia.

Conditions of Socialization

Finally, let me turn to the conditions of socialisation, which are important in answering the question why internalisation, even if to such limited degree, has taken place in Asia. Of the five conditions outlined above, the new and uncertain strategic and economic environment of the post-Cold War era has certainly been an important factor; Khong (2004) has argued that the principal missions of Asian regional institutions have been to reduce and manage uncertainty. Uncertainty (about the US military posture, the rise of China and its strategic intent and behavior, competition between China and Japan, the appearance of regional trade blocs due to NAFTA, and European Union's Single Market) was the key element of the security discourse of the post-Cold

War period and it certainly helps to focus the purpose and direction of Asia's regional institutions. The second condition is consistent with my norm localization argument, that is, norm diffusion is more likely to be successful if it's congruent with the prior beliefs and practices of the norm-taker. Since norms are important to socialisation, it is important to recognize that certain norms promoted by external players (Australia, Canada, Gorbachev's Russia), such as "open regionalism" in the economic arena and "cooperative security" in the security arena, have been accepted in Asia (by ASEAN states and China) because they were congruent (or made to appear as such by norm entrepreneurs from Canada and Australia) with the prior beliefs and practices of the local actors, which included ASEAN's prior multilateralism and its openness to foreign direct investment. By contrast, norms of humanitarian intervention and EU-style free trade failed to diffuse in East Asia because of their clash with prior local norms of non-intervention and developmental regionalism (Acharya 2004, 2009).

The third condition is also relevant in Asia: ASEAN as the chief forum for socialisation had an aura of authoritativeness (at least before the 1997 crisis) which made it attractive for China, India, and Vietnam to participate in ASEAN-led regional institutions. This authoritativeness had to do with ASEAN's relative longevity (the oldest viable regional political grouping in Asia), its role in the Cambodia peace process, its own intra-mural peace, and its system of dialogue relationships with the major powers. ASEAN had also shown both willingness and ability to act out its own norms of non-intervention and non-use of force (notwithstanding the fact that the meaning of non-intervention remains contested here, ASEAN supported fellow regimes facing internal threats, and this particular norm is now subject to increasing challenge). Its authority as a socialiser is also the result of the fact that no other country or group of countries in Asia are in a similar position to provide leadership due to their past failures (India), mutual rivalry (China-Japan), or smallness and security preoccupations (South Korea), or outsider-ness (US, Australia, Canada, Russia, etc.).

The centrality of ASEAN in Asian regionalism also raises the question of the content of norms as a condition for socialisation. In the European context, the examples of such norms which are often cited as conditions of socialisation are minority rights or democratic procedures (Zurn and Checkel 2005, 1055). In Asia, the norms that most influence socialisation are not those of human rights or democracy, but domestic non-interference and regional autonomy. Without the centrality of non-interference in the domestic affairs of states espoused by ASEAN, it is unlikely that China or Vietnam (or

Burma) would have been drawn into APEC, ARF, and EAS. Its sister norm is non-intervention by outside powers in regional affairs, or regional autonomy, and relatedly the intent to explore indigenous solutions to regional problems. This, and the related tendency to localize foreign norms to suit regional context and need in accordance with prior beliefs and practices, has not been that crucial in Europe, but is of considerable salience in Asia's postcolonial context, even though it does not imply the exclusion of outside powers from the region.

Last but not the least is the final condition of socialisation, the importance of having an "in-camera" setting. This condition might suggest that socialisation is more likely to succeed in an authoritarian setting than in a pluralistic one, where the impact of public scrutiny and pressure group influence is more likely to occur and be felt. If this is true, and there is no reason why it should not be (the success of authoritarian ASEAN governments in forming and developing the association is one example), then it challenges those who argue that democracies are more likely to building lasting and more effective institutions, including security communities. And herein lies a possible challenge to the socialising role of Asian regional institutions. As governments in ASEAN and Asia generally increasingly confront the forces of democratization, could their regional institutions keep up with the task of fostering and deepening socialisation? Unlike European institutions, Asian regional groups have not made democracy a condition of membership or rewards. In fact, they have been illiberal and have attracted new members and support by holding up the prospect of non-intervention as a reward. There is a chance that democratization may disrupt this apparent authoritarian bent of Asian regional institutions. But on the positive side, there is no evidence that democratization has induced inter-state war in East Asia and disrupted regionalization or regionalism. On the contrary, it may foster a cooperative security dynamic as evident under recently democratising regimes in South Korea and Indonesia (Acharya 2010).

Of course, socialisation in Asia has not been uniformly successful, as the cases of North Korea and Myanmar demonstrate. But these failures can be explained to some extent by the absence of the scope conditions of socialization, especially frequency and intensity of contact and clash with the prior beliefs of the regimes. In both cases, the prior isolation of the regimes (and hence the low intensity and frequency of contact) is important. ASEAN's policy of Constructive Engagement of Myanmar in the 1990s did not involve direct talks with the regime. The Six-Party Talks with North Korea did provide a forum for contact, but it was clearly limited in scope, failing to address

TABLE 9.3.

Socialisation of Vietnam, China, and India

Institutions/ members	ASEAN	APEC	ARF
Vietnam	Ended occupation of Cambodia in 1989; Signed the Paris Peace Agreement on Cambodia in 1991; Observer status in ASEAN in 1992; Full ASEAN membership in 1995; Chair (rotational) of ASEAN in 2001 and 2010. Leading role in drafting the Hanoi Plan of Action for ASEAN. Abandoned Indochinese federation concept (non-interference); Adheres to One Southeast Asia concept; Seeks peaceful settlement of South China Sea dispute but wants coverage of the South China Sea Code of Conduct to extend to the Paracels; Conservative and staunch champion of non-interference principle.	Joined APEC in 1998. Hosted APEC Summit in 2006 Growing domestic economic liberalisation consistent with open regionalism and market-driven regionalization.	Founding member in 1994; Chair of ARF 2001 and 2010 Inclusiveness: supported North Korea's admission to ARF Cooperative security: regular participation in the ARF's CBMs and capacity-building initiatives; Abandoned military alliance with the former Soviet Union; Seeks to balance but not contain China

China	Agreed to multilateral talks with ASEAN on the South China Sea dispute in 1995; Full Dialogue partner of ASEAN in 1996; Signatory to Treaty of Amity and Cooperation in 2003; Willing to be the first Nuclear Weapon Sate to sign the Southeast Asia Nuclear Weapon–Free Zone Treaty; proposed Free Trade Area with ASEAN in 2002, Agreement to be signed in 2010.	Joined in 1991 along with Taiwan. Accepts Open Regionalism, but supports development-oriented agenda for APEC in preference to trade liberalization	Founding member in 1994. Inclusiveness: supported India's membership in ARF; Cooperative security: regular participation in CBMs and capacity-building initiatives; Leadership: initiated ARF's Security Policy Conference (ASPC–meeting of defence ministry senior officials) in 2004. Excludes Taiwan Issue; Opposes full preventive diplomacy and conflict resolution role for ARF; Opposes raising South China Sea dispute in ARF; Wants ARF to remain consultative, rather than become a problem-solving forum
India	Sectoral Dialogue Partner of ASEAN in 1992; Signatory to Treaty of Amity and Cooperation in 2003; Full dialogue partner in 2005; Willing to sign the Southeast Asian Nuclear Weapon-Free Zone Treaty if asked as a Nuclear Weapon State; India-ASEAN Free Trade agreed in 2008	Sought APEC membership before the membership freeze, but denied. Growing if qualified conformity with Open Regionalism and trade liberalization	Joined the ARF in 1996. Inclusiveness; Cooperative security through participation in confidence-building measures; Leadership in the ARF's maritime security and counter-terrorism initiatives; Seeks to balance but not contain China. Excludes Kashmir issue, even though Pakistan became an ARF member

NOTES: This table incorporates five key indicators of socialisation: (1) partial or full membership; (2) participation in key multilateral agreements with the institution and its members; (3) support for the core norms of the institution; (4) leadership and agenda-setting role (indicating interactive or passive participation); and (5) exclusion of issues from multilateral approach. It should be noted that neither China nor India can join ASEAN whose members alone have the right to host annual ASEAN and APEC leaders meetings and ARF's annual ministerial meeting; the relevant forum for them would be full dialogue partnership with ASEAN.

Pyongyang's regime insecurity, and paling in comparison with the frequency of dialogues among other participants, say between South Korea and US, US and Japan, and even US and China. Also important in both cases is the prior beliefs of the socialisee (which is closely related to regime type). To the extent that socialisation involves overcoming isolationist and autarchic domestic political ideology of the target regimes, the deep-seated paranoia of the regimes in North Korea and Myanmar underpinned by their ideologies of national self-reliance—*Juche* and "Burmese Way to Socialism", respectively—conflicted with the call for openness (economic and political liberalisation, rather than democratisation) from the regional institutions. Finally, and this applies only to North Korea's case, ASEAN and ASEAN-led institutions like the ARF have been somewhat distant and indifferent interlocutors in Northeast Asian security affairs. The Six-Party Talks have been an ad hoc process (in line with the US preference for a la carte multilateralism). A preestablished Northeast Asian subregional institution like ASEAN in Southeast Asia was not around to cushion the dialogue with North Korea. Instead of providing the forum for the socialization of North Korea, such a mechanism is envisaged as a possible outcome of the Six-Party Talks. While the cases of North Korea and Myanmar attest to the failure of socialization by Asian regional institutions, they do suggest the applicability of the conditions of socialisation identified by socialisation theory.

Socialisation and Institutional-Design in Asia

As noted, institutions are central to the constructivist view of international relations, and socialisation is the core function of institutions. But how do the design features of institutions (institutional-design) shape socialisation? What sort of design features are most conducive to socialisation? And conversely, how does having socialisation as their objective shape institutional-design? Socialisation is different from coercion, sanctions, or other types of negative incentives. Hence, different types of institutional design may offer different potential for success of socialisation. Constructivist theory holds that the best chance for success in socialisation lies with institutions which do not coerce or (materially) constrain, but persuade and (socially) pressure. These institutions are more likely to promote behavior on the basis of a logic of appropriateness rather than of consequences.

The literature is not uniform when it comes to identifying the elements of institutional-design, but the following five are important (Acharya and Johnston 2007):

1. Membership (inclusive or exclusive)

2. Scope (range of issue areas, multipurpose or issue-specific)

3. Decision-making rules (e.g., consensus as opposed to majority voting)

4. Ideology (including ideological flexibility)

5. Mandate (brainstorming as opposed to problem solving, distributive versus deliberative, "process over the product")

To this list, one might add institutional foundation and linkages. "These two elements are most important particularly when an institution is at the stage of being proposed or is evolving. Knowing right on which existing regional institutions/agreements a new one should be founded, built on, branch out, and link up to could increase the possibility of its acceptability and success."[2]

The elements of institutional-design can affect the socialisation capacity of institutions. In general, inclusive membership, mutipurposity, decision-making by consensus, and a deliberative mandate are more conducive to socialisation, as they facilitate persuasion. In terms of ideology, ideological flexibility, rather than substance, is more conducive to socialisation. In Asian institutions, the link between socialisation and institution-design has been a two-way process. Prior norms developed through interactions and informal institutions (Bandung Conference, 1955, Association of Southeast Asia) have influenced the design of formal institutions (ASEAN). At the same time, institutions have rendered these designs stable if not permanent. The ASEAN Way thus became the basis for the 'Asia-Pacific Way,' or Asia Pacific institutions like the ARF, APEC, and the East Asian community blueprint. The element of path dependency in the design of Asia regional institutions is especially striking.

It is clear that decision-making rule and mandate have been crucial to the socialising potential of Asian institutions, including ASEAN, APEC, and ARF. All operate by consensus, and have a deliberative, rather than distributive mandate. The effect of scope and membership is less clear. ASEAN expansion has been important to its continued relevance in the post-Cold War era, while the ARF's principle of inclusiveness is what has sustained it so far and resulted in the engagement of China and US. But it's unclear whether APEC's expansion to the Latin American nations has been as fruitful, as it raises the question not only of dilution of regional identity, but also the lower frequency and intensity of contact, which are crucial to socialisation. Ideological flexibility has been common to all Asian groups, which have accommodated different degrees of openness to market economics, political democracy, and state sovereignty. There is no NATO type or EU style ideology binding Asian institutions. And despite growing legalization (Kahler 2004) and formalization (e.g., ASEAN Charter), there is no prospect of major and sudden changes to this situation.

Conclusion

The constructivist turns in international relations theory have influenced and advanced the study of Asian regionalism and regional institutions in important ways. It broadens the understanding of the sources and determinants of Asian regional institutions by giving due play to the role of ideational forces, such as culture, norms, and identity, as opposed to material determinants. By stressing the role of culture and identity, it has helped to link the insights of the traditional area studies approach to Asia or Asian states to the larger domain of international relations theory. Constructivism has also introduced a less static conception of Asia's regional order. By giving greater play to the possibility of peaceful change through socialisation, constructivism has challenged the hitherto centrality of the balance of power perspective. At the very least, it has infused greater theoretical diversity and opened the space for debate, thereby moving the study of Asia's regional relations significantly beyond the traditionally dominant realist perspective.

Like other major theories of IR, constructivism emerged and initially reflected predominantly Western intellectual concerns and debates. But it has found a solid foothold in Asia. Constructivist writings on Asian regionalism have made some distinctive contributions, as highlighted in this essay. One contribution is that ideas and norms that are borrowed from outside go through a localization process, rather than adopted wholesale, before they trigger institutional change. This is seen in the ideas of open regionalism and cooperative security in APEC and ARF, respectively. Second, institutions can emerge and achieve success despite great power indifference or opposition. A corollary is that institutions created and led by weaker actors can engage and socialize stronger states (ASEAN and ARF in relation to the US and China). Third, institutions need not be formal or legalistic in order to play a meaningful role in redefining actor interests and identities (ASEAN Way). Finally, the effects of socialization through international institutions need not be confined to a Type I (tentative and transitional) or a Type II (taken for granted and transformative) outcome, but a Type III outcome in which actors continue to be motivated by both a logic of consequences and a logic of appropriateness on a long-term basis. These insights are not just applicable to the Asian context, but have a wider relevance to the study of regional and international institutions in general.

Notes

1. Not all mechanisms may be present in every case of socialization. There may be overlap among the mechanisms, but the first one (in bold) in the above typology is the mechanism that is most active under different types of internalisation. Because Type III internalisation is a hybrid, mechanisms from Type I and Type III may overlap with those in Type III. This is particularly true of mimicking and social influence; although Johnston considers them mainly as non-rationalist mechanisms, hence theoretically part of Type II, I include them in both Type I and Type II.

2. I am grateful to a reviewer for the ADB for suggesting this variable, and the quote is from the review.

FIVE

CONCLUSION

10

The Future of Asian Regional Institutions

ANDREW MACINTYRE AND JOHN RAVENHILL

An explosion of regional institutional-building across Asia followed in the wake of the financial crisis of 1997–98. One of the conclusions to emerge strongly from the contributions to this volume is that the changes to Asia's regional architecture in the first decade of the 21st century indicate that the well-established view of Asia as presenting only a sparse array of regional institutions is no longer apposite. The new regional cooperation has taken many different forms—ranging from trade agreements among varying combinations of countries within Asia and beyond, through frameworks for financial cooperation, to both sub-regional and pan-regional umbrella frameworks to facilitate high-level political collaboration among different combinations of countries.

In this final chapter of the volume, we seek not to synthesize all that has come before, but instead attempt to look to the future—setting out some ideas and arguments about the primary drivers of change across the region and their implications for the characteristics of the regional institutional architecture that is likely to evolve over the coming five to ten years. We are particularly interested in investigating the extent to which current processes—or institutions themselves—have set in train a self-sustaining momentum that may lead to deeper integration. We give particular attention to the area of greatest activity—trade cooperation.

We begin by considering three of the major possible causal drivers invoked in the literature for what is often styled as Asia's New Regionalism—accelerating regional economic interdependence, direct business pressures in support of regional policy coordination, and a domino-style effect of cascading trade agreements of the sort allegedly occurring elsewhere in the world. We also consider these issues in the context of regional financial cooperation, and we find no real evidence of the sort that would make these compelling explanations—at least as regards the "rush to regionalism" in the first decade of this century. And yet, clearly something has been taking place. A much more plausible explanation for change in this period—which also fits with the nature of the great bulk of Asia's regional institutions themselves—is that international political and security rivalries have been fueling the surge in institution-building.

We use this core insight, together with an analysis of both the most important issues on the regional economic agenda and the changing nature of Asia security environment, to offer a stark set of predictions about the likely direction of regional institution-building in Asia.

Asia's New Regionalism

The regional architecture of Asia has been transformed in the years since the 1997/98 financial crisis. As late as 2000, the region had only one effective FTA in operation: the ASEAN Free Trade Agreement. By 2010, Asian countries were parties to 226 agreements and were negotiating a further 80 (of these, East Asian countries were parties to 124 agreements and were negotiating a further 55) (Asian Development Bank 2011: Table 2.13, pp. 61–63).[1] From being a laggard in regional trade agreements, Asia has become the most active site globally for their negotiation. In addition to the bilateral and minilateral trade agreements, two broader regional/trans-regional arrangements were initiated in the first decade of this century: the ASEAN Plus Three grouping, and the East Asia Summit (EAS), whose membership (which already included Australia, India, and New Zealand) was expanded in 2011 to incorporate Russia and the United States). The US "pivot to Asia" gave prominence to the Trans-Pacific Partnership, a previously obscure trade agreement among four small economies (Brunei, Chile, New Zealand, and Singapore). In a response intended to maintain its centrality in the regional institutional architecture, ASEAN in November 2012 launched a Regional Comprehensive Economic Partnership for a free trade area linking it and all the members of the East Asia Summit with which it currently had a preferential trade agreement (all countries except the United States). Besides the trade agreements, governments in the region have engaged in unprecedented collaboration on monetary matters including (i) the creation of a set of currency swap arrangements, the Chiang

Mai Initiative Multilateralized (CMIM), and (ii) the promotion of domestic and regional bond markets through the Asian Bond Market Initiative (ABMI) and Asian Bond Fund (ABF).

To what extent do the new Asian regional institutions provide a platform for deeper regional cooperation and further institutionalization? What dynamics have the new institutions set in train? To address these questions, we need to consider first what forces have driven the new regionalism and, second, what the consequences have been for participants and non-participants alike.

Economic Interdependence as a Driver of Asia's New Regionalism?

Arguments that increased economic interdependence has driven regionalism have a long pedigree. Functionalist explanations for why governments demand and supply regional institutions continue to enjoy popularity (e.g., Mattli 1999). The relevance of functionalist accounts of regionalism for East Asia has long been questioned, however. Regional integration in the Asia-Pacific, it was frequently argued, was "market-driven." The puzzle was to explain the absence of formal inter-governmental collaboration in the region despite the substantial increase in economic interactions among states. East Asia had experienced regionalization without regionalism. Haggard (1997, 45–46) provided one of the most sophisticated accounts: greater economic interdependence in the region, he suggested, simply had not created the collaboration and coordination problems that would have led to a demand for regional institutions (see also Kahler 1995: 107; Solingen 2008: 288–289).Unilateral action by governments had largely removed obstacles to the development of region-wide supply chains.

Many commentators have suggested, however, that the financial crises of 1997–98 marked a critical juncture in regional collaboration in East Asia. The East Asian regional architecture, writes T. J. Pempel (2008, 164), "today is more complex, more institutionalized, and more Asian than it was when the crisis struck." For some authors, this new regionalism was driven by the imperative of responding to the challenges of increased interdependence. Kawai and Wignaraja (2009, 5) in concluding that deepening market-driven integration had been "first and foremost" among the factors driving East Asian PTAs, assert that "market-driven economic integration has begun to require further liberalization of trade and FDI [foreign direct investment], as well as harmonization of policies, rules, and standards governing trade and FDI" (see also Urata 2009).

But has economic interdependence really increased in the years since the 1997/98 Asian financial crisis? It all depends on how the region and interdependence are measured. If the region is defined as ASEAN Plus Three—the 10 member states of ASEAN plus the People's Republic of China (PRC), Japan, and the Republic of Korea (Korea)—then the share of intra-regional trade in the 10 economies' total trade according to data in the ADB's Asia Regional Integration database [http://aric.adb.org/indicators.php] rose only barely from 37.5% in 1995 to 37.8% in 2008. The figure at the end of the period is substantially below the equivalent for the EU and NAFTA (Kawai and Wignaraja 2008, Table 1). Hamanaka (2012), in a comprehensive analysis of other measures of intra-regional trade integration, similarly found that ASEAN Plus Three was lagging behind Europe and North America. Other studies (for instance, Capannelli, Lee, and Petri 2008) that report much higher values for the intra-regional share in East Asia include trade between Hong Kong and the PRC, which involves a substantial amount of double counting because of the entrepôt role of the city state.

The significance of markets within the East Asian geographical region for the region's exports is also over-stated in the unadjusted market share figures because of substantial double-counting arising from the trade in components. While this problem of double-counting, which arises from a failure to isolate local value added in components trade/assembly, is not confined to East Asia, it is more significant within this region because components trade constitutes a higher share of overall merchandise trade there than in any other part of the world. Athukorala (2011, Table 5) reports that the share of parts and components in intra-regional exports in East Asia in 2006/7 was 47.6% compared with 25% in NAFTA and 24% in the EU.

Of significance to the prospects for institutionalized collaboration in the region is not just the absence of any evidence of a secular trend toward increased economic interdependence but the characteristics of this interdependence. To be sure, production networks and their associated trade within East Asia have been radically reorientated in the years since the 1997/98 financial crisis. The PRC's rapid economic growth has seen it emerge as a major (frequently the single most important) export market for other East Asian economies (Ravenhill 2006). But at the same time, the PRC's own export dependence on East Asian markets has declined dramatically—from 53% in 1996 to 36% in 2007. If Hong Kong is excluded, the East Asian share in China's exports in 2007 was only 20.7%.[2] The consequence is that the dependence of East Asia as a whole on markets outside of the East Asian geographical region changed little in the decade after the Asian financial crises. This dependence on extra-regional markets is disguised by the growth of trade in components: whereas under one-half of East Asian exports in 2006 was shipped directly to European and North American markets, fully two-thirds of the value of total exports ultimately ended up in these markets once the parts and components content of exports were taken into account (Asian Development Bank 2008, 71, Athukorala 2009).

Ideas that East Asia was somehow "decoupling" from the global economy were undermined by the global financial crisis of 2008-9, the effects of which were transmitted to the region primarily through the channel of trade. The countries in the region that were most severely affected by the crisis were those that were most trade-dependent (Singapore, Taiwan, Malaysia); these suffered a dramatic decline in GDP (despite the Chinese economy continuing to grow healthily during the crisis).

If arguments that concerns over the increasing transaction costs from growing interdependence within Asia were the principal driving force behind the new enthusiasm for PTAs were correct, then the expectation would be that countries would have concluded agreements with their major trading partners in the region. To date, this has not happened, particularly for the larger economies of Northeast Asia. The PRC's rapid economic growth has catapulted it to the position of top export market for several East Asian economies—including Japan, Korea, and Taiwan. Yet the Japanese government has completely eschewed a bilateral PTA with the PRC, rejecting a Chinese proposal in 2002. The Korean government has also resisted overtures from the PRC: negotiations sought by Beijing, rather than Seoul, only began in 2012. Of the three Northeast Asian economic powers, only Taiwan has reached agreement with the PRC, an Economic Cooperation Framework Agreement signed in June 2010.

Most of the first generation of PTAs that East Asian governments have concluded or are currently negotiating involve states outside the geographical region. Of the 139 agreements completed, under negotiation, or proposed at the start of 2009, 109 were with countries outside the region (ADB 2008a). Many of these have been with relatively minor trading partners, again suggesting that economics has not been the primary driving force behind these agreements. Japan, for instance, has negotiated PTAs only with ASEAN collectively, the larger ASEAN economies individually, and with Mexico—countries that collectively account for only 14% of Japan's exports. The PRC has a larger number of PTAs, but excluding its agreements with Hong Kong and Taiwan, its PTA partners account for less than 9% of its total exports (Ravenhill and Jiang 2009). The extreme case is Taiwan, whose participation in PTAs has been limited by Beijing's hostility to countries entering agreements with Taipei. Before the negotiation of the ECFA with the PRC, Taiwan's four PTAs collectively covered less than 0.25% of its total exports.[3]

In short, conventional indicators of trade and financial interdependence provide no support for arguments that increasing economic integration has driven the new Asian regionalism. The characteristics of economic integration in Asia affect the trade policy preferences of private sector actors. Components already move freely around the region, facilitated by the tariff concessions provided in export processing zones and by duty-drawback arrangements. In addition, all of the major Asian economies signed on to the WTO's ITA in 1996, which provided for the removal of tariffs on most electronics products, by far the largest single category in Asian trade.[4] Given the dependence on imported components and on extra-regional markets for finished goods, manufacturers may have an unusual combination of trade policy preferences: zero tariffs on imported goods and priority to liberalizing access to the markets of *extra*-regional countries. This combination inevitably affects the resources that they will devote to pushing for closer regional economic cooperation.

Business Interests Driving Trade Cooperation in Asia?

We turn now to consider a second major possible causal driver of Asia's new regionalism, the role of domestic business interests. The starting assumption in the literature on the political economy of trade policy is that governments are utility-maximizing rational actors whose primary concern is re-election to office. Exporting interests will lobby governments for improved access to foreign markets. But why would governments that respond to their pressures, and exporters themselves, choose a regional (preferential) approach to trade liberalization rather than a non-discriminatory global agreement, which all economic modelling suggests would bring larger aggregate economic gains? For governments, the political advantage of PTAs is that they can exploit the lax discipline of the WTO's rules on regional trade agreements to exclude sensitive domestic sectors from the liberalization process, which, consequently, poses fewer political risks for them (Grossman and Helpman 1995).

For firms, the literature predicts that exporting interests are more likely to lobby for regional rather than global liberalization when they are competitive within the proposed regional market but not at the global level. A variant of this argument suggests that a regional trade agreement would be particularly attractive to companies that depend (or would depend) on a regional market to realize economies of scale (Milner 1997, Chase 2005). Although attractive as a theoretical proposition, little empirical support has been offered for arguments based on scale economies. The relatively small additional markets provided by the current PTAs involving Asian economies render such arguments implausible as an explanation for the new Asian interest in regional trade agreements.

An intuitively more persuasive explanation views the support that exporting interests give to PTAs as being driven primarily by "defensive" concerns. For Baldwin (1993), the new enthusiasm of exporting interests for regionalism in the 1990s was triggered by idiosyncratic developments, including formation of the North American Free Trade Association (NAFTA) and the EU's move to a Single Internal Market. A domino effect of proliferating PTAs was created as exporting interests in countries excluded from the new regional arrangements pressured their governments to negotiate their own agreements to level the playing field with their rivals within the PTAs. Ultimately, the proliferation of PTAs will generate its own non-tariff-barriers in the form of incompatible rules of origin. In turn, this will lead businesses that operate increasingly globalized production networks to demand a multilateralization of regional arrangements (Baldwin 2006). A straightforward explanation for the proliferation of trade agreements involving Asian governments follows from the domino theory: it simply reflects a rational response on the part of business groups to their being disadvantaged by preferential arrangements afforded their competitors.

For businesses, the appeal of PTAs is two-fold. They can provide a "positional good" if they afford an advantage that is not available to competitors. Second, PTAs can be regarded as essential for removing disadvantages generated by the PTAs enjoyed by competitors. In the first instance, we would expect to see businesses lobbying to preserve any advantage that PTAs have created. In the second, lobbying would be prompted by desires to level the playing field. For PTAs to have such effects, however, their content must create significant advantages or disadvantages for business groups. For several reasons, skepticism that PTAs involving East Asian economies have had such effects is warranted.

First, many of the first generation of PTAs, particularly those exclusively involving the region's developing economies, had very limited coverage. Taking advantage of the lack of specificity in the WTO's Enabling Clause requirements, the agreements entered into by ASEAN, the PRC, and India are vague in their provisions, frequently failing to clearly specify the products that will be included and the tariff rates that will apply. (ASEAN's definition of free trade is tariffs that fall between zero and 5%.) Moreover, agreements involving these countries typically have lengthy timetables for implementation. They seldom included legally binding provisions or formal dispute settlement mechanisms: many of the PTAs were consistent with the longstanding East Asian preference for "soft law" arrangements (Kahler 2000). India is notorious for seeking to carve out substantial sectors of its economy from its PTAs. In its agreement with Singapore, for instance, only 4.3% of products were granted duty-free access when the agreement was initially implemented, while 56% of all Indian imports were completely excluded from the agreement (Institute of South Asian Studies 2006, 24–25).

Few of the agreements involving the region's less developed economies are WTO Plus in scope; they fail to address issues of deeper integration such as intellectual property rights, investment and competition policies, government procurement, the environment, and labor standards. On services, the region's developing economies have seldom gone beyond a restatement of their existing commitments under GATS. But in their lack of ambition, they are not unique. Although the agreements involving industrialized economies—Japan, Australia, New Zealand, and the US—attempt to extend coverage of trade in services and include provisions on government procurement, competition policy, and environment, unlike NAFTA, they do not include provisions relating to labor standards. And their references to intellectual property rights are typically no more than restatements of the governments' commitments under existing international agreements. Even on services, industrialized countries have failed to extract substantial concessions from the region's developing economies (Ravenhill 2008). Some of the region's more advanced economies have also taken advantage of the lax disciplines of the WTO in regard to regional agreements to carve out sensitive sectors—most notably, agriculture, as well as key service industries—from their liberalization schedules.

One consequence of the relatively limited coverage of the agreements, coupled with the costs of compliance with the rules of origin, is that utilization rates have been low (Ravenhill 2010). And even though much of the computer modeling that has been done of the likely welfare benefits often makes unrealistic assumptions about the extent of liberalization that will take place, it typically finds that the agreements will have a very limited aggregate effect on the economies concerned (Productivity Commission 2010).

All the evidence that points to the likely limited economic impact of existing PTAs and to the failure of businesses to make use of the provisions of existing agreements has significant implications for whether these agreements will generate an economic domino effect. If businesses are not adversely affected by the negotiation of PTAs that favor their rivals, then they are not likely to lobby their governments to negotiate similar arrangements. Similarly, if PTAs do not create significant benefits for domestic businesses, they would not be expected to lobby governments to maintain the positional goods that PTAs are expected to create. As Baldwin (2006, 1469) acknowledges, there is little evidence in the real world that governments have been unwilling to extend the benefits of PTAs to third parties; this willingness suggests that businesses either have not lobbied to prevent the erosion of preferential margins that the proliferation of agreements would generate or that any such lobbying has been ineffective. To the extent that business interests in East Asia have lobbied against the proliferation of PTAs, the pressure has come overwhelmingly from protectionist interests concerned that their position will be further eroded by additional PTAs.

The failure of the vast majority of businesses to take advantage of current PTAs also casts doubt on Baldwin's argument that the proliferation of PTAs will generate a business-led momentum toward multilateralization of the agreements. Faced with potential benefits that are minor compared with the costs of compliance with any agreement, business has simply displayed indifference toward the whole panoply of preferential trading arrangements.

No commentator would be so naïve as to suggest that governments in their foreign economic policy-making give no consideration to the interests of domestic firms. In East Asia, it is often difficult to discern the role that business plays in trade policy-making—as Manger (2009, 21) asserts in a statement that applies across the region, unlike the US case, "lobbying in Japan leaves no visible paper trail." Business leaders often have informal channels through which they can communicate their preferences to governments. Yet, institutional configurations matter. The extensive literature on East Asian political economy suggests that the logic of political action may be different in that part of the world. In particular, researchers have asserted that the state has been both a relatively autonomous actor and the lead player in formulating economic policies—whether of a "developmental" type as in Northeast Asia (Johnson 1982; Deyo 1987; Amsden 1989; Wade 1990; Woo-Cumings 1999) or those that facilitate rent-seeking patrimonialism as in many Southeast Asian countries (Mackie 1988; MacIntyre 1991). Not only does this literature propose that the state enjoys substantial autonomy from domestic interests in formulating foreign economic policies but models of economic policy-making that depend on predictions of the behavior of the median voter are unlikely to have much purchase in East Asia's authoritarian and quasi-democratic polities.

In Singapore, government-linked corporations and the subsidiaries of transnational companies dominate the local economy, providing an opportunity, Lee (2006) notes, for the state to impose its trade policy priorities with little domestic resistance. In Taiwan, Hsueh (2006, 170) asserts, a different logic of state action applies: because of the relative political weakness of sectoral interests and the government's pre-occupation with the Cross-Straits relationship, "the Taiwanese government's trade policy is often made in response not to domestic economic interests, but rather to the international political economic environment of threat under which Taiwan is forced to operate" (see also Dent 2005).

Coupled with the lack of interest of business in many of the first generation of PTAs, the relationship between the state and the private sector in many of the countries in the region produced a trade policy-making process that was state-dominated. In Thailand, where the administration of former Prime Minister Thaksin Shinawatra embarked on an active policy of simultaneously negotiating multiple PTAs with partners as diverse as Croatia and Peru, Nagai (2003, 279) states bluntly that "the private sector does not play an important role in forming FTA policy." Similarly, Chirathivat and Mallikamas (2004) noted that under Thaksin, "academia, policy-makers and even the business sector have difficulties monitoring the longer term development and progress of this FTA strategy"; some of Thailand's PTAs, Hoadley (2008, 111) contends, "seemed impulsive, the result of tourism by Thai leaders, for which the preparatory staff work had not been done." Pongsudhiriak (2010) suggests that civil society groups were more important in trade policy-making in Thailand than were business groups because their opposition to the Thaksin government's approach eventually served to cast doubt on its legitimacy. In Indonesia, Chandra and Hanim (2010) similarly find that business had little influence in trade policy-making. Even in Japan, the initial impetus for its abandonment of its longstanding commitment to non-discrimination came primarily from the government rather than reflecting business lobbying, representing an attempt to (i) stimulate East Asian cooperation in the wake of the 1997/98 Asian financial crisis, and (ii) ensure Japan's centrality within the emerging regional architecture (Munakata 2006b). In Korea, government officials reported that many businesses were either ill-informed about and/or indifferent to the government's strategy.

We do not deny that PTAs hold some attractiveness for Asian governments in the economic opportunities they afford to pursue domestic political advantage (or at least contain domestic political cost), but we do insist that this currently is not the main causal driver of regional trade cooperation.

Rather, much of the explanation for the new enthusiasm for PTAs lies not in economics but in governments' political–strategic considerations. The explosion of PTAs in the region has been driven by a political domino effect, with governments' primary concern being their potential exclusion from a new dimension of regional economic diplomacy. Choi and Lee (2005, 15) note, for instance, that the Korean government expressed increasing concern in the early years of the new millennium at being isolated as the only WTO member besides Mongolia that had not entered into an FTA. With its economy in disarray in the immediate post-financial crisis period, Korea had experienced difficulties in finding potential partners willing to negotiate with it (Park and Koo 2007).

Once the FTA bandwagon started rolling, competitive regionalism became the name of the game. As Munakata (2006a, 133) notes, competing conceptions of the region, rather than a desire to reduce transaction costs, have been the principal driving force. Of particular significance has been the rivalry between the PRC and Japan for leadership in East Asia. The PRC's offer of an FTA to ASEAN was a diplomatic masterstroke. It was designed to assuage ASEAN fears (reinforced by contemporaneous econometric studies) that low-income Southeast Asian economies would be the principal losers from the PRC's accession to the WTO (Ravenhill 2007). But it also served to place Tokyo on the defensive because of the domestic problems Japan faced in negotiating comprehensive agreements with ASEAN economies that were significant exporters of agricultural products. Its status as a framework agreement not only was in keeping with ASEAN's own vague approach to trade liberalization, but also was likely to impose few domestic costs on the PRC's economy. More recently, the proposals for the Trans-Pacific Partnership and the Regional Comprehensive Economic Partnership again reflect political rivalry—this time between alternative visions for the "region" supported by the United States and China, respectively.

With governments unhappy at the prospect of missing out on new diplomatic opportunities, they clamored to enter agreements. Recipients of requests for negotiations faced a dilemma: a negative response would have been regarded as undiplomatic in a region where "saving face" is of great importance. Governments frequently found themselves under pressure to sign on to negotiations with relatively minor partners or with partners in whose capacity or commitment to implement effective arrangements they had little confidence. The proliferation of PTAs has been driven more by a political than an economic domino effect. A survey of elite opinion in eight Asia–Pacific states provides support for the conclusion: Dent's (2006, chapter two) survey found that "strengthening diplomatic relations with key trade partners" was the reason most frequently cited for the negotiation of PTAs.

Financial Cooperation

We have given sustained attention to the dynamics of regional trade cooperation in Asia because there has been so much activity in this sphere and because it has attracted extensive commentary. But a comprehensive review of economic cooperation also requires us to consider developments in the field of regional financial cooperation. The two issue areas are, of course, linked; relatively low levels of intra-regional trade in Asia generate few pressures for monetary integration (Eichengreen 2003). Just as in trade, little evidence exists of increased regional interdependence in finance. Data for Japan, the largest source of FDI within East Asia, show that whereas this geographical region accounted, on average, for 40% of the country's outward FDI flows in the 3 years before the financial crisis, the average for the years 2005–2007 was less than 29% (JETRO 2008) More broadly, ASEAN Plus Three countries accounted for less than one-third of total ASEAN FDI inflows over the years 1995–2006; the percentage actually fell in the years after 2002. In Northeast Asia, the share of intra-regional FDI was much smaller (Hew, et al. 2007). Intra-regional portfolio asset holdings as a share of total assets held by East Asian states is smaller still: in 2006, the share was under 8% of the total in contrast to 37% derived from the US (Kim and Lee 2008, table 5). A similar lack of interdependence is evident in the exchange rate field. Ogawa and Yoshimi (2008) demonstrate that East Asian currencies, rather than moving in alignment with a notional Asian Monetary Unit (a weighted basket of regional currencies) have increasingly deviated from this unit in terms of real exchange rates.

Many of the same political economy arguments apply: because the background conditions for cooperation are unfavorable, regional cooperation in finance, as in trade, has been politically driven. Nonetheless, even though the level of activity is very much less than in trade, cooperation on finance in some ways is even more significant in symbolic terms. Unlike trade cooperation, Asia's institutional frameworks for financial cooperation are organised on a truly pan-regional basis through the ASEAN Plus Three grouping.

Much of the cooperation in the field of finance has involved information exchange, as seen in the work of the ASEAN Plus Three ABMI and the two ABFs of the Executives' Meeting of East Asia Pacific Central Banks (EMEAP). Jennifer Amyx (2008) concludes that both ABMI and ABF "have clearly made progress in pushing forward market reforms and encouraging the strengthening of local currency bond markets in the region." Nonetheless, momentum, in terms of driving and sustaining regional cooperation, has been very modest. EMEAP has undertaken no further projects since the ABF2 launch in June 2005. Meanwhile, the ABMI has stalled, largely because of the unwillingness of governments to permit cross-border local currency bond issues.

In many ways, regional cooperation on finance has the same strengths and weaknesses as APEC's work on trade and, indeed, APEC began its own study on securitized debt instruments in 2003, which was superseded by the ASEAN Plus Three initiative. Grimes's (2008) characterization of the ABMI is apt: despite the regional rationale for these projects, they rest "fundamentally on self-paced liberalization, with actual cooperation confined to some modest cooperative research efforts and demonstration projects, plus a minimalist monitoring process." He added that ABMI relies primarily on "peer pressure, information exchange, and some technical assistance."

The initiatives on financial cooperation resemble those on trade in another dimension: they are government-driven and their momentum depends on governments continuing to maintain enthusiasm for the projects. Those officials who participate in and drive the ABMI have no independent means of implementing their proposals. The involvement of the private sector has been extremely limited. EMEAP's ABF2 project, for instance, attracted little interest from non-EMEAP sources. Despite being open to the public, unlike ABF1, it failed to generate substantial private participation. As Arner, Lejot, and Wang (2009) note: "The commercial sector has been included in Asian financial integration only as a residual matter and, in contrast with the EU pattern, given no transparent role in governance other than any resulting from global initiatives."

Political considerations have also been at the heart of the region's most notable experiment in financial sector cooperation, the Chiang Mai Initiative Multilateralized (CMIM). The CMIM is an innovation in East Asian collaboration in that it is the first regional institution with weighted voting, and one that (at least nominally) is committed to unusually intrusive scrutiny of its members' policies (see Henning, Chapter 7). The multilateralization of the Chiang Mai Initiative (CMI) was a rare instance of institutional deepening in the region in response to previous failure. The CMI emerged in May 2000 from the ashes of the abortive Japanese proposal for an Asian Monetary Fund. The original CMI was a series of bilateral swap agreements. Because East Asian governments were unable to agree on effective mechanisms for surveillance of one another's economies, and for rules to enforce any conditionality, the CMI, despite its origins in criticisms of the global financial institutions, originally depended on the IMF for these functions. In the words of the former Thai finance minister, Chalongphob Sussangkarn (2010, 6) the "CMI was more symbolic than truly effective." The failure of governments to make use of the CMI during the global financial crisis—at a time when Korea and Singapore drew on bilateral swap arrangements offered by the US Federal Reserve—suggested that governments in the region doubted the CMI's value because of the continued linkage of its lending to IMF endorsement.

Proposals for the multilateralization of the CMI long predated the global financial crisis. But it required the humiliation of seeing the flagship ASEAN Plus Three agreement being ignored in precisely those circumstances for which it was originally intended to push East Asian governments into negotiating a more effective (albeit, at the time of writing, untested) arrangement. Although significant issues remain unresolved, particularly relating to the design and implementation of effective surveillance procedures, and the nature of the future relationship between the CMIM and the IMF, the multilateralization of the CMI does mark a major step forward in East Asian cooperation and demonstrates the potential for a new deepening of institutional cooperation in the region.

Yet the impact of the global financial crisis on regional financial cooperation was ambiguous. At the same time as it exposed the ineffectiveness of regional cooperation in finance, the GFC precipitated key changes to the IMF that had long been demanded by developing countries in general and particularly those in East Asia. These included a change in emphasis at the IMF towards proactive lending, and a significant adjustment of voting rights that principally benefited the large developing economies of East Asia. In combination with the raising of the G-20 to summit status, these changes gave countries within the region a greater say in management of the global economy than ever before, and may have the unintended consequence of reducing the perceived need to deepen financial cooperation at the regional level.

Strategic Rivalry, Economic Reform, and the Future of Asian Regional Institutions

In reviewing the underlying dynamics of the surge in activity across Asia to build regional trade and financial institutions, we have argued that economic efficiency considerations have played a relatively minor role and that the primary motivation has been calculations of diplomatic and broader strategic advantage. But how much does Asia's recent past have to tell us about its near future? Quite a lot, we argue. In trying to anticipate how the region's architecture will evolve over the next five to ten years, we expect significant continuity in the underlying factors bearing upon regional institutional arrangements.

First and most importantly, the causal factor to which we have given primacy—regional rivalries—will in all likelihood remain a constant, and may intensify. Major rivalries between China and Japan, and India and China, continue, as well as various more localized rivalries within South and Southeast Asia (particularly between Pakistan and India, but also continuing territorial squabbles between Malaysia and Indonesia, Thailand, and Cambodia) show no sign of abating. And arcing over the top of all of these contests is the increasingly conspicuous competition between the United States and China. These rivalries are crucial factors in likely limiting the willingness of a majority of countries to move toward a major strengthening of regional institutions. Strategic considerations frequently trump economic: for instance, territorial disputes among the Northeast Asian "Big Three"—China, Japan, and the Republic of Korea—in 2011-12 delayed the launch of negotiations for a Trilateral trade agreement.

Second, if ongoing strategic competition imposes major constraints, the prospects for substantial institutional deepening are also weakened by the reality that the biggest and most important items on the economic reform agenda across the high-growth economies of Asia are all likely to be driven primarily on a unilateral basis. The general swing to reduce trade protection in Asia through the late 1980s and 1990s was primarily a unilateral reform process, with APEC playing a modest, retrospectively reinforcing role. Something similar seems likely to pertain for the next decade. While the precise context and configuration varies, from China to Indonesia and from Vietnam to India, the big economic issues for the next five to ten years focus on financial market, labor market, and infrastructure reform. All of these issues are much more likely to be tractable on a unilateral basis rather than through any imaginable multilateral negotiations within the region. Even if strategic rivalries were not such a fundamental obstacle, on the economic issues that will matter most to governments, there is likely to be little incentive to invest in regional strategies.

What of the existing regional institutions themselves? To what extent have they created a self-sustaining momentum for deeper integration? Are the institutions socializing members into new ideas, new modes of interaction that lay the foundation for deeper regional cooperation? We are somewhat skeptical on this matter and do not go as far as the optimism expressed by Amitav Acharya

in Chapter 9. While we do indeed sense a greater propensity on the part of regional elites to think of themselves as being part of a region, we see little solid
evidence linking changed attitudes in a causal way to altered behavior. While
some regional groupings involving Asian countries have played significant roles
in disseminating knowledge and in reinforcing existing proclivities (for instance, APEC's peer pressure that strengthened the hands of pro-liberalization
elements in some of its member economies [Harris 1994]), the "soft law" character of Asian cooperation that Haggard describes in Chapter 8 does very little
to tie governments' hands or to induce behavior change. In looking at instances
where Asian institutions are purported to have socialized governments into
particular actions, it is difficult, probably even more so than in the European
case, to discern behaviors that cannot just as plausibly be explained through
rationalist lenses as the consequence of governments pursuing their perceived
national interests (for a debate on constructivist versus rationalist explanations
in the European context see Checkel and Moravcsik 2001).

We have been pessimistic about the proliferation of preferential trade agreements to create an economic dynamic that will provide momentum toward a
multilateralization (or at least regionalization) of the "noodle bowl." Analysts,
however, are increasingly questioning whether the traditional approach to
PTAs, which focuses on their lowering or removal of border barriers, provides an adequate understanding of the effects of contemporary agreements
and of actors' motivations in entering into them. Richard Baldwin (2011) has
presented the most comprehensive case that "21st century" trade agreements
reflect the internationalization of production networks and therefore about
"disciplines that underpin the trade-investment-service nexus." Whereas 20th
century regionalism was primarily about preferential market access, the new
generation of agreements involve a bargain of "foreign factories for domestic
reforms," that is, they are primarily about foreign direct investment and the
management of supply chains. In a similar vein, Mark Manger (2009) argues
that Japan's recent PTAs have been driven by concerns about enhancing or
defending the interests of its transnational corporations' foreign investments
rather than about securing market access.

To what extent are we seeing a new generation of PTAs involving East
Asian economies that differ substantially from the first generation? And, if so,
what are the political economy forces driving them? An initial point would
be to acknowledge the capacity of economic actors to learn. In Malaysia, for
instance, business groups, which had scarcely mobilized in response to the
government's initial foray into PTAs, became much better informed about
how PTAs might affect their interests and much more active in subsequent

negotiations (Postigo-Angon 2011). We expect interests of this sort will become more significant policy players with time, as political life becomes more pluralistic and more competitive in varying degrees across Asia (MacIntyre, Pempel, and Ravenhill 2008). Governments similarly learned not just from their own experiences in negotiating PTAs but also from that of other countries: agreements typically became more comprehensive and detailed as the first decade of the 21st century progressed. In some instances (most notably Korea—whereas efforts in Japan were far less successful), the institutions for making trade policy were reorganized in an effort to circumvent veto players—the entrenched protectionist interests in some ministries (Choi and Oh 2011).

Arguably the most important development in the second half of the first decade of the new century was the signature of agreements for the first time (the superficial agreements that ASEAN countries individually and collectively had previously negotiated with China notwithstanding) with major trading partners. Of particular importance in this context were the agreements that Korea negotiated first with the United States and then with the EU. These economies are respectively Korea's third and second largest export markets. Moreover, the agreements, following the templates that the larger partners had developed in other negotiations, were particularly comprehensive, containing a large number of legally enforceable provisions on issues not currently covered by WTO texts. Korea's (largely unexpected) success in these negotiations generated considerable concern in other capitals in Northeast and Southeast Asia, particularly in Tokyo—prompting the Japanese government not only to seek its own agreement with the EU (which in 2012 agreed to commence negotiations) but also to contemplate joining the US-led Trans-Pacific Partnership (TPP) agreement.

Again, however, it is important to note that change is coming about primarily through interaction with extra-regional actors, and that closer integration with actors from outside the region will not necessarily have a positive impact on cooperation within it. Consider, for instance, the momentum that the Trans-Pacific Partnership agreement gathered at the 2011 APEC summit in Hawaii. The decision by the government of Japanese Prime Minister Noda to enter the negotiations elevated what had previously been a relatively minor grouping to one that had the potential to exert a significant impact on trade liberalization across the region. Yet Japan's decision to enter the TPP threatened to undermine the nascent steps toward deeper regional cooperation among the Northeast Asian "Big Three" (China, Japan, and Korea) seen in the institutionalization of the Trilateral Summit. Noda's enthusiasm for an Asia-Pacific approach to economic cooperation stood in direct contrast to that of his predecessor, Yukio Hatoyama, whose proposal for an East Asian Community envisaged an Asia-centered foreign policy and a region where the US would have a diminished role.

In demanding that its partners sign up for a high-quality "21st century" agreement in the Trans-Pacific Partnership, the United States is attempting to set the rules that will govern future trade in the region. As Baldwin (2011, 16) notes, only technology-rich countries have the leverage to demand the substantial domestic reforms in their partners that are central to 21st century regionalism. The approach inevitably is divisive—and in East Asia will pit the more advanced economies of the region against those such as China that are unwilling to subscribe to the new rules of the game. Moreover, by making the TPP a central component of its "pivot" to Asia, the Obama administration ensured that regional trade issues would again be entangled with security issues, the TPP being widely perceived as part of a strategy by Washington to "contain" China (Capling and Ravenhill 2012).

We do not, then, expect major change in Asian institutions in the short to medium term. But that does not mean we expect no change at all. We see potential for two main types of incremental enhancement of the regional institutional landscape. One relates to potential developments at the sub-regional and sectoral levels. We expect to see further (often ad hoc) cooperative arrangements to tackle trans-border functional challenges, in areas such as public health and the environment. Such arrangements often go unnoticed in the broader scheme of Asian regional institutions. The other potential development is at the opposite end of the spectrum in terms of membership and scope, relating to the likelihood of further institutional refinement at the pan-regional level. There has been debate for some years about the clutter of overlapping institutional frameworks at the pan regional level, with attention focusing particularly on APEC, the EAS, and the ASEAN Plus Three grouping. The expansion of the EAS to include the United States and Russia from 2011 has been an important development. It follows notable diplomatic entrepreneurship from Japanese and Australian political leaders to achieve a more satisfactory and encompassing framework and a recognition by ASEAN leaders of the need for adjustment if ASEAN itself was to remain at the center of regional architecture.

The advent of an enlarged EAS has not, of itself, dramatically changed the picture. Over time it is likely to shift attention from APEC to EAS as well as putting growing pressure on ASEAN either to adopt stronger organisational norms and procedures or progressively to yield steerage of the EAS to the wider membership of the grouping. Along with medium-term pressures for rationalization of this sort, the expansion of the EAS may also have the effect of adding momentum to ASEAN Plus Three as it will now assume the status of the only large and coherent regional grouping in which Asian leaders are able to meet without their North American and European counterparts present. An initial step in this direction was the 2012 proposal to establish a Regional Comprehensive Economic Partnership.

Changes of this sort will likely take time. For example, rather than showing signs of further deflation upon the US joining the EAS, APEC was the site of an extraordinary surge of activity in 2011. Indeed, President Obama's use of the APEC summit in Honolulu to launch an expanded Trans-Pacific Partnership for trade liberalization overshadowed the achievements of the EAS summit a week later in Bali. To be sure, this particular episode reflects more on the engaged leadership of Obama and the determination of Washington to reassert America's strategic centrality in Asia than it does the importance on APEC itself. Nevertheless, the general point remains that while we can identify logics or incentive effects that will apply over time, in the shorter term there is scope for many different exigencies.

Our core message in this concluding chapter is that for the forseeable future, above all, the central dynamic shaping the evolution of Asian regional institutions will continue to be international political and security rivalries. Our prediction is that the most likely outcome and, in our view, the most prudent way ahead, is ongoing pluralistic experimentation with institutional formats by shifting combinations of players as the world's largest and most diverse region continues to evolve rapidly—in both its economic and political complexion and in the ways it thinks about itself.

Notes

1. Our focus in this chapter is primarily on East Asia because it is the region where most inter-governmental collaboration has occurred. Central and South Asia are not deeply integrated in the regional production networks that have driven economic integration in East Asia (by which we understand the ten ASEAN countries, China, Japan, Korea, and Taiwan).

2. Authors' calculations from IMF *Direction of Trade* data.

3. Authors' calculations from IMF *Direction of Trade* data except for Taiwan where data are from the Bureau of Foreign Trade, available at http://cus93.trade.gov.tw/bftweb/english/FSCE/FSC0011E.ASP

4. The only EAS members that have not signed the ITA are Brunei, Cambodia, the Lao People's Democratic Republic, and Myanmar.

REFERENCE MATTER

Bibliography

Abbott, Frederick M. 2001. "NAFTA and the Legalization of World Politics: A Case Study." In Judith L. Goldstein, Miles Kahler, Robert O. Keohane, and Anne-Marie Slaughter, eds., *Legalization and World Politics*. Cambridge: MIT Press: 135–163.

Abbott, Kenneth W. and Duncan Snidal. 1998. "Why States Act Through Formal International Organizations." *Journal of Conflict Resolution* 42(1):3–32.

Acharya, Amitav. 1997. "Ideas, Identity, and Institution-building: From the 'ASEAN Way' to the 'Asia-Pacific Way'?" The Pacific Review 10(3): 319–346.

Acharya, Amitav. 2000. *The Quest for Identity: International Relations of Southeast Asia*. Singapore: Oxford University Press.

Acharya, Amitav. 2001. *Constructing a Security Community in Southeast Asia: ASEAN and the Problem of Regional Order*. London: Routledge.

Acharya, Amitav. 2003. "Regional Institutions and Asian Security Order: Norms, Power and Prospects for Peaceful Change," in Muthiah Alagappa, *Asian Security Order: Instrumental and Normative Features* Stanford: Stanford University Press 210–240.

Acharya, Amitav. 2004. "How Ideas Spread: Whose Norms Matter? Norm Localization and Institutional Change in Asian Regionalism," *International Organization*, Vol.58, No.2 (Spring): 239–275.

Acharya, Amitav. 2005. "Do Norms and Identity Matter? Community and Power in Southeast Asia's Regional Order," *Pacific Review*, 18(1): 95–118.

Acharya, Amitav. 2009. *Whose Ideas Matter? Agency and Power in Asian Regionalism*. Ithaca: Cornell University Press.

Acharya, Amitav. 2010. "Democracy or Death? Will Democratisation Bring Greater Regional Instability to East Asia?" *Pacific Review*, 23 (3): 335–358.

Acharya, Amitav and Alastair Iain Johnston. 2007a. "Conclusion: Institutional Features, Cooperation Effects, and the Agenda for Further Research on Comparative Regionalism." In *Regional International Institutions in Comparative Perspective*. Cambridge: Cambridge University Press: 244–278.

Acharya, Amitav, and Alastair Iain Johnston. 2007b. "Comparing Regional Institutions: An Introduction," in Amitav Acharya and Alastair Iain Johnston, eds., *Crafting Cooperation: Regional International Institutions in Comparative Perspective*, 1–31. Cambridge: Cambridge University Press.

Acharya, Amitav, and Richard Stubbs, 2006. "Theorising Southeast Asian Relations: An Introduction." *Pacific Review*, Vol. 19, No. 2: 125–134.

Adler, Emanuel and Michael Barnett. eds, 1998. *Security Communities*. Cambridge: Cambridge University Press.

Aggarwal, Vinod and Min Gyo Koo, eds. 2008. *Asia's New Institutional Architecture: Evolving Structures for Managing Trade, Financial and Security Relations*. Berlin: Springer-Verlag.

Aggarwal, Vinod and Shujiro Urata, eds. 2006. *Bilateral Trade Agreements in the Asia-Pacific: Origins, Evolution, and Implications*. London: Routledge.

Aggarwal, Vinod K. and Min Gyo Koo. 2008. "An Institutional Path: Community Building in Northeast Asia." In G. John Ikenberry and Chung-In Moon, eds., *The United States and Northeast Asia*. Lanham, MD: Rowman & Littlefield: 285–307.

Agosin, Manuel R. 2001. Global Integration and Growth in Honduras and Nicaragua. Working Papers UNU-WIDER Research Paper. Helsinki: World Institute for Development Economics Research.

Alesina, Alberto, Ignazio Angeloni, and Federico Etro. 2005. "International Unions." *American Economic Review*, 95, 3 (June): 602–615

Alesina, Alberto and Vittorio Grilli. 1993. "On the Feasibility of a One-Speed or Multi-Speed European Monitary Union." *Economics & Politics* 5(2): 145–165.

Allee, Todd and Paul Huth. 2006. "Legitimizing Dispute Settlement: International Adjudication as Domestic Political Cover." *American Political Science Review* 100(2):219–34.

Allee, Todd and Clint Peinhardt. 2009a. "Delegating Differences: Bilateral Investment Treaties and Bargaining over Dispute Resolution Provisions." *International Studies Quarterly* (forthcoming).

Allee, Todd and Clint Peinhardt. 2009b. Contingent Credibility: The Reputational Effects of Investment Treaty Disputes on Foreign Direct Investment. Manuscript.

Allison, Graham and Philip Zelikow. 1999. *Essence of Decision. Explaining the Cuban Missile Crisis*. 2nd ed. New York: Longman.

Alter, Karen. 1998. "Who Are the 'Masters of the Treaty'? European Governments and the European Court of Justice." *International Organization* 52(1):121–47.

Alter, Karen. 2006. "Private Litigants and the New International Courts." *Comparative Political Studies* 39(1):22–49.

Alter, Karen. 2008. "Courts in Their Political Context." *European Journal of International Relations* (1):33–63.

Alter, Karen. 2009. *The New Terrain of International Law: International Courts in International Politics*. Book manuscript.

America and the Caribbean. José Antonio Ocampo, ed., In *Regional Financial Cooperation*. Washington, D.C.: Brookings Institution Press.

Amsden, Alice H. 1989. *Asia's Next Giant: South Korea and Late Industrialization*. New York: Oxford University Press.

Amyx, Jennifer. 2008. Regional Financial Cooperation in East Asia since the Asian Financial Crisis. In Andrew MacIntyre, T. J. Pempel, and John Ravenhill eds. *Crisis as Catalyst: Asia's Dynamic Political Economy*. Ithaca, NY and London: Cornell University Press.

ANFREL. 2001. East Timor Towards a New Nation Building; Report of International Observation Mission on East Timor Constituent Assembly Elections 25 August–2 September 2001.

Appelbaum, Richard. 1998. "The Future of Law in a Global Economy." *Social & Legal Studies* 7(2):171–92.

Arner, Douglas, Paul Lejot, and Wei Wang. "Assessing East Asian Financial Cooperation and Integration." Asian Institute of International Financial Law Working Paper No. 5. Hong Kong: Faculty of Law, University of Hong Kong, March 2009.

Arocena, Rodrigo. 2009. "Uruguay and the Learning Divides." *DEP: diplomacia, estraté-gia, política* 9 (January-March): 195–214.

Asian Development Bank. 2008. *Emerging Asian Regionalism: A Partnership for Shared Prosperity*. Manila: Asian Development.

Asian Development Bank. 2010. Institutions for Regional Integration: Toward an Asian Economic Community. Manila: Asian Development Bank.

Aspinwall Avery, Mark. 2008. "NAFTA-ization: Regionalization and Domestic Political Adjustment in the North American Economic Area." *Journal of Common Market Studies* 47 (1): 1–24.

Athukorala, Prema-chandra. 2011. "Production Networks and Trade Patterns in East Asia: Regionalization or Globalization?" *Asian Economic Papers* 10, no. 1 (Winter/Spring): 65–95.

Athukorala, Premachandra. 2009. "The Rise of China and East Asian Export Performance: Is the Crowding-out Fear Warranted?" *The World Economy* 32, no. 2 (February): 234–66.

Avery, William and James Cochrane. 1973. "Innovation in Latin American Regionalism: The Andean Common Market." *International Organization* 27:1 (Winter): 181–223.

Ba, Alice D. 2009. *(Re)Negotiating East and Southeast Asia: Region, Regionalism and the Association of Southeast Asian Nations*. Stanford: Stanford University Press.

Balassa, Bela. 1971. "Regional Integration and Trade Liberalization in Latin America." *Journal of Common Market Studies* 10:1 (September): 58–77.

Baldwin, R. 1993. A Domino Theory of Regionalism. *NBER Working Paper* 4465.

Baldwin, R. 1994. *Towards an Integrated Europe*. London: CEPR.

Baldwin, R. 2011. Sequencing Regionalism: Theory, European Practice, and Lessons for Asia. ADB Working Paper Series on Regional Economic Integration 80.

Baldwin, Richard. 1993. "A Domino Theory of Regionalism." National Bureau of Economic Research, Working Paper 4465.

Baldwin, Richard. 1997. "The Cause of Regionalism." *The World Economy* 20: 865–888.

Baldwin, Richard. 2009. Sequencing Regionalism: Theory, European Practice and Lessons for Asia, paper prepared for Asian Development Bank.

Baldwin, Richard. 2010. "Sequencing Regionalism: Theory, European Practice and Lessons for Asia, Asian Development Bank." Asian Development Bank Working Paper Series on Regional Economic Integration.

Baldwin, Richard. 2011a. "Sequencing Regionalism: Theory, European Practice, and Lessons for Asia." ADB Working Paper Series on Regional Economic Integration. No. 80 (May). Manila: Asian Development Bank.

Baldwin, Richard. 2011b. "21st Century Regionalism: Filling the Gap between 21st Century Trade and 20th Century Trade Rules." No. 56. London: Centre for Economic Policy Research, May.

Baldwin, Richard E. 2004. The Spoke Trap: Hub-and-Spoke Bilateralism in East Asia. CNAEC Research Series 04–02 Seoul: Korea Institute for International Economic Policy.

Baldwin, Richard E. 2006. "Multilateralising Regionalism: Spaghetti Bowls as Building Blocs on the Path to Global Free Trade." *World Economy* 29, no. 11: 1451–518.

Baldwin, Richard E. 2008. Big-Think Regionalism: A Critical Survey. NBER Working Paper No. 14056. June.

Banco Interamericano de Desarrollo. 2002. *Más allá de las fronteras: El Nuevo regionalismo en América Latina. Progreso económico y social en América Latina: Informe 2002.* Washington: Banco Interamericano de Desarrollo.

Banzhaf, John F. (1965) "Weighted Voting Doesn't Work: A Mathematical Analysis." *Rutgers Law Review* 19: 317–343.

Barnett, Michael and Etel Solingen. 2007. Designed to Fail or Failure of Design? The Origins and Legacy of the Arab League. A. Acharya and I. Johnston. *Crafting Cooperation: The Design and Effect of Regional Institutions in Comparative Perspective.* Cambridge, Cambridge University Press: 180–220.

Barton, John H., Judith L. Goldstein, Timothy E. Josling, and Richard H. Steinberg. 2006. *The Evolution of the Trade Regime: Politics, Law, and Economics of the GATT and the WTO.* Princeton: Princeton University Press.

Bayoumi, Tamim and Barry Eichengreen. 1992. "Is There a Conflict between EC Enlargement and European Monetary Unification?" NBER Working Paper 3950.

Bearce, David and Stacy Bondanella. 2007. "Intergovernmental Organizations, Socialization, and Member-State Interest Convergence." *International Organization* 61(04): 703–733.

Berglof, Erik, Mike Burkart, Guido Friebel, and Elena Paltseva. 2008. "Widening and Deepening: Reforming the European Union." *American Economic Review: Papers & Proceedings* 98, 2: 133–137.

Bergsten, C. Fred and Yung Chul Park. 2002. *Toward Creating a Regional Monetary Arrangement in East Asia.* Research Paper 50. Tokyo: Asian Development Bank Institute.

Beyers, Jan. 2005. "Multiple Embeddedness and Socialization in Europe: The Case of Council Officials." *International Organization* 59(04): 899–936.

Bhagwati, Jagdish. 2008. *Termites in the Trading System: How Preferential Agreements Undermine Free Trade.* New York: Oxford University Press.

Blejer, Mario I. 1984. "Economic Integration: An Analytical Overview." In *Economic and Social Progress in Latin America: 1984 Report.* Washington: Inter-American Development Bank.

Boehmer, Charles, Erik Gartzke, and Timothy Nordstrom. 2004. "Do Intergovernmental Organizations Promote Peace?" *World Politics* 57(1): 1–38.

Borensztein, Eduardo, Eduardo Levy and Ugo Panizza. 2006. *Living with Debt: How to Limit the Risks of Sovereign Finance. Economic and Social Progress in Latin America, 2007 Report.* Washington: Inter-American Development Bank.

Börzel, Tanja A. 2001. "Non-Compliance in the European Union: Pathology or Statistical Artifact?" *Journal of European Public Policy* 8(5):803–24.

Bouzas, Roberto, and José María Fanelli. 2002. *MERCOSUR: Integración y crecimiento.* Buenos Aires: Fundación OSDE y Grupo Editor Altamira.

Bouzas, Roberto, Pedro da Motta Veiga, and Sandra Ríos. 2008. Crisis y perspectivas de la integración en América del sur. In Ricardo Lagos ed. *América Latina: ¿Integración o Fragmentación?*, Buenos Aires: Fundación Grupo Mayan.

Bradley, Curtis and Judith Kelly. 2008. "The Concept of International Delegation." *Law and Contemporary Problems* 71, 1: 1–36.

Bräuninger, Thomas and Thomas König. 2005. *Indices of Power IOP 2.0* [computer program]. Konstanz: University of Konstanz [http://www.tbraeuninger.de/IOP.html].

Broadberry, S.N. and M. Harrison. 2005. The Economics of World War I: An Overview. In S.N. Broadberry and M. Harrison eds. *The Economics of World War I*, Cambridge: Cambridge University Press.

Burley, Anne-Marie and Walter Mattli. 1993. "Europe Before the Court: A Political Theory of Legal Integration." *International Organization* (47): 41–76.

Buscaneanu, Sergiu. 2006. "How Far is the European Neighbourhood Policy a Susbstantial Offer for Moldova?" *Journal of Foreign Policy of Moldova* (09/2006).

Busch, Marc L. 2007. "Overlapping institutions, forum shopping, and dispute settlement in international trade." *International Organization*: 735–761.

Busch, Marc, Eric Reinhardt, and Gregory Shaffer. 2009. "Does Legal Capacity Matter? A Survey of WTO Members." *World Trade Review* (8):559–77.

Büthe, Tim and Helen V. Milner. 2009. Bilateral Investment Treaties and Foreign Direct Investment: A Political Analysis. In Karl P. Sauvant and Lisa Sachs eds. *The Effect of Bilateral Investment Treaties and Double Taxation Treaties on Foreign Direct Investment Flows*. New York: Oxford University Press, 171–224.

Buti, Marco and Lucio Pench. 2004. "Why Do Large Countries Flout the Stability Pact? And What Can Be Done About It?" *Journal of Common Market Studies* 42(5): 1025–1032.

Caballero-Anthony, Mely. 2005. *Regional Security in Southeast Asia: Beyond the ASEAN Way*. Singapore: Institute of Southeast Asian Studies.

Caetano, Gerardo. 2007. MERCOSUR: Quo Vadis? *DEP: diplomacia, estratégia, política* 5 (January-March): 137–170.

Calder, Kenneth and Min Ye. 2010. The Making of Northeast Asia. Stanford: Stanford University Press.

Calder, Kent and Francis Fukuyama, eds. 2008. *East Asian Multilateralism: Prospects for Regional Stability*. Baltimore: Johns Hopkins University Press.

Calder, Kent and Min Ye. 2004. "Regionalism and Critical Junctures: Explaining the "Organization Gap" in Northeast Asia." *Journal of East Asian Studies* 4 (2004), 191–226

Campbell, Jorge, ed. 1999. *MERCOSUR: Entre la utopia y la realidad*. Buenos Aires: Grupo Editor Latinoamericano.

Camps, M. 1964. *Britain and the European Community 1955–63*. London: Oxford University Press.

Capannelli, Giovanni. 2009. Regional Financial Arrangements. Presentation to the Institutions for Regionalism workshop, ADB, Honolulu, August 10–11.

Capannelli, Giovanni and Carlo Filippini. 2009. East Asian and European Economic Integration: A Comparative Analysis, Asian Development Bank Working Paper Series on Regional EconomicIntegration, no. 29.

Capannelli, Giovanni, Jong-Wha Lee, and Peter A. Petri. "Extent of Economic Interdependence in Asia: Developing Indicators for Regional Integration and Cooperation." In *Symposium on Asian Economic Integration*. Nanyang Technological University, Singapore, 2008.

Caparaso, James and Young Choi. 2002. In W. Carlsnaes, T. Risse-Kappen and B. Simmons. *Comparative Regional Integration. Handbook of international relations*. London, Sage Pubns Ltd: 480–499.

Capling, Ann and John Ravenhill. "The TPP: Multilateralizing Regionalism or the Securitization of Trade Policy?" In C.L. Lim, Deborah Kay Elms and Patrick Low eds. *The Trans-Pacific Partnership: A Quest for a Twenty-First Century Trade Agreement*, Cambridge: Cambridge University Press, 2012: 279–98. Carter Center. 2007. Carter Center Preliminary Statement: Timor-Leste Parliamentary Election Democratic and Peaceful. Atlanta, Georgia.

Caporaso, James. A. 2007. The Three Worlds of Regional Integration Theory. In Paolo Graziano and Maarten P. Vink, eds. *Europeanization: New Research Agendas*. Basingstoke: Palgrave Macmillan.

Casas Gragea, Ángel María. 2002. "International Economic Policy in the New Regional Integration of the Americas: The Community Case." *Integration and Trade* 16 (January-June): 95-156.

Cecchini, Paolo, Michael Catinat, and Alexis Jacquemin (1988) *The European Challenge 1992: The Benefits of a Single Market*. Aldershot: Gower.

Cha, Victor. 2009/10. "Powerplay: Origins of the U.S. Alliance System in Asia," *International Security*, 34, 3 (Winter):158–196.

Chandra, A.C. and L. Hanim. "Indonesia." In Ann Capling and Patrick Low eds. *Governments, Non-State Actors and Trade Policy-Making: Negotiating Preferentially or Multilaterally?* Cambridge: Cambridge University Press, 2010: 125–60.

Chase, Kerry A. *Trading Blocs: States, Firms, and Regions in the World Economy*. Michigan Studies in International Political Economy. Ann Arbor: University of Michigan Press, 2005.

Chayes, Abram and Antonia Handler Chayes. 1993. "On Compliance." *International Organization*, 47, 2 (March): 175–205

Chayes, Abram and Antonia Handler Chayes. 1995. *The New Sovereignty: Compliance with International Regulatory Agreements*. Cambridge, MA: Harvard University Press.

Checkel, Jeffrey. 1998a. "Norms, Institutions and National Identity in Contemporary Europe." *ARENA Working Papers*, 98/16. Oslo: Advanced Research on the Europeanization of the Nation-State, University of Oslo.

Checkel, Jeffrey. 1998b. "The *Constructivist Turn* in International Relations Theory." *World Politics*, Vol. 50, No. 2: 324–348.

Checkel, Jeffrey. 1999. "Social construction and integration." Journal of European Public Policy 6(4): 545–560.

Checkel, Jeffrey. 2005. "International institutions and socialization in Europe: Introduction and framework." *International Organization* 59(4): 801-826.

Checkel, Jeffrey and Andrew Moravcsik. 2001. "A Constructivist Research Program in EU Studies?" European Union Politics 2: 219–249.

Chirathivat, Suthiphand and Sothitorn Mallikamas. 2004. "Thailand's FTA Strategy: Current Development and Future Challenges." *ASEAN Economic Bulletin* 21, no. 1 (April): 37–53.

Choi, Byung-il and Kong-Jin Lee. 2005. "A Long and Winding Road: Ratification of Korea's First FTA." In *Korea and International Conflicts: Case Studies—Volume 1*, edited by Byung-il Choi. Seoul: Institute for International Trade and Cooperation, Ewha Womans University, 11–47.

Choi, Byung-il and Jennifer Sejin Oh. 2011. "Asymmetry in Japan and Korea's Agricultural Liberalization in FTA: Domestic Trade Governance Perspective." *The Pacific Review* 24, no. 5 (December): 505–27.

Christiansen, Thomas, Knud Erik Jorgensen, and Antje Wiener. 2001. "Introduction" in Christiansen, Jorgensen and Wiener, eds., *The Social Construction of Europe*. 1–21. London: Sage Publications.

Clarkson, Stephen. 2007. "Does North America Exist? Transborder Governance after NAFTA and the Security and Prosperity Partnership." *Norteamérica* 2:2 (July–December): 85–104.

Cochrane, James D. and John W. Sloan. 1973. "LAFTA and the CACM: A Comparative Analysis of Integration in Latin America." *Journal of Developing Areas* 8:1 (October): 13–38.

COE. 1994. Information Report on the Parliamantary Elections in Moldova (27 February).

COE. 1998. Information Report on the Parliamentary Elections in Moldova (Chisinau, 19–24 March).

Cohen, Benjamin J. 1993. "Beyond EMU: the Problem of Sustainability." *Economics and Politics* 5 (July): 187–202.

Cohen. 1992. U.S. Debt Policy in Latin America: The Melody. In Robert Bottome et al. eds. *In The Shadow of Emerging Debt*. New York: The Twentieth Century Fund Press.

Cooper, Andrew and Thomas Legler. 2001. "The OAS Democratic Solidarity Paradigm: Questions of Collective and National Leadership." *Latin American Politics and Society* 43(1): 103–126.

Corporación Andina de Fomento. 2009. www.caf.com/view/index.asp?pageMS=34163&ms =17 accessed 7 September 2009.

Coskun, Bezen Balamir. 2006. Region and Region Building in the Middle East Problems and Prospects. UNU-CRIS Occasional Papers, United Nations University.

Crawford, Gordon. 1997. "Foreign Aid and Political Conditionality: Issues of Effectiveness and Consistency." *Democratization* 4(3): 69–108.

Dai, Xinyuan. 2007. *International Institutions and National Policies*. Cambridge: Cambridge University Press.

Danilenko, Gennady M. 1999. "The Economic Court of the Commonwealth of Independent States." *New York University Journal of International Law and Politics* 31:893–918.

Davis, Christina and Sarah Blodgett Bermeo. 2009. "Who Files? Developing Country Participation in GATT/WTO Adjudiciation." *Journal of Politics* (71):1033–49.

Davis, Christina and Yuri Shirato. 2007. "Firms, Governments, and WTO Adjudication: Japan's Selection of WTO Disputes." *World Politics* 59(2): 274–313.

de Brouwer, Gordon. 2004. *Institutions to Promote Financial Stability: Reflections on East Asia and an Asian Monetary Fund*. Australian Treasury Working Paper 2004–02 (September).

Debroy, Bibek. 2009. "Linking South and East Asian Economies: Markets and Institutions." Background Paper prepared for the Asian Development Bank Flagship Study "Institutions for Regionalism: Enhancing Asia's Economic Cooperation and Integration."

Dehousse, Renaud (1992) "Integration v. Regulation? On the Dynamics of Regulation in the European Community." *Journal of Common Market Studies* 30(4): 383–402.

Delich, Valentina. 2006. "Trade and Dispute Settlement in South America: Concerns and Challenges in the Way of the FTAA." *Integration and Trade* 24 (January–June): 3–25.

Dent, C. 2010. Organizing the Wider East Asia Region. ADB Working Paper Series on Regional Economic Integration 62.

Dent, Christopher M. 2005. "Taiwan and the New Regional Political Economy of East Asia." *The China Quarterly* 182: 385–406.

Dent, Christopher M. 2006. *New Free Trade Agreements in the Asia-Pacific*. Basingstoke: Palgrave McMillan.

Dent, Christopher M. 2008. *East Asian Regionalism*. London: Routledge.

Destler, I.M. and C. Randall Henning. 1989. *Dollar Politics: Exchange Rate Policymaking in the United States*. Washington: Institute for International Economics.

Deutsch, Karl and Sidney Burrell, Robert Kann, Maurice Lee, Martin Lichterman, Raymond Lindgren, Francis Loewenheim, and Richard Van Wagenen. 1957. *Political Community and the North Atlantic Area*. Princeton: Princeton University Press.

Devlin, Robert and Antoni Estevadeordal. 2001. *What's New in the New Regionalism in the Americas?* INTAL-ITD-STA Working Paper, no. 6: 1–40.

Devlin, Robert, Antoni Estevadeordal, and Luis Jorge Garay. 2000. Some Economic and Strategic Issues in the Face of the Emerging FTAA. In Jorge I. Domínguez ed. *The Future of Inter-American Relations*. New York: Routledge.

Deyo, Frederic C., ed. *The Political Economy of the New Asian Industrialism*, Cornell Studies in Political Economy. Ithaca, NY: Cornell University Press, 1987.

Dickerson, Claire Moore. 2005. "Harmonizing Business Laws in Africa: OHADA calls the tune." *Columbia Journal of Transitional Law* 44(1):17–73.

Dietz, James. 1987. "The Latin American Economies and Debt: Institutional and Structural Response to Crisis." *Journal of Economic Issues* 21, no. 2: 827–836.

Dinan, Desmond. 2004. *Europe Recast: A History of European Union*. London: Lynne Rienner Publishers.

Dirlik, Arif. 1992. "The Asia-Pacific Idea: Reality and Representation in the Invention of a Regional Structure." *Journal of World History* 3.1: 55–79.

Domínguez, Jorge I. 2003. *Boundary Disputes in Latin America*. Peaceworks 50. Washington: United States Institute of Peace.

Dominguez, Jorge I. 2007. "International Cooperation in Latin America: The Design of Regional Institutions by Slow Accretion." In Amitav Acharya and Alastair Iain Johnston, eds., *Crafting Cooperation: Regional International Institutions in Comparative Perspective*. Cambridge: Cambridge University Press: 83–128.

Domínguez, Jorge I and Rafael Fernández de Castro. 2009. *The United States and Mexico: Between Partnership and Conflict*. 2nd. ed. New York: Routledge.

Downs, George W., David M. Rocke, and Peter N. Barsoom. 1996. "Is the Good News about Compliance Good News about Cooperation? *International Organization* 50:379–406.

Dragneva, Rilka and Joop de Kort. 2007. "The Legal Regime for Free Trade in the Commonwealth of Independent States." *International & Comparative Law Quarterly* 56(2):233–66.

Dura, George and Vitu, Liliana. 2008. *Country Report—Moldova*. Freedom House.

East Asia Study Group. 2002. *Final Report of the East Asia Study Group*, 4 November 2002. Available at: http://www.mofa.go.jp/region/asia-paci/asean/pmv0211/report.pdf.

East Asia Vision Group. 2001. *Towards an East Asian Community*, Report of the East Asia Vision Group, 2001. Available at: http://www.mofa.go.jp/region/asia-paci/report2001.pdf.

Eichengreen, B. 2007. *The European Economy Since 1945: Coordinated Capitalism and Beyond*. Princeton: Princeton University Press.

Eichengreen, B. and A. Boltho. 2010. The Economic Impact of European Integration. In S.N. Broadberry and K.H. O'Rourke eds. *The Cambridge Economic History of Modern Europe*. Cambridge: Cambridge University Press.

Eichengreen, Barry. 1992. Should the Maastricht Treaty Be Saved? *Princeton Studies in International Finance* (International Finance Section, Princeton University).

Eichengreen, Barry. 1996. *A More Perfect Union? The Logic of Economic Integration*. Princeton: Princeton University, Essays in International Finance.

Eichengreen, Barry. 2002a. *Financial Crises and What to Do about Them.* Oxford: Oxford University Press.

Eichengreen, Barry. 2002b. "What to Do with the Chiang Mai Initiative?" *Asian Economic Papers* 2: 1–52.

Eichengreen, Barry. 2006. European Integration. In Barry R. Weingast and Donald Wittman (eds.), *The Oxford Handbook of Political Economy.* Oxford: Oxford University Press, pp. 799–813.

Eichengreen, Barry and Jeffry A. Frieden. 1994. The Political Economy of European Monetary Unification: An Analytical Introduction. In Barry Eichengreen and Jeffry A. Frieden (eds.) *The Political Economy of European Monetary Unification,* 2nd edition. Boulder, CO: Westview Press. (pp. 1–23).

Eichengreen, Barry, and Peter H. Lindert (eds.), 1989. *The International Debt Crisis in Historical Perspective.* Cambridge: MIT Press.

Ellison, J. 2000. *Threatening Europe: Britain and the Creation of the European Community, 1955-58.* London: Macmillan Press.

Eilstrup-Sangiovanni, M. and D. Verdier. 2005. "European Integration as a Solution to War." *European Journal of International Relations* 11: 99–135.

Epstein, David and Sharon O'Halloran. 2008. "Sovereignty and Delegation in International Organizations." *Law and Contemporary Problems* 71, 1: 77–92.

Escudé, Carlos and Andrés Fontana. 1998. Argentina's Security Policies: Their Rationale and Regional Context. In Jorge I. Domínguez ed. *International Security and Democracy: Latin America and the Caribbean in the Post-Cold War Era.* Pittsburgh: University of Pittsburgh Press.

EU. 2001. Final Report of the European Union Electoral Observation Mission in East Timor; 30 August 2001 Constituent Assembly Elections.

EU. 2002. East Timor Presidential Elections 14 April 2002.

European Commission (1985) *Completing the Internal Market: White Paper of the Commission the European Council,* COM(85) 310, Luxembourg: Office of Official Publications of the European Communities.

European Parliament. 2001. European Parliament resolution on the Commission communication on EU Election Assistance and Observation (COM(2000) 191–C5-0259/ 2000–2000/2137 (COS)). Strasbourg.

Evans, Paul. 1999. "The Concept of Eastern Asia." In Colin Mackerras, eds., *Eastern Asia: An Introductory History.* 2nd ed. Chapter 2. Melbourne: Longman Australia.

Farber, Daniel A. 2002. "Rights as Signals." *Journal of Legal Studies* 31(1):83–98.

Farer, Tom. 1996. Collectively Defending Democracy in the Western Hemisphere: Introduction and Overview. In T. Farer, *Beyond Sovereignty: Collectively Defending Democracy in the Americas.* Baltimore, MD: Johns Hopkins University Press: 1–25.

Fearon, James D. 1998. "Bargaining, Enforcement and International Cooperation." *International Organization,* 52(2):269–305.

Feinberg, Richard, ed. 2003. *APEC as an Institution: Multilateral Governance in the Asia-Pacific.* Singapore: Institute of Southeast Asian Studies.

Felsenthal, Dan and Moshe Machover. 2001. "The Treaty of Nice and Qualified Majority Voting." London: LSE Research Online. [http://eprints.lse.ac.uk/archive/00000420].

Felsenthal, Dan and Moshe Machover. 2007. "Analysis of QM Rule adopted by the Council of the European Union." London: LSE Research Online. [http://eprints.lse .ac.uk/2531].

Ffrench-Davis, Ricardo, Oscar Muñoz, and José Gabriel Palma. 1994. The Latin American Economies, 1950–1990. In Leslie Bethell ed. *The Cambridge History of Latin America*. Cambridge: Cambridge University Press.

Findlay, R. and K.H. O'Rourke. 2007. *Power and Plenty: Trade, War, and the World Economy in the Second Millennium*. Princeton: Princeton University Press.

Finnemore, Martha and Kathryn Sikkink. 1998. "International Norm Dynamics and Political Change." *International Organization*, Vol. 52, No. 4: 887–917.

Finnemore, Martha. 1993. "International Organizations as Teachers of Norms: the United Nations Educational, Scientific, and Cutural Organization and Science Policy." *International Organization* 47(4): 565–597.

Floreal González, Flavio. 1999. "MERCOSUR: The Incompatibilities between its Institutions and the Need to Complete the Customs Union." *Integration and Trade* 9 (September-December): 83–104.

Fondo Latinoamericano de Reservas. 2008. www.flar.net/contenido/contenido.aspx?catID =138&conID=196 accessed 7 September 2009.

Franchino, Fabio 2007. *The Powers of the Union: Delegation in the EU*. Cambridge: Cambridge University Press.

Franck, Susan. 2007. "Foreign Direct Investment, Investment Treaty Arbitration and the Rule of Law." *McGeorge Global Business and Development Law Journal* 19:337–68.

Franck, Susan. 2009. "Development and Outcomes of Investment Arbitration." *Harvard International Law Journal* 50(2):435–90.

Frieden, Jeffry. 1991. "Invested Interests: The Politics of National Economic Policies in a World of Global Finance." *International Organization*, 45, 4 (Autumn): 425–451.

Frieden, Jeffry A. 1991. *Debt, Development, and Democracy: Modern Political Economy and Latin America, 1965–1985*. Princeton: Princeton University Press.

Frieden, Jeffry A. 2002. "Real Sources of European Currency Policy: Sectoral Interests and European Monetary Integration." *International Organization* 56, no. 4: 831–860.

Gauhar, Altaf. 1985. *Regional Integration: The Latin American Experience*. Boulder, CO: Westview Press.

Gersen, Jacob and Eric Posner. 2008. "Soft Law." Public Law and Legal Theory Working Paper No. 213, University of Chicago Law School at http://www.law.uchicago.edu/ academics/publiclaw/index.html

Gheciu, Alexandra. 2005. "Security Institutions as Agents of Socialization? NATO and the." *International Organization* 59(04): 973–1012.

Giavazzi, Francesco and Marco Pagano. 1988. "The Advantage of Tying One's Hands: EMS Discipline and Central Bank Credibility." *European Economic Review* 32: 1055–1082.

Gillingham, J. 1995. The European Coal and Steel Community: An Object Lesson? In B. Eichengreen ed. *Europe's Post-War Recovery*. Cambridge: Cambridge University Press.

Ginsburg, Tom and Albert H.Y. Chen, eds. 2008. *Administrative Law and Governance in Asia: Comparative Perspectives*. London: Routledge.

Goertz, Gary. 2006. *Social Science Concepts: A User's Guide*. Princeton, NJ: Princeton University Press.

Goldstein, Avery. 2005. *Rising to the Challenge: China's Grand Strategy and International Security*. Stanford:Stanford University Press.

Goldstein, Judith L., Miles Kahler, Robert O. Keohane, and Anne-Marie Slaughter, eds. 2001. *Legalization in World Politics*. Cambridge, MA: MIT Press.

Golob, Stephanie. 2003. "Beyond the Policy Frontier: Canada, Mexico, and the Ideological Origins of NAFTA." *World Politics* 55:3 (April): 361–398.

Gomez Mera, Laura. 2005. "Explaining Mercosur's Survival: Strategic Sources of Argentine-Brazilian Convergence." *Journal of Latin American Studies* 37 (2005): 109–140.

Gourevitch, Peter. 1983. *Politics in Hard Times: Comparative Responses to International Economic Crises.* Ithaca: Cornell University Press.

Grabbe, Heather. 2002. Europeanization goes east: power and uncertainty in the EU accession process. ECPR Joint Sessions of Workshops. Turin.

Granados, Jaime. 2001. *La integración comercial centroamericana: Un marco interpretativo y cursos de acción plausible.* INTAL-ITD-STA Working Paper 8: 1–36.

Grandi, Jorge, and Lincoln Bizzózero. 1997. "Towards a MERCOSUR Civil Society: Old and New Actors in the Sub-regional Fabric." *Integration and Trade* 3 (September-December): 31–43.

Green, Carl J. 1994. "APEC and Trans-Pacific Dispute Management." *Georgetown Journal of International Law* (26): 719

Green, Michael and Bates Gil, eds. 2009. *Asia's New Multilateralism: Cooperation, Competition and the Search for Community.* New York: Columbia University Press.

Grieco, Joseph. (1997) "Systemic Sources of Variation in Regional Institutionalization in Western Europe, East Asia, and the Americas," in Helen Milner and Edward Mansfield eds. *The Political Economy of Regionalism.* New York: Columbia University Press.

Griffin, Keith, and Ricardo Ffrench-Davis. 1965. "Customs Unions and Latin American Integration." *Journal of Common Market Studies* 4:1 (October): 1–21.

Grimes, William. 2009. *Currency and Contest in East Asia: the Great Power Politics of Financial Regionalism.* Ithaca: Cornell University Press.

Grimes, William W. "Political Economy of Bond Market Initiatives in Asia." In *American Political Science Association.* Boston, 2008.

Gros, Daniel, and Niels Thygesen. 1992. *European monetary Integration: From the European Monetary System to European Monetary Union.* London: Longman; and New York: St. Martin's Press.

Grossman, Gene M., and Elhanan Helpman. "The Politics of Free Trade Agreements." *American Economic Review* 85, no. 4 (September): 667–90.

Haacke, Jürgen. 2003. *ASEAN's Diplomatic and Security Culture: Origins, Developments and Prospects.* London: RoutledgeCurzon.

Haas, Ernst, 2001. "Does Constructivism Subsume Neo-Functionalism?" in Thomas Christiansen, Knud Erik Jørgensen, and Antje Wiener, eds., *The Social Construction of Europe. 22–31.* London: Sage Publications.

Haas, Ernst B. 1970. "The Study of Regional Integration: Reflections on the Joy and Anguish of Pretheorizing." International Organization 24(4): 607–646.

Haas, Ernst and Philippe Schmitter. 1964. "Economics and Differential Patterns of Political Integration: Projections about Unity in Latin America." International Organization 18(3): 705–737.

Haggard, Stephan. 2000. *The Political Economy of the Asian Financial Crisis.* Washington, D.C.: Institute for International Economics.

Haggard, Stephan. "Regionalism in Asia and the Americas." In Edward D. Mansfield and Helen V. Milner eds. *The Political Economy of Regionalism.* New York: Columbia University Press, 1997: 20–49.

Haggard, Stephan and Noland, Marcus. 2009. "A Security and Peace Mechanism for Northeast Asia: the Economic Dimension." *The Pacific Review,* 22, 2:119–137

Hamanaka, Shintaro. "Is Trade in Asia Really Integrating?". Mandaluyong City: Asian Development Bank, ADB Working Paper Series on Regional Economic Integration 91, January2012.

Harris, Stuart. "Policy Networks and Economic Cooperation: Policy Coordination in the Asia-Pacific Region." *The Pacific Review* 7, no. 4 (1994): 381–96.

Hausken, Kjell, Walter Mattli, and Thomas Plümper. 2006. "Widening Versus Deepening of International Unions." SSRN eLibrary.

Hawkins, Darren, David Lake, Daniel Nielson, and Michael Tierney, eds. 2006. *Delegation and Agency in International Organizations.* Cambridge: Cambridge University Press.

Hayes-Renshaw, Fiona and Helen Wallace. 2006. *The Council of Ministers*, 2nd ed. London: Palgrave.

Helfer, Laurence R. 2002. "Overlegalizing Human Rights: International Relations Theory and the Commonwealth Caribbean Backlash against Human Rights Regimes." *Columbia Law Review* 102 (7): 1832–1911.

Helfer, Laurence R. and Karen J. Alter. 2009. "The Andean Tribunal of Justice and Its Interlocutors: Understanding Preliminary Reference Patterns in the Andean Community." *New York University Journal of International Law* 41:1–46.

Helfer, Laurence R., Karen J. Alter, and Florencia M. Guerzovich. 2009. "Islands of Effective International Adjudication: Constructing an Intellectual Property Rule of Law in the Andean Community." *American Journal of International Law* 103:1–47.

Helfer, Laurence R. and Anne-Marie Slaughter. 1997. Toward a Theory of Effective Supranational Adjudication. *The Yale Law Journal* 107:273–391.

Helfer, Laurence R. and Anne-Marie Slaughter. 2005. Of States, Bargains and Judges: A Response to Professors Posner and Yoo. *California Law Review* 93:899–956.

Helleiner, Eric. 2006. *Towards North American Monetary Union? The Politics and History of Canada's Exchange Rate Regime.* Montreal & Kingston: McGill-Queen's University Press.

Hemmer, Christopher M. and Peter J. Katzenstein. 2002. "Why Is There No NATO in Asia? Collective Identity, Regionalism, and the Origins of Multilateralism." *International Organization*, Vol. 56, No.3 (Summer): 575–607.

Henning, C. Randall. 1994. *Currencies and Politics in the United States, Japan and Germany.* Washington, D.C.: Institute for International Economics.

Henning, C. Randall. 1998. Systemic Conflict and Regional Monetary Integration: The Case of Europe. *International Organization* 52: 537–573.

Henning, C. Randall. 1999. *The Exchange Stabilization Fund: Slush Money or War Chest?* Policy Analyses In International Economics 57. Washington: Institute for International Economics.

Henning, C. Randall. 2002. *East Asian Financial Cooperation.* Policy Analyses in International Economics 68. Washington: Institute for International Economics.

Henning, C. Randall. 2005. Regional Economic Integration and Institution Building. In Julie McKay, Maria Oliva Armengol, and Georges Pineau, eds. *Regional Economic Integration in a Global Framework.* Frankfurt: European Central Bank and People's Bank of China. (pp. 79–100).

Henning, C. Randall. 2006a. The Exchange Rate Weapon and Macroeconomic Conflict. In David M. Andrews, ed. *International Monetary Power.* Ithaca, NY: Cornel University Press. (pp. 117–38)

Henning, C. Randall. 2006b. "Regional Arrangements and the International Monetary Fund." In Edwin M. Truman, ed., *Reforming the IMF for the 21st Century.* Washington, D. C.: Institute for International Economics: 171–184.

Henning, C. Randall. 2008. Multilateral Context and Financial Regionalism: The Case of East Asia. Presented to the annual meetings of the American Political Science Association, September. Manuscript.

Henning, C. Randall. 2009. "The Future of the Chiang Mai Initiative: An Asian Monetary Fund?" Policy Brief Number PB09-5 (February). Washington, D. C.: Peterson Institute for International Economics.

Henning, C. Randall. 2009. "The Future of the Chiang Mai Initiative: An Asian Monetary Fund?" *Peterson Institute Policy Brief* No. 09–5. Feburary.

Herbst, Jeffrey. 2007. "Crafting Regional Cooperation in Africa." In Amitav Acharya and Alastair Iain Johnston, eds. *Crafting Cooperation: Regional International Institutions in Comparative Perspective*. Cambridge: Cambridge University Press: 129–144.

Hew, Denis, Soedradjad Djiwandono, Stephen Grenville, Andrew Sheng, Masahiro Kawai, Melanie Milo, Sakulrat Montreevat, and Sahchita Basu Das. "Options for EAS Finance Cooperation: A Scoping Study." REPSF II Project No. 07/001. Jakarta: ASEAN Secretariat, September 2007.

Hirst, Mônica. 1998. Security Policies, Democratization, and Regional Integration in the Southern Cone. In Jorge I. Domínguez ed. *International Security and Democracy: Latin America and the Caribbean in the Post-Cold War Era*. Pittsburgh: University of Pittsburgh Press.

Hix, Simon. 2005. *The Political System of the European Union*. New York: Palgrave MacMillan. Second edition.

Hix, Simon, Abdul Noury, and Gerard Roland. 2007. *Democratic Politics in the European Parliament*. Cambridge: Cambridge University Press.

Hix, Simon, Abdul Noury, and Gerard Roland. 2009. "Voting Patterns and Alliance Formation in the European Parliament." *Philosophical Transactions of the Royal Society B* 364: 821–831.

Hoadley, Stephen. "Thailand's and Malaysia's Cross-Regional FTA Initiatives." In Saori N. Katada and Mireya Solis eds. *Cross Regional Trade Agreements: Understanding Permeated Regionalism in East Asia*. Berlin: Springer-Verlag, 2008: 95–121.

Hojman, David. 1987. "Why the Latin American Countries Will Never Form a Debtors' Cartel." *Kyklos* vol. 40, issue 2:198–218

Hooghe, Liesbet. 2005. "Several Roads Lead to International Norms, but Few Via International Socialization: A Case Study of the European Commission." *International Organization* 59(04): 861–898.

Hopf, Ted. 1998. "The Promise of Constructivism in International Relations Theory." *International Security* 23, No.1 (Summer): 170–200.

Hsu, Locknie. 2006. "Government Procurement under RTAs and Asian Perspectives and Practices." *Asian Journal of WTO & International Health Law and Policy*, 1, 2, 379–396

Hsueh, Roselyn Y. "Who Rules the International Economy? Taiwan's Daunting Attempts at Bialteralism." In Vinod K. Aggarwal and Shujiro Urata eds. *Bilateral Trade Agreements in the Asia-Pacific: Origins, Evolution, and Implications*. London: Routledge, 2006: 160–83.

Hufbauer, Gary, and Jeffrey Schott. 2005. *NAFTA Revisited: Achievements and Challenges*. Washington: Institute for International Economics.

Hufbauer, Gary, Jeffrey Schott, Kimberly Elliott, and Barbara Oegg. 2007. *Economic sanctions reconsidered*. Washington, DC, Peterson Institute for International Economics.

Hufbauer, Gary Clyde and Jeffrey J. Schott. 2007. "Fitting Asia-Pacific Agreements into the WTO System," paper presented at the Joint Conference of The Japan Economic

Foundation and Peterson Institute for International Economics on "New Asia-Pacific Trade Initiatives," Washington, DC (November 27).

Hurrell, Andrew. 1998. "An Emerging Security Community in South America." In *Security Communities*, Emanuel Adler and Michael Barnett ed. Cambridge: Cambridge University Press.

Huth, Paul and Todd Allee. 2002. *The Democratic Peace and Territorial Conflict in the Twentieth Century.* New York: Cambridge University Press.

Hymans, Jacques. 2001. "Of Gauchos and Gringos: Why Argentina Never Wanted the Bomb, and Why the United States Thought it Did?" *Security Studies* 10:3 (Spring): 153–185.

IFES. 2007. Election Violence Education and Resolution (EVER) in Timor-Leste.

Ikenberry, John. 2001. *After Victory: Institutions, Strategic Constraint, and the Rebuilding of Order After Major Wars.* Princeton: Princeton University Press.

Ikenberry, John. 2003. 'America in East Asia: Power, Markets, and Grand Strategy,' in T. J. Pempel and Ellis Kraus, eds., *Beyond Bilateralism: The Emerging East Asian Regionalism.* Stanford: Stanford University Press.

Ikenberry, John and Chung-in Moon, eds. 2008. *The United States and Northeast Asia: Debates, Issues and New Order.* London: Rowman and Littlefield.

Ikenberry, John G. and Charles A. Kupchan. 1990. "Socialization and Hegemonic Power," *International Organization* 44 (3), 283–315.

Institute for International Monetary Affairs. 2005. *Economic Surveillance and Policy Dialogue in East Asia.* ASEAN+3 Research Group Studies, 2004–2005. Tokyo.

Institute of South Asian Studies, National University of Singapore. *Guide to the Singapore-India Comprehensive Economic Cooperation Agreement.* Singapore: Rajah and Tann, 2006.

Inter-American Development Bank. 1984. *Economic and Social Progress in Latin America: Economic Integration.* Washington: Inter-American Development Bank.

Inter-American Development Bank. 2001. *Ecuador: Country Paper.* Washington: Inter-American Development Bank.

Inter-American Development Bank. 2004. *Country Program Evaluation, Ecuador 1990-2002*, RE-295. Washington: Inter-American Development Bank.

International Court of Justice. 2009. Pulp Mills on the River Uruguay: Argentina v. Uruguay, www.icj-cij.org accessed 29 July 2009.

International Monetary Fund. Various years. *Direction of Trade Statistics*, www.imfstatistics .org.ezp-prod1.hul.harvard.edu/DOT/.

Irwin, D.A. 1995. The GATT's Contribution to Economic Recovery in Post-war Western Europe. In B. Eichengreen ed. *Europe's Post-war Recovery.* Cambridge: Cambridge University Press.

Jacoby, Wade. 2004. *The Enlargement of the European Union and NATO: Ordering from the Menu in Central Europe.* Cambridge University Press.

Jayasurya, Kanishka. 2007. "Riding the Accountability Wave? Politics of Global Administrative Law." Asia Research Centre Working Paper, n. 142, June 2007 (http://www.arc .murdoch.edu.au/wp/wp142.pdf)

JETRO. "Japan's Outward and Inward Foreign Direct Investment." 2008.

Johnson, Chalmers. *MITI and the Japanese Miracle.* Stanford, CA: Stanford University Press, 1982.

Johnston, Alastair Iain. 1998. *Cultural Realism: Strategic Culture and Grand Strategy in Chinese History.* Princeton: Princeton University Press.

Johnston, Alastair Iain. 1999. "The Myth of the ASEAN Way: Explaining the Evolution of the ARF." In Helga Haftendor, Robert O. Keohane and Celeste Wallander, eds. *Imperfect Unions: Security Institutions Over Time and Space.* Oxford: Oxford University Press. 287–324.

Johnston, Alastair Iain. 2001. "Treating Transnational Institutions as Social Environments." *International Studies Quarterly,* vol. 45(December): 487–515.

Johnston, Alastair Iain. 2008. *Social States: China in International Institutions: 1980–2000.* Princeton: Princeton University Press.

Johnston, Richard, André Blais, Henry Brady, and Jean Crête. 1992. *Letting the People Decide: Dynamics of a Canadian Election.* Stanford, CA: Stanford University Press.

Jones, David Martin and Michael L.R. Smith. 2007. "Making Process, Not Progress: ASEAN and the Evolving East Asian Regional Order." *International Security* 32, 1 (Summer):148–184

Jones, E.L. 2003. *The European Miracle: Environments, Economies and Geopolitics in the History of Europe and Asia.* Third Edition. Cambridge: Cambridge University Press.

Journal of European Public Policy. 2005. Vol. 12, no. 2 (April).

Kahhat, Farid. 2008. ¿Guerra Fría en los Andes? *Foreign Affairs Latinoamérica* 8 (3): 35–41.

Kahler, Miles (2009) "Institutionalizing Economic Cooperation in Asia: Regional Comparisons." In Barry Eichengreen and Jong-Wha Lee (eds), *Institutions for Regionalism: Enhancing Asia's Economic Cooperation and Integration,* Manila: Asian Development Bank.

Kahler, Miles. 1992. "Multilateralism with Small and Large Numbers." *International Organization* 46(3): 681–708.

Kahler, Miles. 1995. *International Institutions and the Political Economy of Integration.* Washington, D. C.: The Brookings Institution.

Kahler, Miles. 2000. "Legalization as Strategy: The Asia-Pacific Case," *International Organization* 54, 3 (Summer): 549–571.

Kahler, Miles. 2001. "The Causes and Consequences of Legalization." In Judith L. Goldstein, Miles Kahler, Robert O. Keohane, and Anne-Marie Slaughter, eds., *Legalization and World Politics.* Cambridge: MIT Press: 277–299.

Kahler, Miles. 2012. "Regional Economic Institutions and East Asian Security." In Avery Goldstein and Edward D. Mansfield, eds. *The Nexus of Economics, Security, and International Relations in East Asia.* Stanford: Stanford University Press.

Kaiser, W. 1996. *Using Europe, Abusing the Europeans: Britain and European Integration, 1945-63.* London: Macmillan.

Kaiser, W. 2007. *Christian Democracy and the Origins of European Union.* Cambridge: Cambridge University Press.

Kang, David C. 2003. "Getting Asia Wrong: The Need for New Analytical Frameworks." *International Security* 27, no. 4 (Spring): 57–85.

Katada, Saori N. 2001. *Banking on Stability: Japan and the Cross-Pacific Dynamics of International Financial Crisis Management.* Ann Arbor: University of Michigan Press.

Katada, Saori N. 2004. Japan's Counterweight Strategy: U.S.-Japan Cooperation and Competition in International Finance. In Ellis S. Krauss and T. J. Pempel, eds., *Beyond Bilateralism: U.S.-Japan Relations in the New Asia-Pacific.* Stanford, CA: Stanford University Press. 176–197.

Katsumata, Hiro. 2006. "Establishment of the ASEAN Regional Forum: Constructing a 'Talking Shop' or a 'Norm Brewery'?" *The Pacific Review,* Volume: 19, Issue: 2: 181–198.

Katsumata, Hiro. 2009. *ASEAN Regional Forum.* Basingstoke: Palgrave-Macmillan.

Katzenstein, Peter J. 1996. *The Culture of National Security: Norms and Identity in World Politics.* New York: Columbia University Press.

Katzenstein, Peter J. 2005. *A World of Regions: Asia and Europe in the American Imperium.* Ithaca, NY: Cornell University Press.

Kawai, Masahiro, and Cindy Houser. 2007. *Evolving ASEAN+3 ERPD: Towards Peer Reviews or Due Diligence?* ADB Institute Discussion Paper 79 (September). Tokyo: Asian Development Bank Institute.

Kawai, Masahiro, and Ganeshan Wignaraja. 2008. "Regionalism as an Engine of Multilateralism: A Case for a Single East Asian FTA." Working Paper Series on Regional Economic Integration No. No. 14. Mandaluyong City: Asian Development Bank.

Kawai, Masahiro, and Ganeshan Wignaraja. 2009. "The Asian "Noodle Bowl": Is It Serious for Business?" Working Paper Series No. No. 136. Tokyo: Asian Development Bank Institute, April.

Kelley, Judith G. 2004a. *Ethnic Politics in Europe: The Power of Norms and Incentives.* Princeton: Princeton University Press.

Kelley, Judith. 2004b. "International Actors on the Domestic Scene: Membership Conditionality and Socialization by International Institutions." *International Organization* 58(03): 425.

Kelley, Judith. 2007. "Who Keeps International Commitments and Why? The International Criminal Court and Bilateral Nonsurrender Agreements." *American Political Science Review* 101(3): 573–589.

Kelley, Judith. 2012. *Monitoring Democracy: When International Election Observation Works and Why It Often Fails.* Princeton, New Jersey, Princeton University Press.

Kent, Ann. 2002. "China's International Socialization: The Role of International Organizations." *Global Governance* 8(3): 343.

Keohane, Robert 2001, "Governance in a Partially Globalized World." *American Political Science Review* 95(1), pp. 1–13.

Keohane, Robert and Elinor Ostrom. 1995. *Introduction. Local Commons and Global Interdependence: Heterogeneity and Cooperation in Two Domains.* R. Keohane and E. Ostrom. London, Sage Publications: 1–26.

Keohane, Robert O. 1984. *After Hegemony: Cooperation and Discord in the World Political Economy.* Princeton: Princeton University Press.

Keohane, Robert O. 1989. *International Institutions and State Power.* Boulder, CO: Westview Press.

Keohane, Robert O., Andrew Moravcsik, and Anne-Marie Slaughter. 2000. "Legalized Dispute Resolution: Interstate and Transnational." *International Organization* 54(3): 457–88.

Khadiagala, Gilbert M. 2009. "Institution-Building for African Regionalism." Background Paper prepared for the Asian Development Bank Flagship Study "Institutions for Regionalism: Enhancing Asia's Economic Cooperation and Integration."

Khong, Yuen Foong. 2004. "Coping with Strategic Uncertainty: Institutions and Soft Balancing in Southeast Asia's Post-Cold War Strategy." In J.J. Suh, Peter Katzenstein, and Allen Carlson eds. *Rethinking Security in East Asia: Identity, Power and Efficiency.* Stanford, CA: Stanford University Press. 172–208.

Khong, Yuen Foong and Helen E. S. Nesadurai. 2007. "Hanging Together, Institutional Design, and Cooperation in Southeast Asia: ASEAN and the ARF." In Amitav Acharya and Alastair Iain Johnston eds. *Crafting Cooperation: Regional International Institutions in Comparative Perspective.* Cambridge: Cambridge University Press: 32–82.

Kim, Soyoung, and Jong-Wha Lee. "Real and Financial Integration in East Asia." Working Paper Series on Regional Economic Integration No. 17. Manila: Office of Regional Economic Integration, Asian Development Bank, June 2008.

König, Thomas and Thomas Bräuninger (1998) "The Inclusiveness of European Decision Rules," *Journal of Theoretical Politics* 10(1): 125–141.

Kono, Daniel. 2007. "Making Anarchy Work: International Legal Institutions and Trade Cooperation." *The Journal of Politics* 69(3):746–59.

Koremenos, Barbara, Charles Lipson, and Duncan Snidal, eds. 2003. *The Rational Design of International Institutions*. New York: Cambridge University Press.

Koremenos, Barbara, Charles Lipson, and Duncan Snidal. 2001. "The Rational Design of International Institutions." *International Organization* 55(4):761–799.

Krasner, Stephen. 2001. "Sovereignty." *Foreign Policy* 122(Jan.–Feb.): 20–29.

Krasner, Steven D. 1983. *International Regimes*. Ithaca, NY: Cornell University Press.

Krauss, Ellis. 2004. "The United States and Japan in APEC's EVSL Negotiations: Regional Multilateralism and Trade," in Krauss and T.J. Pempel, eds. *Beyond Bilateralism: US-Japan Relations in the New Asia-Pacific*. Stanford: Stanford University Press.

Kugler, Jacek. 1987. "The Politics of Foreign Debt in Latin America: A Study of the Debtors' Cartel." *International Interactions*, vol. 13 no. 2: 115–144.

Kuroda, Haruhiko, and Masahiro Kawai. 2004. Strengthening Regional Financial Cooperation in East Asia. In Gordon de Brouwer and Yunjong Wang eds. *Financial Governance in East Asia: Policy Dialogue, Surveillance and Cooperation*. London: Routledge.

Kydd, Andrew. 2001. "Trust Building, Trust Breaking: The Dilemma of NATO Enlargement." *International Organization* 55(04): 801–828.

La Porta, Rafael, Florencio Lopez de Silanes, Cristian Pop-Eleches, and Andrei Shleifer, 2004. "Judicial Checks and Balances" *Journal of Political Economy* 112(2):445–70.

Lake, David. 2007. "Delegating Divisible Sovereignty: Sweeping a Conceptual Minefield." *Review of International Organizations* 2: 219–237.

Lawrence, Robert Z. 1996. *Regionalism, Multilateralism, and Deeper Integration*. Washington, D. C.: The Brookings Institution.

Lee, Seungjoo. "Singapore Trade Bilateralism: A Two Track Strategy." In Vinod K. Aggarwal and Shujiro Urata eds. *Bilateral Trade Agreements in the Asia-Pacific: Origins, Evolution, and Implications*. London: Routledge, 2006: 184–205.

Lee, Yong Wook. 2006. Japan and the Asian Monetary Fund: An Identity-Intention Approach. *International Studies Quarterly*, vol. 50 (2): 339–366.

Leifer, Michael.1989. *ASEAN and the Security of South-East Asia*. London and New York: Routledge.

Leifer, Michael. 1996. "The ASEAN Regional Forum," *Adelphi Paper*, No. 302. London: International Institute for Strategic Studies.

Lindert, Peter. 1989. Response to the Debt Crisis: What Is Different about the 1980s? In Barry Eichengreen and Peter H. Lindert eds. *The International Debt Crisis in Historical Perspective*. Cambridge: MIT Press.

Lissakers, Karin. 1991. *Banks, Borrowers, and the Establishment: A Revisionist Account of the International Debt Crisis*. New York: Basic Books.

Lustig, Nora. 1998. Introduction: Economic Shocks, Inequality and Poverty: The Need for Safety Nets. In N. Lustig ed. *Coping With Austerity. Poverty and Inequality in Latin America*. Washington: Brookings Institution.

Lynch, F.M.B. 2000. De Gaulle's First Veto: France, the Rueff Plan and the Free Trade Area. *Contemporary European History* 9: 111–35.

Lyne, Mona, Daniel Nielson, and Michael J. Tierney. 2006. "Who Delegates? Alternative Models of Principals in Development Aid," in Hawkins et. al. *Delegation and Agency in International Organizations*. Cambridge: Cambridge University Press.

MacIntyre, Andrew. *Business and Politics in Indonesia*. Sydney: Allen and Unwin, 1991.

MacIntyre, Andrew, T.J. Pempel, and John Ravenhill, eds. *Crisis as Catalyst: Asia's Dynamic Political Economy*. Ithaca NY: Cornell University Press, 2008.

Mackie, J.A.C. "Economic Growth in the ASEAN Region: The Political Underpinnings." In Helen Hughes ed. *Achieving Industrialization in East Asia*. Cambridge: Cambridge University Press, 1988: 283–326.

Maddison, Angus. 2003. *The World Economy: Historical Statistics*, London: Development Center, Organization for Economic Cooperation and Development.

Maggi, Giovanni and Massimo Morelli. 2006. "Self-Enforcing Voting in International Organizations." *American Economic Review* 96(4):1137–1158.

Maher, D.J. 1986. *The Tortuous Path: The Course of Ireland's Entry into the EEC 1948–73*. Dublin: Institute of Public Administration.

Majone, Giandomenico. 1994. "The Rise of the Regulatory State in Europe." *West European Politics* 17(3):77–101.

Majone, Giandomenico 1996. *Regulating Europe*, London: Routledge.

Majone, Giandomenico. 2001. "Two Logics of Delegation: Agency and Fiduciary Relations in EU Governance." *European Union Politics* 2(1):103–22.

Malamud, Andrés. 2005. "Presidential Diplomacy and the Institutional Underpinnings of MERCOSUR: An Empirical Examination." *Latin American Research Review* 40:1 (February): 138–164.

Mancuso, Salvatore. 2007. "Trends on the Harmonization of Contract Law in Africa." *Annual Survey of International & Comparative Law* 13:157.

Manger, Mark S. *Investing in Protection: The Politics of Preferential Trade Agreements between North and South*. Cambridge: Cambridge University Press, 2009.

Mansfield, Edward D., Helen V. Milner, and Jon C. Pevehouse. 2008. "Democracy, Veto Players and the Depth of Regional Integration." *World Economy* 31(1): 67–96.

Mares, David. 2001. *Violent Peace: Militarized Interstate Bargaining in Latin America*. New York: Columbia University Press.

Mares, David. 2008. Los temas tradicionales y la agenda latinoamericana. *Foreign Affairs Latinoamérica* 8 (3): 2008: 2–11.

Martin, Lisa. 2000. *Democratic Commitments: Legislatures and International Cooperation*. Princeton: Princeton University Press.

Martin, Lisa and Beth A. Simmons. 1998. "Theories and Empirical Studies of International Institutions." *International Organization*, Volume 52, Issue 04, October, pp 729–757.

Mattila, Mikko and Jan-Erik Lane. 2001. "Why Unanimity in the Council? A Roll Call Analysis of Council Voting," *European Union Politics* 2(1): 31–52.

Mattli, Walter (1999) *The Logic of Regional Integration: Europe and Beyond*, Cambridge: Cambridge University Press.

Mattli, Walter and Anne-Marie Slaughter. 1998. Revisiting the European Court of Justice. *International Organization* 52(1):177–209.

McCubbins, Mathew D. and Thomas Schwartz. 1984. "Congressional Oversight Overlooked: Police Patrols versus Fire Alarms." *American Journal of Political Science* 28(1): 165–179.

McNamara, Kathleen. 1998. *The Currency of Ideas: Monetary Politics in the European Union*. Ithaca, NY: Cornell University Press.

McSherry, J. Patrice. 1999. Operation Condor: Clandestine Inter-American System. *Social Justice* 26 (Winter): 144–174.

Middlemas, Keith (1995) *Orchestrating Europe: The Informal Politics of the European Union, 1943–95*, London: Fontana Press.

Milner, Helen V. "Industries, Governments, and the Creation of Regional Trading Blocs." In Edward D. Mansfield and Helen V. Milner eds. *The Political Economy of Regionalism*. New York: Columbia University Press, 1997: 77–106.

Milner, Helen V. 1998. "Rationalizing Politics: The Emerging Synthesis among International Politics and American and Comparative Politics." *International Organization* 52 no. 4: 759–786.

Milward, A.S. 2000. *The European Rescue of the Nation-State*. Second edition. London: Routledge.

Minzarari, Dumitru. 2008a. "False Hope."

Minzarari, Dumitru. 2008b. "Moldova: Under the West's Radar."

Mitchell, Ronald and Patricia Keilbach. 2001. "Situation Structure and Institutional Design: Reciprocity, Coercion, and Exchange." *International Organization* 55(4): 891–917.

Mitnick, Barry M. (1980) *The Political Economy of Regulation: Creating, Designing and Removing Regulatory Forms*. New York: Columbia University Press.

Moravcsik, A. 1998. *The Choice for Europe: Social Purpose & State Power from Messina to Maastricht*. Ithaca NY: Cornell University Press.

Moravcsik, A. 2000. "De Gaulle Between Grain and Grandeur: The Political Economy of French EC Policy, 1958–1970." *Journal of Cold War Studies* 2(2): 3–43 and 2(3): 4–68.

Moravcsik, Andrew. 1999. "A New Statecraft? Supranational Entrepreneurs and International Cooperation." *International Organization* 53(2): 267–306.

Moravcsik, Andrew. 2001. "Constructivism and European Integration: A Critique," in *The Social Construction of Europe*. by Thomas Christiansen, Knud Erik Jorgensen and Antje Wiener eds. London: Sage Publications. 176–188.

Moravcsik, Andrew. 2003. "The Origins of Human Rights Regimes: Democratic Delegation in Postwar Europe." *International Organization* 54(2): 217–252.

Munakata, Naoko. 2006a. "Has Politics Caught up with Markets? In Search of East Asian Economic Regionalism." In Peter J. Katzenstein and Takashi Shiraishi eds. *Beyond Japan: The Dynamics of East Asian Regionalism*, Ithaca, NY: Cornell University Press. 130–57.

Munakata, Naoko. 2006b. *Transforming East Asia: The Evolution of Regional Economic Integration*. Washington, D.C.: Brookings Institution Press.

Nagai, Fumio. "Thailand's FTA Policy: Continuity and Change between the Chuan and Thaksin Governments." In Jiro Okamoto ed. *Whither Free Trade Agreements? Proliferation, Evaluation and Multilateralization*. Chiba, Japan: Institute of Developing Economies Japan External Trade Organization, 2003: 252–84.

NDI. 1990. 1990 Elections in the Dominican Republic.

NDI. 1994. Interim Report on the May 16, 1994 Elections in the Dominican Republic.

Nesadurai, Helen. 2003. *Globalisation, Domestic Politics and Regionalism: The ASEAN Free Trade Area*. London and New York: Routledge.

Nesadurai, Helen. 2010. "Labour and Grassroots Civic Interests in Regional Institutions." ADB Working Paper Series on Regional Economic Integration. No. 63 (November). Manila: Asian Development Bank.

Nielson, Daniel and Michael Tierney. 2003. "Delegation to International Organizations: Agency Theory and World Bank Environmental Reform." *International Organization* 57, 2: 241–276.

Nye, Joseph S. 1968. Central American Regional Integration. In Joseph S. Nye ed. *International Regionalism*. Boston: Little, Brown.

OAS. 1996. Report of the Electoral Observation Mission of the OAS in the Dominican Republic.

OAS. 2000. Report of the Electoral Observation Mission on the Presidential Elections in the Dominican Republic.

OAS. 2008. Report of the Mission of the OAS Electoral Observation in the Dominican Republic.

Ocampo, Jose Antonio. 2002. Recasting the International Financial Agenda. In John Eatwell and Lance Taylor eds. *International Capital Markets: Systems in Transition*. Oxford University Press.

OECD. 2003. *Regionalism and the Multilateral Trading System*. Paris: OECD.

Ogawa, Eiji and Taiyo Yoshimi. "Widening Deviation among East Asian Currencies." Discussion Paper Series No. 08-E-010. Tokyo: Research Institute of Economy, Trade and Industry, Ministry of Economy Trade and Industry, 15 March 2008.

Olson, Mancur. 1965. *The Logic of Collective Action*. Cambridge, MA: Harvard University Press.

OSCE. 1994. ODIHR Report on the Parliamentary Elections in Moldova (27 February).

OSCE. 2007. Interim Report on the Election Observation Mission; Republic of Moldova Local Election.

Padoa-Schioppa, Tommaso. 2004. *The Euro and Its Central Bank*. Cambridge, MA: MIT Press.

Park, Sung-Hoon and Ming Gyo Koo. "Forming a Cross-Regional Partnership: The South Korea-Chile FTA and Its Implications." *Pacific Affairs* 80, no. 2 (2007): 259–78.

Pastor, Robert A. 2001. *Toward a North American Community: Lessons from the Old World for the New*. Washington: Institute for International Economics.

Pauly, Louis W. 1997. *Who Elected the Bankers? Surveillance and Control in the World Economy*. Ithaca, NY: Cornell University Press.

Pearson, Margaret. 2005. "Institutions and Norms of the Emerging Regulatory State The Business of Governing Business in China." *World Politics* 57(2):296–322.

Pempel, T.J., ed. 1999. *The Politics of the Asian Economic Crisis*. Ithaca, NY: Cornell University Press.

Pempel, T.J. 2005. *Remapping East Asia: The Construction of a Region*. Ithaca, NY: Cornell University Press.

Pempel, T.J. 2008. "Restructuring Regional Ties." In Andrew Macintyre, T.J. Pempel and John Ravenhill eds. *Crisis as Catalyst: Asia's Dynamic Political Economy*, Ithaca NY: Cornell University Press. 164–80.

Peña, Félix. 1973. El Grupo Andino: Un nuevo enfoque de la participación internacional de los países en desarrollo. *Estudios internacionales* 6:22 (April-June): 44–81.

Peña, Félix. 1992. The MERCOSUR and its Prospects: An Option for Competitive Insertion in the World Economy. In *Prospects for the Processes of Sub-Regional Integration in Central and South America*. Madrid: Institute for European-Latin American Relations.

Peña, Félix. 2003. Concertación de intereses, efectividad de las reglas del juego y calidad institucional, www.fundacionbankboston.com.ar accessed 29 July 2009.

Peng, Shin-yi, 2000. "The WTO Legalistic Approach and East Asia: From the Legal Culture Perspective." *Asian-Pacific Law & Policy Journal* 1(2):1–69.

Penrose, Lionel (1946) "The Elementary Statistics of Majority Voting," *Journal of the Royal Statistical Society* 109(1): 53–57.

Perry, Valery. 1998. "The OSCE Suspension of the Federal Republic of Yugoslavia." Helsinki Monitor 9(4): 44–54.

Pevehouse, Jon. 2003. "Democracy from the Outside-In? International Organizations and Democratization." *International Organization* 56(03): 515–549.

Pevehouse, Jon. 2009. International Institutions and the Rule of Law: The Case of National Corruption, Background Paper, ADB Flagship Study, Institutions for Regionalism: Enhancing Asia's Economic Cooperation and Integration, Asian Development Bank.

Phillips, Nicola. 2004. *The Southern Cone Model: The Political Economy of Regional Capitalist Development in Latin America.* London: Routledge.

Phillips, Warren and Richard Rimkumnas. 1978. "The Concept of Crisis in International Politics." *Journal of Peace Research,* vol. no.3: 259–272.

Pollack, Mark A. 1997. "Delegation, Agency and Agenda Setting in the European Community." *International Organization* 51(1): 99–134.

Pollack, Mark A. 2003. *The Engines of Integration: Delegation, Agency, and Agency Setting in the European Union,* Oxford: Oxford University Press.

Pongsudhiriak, T. "Thailand." In Ann Capling and Patrick Low eds. *Governments, Non-State Actors and Trade Policy-Making: Negotiating Preferentially or Multilaterally?,* Cambridge: Cambridge University Press, 2010: 161–85.

Poon, Jessie P.H. 2001. "Regionalism in the Asia Pacific: Is Geography Destiny?" *Area* 33(3):252–60.

Postigo-Angon, Antonio. "Policymaking of FTAs in Thailand and Malaysia." unpublished manuscript, London School of Economics: January 2011.

Prebisch, Raúl. 1959. *The Latin American Common Market.* New York: United Nations, Economic Commission for Latin America.

Productivity Commission, Commonwealth of Australia. "Bilateral and Regional Trade Agreements, Draft Report." Melbourne: Productivity Commission 2010.

Pryles, Michael. 2006. *Dispute Resolution in Asia. 3rd ed.,* Kluwer Law International.

Putnam, Robert D. and C. Randall Henning. 1989. "The Bonn Summit of 1978: A Case Study in Coordination." In Richard N. Cooper, Robert D. Putnam, C. Randall Henning, and Gerald Holtham, eds., *Can Nations Agree? Issues in International Economic Cooperation.* Washington, D.C.: Brookings Institution. 12–140.

Rajan, Ramkishen and Reza Sirigar. 2004. Centralized Reserve Pooling for the ASEAN+3 Countries. In *Monetary and Financial Integration in East Asia: The Way Ahead* 2. Asian Development Bank. Basingstoke: Palgrave MacMillan.

Raustiala, Kal and Anne-Marie Slaughter. 2002. International Law, International Relations and Compliance. Princeton Law & Public Affairs Paper No. 02-2. In Walter Carlnaes, Thomas Risse and Beth A. Simmons, eds. *The Handbook of International Relations.* London: Sage Publications.

Ravenhill, John. 2001. *APEC and the Construction of Pacific Rim Regionalism.* Cambridge: Cambridge University Press.

Ravenhill, John. 2006 "Is China an Economic Threat to Southeast Asia?" *Asian Survey* 46, no. 5 (October): 653–74.

Ravenhill, John. 2007a. "Fighting Irrelevance: An Economic Community 'with ASEAN Characteristics'" Canberra: Australian National University Department of International Relations Working Paper 2007/3.

Ravenhill, John. 2007b "China's 'Peaceful Development' and Southeast Asia: A Positive Sum Game?". In William W. Keller and Thomas G. Rawski eds. *China's Rise and the Balance of Influence in Asia*. Pittsburgh: University of Pittsburgh Press. 162–92.

Ravenhill, John. 2008. "The Move to Preferential Trade on the Western Pacific Rim: Some Initial Conclusions." *Australian Journal of International Affairs* 62, no. 2 (June): 129–50.

Ravenhill, John. 2009a. 'East Asian Regionalism: Much Ado About Nothing?', in Rick Fawn (ed.) *Globalising the Regional: Regionalising the Global*, Cambridge: Cambridge University Press.

Ravenhill, John. 2009b. "The Political Economy of Asian Regionalism," paper prepared for the Asian Development Bank Workshop on Institutions for Regionalism in Asia and the Pacific, Shanghai, December 2–3.

Ravenhill, John. 2010. "The Political Economy of Asian Regionalism." Working Paper No. 57. Manila: Asian Development Bank, September.

Reh, Christine. 2009. "The Lisbon Treaty: De-Constitutionalizing the European Union?" *Journal of Common Market Studies* 47 no. 3: 625–650.

Reinhardt, Eric. 2002. Tying Hands without a Rope: Rational Domestic Response to International Institutional Constraints. In *Locating the Proper Authorities: The Interaction of Domestic and International Institutions*, Daniel Drezner ed. Ann Arbor: University of Michigan Press, 77–104.

Risse, Thomas. 1997. "Let's Talk." Paper Presented to the American Political Science Association Annual Conference, Washington, DC, August 28–31.

Risse, Thomas and Wiener Antje. 2001. "The Social Construction of Social Constructivism." In Thomas Christiansen, Knud Erik Jorgensen and Antje Wiener, eds., *The Social Construction of Europe*. London: Sage Publications. 199-205.

Risse, Thomas, Stephen C. Ropp, and Kathryn Sikkink. 1999. *The Power of Human Rights: International Norms and Domestic Change*. Cambridge, UK: Cambridge University Press.

Rittberger, Berthold (2005) *Building Europe's Parliament: Democratic Representation Beyond the Nation State*. Oxford: Oxford University Press.

Rose, Andrew. 2004. "Do We Really Know that the WTO Increases Trade?" *American Economic Review* 94(1):98–114.

Rozman, Gilbert. 2004. *Northeast Asia's Stunted Regionalism: Bilateral Distrust in the Shadow of Globalization*. New York: Cambridge University Press.

Russett, Bruce. 1967. *International Regions and the International System: A Study in Political Ecology*. Chicago: Rand McNally.

Ryan, Lisa M. 1996. "Convention on the International Sale of Goods: Divergent Interpretations." *Tulane Journal of International Law* 4:99–118.

Sánchez Sánchez, Rafael. 2003. "The Central American Integration System as the Outcome of Asymmetrical Bargaining between States: An Intergovernmental Perspective of Regional Integration." *Integration and Trade* 19 (July-December): 45–72.

Sandholtz, Wayne. 1993. Choosing Union: Monetary Politics and Maastricht. *International Organization* 47 (winter): 1–39.

Sandholtz, Wayne. 1996. "Membership Matters: Limits of the Functional Approach to European Institutions." *Journal of Common Market Studies* 34(3): 403–429.

Sandholtz, Wayne and Alec Stone Sweet. 1998. "Integration, Supranational Governmance, and the Institutionalization of the European Polity." In W. Sandholtz and A. Stone Sweet, *European Integration and Supranational Governance*. Oxford, Oxford University Press: 1–26.

Sandholtz, Wayne and John Zysman (1989) "1992: Recasting the European Bargain." *World Politics* 42(1): 95–128.

Sanguinetti, Pablo and Eduardo Bianchi. 2006. "Trade Liberalization, Macroeconomic Fluctuations, and Contingent Protection in Latin America." *Integration and Trade* (Spring): 147–183.

Schaad, M. 1998. "Plan G—A 'Counterblast'? British Policy Towards the Messina Countries, 1956." *Contemporary European History* 7: 39–60.

Schmitter, Philippe. 1970. "Central American Integration: Spill-over, Spill-around or Encapsulation?" *Journal of Common Market Studies* 9:1 (September): 1–48.

Severino, Rodolfo C. 2006. *Southeast Asia in Search of an ASEAN Community.* Singapore: Institute for Southeast Asian Studies.

Severino, Rodolfo C. 2009. "Regional Institutions in Southeast Asia: The First Movers and Their Challenges." Background Paper prepared for the Asian Development Bank Flagship Study "Institutions for Regionalism: Enhancing Asia's Economic Cooperation and Integration."

Shin, Gi-wook and Daniel Sneider. 2007. *Cross Currents: Regionalism and Nationalism in Northeast Asia.* Stanford: Walter H. Shorenstein Asia-Pacific Research Center.

Simmons, Beth. 2000. "International Law and State Behavior: Commitment and Compliance in International Monetary Affairs." *American Political Science Review* 94(4): 819–835.

Simmons, Beth A. 2001. "The Legalization of International Monetary Affairs." In Judith L. Goldstein, Miles Kahler, Robert O. Keohane, and Anne-Marie Slaughter, eds., *Legalization and World Politics.* Cambridge: MIT Press: 189–218.

Simmons, Beth A. 2006. "Trade and Territorial Conflict in Latin America: International Borders as Institutions." In Miles Kahler and Barbara Walter, eds., *Territoriality and Conflict in an Era of Globalization.* Cambridge: Cambridge University Press.

Slomczynski, Wojciech and Karol Zyczkowski. 2007. "Jagiellonian Compromise: An Alternative Voting System for the Council of the European Union." http://chaos.if.uj.edu.pl/ karol/pdf/JagComo7.pdf.

Smith, Anthony. 2004. "East Timor: Elections in the World's Newest Nation." *Journal of Democracy* 15.

Smith, James McCall. 2000. "The Politics of Dispute Settlement Design: Explaining Legalism in Regional Trade Pacts." *International Organization* 54, 1 (Winter): 137–180.

Snidal, Duncan. 1995. The Politics of Scope: Endogenous Actors, Heterogeity and Institutions. In R. Keohane and E. Ostrom, *Local Commons and Global Interdependence: Heterogeneity and Cooperation in Two Domains.* London, Sage Publications: 47–70.

Solingen, Etel. 2008. "The Genesis, Design and Effects of Regional Institutions: Lessons from East Asia and the Middle East." *International Studies Quarterly* 52, no. 2 (June): 261–94.

Solingen, Etel. 2009. "Institutions for Regionalism in East Asia and the Middle East." Background Paper prepared for the Asian Development Bank Flagship Study "Institutions for Regionalism: Enhancing Asia's Economic Cooperation and Integration."

Solis, Mireya, Barbara Stallings and Saori Katada, eds. 2009. *Competitive Regionalism: FTA Diffusion in the Pacific Rim (International Political Economy).* Basingstoke (UK), New York: Palgrave Macmillan.

Sotomayor Velázquez, Arturo. 2004. "Civil-Military Affairs and Security Institutions in the Southern Cone: The Sources of Argentine-Brazilian Nuclear Cooperation." *Latin American Politics and Society* 46:4 (Winter): 29–60.

Stigler, George J. (1971) "The Theory of Economic Regulation," *Bell Journal of Economics and Management Science* 6(2): 3–21.

Stone, Randall. 2011. *Controlling Institutions: International Organizations and the Global Economy.* Cambridge: Cambridge University Press.

Stone Sweet, Alec. 2005. "European Integration and the Legal System. IHS Political Science Series: 2005, No. 101": 78.

Stubb, Alexander. 1996. "A Categorization of Differentiated Integration." Journal of Common Market Studies 34(2): 283–295.

Sunstein, Cass R. (1990) *After the Rights Revolution: Reconsidering the Regulatory State,* Cambridge, MA: Harvard University Press.

Suominen, Kati. 2009. "The Changing Anatomy of Regional Trade Agreements in East Asia." *Journal of East Asian Studies* 9: 29–56

Sussangkarn, Chalongphob. "The Chiang Mai Initiative Multilateralization: Origin, Development and Outlook." ADBI Working Paper Series No. 230. Tokyo: Asian Development Bank Institute, July 2010.

Svensson, P. 1986. "Stability, Crisis and Breakdown: Some Notes on the Concept of Crisis in Political Analysis." *Scandinavian Political Studies,* vol. 9, no.2.

Tallberg, Jonas. 2002. "Paths to Compliance: Enforcement, Management, and the European Union." *International Organization* 56(3): 609–643.

Tallberg, Jonas. 2003. "Paths to Compliance: Enforcement, Management, and the European Union." *International Organization* 56(3): 609–643.

Thomas, Daniel. 2001. *The Helsinki Effect: International Norms, Human Rights, and the Demise of Communism.* Princeton University Press.

Thomas, Daniel. 2005. "Human Rights Ideas, the Demise of Communism, and the End of the Cold War." *Journal of Cold War Studies* 7(2): 110–141.

Titelman, Daniel. 2006. Subregional Financial Cooperation: The Experiences of Latin

Tomz, Mike, Judith Goldstein, and Doug Rivers. 2007. "Do We Really Know that the WTO Increases Trade?" *American Economic Review* 97(5):2005–18.

Tracy, M. 1989. *Government and Agriculture in Western Europe 1880-1988,* 3rd Ed. New York: Harvester Wheatsheaf.

Turcotte, Sylvain. 2008. La política de Brasil hacia Sudamérica: Entre voluntarismo y resistencias. Foro Internacional 48:4 (October-December): 785–806.

U.S. Department of the Treasury, Office of International Affairs. 2009. Exchange Stabilization Fund: History. http://www.treasury.gov/offices/international-affairs/esf/history/ accessed 24 October 2009.

Urata, Shujiro. "Exclusion Fears and Competitive Regionalism in East Asia." In Mireya Solís, Barbara Stallings and Saori N. Katada eds. *Competitive Regionalism: FTA Diffusion in the Pacific Rim,* New York: Palgrave Macmillan, 2009: 27–53.

Urwin, D.W. 1995. *The Community of Europe: A History of European Integration since 1945.* 2nd Ed. London: Longman.

Vaubel, Roland. 2006. "Principal-Agent Problems in International Organizations," *Review of International Organizations,* 1: 125–138

Vernon, Raymond. 1971. *Sovereignty at Bay: The Multinational Spread of U.S. Enterprises.* New York: Basic Books.

Vervaele, John A.E. 2005. "Mercosur and Regional Integration in South America." *International & Comparative Law Quarterly* 54:387–410.

Voeten, Erik. 2007. "The Politics of International Judicial Appointments: Evidence from the European Court of Human Rights." *International Organization* 61(4):669–701.

Voeten, Erik. 2008. "The Impartiality of International Judges: Evidence from the European Court of Human Rights." *American Political Science Review* 102(4):417–33.

Voeten, Erik. 2009. "The Politics of International Judicial Appointments." *Chicago Journal of International Law* 9(2):387–406.

Wade, Robert. *Governing the Market: Economic Theory and the Role of Government in East Asian Industrialization.* Princeton, NJ: Princeton University Press, 1990.

Wallace, Helen, W. Wallace and M. Pollack, eds. 2005. *Policy Making in the European Union.* 5th Ed. Oxford: Oxford University Press.

Warlouzet, L. 2008. Négocier au pied du mur: la France et le projet britannique de zone de libre-échange (1956–1958). *Relations internationales* 136 : 33–50.

Weiler, Joseph. 1994. "A Quiet Revolution: The European Court of Justice and Its Interlocutors." *Comparative Political Studies* 26(4):510–34.

Wendt, Alexander. 1992. "Anarchy Is what States Make of it: The Social Construction of Power Politics." *International Organization* 46, 2 (Spring): 391–425.

Wendt, Alexander. 1999. *Social Theory of International Politics.* Cambridge: Cambridge University Press.

Wildhaber, Luzius. 2000. Precedent in the European Court of Human Rights. In Rolv Ryssdal ed. *Protection des droits de l'homm : la perspective européenne, mélanges à la mémoire,* 1529–45.

Willett, Thomas D. and David M. Andrews. 1997. "Financial Interdependence and the State: International Monetary Relations at Century's End." *International Organization* 51: 479–511.

Williamson, Oliver. 1985. *The Economic Institutions of Capitalism: Firms, Markets, Relational Contracting.* New York: Free Press.

Willmore, Larry N. 1976. "Trade Creation, Trade Diversion and Effective Protection in the Central American Common Market." *The Journal of Development Studies* 12:4 (July): 396–414.

Winters, L. Alan. 1997. "What Can European Experience Teach Developing Countries About Integration?" *The World Economy* 20(7): 889–912.

Wionczek, Miguel S. 1970. "The Rise and Decline of Latin American Economic Integration." *Journal of Common Market Studies* 9:1 (September): 49–66.

Woo-Cumings, Meredith, ed. *The Developmental State.* Cornell Studies in Political Economy. Ithaca, NY: Cornell University Press, 1999.

Wu, Xinbo. 2009. "Chinese Perspectivs on Building an East Asian Community in the Twenty-First Century." In Michael Green and Bates Gil, eds., *Asia's New Multilateralism: Cooperation, Competition and the Search for Community.* New York: Columbia University Press.

Wyplosz, Charles. 2006. "Deep Economic Integration: Is Europe a Blueprint?" *Asian Economic Policy Review,* 1: 259–279.

Yamazawa, Ippei. 2008. "APEC FTA vs. East Asian Summit FTA: Free Trade Agreements in the Asia Pacific", Australian APEC Study Center ed. *Driving Growth—APEC's Destiny: Priorities and Strategies for APEC's Future in the 21st Century*, Melbourne.

Yarbrough, Beth V., and Robert M. Yarbrough. 1992. *Cooperation and Governance in International Trade.* Princeton, NJ: Princeton University Press.

Yourow. Howard Charles. 1996. *The Margin of Appreciation Doctrine in the Dynamics of European Human Rights Jurisprudence.* Leiden, Netherlands: Martinus Nijhoff.

Zamora, Stephen. 1980. "Voting in International Economic Organizations." *American Journal of International Law* 74:566–608.

Zurn, Michael and Jeffrey Checkel. 2005. "Getting Socialized to Build Bridges: Constructivism and Rationalism, Europe and the Nation-State." *International Organization,* Vol. 59, No.4: 1045-1079.

Index